THE
GINGERBREAD
RACE

ANDREI NAVROZOV

THE GINGERBREAD RACE

A LIFE IN THE CLOSING WORLD ONCE CALLED FREE

PICADOR ORIGINAL

A Picador original
First published 1993 by Pan Books Limited

a division of Pan Macmillan Publishers Limited
Cavaye Place London SW10 9PG
and Basingstoke

Associated companies throughout the world

ISBN 0 330 37636 8

1 3 5 7 9 8 6 4 2

A CIP catalogue record for this book is available from
the British Library

Designed by Hayley Cove
Typeset by Cambridge Composing (UK) Limited, Cambridge
Printed by Mackays of Chatham plc, Kent

I do not say to people *you are to be forgiven or condemned*,
I say to them *you are dying*.

– Arthur de Gobineau to Alexis de Tocqueville, 1856.

PART ONE

OUT
OF PARADISE

PART ONE

OUT
OF PARADISE

1

The sun sets and lengthens the shadow on the dial. I understand what this means because time is so easily read. It is a culture. In the language to which I was born, it is the Sanskrit word for the track of the wheel, left in the dust of the ritual chariot races, *vartanna,* a millennium before the birth of Plato. The atavistic spokes on the face of a clock are remnants of its revolutionary past. It passes, and an artist composes a still life of ripe fruit on the wooden planks of a rustic table. Now it is early morning. As he begins painting, his light changes and declines. His hand, even if it is a hand of genius, is no match for his honesty. Hence his yearning for the ideal, which alone captures time, for in order to depict subjects in their true light he must know their ultimate destiny. Let us rejoice. This yearning runs from our purest Indo-European wellsprings, and it alone makes the present worth living. But now the chariot wheel is in its last revolution. Then let us mourn, because the *vartanna* of Western civilization is not eternal. Another culture is on the move, and with our own dying eyes we may yet see what sort of imprint it leaves on the asphalt. From where I write, it looks like the caterpillar track of an armoured personnel carrier. The artist may protest, as the still life before me could not have seemed more picturesque. Yet I now commend it into his hands, for he alone exhibits a vital interest in the ultimate destiny of such subjects as ripe fruit, farthingales and individual liberty.

2

If power is a culture, then Vnukovo was the Pieria of its muses. But this hardly captures the glamour. If Moscow is the Hollywood of power, Vnukovo was Beverly Hills. But this empties it of the mystery.

3

Moscow was Versailles and Vnukovo was one of its finest grottoes, though the whereabouts of several other retreats that fitted this description was better known to the general public. Peredelkino, just two bucolic whistlestops away on our railway line, had recently buried Boris Pasternak. We still used his septic tank man. He arrived every spring to pump our sewage into his cistern, his literary loyalties evenly divided among his customers. He admired our late neighbour, the poet with the pen name meaning Crimson who once wrote a song called 'Broad is My Native Land'. It was the logical equivalent of 'America the Beautiful', but much more famous:

> Broad is my native land,
> With forests, rivers, fields aplenty.

Crimson himself was roughly as famous as Walt Disney, and the architectural follies of his house, whose peaked orange roof would be visible from our terrace after the leaves fell in autumn, reflected something of his analogue's distant world. Each house stood on its own land, usually ten or fifteen acres, surrounded by a picket fence that was painted green if the original owner was still alive, or weather-beaten and with long splinters if he was dead. Crimson's, where it connected with ours forming a kind of narrow wedge, had crumbled out altogether, and there you could crawl through to his thicket of raspberry bushes, peacefully going wild in the totalitarian gloom. To get to the opening you passed under the apple trees of our orchard, sixty-five in all. We also had three pear trees, and a thicket of gooseberries and currants to rival his raspberries. But it was what lay to the side that made our house the grandest in Vnukovo. To the side lay a birch grove, vestals in white improbably edged in black Catalan lace, running away from the eye every time it blinked to stop them. At the end of the grove was another fence and another dead owner, a novelist by the name of Cymbal. That is what the name meant, anyway. Cymbal's famous novel was called *The White Birch*, and sharp tongues would recite a limerick whose hero progressed from the white birch of Vnukovo to the white silverfoil top of the vodka bottle to the white heat of delirium tremens and finally to White Posts, a mental hospital of distinction not far from Moscow. Be that as it may, Cymbal's neglected property had nothing to offer. The birch grove receded just before it reached his fence, and even the mushrooms seemed to disappear as you approached the fence from our side. The best places to find them in the grove were along the fence which separated us from the composer who bore the name of the River Danube, or else near the front fence, beyond which ran the road called Mayakovsky Street. Ours was No. 4, Cymbal's was No. 6. Across the road, at No. 3, was the house of another writer, also very famous, although nobody remembered why. No. 5, down the street, was owned by a poet whose name would be Marmot in English translation. His wartime lyric, about fire beating in the stove, was not quite as famous as 'Broad is My Native Land', but songs, after all, are supposed to be more popular than poems:

> Fire beats in the narrow stove,
> And the resin is like a tear.

Perhaps I simplify. Still, Marmot's poems were not meant to be difficult. Further down at No. 7, on the assumption of relative equality among the muses, lived the founder of the puppet theatre, a Diaghilev of the inanimate. It was said that he kept pet alligators, but to what extent this was true is now hard to say since we never visited our neighbours. Except our immediate neighbours, both women. One lived at No. 2 with her husband, a film director. She was Vnukovo's movie star, and as the country's film industry was never very prolific even in the good old days, it followed that she had to combine the beauty of Marilyn Monroe and the intellect of Katharine Hepburn with all the permutations of charm and sophistication imaginable in between. Her Christian name was Love, of course, and the surname can be rendered as Eagle. Together with Danube, Crimson and the original owner of our own No. 4, a Frank Sinatra figure who may be recalled as Cliff, Miss Eagle and her husband had made the film industry what it was. Their happiest collaboration, indeed a masterpiece of optimism, was called *Jolly Fellows*. It accounted for roughly one-third of all famous comedies ever produced, the other two also starring Miss Eagle and directed by her husband, who started his career with Eisenstein on the *Battleship Potemkin* and was later entrusted with such sensitive subjects as *Encounter on the Elbe*. The other woman we visited lived at No. 1. She was a distant relation of the original owner, a scientist who discovered the secret of immortality. This secret was of great interest to the ruler of a vast and powerful country like ours, and he showered her with honours until his death from cerebral haemorrhage. Sharp tongues later explained that, simply put, the scientist's secret was a highly diluted solution of caustic soda in which you bathed regularly. But as she too had now

5

died, of old age or a broken heart or some other cause embarrassingly unbecoming a person of such uncompromisingly scientific outlook, only the rumours of people with severe burns caused by their pursuit of immortality still circulated, while the older rumours, the glorious old rumours of her incontrovertible successes, had apparently died with her. Zina, who inherited the villa that was once a personal gift from the ruler, must have thought the whole thing terribly unfair because she was kind and kind people think most things terribly unfair. In a way it was, but we never discussed the matter. Zina had sixteen cats and, bless her kind heart, looked like one, although it was difficult to decide which one. It varied from day to day. The animals, as she called them, were all deformed and quiet, and since I already knew Dostoevsky's novel it was impossible not to think of them as the insulted and injured of the title. Zina was the only truly obscure inhabitant of Vnukovo, and the only one who was poor. For the animals she cooked a kind of nightmare stew, although at times it resembled plain gruel, perhaps simply oatmeal porridge with lots of innocent water, which was sticky and therefore frightening to a child who had never been exposed to life in the raw. She served the gruel at dusk, on the front porch of the crumbling house, with a heart-rending cry of 'Animals!' And, from the four corners of the garden, the animals would leap, hobble, or crawl, depending on the nature and extent of the injuries they had sustained in their formative years, meekly and noiselessly. In the evenings she watched television with her husband, a tired older man who, like her, never did or said a cruel thing in his life. What bile Kolya had in him he reserved for the television. If a singer sang, he would laugh demonically and exclaim: 'Is this singing?' If the news came on, he would snort: 'Is this news?' The only exception was what he called modern art, which he loathed despite the fact that it never appeared on the screen. To compensate, he had a reproduction of the Picasso etching of Don Quixote tacked, upside-down, to the wall above the television set, presumably in order to say 'Is this art?', or even 'Is this Don Quixote?', and to enjoy its humiliation when nothing on the screen diverted his selectively jaundiced eye. Their garden had very late apples, which lasted even longer into the winter than our own Antonov variety, and as we munched them Kolya would occasionally hurl a core at the etching, making even more of a mess of Don Quixote, he explained, than the artist had. From their gate to ours was a few hundred yards, but at midnight in winter it seemed much farther. During the day, in

6

summer, to bicycle from one gate to the next on the asphalted road took only a second. Such was the topography, or at any rate the social topography, of Mayakovsky Street.

3

If Vnukovo seems at all like heaven then our part of it, with a fence freshly painted forest green from Miss Eagle's to Cymbal's, was, as the etymology of the word suggests, paradise. This Persian term for 'enclave' specifically refers to a fence, at once confining bliss and excluding the interloper: 'What is out there?' our guests would ask. 'Out there?' my father would repeat absentmindedly, pretending that he was trying to think of an answer. 'Out there is power.' That, of course, was God's own truth. From the puppeteer to the director, from 'Broad is My Native Land' to *The White Birch* and the poem of the stove, from the martial splendour of Danube the composer of gay marches to the *prima ballerina assoluta* coquetry of Miss Eagle the comedienne, stretched Vnukovo, a cornerstone of the establishment upon which that power stood. It was now touched by decay, this grandiose monument to the arts of the empire. An airport had been built several miles away, a blight in the sense that the pharmaceutical enterprises dotting the environs of Versailles are a blight. Here too the locals had changed. Government worthies now had their dachas at the top of Mayakovsky Street, where the road curved towards town past Miss Eagle's, and it almost seemed that their rank was measured by their proximity to her. Gromyko, the venerable foreign minister, was nearest, with smaller fry at the other end. Overt encroachment of politics on the arts, if that is what it was, continued on the puppeteer's side of the colony, where Ponomarenko, a kindly secret policeman who founded SMERSH, had a house. His job description, when I looked it up years later in a Western reference book, read 'Head of NKVD control of Partisan Operations as head of Central HQ of the partisan movement, 1942–44'. He was, of course, a mass murderer, and like Hans Frank, Hitler's overseer in Poland whose granddaughter I later met at Peterhouse in Cambridge, an interesting man. Franziska Frank, who did not know her grandfather and never bothered to read his diaries, was not amused when I told her that just because a man is hanged at Nuremberg he should not be thought of as dull. And old Ponomarenko, to all appearances an average man, was certainly far more intelligent than the average. Father would often stop to chat with him in Mayakovsky Street. 'I told Iosif Vissarionovich to grab hold of Yugoslavia,' I remember once overhearing. But my mother was waiting for us to bring home the milk we had gone out to buy from the shop in town, and a few minutes later the conversation fizzled. We went home, the milk was boiled, and our guests could at last have their coffee. 'And what is out there?' one of them asked, as always, pointing to the edge of our grove. 'Out there', my father said, his eyes, as always, narrowing at the question, 'is power.' Moscow was Versailles, a Hollywood stage set, a dummy inflated to befuddle outsiders, a Potemkin village for foreigners to deceive themselves by observing understandable forms of life, when natives knew all the while that a hundred paces due north there began a different country, where nobody had ever seen a sofa or an orange and militarization held sway over tens of thousands of underground cities called bases, installations called closed towns and secret factories called postboxes, where man lived the totalitarian nightmare every waking moment, perpetuating and helping to perpetuate power and having no choice but death, grimy and terrible yet as ordinary and inconsequential as the death of a stingless insect. Why, even Moscow was known to conceal beneath itself a secret city skyscraper-deep, with underground buildings, railways and motorways, including one that ran from the Kremlin to the Vnukovo airport twenty-six steel-girded kilometres of tunnel away. Vnukovo, our charming grotto, sat on the pinhead summit of that iceberg of a world, and from its vantage point an active imagination could easily reconstruct the submerged whole as though measuring the entire monolith with a single blind guess.

> Broad is my native land,
> With forests, rivers, fields aplenty.

In that world, in this new civilization that was in reality militarization, we too were foreigners, as we were foreigners in Vnukovo. Not literally, of course, although many of our guests, the guests who asked 'What is out there?', were visitors from abroad. Ennobled by Ivan the Terrible for their service to Russian commerce, my paternal ancestors came from Persia and settled here centuries ago. Father was an hereditary Muscovite. He met my mother at the élite Foreign Languages Faculty, established at Moscow University by the omniscient ruler's personal command. All of which meant that my parents were natural insiders, raised and educated at Versailles. Cliff's house, when we bought it, cost the equivalent of what an average toiler would earn in eight hundred years, a generation more than it took mankind to progress from the Athens of Solon to the Rome of Marcus Aurelius. What better proof of belonging? Yet we lived as exiles, with the foreign feeling unique to the interloper, unique, perhaps, to paradise. Hence the power, out there, where the handmaiden of totalitarianism, art, strolled through the woods in the guise of a shepherdess, where Miss Eagle's daily chatted with her counterpart in the Gromyko household about men and the hardships of kitchen life, where old Ponomarenko turned the corner leaning on a cane which may or may not have grazed a prisoner's face already disfigured by torture. The power was objective, permanent and absolute. The feeling was fleeting yet recurrent, reflected in my father's narrowed eyes and instantly tired voice whenever he answered the question about what lay out there. Once in a while the ambiguity had unexpectedly comic overtones, as when, at the end of each winter month, time came for us to restock on coal for the central heating. The procedure was simple. You walked out on the main road and waved your fists, thumbs up, at the first lorry you happened to see going in the direction of the airport. The lorry would pull over because it was obvious that my father was a gentleman, in need of something that could be stolen, and the driver would then ask how much of it was needed. A gentleman's vague 'couple of tonnes' was the traditional reply. By contrast, Gromyko could not very well flag down a lorry on the motorway, and the veteran foreign minister had to go through official channels. Our coal, highest quality anthracite in perfectly shaped, egg-size sparkling lumps, would arrive just hours after it was stolen. His coal would come weeks or months after it was requisitioned, in huge dull-grey boulders mixed with completely useless coal dust. Through an opening in Gromyko's fence, glimpses of the foreign minister's maid hacking away at the boulders with a pickaxe illustrated the impotence of bureaucracy or the beauty of free enterprise, depending on the on-looker's mood. This particular comic source, however, ran dry when the government side of the enclave eventually arranged for mainline gas to be supplied to their villas, and the cultural side was joined up in due course. Out there was power, and though at times we laughed at its clumsy ways or mocked its invisible transience from behind the fence freshly painted forest green, it was there all the same. Power lay beyond the gates of our paradise, where a fresh-faced servant girl served coffee to a crowd of Russians and foreigners, our guests, after a dinner which rewarded them for the day's skiing or mushrooming exertions with sturgeon in aspic, roast grouse, apple charlotte *à la russe* and bottles of Georgian Tsinandali. Years later I met an Englishman, Lord Bethell, who remembered one of those dinners. He distinctly remembered the grouse. An American, Daniel Rose, was present at another. He took a Polaroid picture. It is the only photograph of our house which has survived.

4

Father thought photography vulgar and discouraged the practice, but here it is, the white house in the background, its stuccoed walls three bricks thick, an Italianate villa with twelve rooms, two open and two covered terraces. The windows of the dining room are just visible behind us three, father, mother and son posing for the camera in the foreground. If you took the side entrance we used, you would pass the kitchen on the left and down the corridor into my laboratory. There, when other children visited, though like photography other children were thought vulgar and rarely did, I too narrowed my eyes in response to their inevitable 'Can you make an explosion?' 'I can,' went the stock answer, 'but my interest is quantitative microanalysis.' I was contemptuous because my parents, who as my sole constant companions in paradise were my natural equals, never regarded me as a child in all those years, twelve of which had already passed and seemed like a lifetime in retrospect. Some had been spent elsewhere in paradise, in other summer enclaves where houses were rented, or in Moscow in the winter. In Moscow, a government inspector came because it was reported to the board of education that a child is being deliberately kept out of school. I was struggling with Xenophon's *Anabasis*. 'Can the child read Greek?' asked the inspector. 'Only with a dictionary,' the child interjected with crushing modesty, pointing to the old volume with the purple library stamp of a defunct ladies' college. Power temporarily retreated at the sight of such nauseatingly well-mannered monasticism, but it was decided that Moscow is no place to lead a secret life, what with the transparent social landscape, the nosy neighbours and, most menacing, the various uncles and aunts intent on wasting everyone's time with children's toys, other children of the same age, and pointedly generalized observations concerning the education of children, all of which were equally sterile, absurd and impertinent. Greek was a suitable obstacle in the path of these intrusions, but in case the relatives missed the point and still considered the child common property, he was instructed to intimate that, as he was busy with Henry Thomas Buckle's *A History of Civilization in England*, he would not accompany them to the May Day parade. Birthday toys were disembowelled on arrival, their tinpot mysteries exposed, a joyful procedure meant to encourage the deconstructive, experimental impulse. Books were received with suspicion and a warning to weed out anything intended for children. Fairy tales were on a par with Xenophon, of course, but Dumas was viewed as dangerously infantile and only narrowly escaped expulsion. Thus the basic attitude to the family as the individualist's last refuge under siege was established long before Vnukovo, with blood relations as the earliest philistines of a story not incompatible with the Gospels. Didactic and conceited, strong in numbers, relatives were swarming the gates, poised to overrun the family enclave with their plebeian pragmatism, their eternal values, myopic and cowardly, presented as well-meaning practical hints. Theirs was a world of furniture and furnishings, of good and still better jobs, of holidays in the Crimea and trips to Hungary, of new foreign films and the complete works of Tolstoy bound in imitation leather, of downhill skiing and other tribal rites that punctuate the sanctimonious ordeal of human existence. In the land where their parents might have disappeared without a trace and their own children might still be forced to swallow shards of glass in a cellar, they feared thieves. In the land where their parents had become movable property, totalitarian chattels, they saved money and hoped to pass it on to their children. They locked the door at night and counted their change when shopping. They wanted to teach us to be normal. But we saw them as philistines, and would not let them: 'Don't teach us how to live!' Father would yell, 'Damn philistines!' At the time of the shouting, however, when the family enclave was still based in Moscow, deep down we felt vulnerable and on occasion they had the upper hand. Father would work one or two days a month, writing the rest of the time, in longhand, on reams of white paper which would be regularly burnt in the building's litter-strewn rear courtyard. It was only when Moscow finally became unbearable,

11

despite our summer escapes to the countryside which usually began in early spring and ended in late autumn, that he started working for money. Where one or two days of work used to pay for a month of leisure, a year or two of work round the clock paid for Cliff's estate in Vnukovo. The philistines, who had earlier felt their criticism of his selfish idleness justified because Moscow may be Versailles but all the same a man must get ahead, were left gaping, and the gate in the fence painted forest green shut them out for ever. The primacy of spirit over blood was asserted. The principle of the family as a voluntary assembly of peers was upheld. It stands to reason that no member of such a body could be treated as a child, or for that matter as a parent. We were all in it together, united by the common task of keeping out the philistines who stood ready to invade the privacy of the study, the library and the laboratory with a pig snout as big as the world. I was gathering fallen apples, washing my test-tubes, reading the great and wise philosophers. Our freshly painted fence was there to remind me of Tom Sawyer's celebrated relay of the long-handled brush, and of the ambiguity, cultivated in our household with an almost religious zeal, of the distinction between work and play, an ugly distinction, I had been brought up to believe, made in Philistia. If Tom Sawyer 'had been a great and wise philosopher like the writer of this book,' wrote Mark Twain, 'he would now have comprehended that work consists of whatever a body is *obliged* to do, and that play consists of whatever a body is not obliged to do. And this would help him to understand why constructing artificial flowers or performing on a treadmill is work, while rolling ten-pins or climbing Mont Blanc is only amusement.' That was the practical basis of the family's daily routine, yet to this day I think of it as the divine *apeiron* of individual liberty. Father, when not working for money, was scissoring his way through the voluminous self-incriminations of Lenin's correspondence, or reading John Stuart Mill upon whose childhood my own education was to be based. Mother was typing away the afternoons, her electric Smith Corona the magical anode in our accumulation of fabulous wealth. The cathode was my father's youthful resistance to the wisdom of the philistines, who wanted him to become an engineer. He wanted to think, and to think meant to transplant oneself secretly to civilization, which in turn meant its language. If civilization is made by the individual, supreme in his right in law to defend his private caprices against the society which is ever intent on imposing upon him its public caprices, then England was the civilization of my father's

12

youth, and English its language. Others studied English, learning it as one learns engineering, making word lists, memorizing phrases like 'The struggle of the world proletariat will end with its victory' or 'The White House is the official residence of the President of the United States'. They knew English as a means of communication, a kind of invisible money, something to do with success in life, with foreign travel, with indoor plumbing. But no language opens its soul to exploitation, and they all died in the jungle, bogged down in the subjunctive, felled in droves by pronunciation and other native diseases. Father read the dictionary, entry by entry. This held the soul of civilization, these were the words of *Areopagitica*, these the shadows of the Magna Carta and the Corpus Juris Civilis. None was too archaic or obsolete, these natives of civilization among whom he dreamt of living. In the end they accepted him, and every word in the *Oxford Dictionary* knew his shortsighted way of fumbling about, recalling with a bemused smile the last time the eccentric Russian rustled past. My mother, when he was courting her, once agreed to meet him at a railway station at eleven in the evening. The reason she was angry to find him there, reading the dictionary, was because he had been there since eleven that morning and never noticed that she was late. The unanticipated result of his amatory flight into civilization was recognition by the very power which he was hoping to flee, the militarization which eyed the civilization as a parasite follows its host or a predator tracks its once and future prey. On leaving university he was offered the post of embassy secretary in London, provided, as the symbolism of allegiance dictated at the time, he joined the relevant organization. He refused, but the relevant organization bore no grudges, knowing that a unique talent would serve its aims regardless of how that talent was bureaucratically channelled. It had nowhere else to go. The gargantuan industry of communications with the West, whose main language was English, was then operated by native English speakers, its more sophisticated functions overseen by men like Kim Philby. Father entered the industry as a freelance, after submitting a translation anonymously and then revealing himself as a humble denizen of Muscovy who had never spent a day of his life abroad. Philby's fellow natives had failed to find fault with the translation, and this freak of nature became the first and only Russian ever to be accredited by their guild. By the time Vnukovo offered its seclusion, he was translating everything from Dostoevsky, Herzen and Prishvin to marine biology and mathematical linguistics. The entire

13

content of journals like *Nuclear Physics* would be delivered to the Vnukovo house in Russian, to be collected by messenger in English and ready for publication in the West a few days later. Using special dictaphones, which, as a sometime engineer *manqué*, he designed and built for his typists, he overtook the combined productivity of the whole guild and was able to negotiate his own fees, earning an engineer's annual wages in one day. Yet the seclusion of Vnukovo, so dearly bought, was an illusion. Out there lay power, and our independence from it was as conditional as my father's release from all social obligations which he passed on to his only son as a nobleman might a title. I was probably alone in all of Russia never to attend school or participate in anything 'collective', 'obligatory' or 'relevant'. Science became the official cover for my introspection, as the unexpectedly practical applications of my father's talent were a cover for his, when I was invited at age twelve to read analytical chemistry at Moscow University after winning a national competition. But again, on closer scrutiny these freedoms were little more than latitudes, and it is hardly surprising that the relationship between the two, considered from the vantage point of freethinking individualism, was the main topic at the Vnukovo symposia attended by our foreign and Russian guests. Those interested in the subject, often to the exclusion of all others, comprised our natural milieu. They were our extended family.

5

The Vnukovo dialogues were Socratic not merely in genre, dominated as these were by the fundamental problem of differentiating between reality and appearance, fact and verisimilitude. All foreigners were welcome, as each was thought potentially capable of contributing to the discussion a new insight into civilization, revealing something unknown about its power to save or to sustain the individual. Assuming perhaps that it contained some of the answers we sought so anxiously, on his return home the American who took the Polaroid picture sent us a full set of the reassuringly voluminous *Encyclopaedia Britannica*. Our Russian guests belonged to what is known as the intelligentsia, but it would have been inaccurate to describe them as 'dissidents'. Most were beyond rebellion, too hardened in their cynicism, too sceptical about the individual's prospects in a totalitarian world, and the occasional underground activist to munch on our grouse was viewed with a mixture of sympathy and apprehension. One such activist rented Zina's summer cottage. On weekends the womanly falsetto of a relation of his, the author of a recent *succès de scandale*, a novella about a single day in the life of a camp inmate, wafted Cliffwards. The novella was published at the instigation of the last ruler, who in the usual byzantine way wanted to vilify his predecessor but then decided that enough was enough, turning on both the author, who by then had all but pocketed the literary prize named after the already-vilified predecessor's as-yet-unvilified predecessor, and the editor of the magazine which had printed the novella, who soon died at his dacha in Vnukovo on the other side of a ravine that ran parallel to Mayakovsky Street. It was the usual Vnukovo story, its provisional moral only marginally more puzzling than the death of the scientist who discovered immortality, and slightly complicated by our own recognition that the novella showed unmistakable signs of talent. Our guests would have been unlikely to appreciate these subtleties even if the voice of the rebellious author, who now had a xenophobic beard and consorted with underground activists, had not been so damn loud. They had only to reflect that if a supremely apolitical life, such as my father's, could fulfil the aims of power so inexorably and invisibly, then underground political activism was hardly more than a hoax, directly fulfilling those aims despite the noblest intentions of the participants and their naively clandestine associations. In his youth, when the penalty for the offence was death under torture, my father experimented with 'dissidence' in this sense by slipping a leaflet, which he had prepared after consulting a standard work on forensics, into the ballot box. Since then, as surely as the rulers came and went, the power he had offended in private had grown stronger, with the result that the penalty for offending it, even publicly, was now no longer death under torture, but merely arrest, deportation, exile. This is why those who were not born individualists, or hardened into cynics, were organically incapable of participating in the Socratic symposium on human motivations and limitations. They dared not to observe that the noble intentions never stirred in their breast, or the breast of any other shrill-voiced rebel, when the price was death under torture. That these noble intentions stirred there now, braving arrest, deportation, exile, was an insult to the freethinking individualist, who could well anticipate a future when the offended power would become so strong that even the mildest penalty for the offence would be lifted. What then? Gazing into these troubled waters, the individualist saw his ultimate nightmare, a deep stillness of power more quiet than time itself, eternal and invulnerable for millennia. Yet elsewhere, it seemed, civilization lingered, and in the West, beyond the power that lay out there, was hope and salvation. Hence the foreigners at our table, robustly interrogated well into the night, as the violet snow turned a screechy white and retired at twenty below, having gently wrapped the windows of our dining room and the wheels of their sleeping Mercedes, dainty as Cinderella's slipper, in cottonwool and tinsel. On more than one occasion I remember them bursting into tears under the stress of Socratic questioning by the Russians. The war which the West was then losing in South-east Asia was a war which the intelligentsia hoped it would win, as it had won the war in the Middle East. I merely record the facts. I never met anyone in my childhood who did not believe that South Vietnam and Israel alike belonged to the West and to civilization, and equally that the opponent seeking their destruction was the very power which we in Vnukovo knew lay beyond the fence freshly painted forest green. Civilization's victories meant that this earthly power had limits just as real, that it could not crush our enclave and all other enclaves like ours with absolute equanimity. The power tolerated individuals for as long as it needed them, for as long as militarization had not devoured civilization globally, while we, if only by remaining individuals, were helping it to achieve this end and hence to bring about our own eventual destruction. Conversely, civilization's defeats meant that the process was far more advanced than we knew or hoped. Civilization, in short, was God, and our interest in the West was as vital as theology had been in centuries past. Doubting the godhead's power was psychologically suicidal, as was doubting its wisdom, and yet the foreigners' tears and often incoherent expostulations were ample proof that all was not well in the heaven which the newspapers called 'capitalist paradise' in inverted commas and of which No. 4 Mayakovsky Street was a miniature replica. The angels themselves appeared quite ignorant of their God's mysterious ways, though as far as my father and his fellow exegetes were concerned, as I said, doubt was tantamount to suicide. That was *our* limit.

6

Even with unlimited hindsight it is difficult to see how the abstract West could have failed to become the living God of the intelligentsia under totalitarianism, and of our family paradise in particular. In the beginning was the word, and Russians of my grandfather's generation were the first to discern, more or less dimly, that the word was there to breathe life into an otherwise tendentious account of creation. My grandfather was a playwright, a friend of Zamyatin whose novel, *We*, anticipated and corroborated Orwell's conception of the future. He volunteered and was killed in 1941. From him we inherited our family library, not in the bourgeois sense of mahogany and morocco, but as an arc of covenant, a ten-foot ream of battered and dusty remnants of books, pamphlets and magazines which appeared in his early days as a writer and represented his generation. Because this generation was the last legitimate representative of Russian culture, the sisyphean burden of seeing a beginning in its own end fell on its shoulders. For my father and later for me, it was vital to feel that weight as our own, to learn the myth in every minute detail. From the layers of obfuscation, from the dust that was often ashes and contained charred human bones, first to emerge was the truth articulated by Mandelstam in lines addressed to totalitarian power when many of that generation had already fallen silent:

> Whom will you kill? Whom will you rule divine?
> What new deception have you planned?
> Pluck out the typing key. Return to find
> A fishbone buried in the gaping land.

It was the truth of universal provocation. Everything on earth, all acts of volition, everything done or attempted, openly or in secret, for this, that or another reason, serves the ruler in a totalitarian world, the omniscient demiurge who is God on earth. A totalitarian world is the world without free will. You paint a picture that is a masterpiece, and this pleases the ruler. You conspire to assassinate the ruler, and this pleases him even more, because he exposes a genuine conspiracy. You live like Diogenes, and the ruler makes an example of you to teach other vagrants a lesson. You marry, and bear the ruler another pair of subjects. You become a doctor, a priest, an engineer, a caretaker or a chef, you study ancient languages or fluid mechanics, you eat, drink and make merry, you write limericks or *vers libre*, you plot revenge against your neighbour or turn the other cheek, you go mad or feign insanity, you are drafted into the army or sign on as a volunteer, all these choices, decisions and outcomes are equally illusory and destined to serve the same end. But the corollary truth, which emerged as though from a wellspring of living water to cure total despair, was that the dominion of the God on earth had limits and did not extend to heaven. 'The West, the West!' There the true God ruled, and if only these supplications could reach him, life on earth would have meaning. The painter would be recorded in his book of being, as would the martyr and the saintly vagrant, the simple father of two and the professional man. The scholar's scribblings and the poet's intuitions would be judged, the grievances of neighbours settled, the fool pronounced sane and the toady a fool, the soldier decorated and the general pardoned. The truth of this corollary was easily proven by historical observation. Everything on earth, all acts of its totalitarian demiurge, everything done or attempted, openly or in secret, for whatever stated reason, by the ruler and his satraps, had the West as its intended audience. Since the ultimate aim of all earthly power is to destroy God and rule heaven, for all these years our rulers had been trying to talk him into coming down to earth. He would take our word for it and come down some day, all human, unarmed, a hostage. Their summit, their total power, their final turn in the eternal return of the Mahabharata, their earth, already a lion's share of the globe with satrapies from ocean to ocean, and now their heaven as well. And all because of our word, which had been there since the beginning of totalitarian time as the main semiotic component of each successive ruler's 'dialogue with the West', our word, Russian culture, artificially grafted like a human mouth on a waxwork idol, a living *logos* on an *eikon basilikon,* and conserved in timelessness until the day when such idols, representing the individual and fashioned in his image, would no longer be needed. All was grist to the mill. The popular singer sang the word and, under her husband's direction, the popular comedienne acted it out to the popular tune of her Vnukovo neighbour, and all this was terribly, terribly democratic and lowbrow and just like in the West:

> 'Cuz we got the chicken and we got the oven,
> And everybody is a Be-e-e-t-hoven!

18

And, two whistlestops away, in Peredelkino, a poet of genius by whose intuitions world culture can be measured as it is measured by Shakespeare's, wrote the word, and it was all terribly, terribly aristocratic and highbrow, just like in the Russia which was once the West:

> Oh, that this too too solid flesh would melt,
> Thaw and resolve itself into a dew.

More grist to the mill. And in another enclave, on another suburban railway line, a Beethoven of the twentieth century composed the word, just as he once composed it in the Russia where he had been born, and it too lived on and was that selfsame totalitarian word which finally convinced the true God in heaven to come down to earth and be crucified with no hope of resurrection.

7

Prokofiev's dacha in Nikolina Gora was one of those we had looked at before buying the house in Vnukovo. Who knows how many a mock paradise the ruler had built for the coryphaei of the word in the environs of Moscow. Prokofiev's son, Oleg, was a family friend with whom my father in the days of his youth studied painting. I never knew Khazanov or Falk, their teachers. Only one of my father's bathers survived to substantiate his bemused recollections of Khazanov, and only a still life with cherries by Falk. Oleg remembered how old Falk, emaciated, in a paint-spattered smock, tried to persuade his father, orotund and prosperous, not to put him through institutionalized art training in draughty Moscow. In such tales lay the object lesson for my own future, though at Nikolina Gora it was the grapes overgrowing Prokofiev's glass veranda which seemed more apposite. But later, when I heard Prokofiev's music, when I came to know by heart every line Pasternak had written, when I read through my grandfather's library and exhumed other family histories like his, it all fitted together. Grist to the mill, no doubt, but so much more complex and confusing than Kolya's visceral denial of television, or of Picasso! Nikolina Gora became part of an unwritten cosmogony, and in the

streaming consciousness of adolescence its Dionysian grapevines inter-
twined with the Apollonian birches of Vnukovo. Take Prokofiev's
'Lieutenant Kizhé'. This was based on a satirical novella by a writer
my grandfather knew, who was among Pasternak's earliest admirers.
Yet was not the novella published because it satirized 'old' Russia,
where Prokofiev's genius had been engendered, nursed and understood? And did not Prokofiev compose the suite for a film? A film! The
cine-mah, which to Pasternak or Mandelstam would in itself have
been lowbrow anathema, while Mayakovsky and Meyerhold lapped it
up. As Mandelstam summed up the genre:

> The cinema. Three empty benches.
> A lot of sentimental bother.
> A nob, a moneybags. Two wenches
> Trapped in the intrigue of another.

Did not Prokofiev later collaborate with Eisenstein, every bit as
seriously as Miss Eagle and as bemedalled as the worst of them? In
America, he even imagined working with Walt Disney, the local
equivalent of our Crimson. His only peer, Shostakovich, composed
the music for more than thirty films. And did not our lighthearted
Danube conduct the première of 'Kizhé' for the soundtrack? Did not
Konchalovsky, a friend of the Pasternaks, paint that portrait of
Prokofiev under the pine tree? Did not Pasternak's brother design the
mausoleum in Red Square? And where was that pine tree, anyway?
In what other mock paradise in this web of enclaves, spanning the
corners of the earth and spun by power to perpetuate power? Did God
in heaven, we wondered, so much as possess a culture unentangled in
this web, independent of the word uttered here, a culture that really
was what Russia's had been? Those who made it to heaven, at any
rate to have a good look, Zamyatins and Nabokovs, Diaghilevs and
Rachmaninoffs, Prokofievs and Pasternaks, Chagalls and Stravinskys,
told no tales. 'Do not return to Russia, it is draughty there, Marina,'
was all that Pasternak's bloodless lips whispered to Tsvetaeva in
Paris. It was not convincing, and she returned to her death. The
infinitely wise Zamyatin – who said that Russian literature had only
one future, its past – returned and mocked England in *The Islanders*. It
was not convincing either. Yet Zamyatin, fortunate in that he was
allowed out once more, died in France in total obscurity. But were not
France and England, in our view, different names for heaven? Besides,
did not Zamyatin inspire Orwell? We knew there was no better

description of life on earth than Orwell's. And yet again, some of the foreign visitors to Vnukovo insisted that what Orwell had described was life in heaven. Were the angels to be believed? But doubt was suicide:

> Oh, that this too too solid flesh would melt,
> Thaw and resolve itself into a dew.

8

The word which renders into Russian the English notional triad of 'power, force, strength' sounds like and is etymologically related to the Germanic word 'soul', which evolved from the idea of resilience, such as that of a tree branch in the face of the elements, perceived by the primitive Indo-European mind as a useful, positive quality. As this meaning grew more specific, it gave rise to other Russian words, such as the one meaning 'rape', literally the imposition of power, force, strength upon another, a connotation lost in English when even in polite discourse the rude Anglo-Saxon word displaced 'violation', so transparently akin to 'violence'. As a result, to the modern English ear 'rape' is an abstraction, while the Russian cannot but feel for the victim's violated soul etymologically, which is to say literally. The word used by my father, however, when he explained that power lay out there, was not this vivid, concrete Russian counterpart of the abstractly opaque English notions. He used instead the dark, vague, all-encompassing word with a meaning akin to 'ownership' or 'possession' which sounds like and is etymologically related to the English 'wield', from the Anglo-Saxon verb meaning 'to have power over, rule, possess'. One of the most powerful gods in the pagan pantheon of the ancient Slavs was the god of cattle named Veles, from whom, of course, it is only a young calf's skip to 'wealth'. The word for 'God', tied to the notion of 'good' in English, is likewise tied to 'wealth' in Russian, while its Russian antonym, 'poverty', sounds like and is etymologically related to the English 'bad'. Thus from the ownership of people to the ownership of things is the skip of civilization, with its implicit meaning of civic evolution. The noun form of 'wield', that dark, all-encompassing word which my father used, antedated this evolution. Ownership, out there, meant ownership of people, man's power over man. How did I know all this?

> Oh, that this too too solid flesh would melt,
> Thaw and resolve itself into a dew.

Every morning the gramophone needle would follow the groove, surprisingly large when your eye was right next to the thumb that lifted the tone-arm. We never went to the opera in those Vnukovo days, but when I heard the recorded voices of Smirnov and Caruso the melting of the flesh which I knew to be the aim of music could never equal the original. The original was called *Gamlet* in Russian. What made my resolution into a dew historically inevitable, as a follower of Gegel – I mean, of Hegel – might say, was the effortless disdain of Laurence Olivier when, after a few rasps and scratches, his invisible mouth, almost without moving, began to form the syllables bitter as wormwood. In the Russian idea of nobility, disdain and sadness are fused so that it is impossible to tell where one ends and the other begins. And this is how it ought to be, of course, because the world is divided into those who are stronger than I (for them, like the flat of a blade, my disdain) and those who are weaker (I give them my sadness). The idea did not originate in Russia, it merely survived in Russian culture longer than elsewhere in Europe, and the prince's voice resuscitated this anachronism with the force of universal tragedy. Was there in all Russian literature, this product of an aristocratic culture, a single joke at the expense of a woman deceived? A child? A pauper? No, as I read somewhere and thought it was true, our literature is a paean to the insulted and injured, and even the thief of Dostoevsky's *Honest Thief* is honest. Literature is the creation of novel hierarchies. Forever imitating the Gospels, it redistributes power in the worlds it creates, worlds which are like the earth yet as theoretical as heaven. *Scandalum magnatum*, offending the great, is at the heart of its being. Uplifting the meek is its essence. This was the ghost that haunted Vnukovo, and though Zina was so powerless she had only cats to uplift, and Kolya only apple cores with which to defend Don Quixote's dignity, even our own Mayakovsky Street was not unlike Elsinore. I had read the play in the Russian translation made by Pasternak in spiritual dotage, a satyr to the Hyperion of his youth. Much closer to the truth of the original was a line of Mandelstam, whose poems were then still known only in typescript, which mentioned the Englishwoman's red-maned disdain, 'and the quinine of

22

distant colonies' in the next line. That was just it, red-maned disdain becoming a prince was the foundation of our common European culture. And this meant I would be able to learn English, which is how the same children who asked for explosions in the laboratory would describe my morning efforts to fuse the tones of condescension and humility in the Olivier manner. I had not, in fact, been given the English text of the play. The object was to piece it together by listening to the record and looking up each word in my father's 'big blue' English–Russian dictionary. Although I never did discover what *fieont* was, nor *ofie* for that matter, the ordeal of many months was an education in the rhythm and timbre of the language. I did not know the words, but I could parrot them with the mixture of disdain and sadness that satisfied the Romantic craving. Earlier in childhood I had learned to read Russian poetry in the same way, imitating the imagined sound of Pasternak, Mandelstam or Tsvetaeva as the words themselves, many of which then eluded my understanding, were written to make the reader do. When an adult reads, unless he is Olivier, he cannot hear the poem for the words, whereas a child may rely entirely on the inner ear of the imagination to guide him through the verbal underwood. Camellia, to both the Russian and the English ear, sounds just as it should, far less delicate than it is made out to be and pale for the fear that this will be discovered, so how important can it really be to know what the word actually means? Therein lay my whole method of learning English, as those children would have called my disastrous affair with Ophelia, which sounds like camellia and has at its root the Greek word for snake. I found a small English–Russian dictionary, no more than ten thousand words, and with Father's approval began the year-long project. After copying out a word in a notebook, I hunted for its cognates in etymological dictionaries, noting the entries which often yielded a whole series of kindred Slavic meanings. By the time I was finished with each word I knew its whole Indo-European history, and dozens of new English words besides. And so I learnt that *Graf*, the princely title from Europe's tribal Germanic past, is the English 'grab' in disguise, and the Russian for 'loot'. Between Prince Hamlet and his people stood civilization. That in German 'kiss' is *Kuss*, which in Russian means 'bite'. How like Ophelia! That in Russian the word which is literally 'yearning to bite' means both 'temptation' and 'art', eternal in the English of 'attempt'. That poetry, as Pasternak once wrote to Tsvetaeva, is the etymology of feeling.

23

9

The grassy ravine ran parallel to Mayakovsky Street and away from the pond, which everyone respectfully called the lake, at the bottom of Zina's garden. Marmot's back fence, at the ravine's other end, had a gate, and there I saw Katya. I think there was a swing, but perhaps she was only leaning on her bicycle. She was with her girl friends, one of whom was the daughter of a man groomed to become the next ambassador to the Court of St James's. We were enemies, I and they. If only because every one of our Russian guests grimaced contempt on hearing Marmot's name, whereas the mention of a mass murderer like Ponomarenko evinced merely curiosity. Marmot was known as Pasternak's murderer, which was not strictly speaking true but seemed plausible because, emboldened by the moral of the Mozart story, popular ignorance likes to pit the mediocrity it is itself incapable of identifying against the genius it only belatedly recognizes, with consequences sufficiently bloody and appealing for it to appreciate. The story of Pasternak was likewise misconstrued. In fact, some thirty years earlier, when the poet was still the genius of his own story, Marmot venerated him publicly as a 'master'. By the time the scandal of *Zhivago* erupted and Marmot organized the murderous campaign of denunciation against its author, long dead as the poet who had been the genius of his own story, few realized that it was the case of Salieri poisoning one of his own kind, a Vnukovo story. Certainly neither we nor any of our guests realized this, preferring to see Pasternak as he had been, and Marmot for what he always was. And here was Katya, who called the poetaster with the poet's blood on his hands grandpa, tanned and thin in the swing, surrounded by the equally high-born offspring of Vnukovo. They called me over. 'So what makes you think you know English?' said the Red Queen, with a conspiratorial glance at her friend who, I was told, had been schooled in America. 'What is the English for "girl?"' The taunt was unbearable, my family honour at stake, Pasternak unavenged. If they had asked about the word 'blossom', I would have astonished them with a semantic play within a play, since earlier that morning I had been investigating the etymological links between 'bloom' and 'blood', as well as the connections between the Russian word for blood and the English 'crude' and 'raw'. Of course I knew the word 'girl', but to answer the question straightforwardly, like a coward or a soldier, would have meant acknowledging their mastery over my vocabulary. I had not reached the seventh letter of the dictionary in those semantic exercises, but anyway my intuition told me that even if I had, 'girl' was sure to mire me in some Anglo-Saxon bog. The *jeunesse dorée* of Vnukovo waited, gloating. The *sans-culotte* intellectual, trembling, said he did not know. Probably because she had recently heard the phrase somewhere, Katya said theatrically: 'Well, that's that. I wash my hands of him.' Did I let the poet down? There is, I learnt later, an American television show famous for the host's cathartic, tell-the-truth exhortation to the 'real' guest to stand up, while the impostors, invited to impersonate him, remain seated. Nothing odd about imagining Pasternak on the show. 'What is poetry?' he would be asked. 'I don't know, it's difficult to say, I've been thinking about that myself just now . . .' he would plead, looking sideways at the studio audience. 'All right, then. What is life?' Again total bewilderment, while Marmot and other impersonators rattled off their answers: 'The etymology of feeling!' or 'My sister!' Nothing sacrilegious about imagining the appearance of Christ on the show either, especially if the circumstances of the second coming are at all like the first, transposed, naturally, to our own existential frame of reference with television studios as the houses of prayer or the market squares of antiquity. Flanked on the screen, symbolically enough, by two impostors, Jesus would be asked: 'Tell us, what were you doing in the Garden of Gethsemane?' He would pause, stammer. 'I can't remember.' The robbers would answer, without a moment's hesitation, that they were praying. I do not mean that the Vnukovo ravine was my Galilee. I merely note the essential clumsiness of all that is genuine, and what an evanescent thing is truth.

10

Peredelkino and Vnukovo were two whistlestops apart and no one bothered to remember the life outside, a life to which I, even I, had been born. Only my mother still strung those days together, obliquely, sporadically, maternally, like the illiterate village woman her own mother had been, yawning and making the sign of the cross over her mouth to keep petty devils from hopping in. You were born in autumn, she said. It was in October, and the first year was hard for both of us because you had to be nursed to life. That summer we rented in Zagoryanka, on the Northern line, together with old Khazanov. He and your father went out to the river every morning to paint their landscapes. In the evenings Khazanov liked to have proper Russian buckwheat, steamed in a cast-iron pot in a peasant stove, and we always supped with him and the maids. Ours was called Valya, a young girl, from the deepest provinces. One day the seizures started, I was only on my sixth month and everybody knows that at seven they survive and at six they do not. The evening of Saturday I was in the village hospital, no doctor and none expected till Monday. It was a one-storey building, with windows facing the road, and at night when I turned on the light the sheet was crawling with lice and I started screaming. Everybody just stared, why such commotion, they were used to living all covered in vermin from head to foot. I had no money with me, but I told the nurse I would give her my diamond ring if she phoned my aunt in Moscow to come and take me away from there. What do I want with your diamond, she answered, give me a fiver. And I had nothing. By now it was getting light, and all of a sudden there was Valya poking her head in through the window: 'I've been guarding you all night.' 'Run for my husband,' I said, 'tell him to come and save me.' He came and carried me to the station in his arms. We took the train to Moscow, then a taxi to the Arbat clinic where my doctor, an old Armenian, Tsevyanov by name, was the consulting physician. He is my doctor, I told them. 'You're lying,' they said, 'and anyways it's now Sunday and he ain't here, so we are ordering you to municipal clinic 13.' I locked myself in the toilet. They broke the lock. I pretended I had fainted, your father started yelling at them that he would not let me go by myself, and finally they allowed him and Valya to come with me in the ambulance. A nurse sat with the driver. We drive along the Garden Ring, past our house in Red Gates, where the car stops at the light and your father swings open the door and yells 'Run!' Then the ambulance driver and the nurse jump out, he starts fighting with the driver and Valya with the nurse, and the driver grabs my dress and the dress tears and falls to the ground in shreds, and the traffic stops, and some policemen come running. I hid in the lobby of the Ministry of Transport, watching your father being arrested and shoved into a police car, watching Valya on her knees, picking up our scattered belongings, a toothbrush, a handkerchief. I had nothing on except my belly, so I asked people who passed by to cover me, to help me cross the Ring, but they only looked away, until at last some man lent me his overcoat and took me home. The next day Tsevyanov arrived, we gave him a thousand roubles, he said at clinic 13 you would have been routinely aborted. He told me to stay in bed, and I did. Your father left every morning to paint with Khazanov at the dacha, returning by afternoon train. A month passed, your seventh. Then another, and again I started worrying, because everybody knows that at seven they survive and at eight they do not, because it can be seven and it can be nine, but it cannot be eight. Then comes October, my real seizures start, and I am taken to Tsevyanov's clinic. He says you have turned upside-down, and that there are all sorts of complications besides, and I trust him because he is a master, an artist, a man of genius, the only one of his kind in Moscow. The trouble is, he is a consultant to the clinic and cannot operate there unless he is teaching his students, so he brings his whole university class and 'chooses' me to demonstrate a particularly complex procedure. And thanks to that demonstration you were born, alive and whole, and I heard you crying. But then they took you away, and I did not see you for many days. Day and night I wept, with my head under the covers because I could not bear to watch the other women feeding theirs. But then a woman next to me said, 'You fool, get out from under those covers, you bloody fool, they brought him in just now and you missed him, they thought you was sleeping.' At last they brought you to me, and I took you home to nurse you to life because Tsevyanov said you were so weak it was all in my hands now. And I nursed you for a whole year, not leaving the room until the following summer, you were still so weak. Later, when another year went by and you refused to eat food, your father would make paper ships and set them alight in a basin of water, and you watched with amazement, sometimes opening your mouth to my spoon. Your father kept saying Homer, Homer, and I kept thinking Tsevyanov, Tsevyanov, he saved you, I must give him a present, something equally miraculous, but time passed, I never got round to it, and then I heard he was dead, and again I kept thinking I must go to the cemetery and put some flowers on his grave, a huge, huge wreath, but I never went. It seemed so difficult then, life did. But even when you started walking and we would go to the park near by, the one used to be called Three Saints in the old days, or to Clear Ponds where my aunt lived, God be my witness I still thought we would visit his grave some day. It never happened, perhaps it was unimportant.

The important thing is what I am telling you now in his memory, because if you want something locked up in a bank vault I can eat through the metal like acid, yet even this love which stops at nothing, a mother's love, cannot save a life without an art like his and for that may his blessed soul rest in paradise.

11

Miraculous the present she gave me instead of Tsevyanov, though again a doctor was in the background, because love is a miracle which must be safeguarded with gifts, just as life is by those who have the gift of an art like medicine. I had found the knife every child wanted, a thief's knife called 'Finnish' in Russian, with a long thin blade and a handle of coloured pieces of translucent plastic, bright as a necklace of beads, and I had been amusing myself by throwing household objects into the air, the better to stab them, when I cut in half the index finger of my left hand. At the hospital the doctor said that the finger would mend, and then something that pleased Father still more. He offered to let me stitch it together myself, under his supervision at the hospital, which was so scientifically exciting that I did not feel any pain. Father said he was sure that if John Stuart Mill had been in the same predicament, this is just what *his* doctor would have done. From that moment on, Shura became our family physician, and when my appendix almost burst and everyone thought I had eaten a wrong mushroom, he said there was a danger of peritonitis but it might still go away and the logical thing was to let me decide. Do you want your appendix out, he said by my pillow, or do you prefer to take the risk of peritonitis? Can I take it out myself at your hospital? I asked. No, he said, but I can tilt a mirror so you can watch the operation. Shura was the chief surgeon of a ward, and while after routine operations of this kind patients are moved to a huge hall with twenty or thirty beds, he knew what my mother wanted and I had a room to myself. Mother stayed with me in the room until the stitches had to come out, and of course hospital food never crossed the threshold. She asked Shura if she could cook in the hospital kitchen: 'What if somebody tells me I can't?' Spit in his dumb savage face, said Shura. And after all these miracles had been wrought, life and love made safe from the barbarism beyond, there came the greatest miracle and the greatest gift, three tomatoes and a cucumber. In November. The cucumber I ate right away, but the tomatoes, November tomatoes, grown somewhere in the south by dark-faced Abkhazians, smuggled into Moscow in overstuffed bags in the dead of night, sold like perfume or silk stockings, but more precious because the love they symbolized was rarer and more visceral, and besides they did not keep, the tomatoes I kept by my bedside for a day or two. *Tomatl*, fruit of Atlantis. Huge and misshapen they were, red and green like the map of a civil war, with ingrown scars for rivers. When you bit into one, its juice and its yellow seeds would rush to the surface, as if you were the earth and it a volcano, as if you were the lion that had ruptured the aorta of a stray lamb, as if you were the priest called to make a ritual offering. And then you added the salt, to make the second bite more like a human meal, because you were neither a god nor an animal, and also some bread and butter. Oh what divine hand healed my wounds in that hospital room, it was as nothing next to the hand that proffered this gift, the hand that cultivated and transported and paid. No matter how much salt I added, no matter how much bread and butter I ate, the sacrifice belonged to the Indo-European myth of the earth, the genius who bears fruit because such is her art, suffering because she knows that if she should ever stop, her paradise will be overrun by savage time and barbarian probability.

12

Peredelkino and Vnukovo were two whistlestops apart, and no one knew how many a mock paradise there was besides. I recall another such enclave, where we had a house before Vnukovo, curiously enough near the other Moscow airport, Sheremetevo, and an evening at Arseny Tarkovsky's, or perhaps the house was actually rented by his son Andrei, then making a film about the icon painter Rublev during the shooting of which, it was said in alarmed whispers, a cow had been burnt alive. There was a large room, and everyone sat on the floor by candlelight, as the aesthetics of the decade demanded, eating a kind of pot-luck supper of which I remember only the dazzling green of coriander, then fashionable because it came from freewheeling

Georgia, as did the evening's entertainment, Bulat Okudzhava, a Moscow poet who sang his verse accompanying himself on a guitar:

> There lived on earth a soldier boy,
> So fine he was, so dapper —

he declaimed, reaching for the instrument with an air of calculated laziness. Then he touched the strings, and a little mechanical tune began to unravel the words:

> But children thought he was a toy,
> A soldier made of paper.

The banality was deliberate, and the singer's beautiful voice so hopelessly cynical that even a child could take his meaning:

> He lived to make us unafraid,
> He lived to make us happy . . .

Pause. Total silence.

> But he himself hung on a thread,
> The soldier made of paper.

I think there was another verse or two, as the words came faster and faster off the song's unravelling spool:

> Then he, as fate decreed he might,
> Wished for just one great caper,
> And begged and begged: 'Let there be light!'

This last was sung with a kind of plaintive tremolo, followed by the inevitably mechanical:

> Forgetting he was paper.

We were by now expecting the denouement, one final verse, sung so quickly that only after the applause and the shouts died down was a sadness felt in the room, though many of the guests, if a child can read adult faces, thought it was only a song, which, once over, meant they could safely get back to the communal coriander.

> Is that your wish? All right then, go.
> He marched straight at the taper
> And in its flame burnt up for naught,
> The soldier made of paper.

Okudzhava's ballad later became the intelligentsia's, although few understood its meaning in all its utter and inescapable pessimism, which I think I glimpsed at the age of six. The other improbable memory of Sheremetevo was an afternoon walk in the woods in the company of my nanny, when I met two similarly escorted girls. I had heard somewhere that one could construct a theatre of shadows using paper cut-outs which moved behind a transparent paper screen with an ordinary candle for illumination. At a loss for how to engage their attention, I blurted out to the girls that such a theatre had already been built by me, and that I would entertain them, rather as Okudzhava entertained Tarkovsky's guests, with an adaptation for the shadow stage of the novel about the War of the Roses I was then reading, Stevenson's *Black Arrow*. It is really heaven, I promised, this theatre of mine is heaven. My nanny, who had firm instructions not to interfere in my personal life, did not object when I went on to tell the girls that performances began promptly at eight. But since the very process of telling them about my shadow theatre fully satisfied the Platonic yearning which our chance meeting had awakened, I forgot all about it. My humiliation at a quarter to eight when the girls, again accompanied by their nanny, appeared on our doorstep, just in time to buy the tickets and have a quick drink at the bar I suppose, was indescribable. Humbled by both the literalism and the blindness of their faith in the paradise I had invented, I improvised a screen, some cut-outs and a candle, but in the end the applause was thin and the disappointment unconcealed. My mother made cocoa. It was the only time in my life when I felt like a child. The burn smarted until I read the Huysmans novel whose asthenic hero intends to travel to England but stops short in Calais, where the oxtail soup of an English pub satiates his yearning as fully as the shadow theatre of my boast extinguished the desire, which I had irresponsibly ignited in others, to see heaven. The languid Des Esseintes had grasped the principle, as it were, and this made the Channel crossing itself at best superfluous and at worst simply tiring. The thing about the West which made any voyage there as original as Columbus's and as irreversible as the immolation of the paper soldier was that none of us had as yet grasped the principle. How ironic that my theatre of shadows should have gone bust near an international airport, where on our heavenless earth such voyages invariably begin.

13

For those early dabblers in shadow theatre like Mayakovsky and Meyerhold, film was a mere symbol of mass culture. They had to live with such a culture no more than an animal rights activist has to live the way Zina did. As in the case of similar symbols, such as Mayakovsky's manufacture of 'agitprop' posters, or 'audience participation' in the Meyerhold productions, these artists were in the enviable position of enjoying the hierarchic safety of an aristocratic culture while making what seemed like innovative, reckless, populist gestures. It hardly occurred to them that the aristocratic culture into which they had been born, and which now provided the opulent setting without which these gestures would have had no context and hence no meaning, was being preserved deliberately and artificially, conserved like a medical specimen in formaldehyde, ingrafted like a human mouth on the inanimate representation of power's omnipotence. It was a hoax. A woman approaches a man in a nightclub and tells him that he is a magnificent animal. He does not murmur, 'No, I am not like that at all.' He does not demur, or measure himself anew with a stage aside: 'How his arms and legs are thin!' 'Am I really?' he says, grinning contentedly in the darkness. Only in this case the hoax was gigantic, epochal, and even minds endowed with the intuition of genius were duped. They were taken in because the power of the hoaxer was incalculable in terms of ordinary human intercourse, as if a thousand women approached the man in the nightclub and, in unison, began whispering sweet nothings into his ear with the roar of a landing Concorde. With the passing of years, power's needs evolved. Many of the initial beneficiaries of the hoax suffocated like Mayakovsky, or were suffocated like Meyerhold. But no matter how the culture was distended or reshaped, so long as the idol of power needed a living mouth the hoax would continue. As a diabolical ritual relies on a sacred text, adapting it to a new and unanticipated context, the aristocratic substance of European culture was adapted, yet preserved, within the form of totalitarianism. I mentioned film because had Russia, historically the last vessel without cracks to hold the aristocratic substance of European culture, gone on to exist outside that unforeseen form, film would never have become an organic part of its heritage. But in the totalitarian Russia it never did either, if only because the mouthpiece of culture was there to chat

32

up the élites in the West and only incidentally to seduce the populace. Film, despite Miss Eagle and all her charm, was not permitted to displace the arts.

> A nob, a moneybags. Two wenches
> Trapped in the intrigue of another.

The Russian word for 'art' mirrors the English 'attempt'. Film is not an art for the obvious reason that creation cannot begin where the artist ends, with the audience. Like printing or engraving, film is only a technical means of disseminating something already created: an idea or an image, an actor's voice. The possible feat, an 'attempt' so predictable that even the uninitiated know it will succeed, is a diverting contradiction which belongs in the circus and in the stadium. One cannot make a thought out of the means of its dissemination any more than one can draw a pint of bitter out of its price in pounds and pence. The very cost of making a film presupposes an audience for its conception, an audience, furthermore, presupposed to be large enough to justify the production. In practical terms this means an audience in the millions, though the operative contradiction here is that the size of the audience should play any part at all in the attempt at creation. It is equally obvious that if Flaubert had known all along what would become of Emma Bovary, she would not have outlived him. The attempt cannot be made in film because the maker, unlike God, is in the possession of a written or unwritten script, an anterior scripture that gives him total insight into his subjects, and even if spontaneity extends to the conception, mediocrity will rule over the creation. Unlike the artist, who imitates God even when he fails, it is the success of a totalitarian demiurge and of the institutions of established religion that the film maker emulates. In somewhat more modest terms, film is to the theatre arts what sport is to the arts of war.

14

Having to explain in the West today what would have been axiomatic for my grandfather's generation in Russia is tiresome and embarrassing. It may therefore be instructive to recall what the culture into which he was born had been like, before it became a totalitarian mouthpiece. To recall this is not to rattle off the names of poets, but to turn for a moment to the prose of its inner 'arrangement', which is the literal meaning of the Greek word from which the English 'art' is derived. Imagine any country in Europe. The yard of a coaching inn in its dreariest province well over a century ago. Smells of tar, leather, manure. Dirt, poverty. Mortality. Barefooted children. One of them, a boy of six, plays with loose bits of pencil and charcoal. A porter on his day off sees the boy sketching, and offers him half a crown if he will draw a scene to which the porter is mysteriously attached, a hare pursued by hounds. The artist accepts the commission, and buys paints with the money. Later he attends a local school, where the headmaster beats children black and blue for the slightest transgression. In class the boy draws a pair of Siamese twins, objects of fascination for readers of popular almanacs including the headmaster. So charmed are this Dickensian personage and his suitably quarrelsome wife by the boy's talent that they become his patrons. He leaves the provincial town and travels abroad to study, then returns home and settles in one of the capital cities, where he gradually acquires a following. Later he marries the girl next door, a concert pianist whose own progress in the world has resembled his. She bears him four children: Boris, Alexander, Josephine and Lydia. They are born to prosperity in Moscow, Tolstoy is a friend of their father's. When Rainer Maria Rilke visits in 1900, Boris Pasternak is ten. The crucial disparity between his world and that of his father, as well as the moral of the fairy tale, is glimpsed in the juxtapositon of poetry and painting. The latter, despite all of this century's attempts to prove otherwise, was and is the production of tangible objects that are exhibited, bought and subsequently hung on special hooks in the houses of people rich enough to have houses. However equal the muses, however comparable the spiritual values generated by those whom they inspire, a child able to draw a hare pursued by hounds can be imagined receiving, even amid the unimaginable squalor of provincial life, a few coppers from an illiterate porter by way of patronage. Such patronage, however, is not the destiny of a poet. To survive he needs peers, not patrons. He needs an aristocratic milieu, one to which Pasternak was born as though to a manner. It was a culture in which a new book of verse was either the gift of the author or so practically unattainable that a schoolgirl of seventeen, my father's mother from whom we inherited the edition of Blok in the margins of which she had copied all known variants of each poem, had to save money for a year in order to come to possess it. A writer explained why books were dear: 'Because books ought to be dear. A book is not vodka, not a woman walking the street.' Naturally, only a viable aristocratic milieu could impose such an attitude upon the public and sustain a culture in which, as an economist would say, supply led demand. Yet, as many aristocratic institutions are in practice though not in theory, publishing in 'aristocratic' Russia was in reality more democratic, and no less commercial, than its future counterpart elsewhere in increasingly 'democratic' Europe or America. It is just that the institution favoured the producer at the expense of the consumer, not the other way round. At something like a thousand guineas a copy, the exorbitant price of books in their first editions allowed the writer to survive, not merely physically but with his dignity uncompromised, through the sale of several hundred copies to the public. A poet, after all, cannot be expected to be understood by more than a few hundred contemporaries. And even if he is, he can hardly be expected to put pen to paper in the knowledge that unless he is understood by more than a few hundred people, he will not only starve but allow his dignity to be compromised. If a writer's words were subsequently seen to attract more readers than publishers or booksellers had anticipated, subsequent printings of his book would be priced more modestly, and the achyropoetic *haute couture* of the previous season would soon arrive in the shops as ordinary merchandise. But in any event the essential miracle of voluntary public patronage for which his aristocratic milieu set the tone would by then have already occurred. The existence of a sophisticated aristocracy in the twentieth century may be seen as a quaint anachronism, or at any rate a negligible anomaly, but it was this which made the culture into which my grandfather was born what it was. From the point of view of that culture's producers, the anomaly was the natural order of things. From the point of view of future generations, the anachronism amounted to an innovation, an experiment which crossed the commercial with the noble and forced a flowering of genius unprecedented in European literature since Elizabethan England. Unlike the written word, however, which was the principal beneficiary of this innovation, by the time Pasternak was born the fine arts had not developed a comparably ingenious and modern relationship between producer and consumer. The process of the artist's survival had not undergone a fundamental transformation since the earliest days of private patronage: patrons might have changed, industrialists might have replaced princes, but the need to attract them remained an essential feature of the artist's life. In the coming modern era the relationship would still belong to the Renaissance, with the result that it would be increasingly difficult for the artist to reach his audience without compromising his dignity. That is to say, without becoming a kept man, a circus clown or a university professor. Thus culturally epiperipheral activities like 'publicity' and 'promotion' came to the fore. In *fin de siècle* Russia, to drag the name of a poet like Blok into such activities would have been puzzling and absurd, if not deliberately sacrilegious. A contemporary painter, by contrast, realized that without dealers, impresarios, critics, patrons, connections and the other traditional paraphernalia of public mediation he would not advance beyond the physical survival which, from the outset, the talent of a boy able to draw a hare pursued by hounds can all but guarantee. Unlike the poet in Russia, in Russia as elsewhere in Europe the painter had a career to make. His future, consequently, depended on his ability to make it – using skills other than the one he was born to practice – and the notorious coincidence of genius and obscurity symbolized throughout Europe by the man surviving in a freezing garret is but one example of the debilitating consequences of that dependence. In the world of Balzac, which is to say all of Europe in the nineteenth century, no cultural domain was safe from these consequences. In my grandfather's world, which only existed intact for the first twenty-seven years of Pasternak's life, at least literature was safe. It was a silk cocoon, an Atlantis, a glass veranda.

> We were music of the tea-cups
> That in the darkness take their tea,
> Which forest gloom and nights of weakness
> And awkward mystery distil.

By the time the Great War brought about the collapse of civilization and the subsequent imposition of the militarized wield, Russian literature was *sui generis* and centuries ahead of the rest of Europe, while even at its most advanced, Russian painting was European and belonged to its time. The two worlds, Balzac's vast continent of the West and Pasternak's tiny native milieu, went on to lead separate lives, one natural and the other artificial, yet each would be rooted in its own inheritance. Logically enough, it was the literary aspect of Russian culture, the one perceived as most dynamic, original, futurist, that the militarized wield absorbed and assimilated to its initial propaganda aims. Everything 'new' could be associated with social innovation and international revolution, while everything 'old' could be linked with chauvinist reaction or bourgeois stagnation. Paradoxically, it was the achievement of an aristocratic culture which was upheld in the process. Equally, when some decades later the engines of propaganda went into reverse, it was the other aspect of Russian culture which would be exhumed and exhibited. Everything 'new' could now be presented as socially corrupt and redolent of European decadence, while everything 'old' could be tied to ancient tradition and national heritage. Paradoxically, it was the moth-eaten old hat of bourgeois Europe which was upheld in the turnabout. Thus the imperial art of Vnukovo was the resuscitated heritage of Papa Biedermeier and his global successors-in-interest, chocolate boxes and crystal swans, *Boy's Own Paper* and the Salvation Army, Viennese dentists' waiting-rooms and the League of Nations, buttery genre in *Die Kunst* and Eugene Sue's Parisian mysteries, Havelock Ellis's *Man and Woman* and the London music hall, Darwinist atheism and Dr Freud, phrenology and Sherlock Holmes instalments, Sir Henry Rider Haggard's romances and the magic of Broadway. And yes, film. Yet neither the original cataclysm nor the decades of totalitarian manipulation of what had been the last aristocratic culture in history would make film, in the absentmindedly narrowed eyes of the Russian intelligentsia, anything more than a philistine medium for the dissemination of moth-eaten images and ideas. Whatever their agenda of the moment, to totalitarian rulers the value of a genuine culture was simply too great to allow its displacement by a bourgeois facsimile. And when, in the eighth decade of the twentieth century of the common era, I arrived in the West, I understood their wisdom, because in the era of universal provocation it is the phantom of culture that either saves civilization or delivers it in a box-car to the totalitarian Calvary.

15

The first film I saw in the West was *Nicholas and Alexandra* dubbed into Italian. I turned sixteen as the plane left Sheremetevo airport, and I deliberately foreshorten the perspective of this narrative at the moment of our departure. For the rest of my natural life, it seemed, I would hear myself answering in English the question: 'Can you get out of Russia?', closely followed by: 'Was it very difficult?' 'I can,' my lips moved to answer, 'but my interest is quantitative micro-analysis.' I answered, truthfully, that it was as easy, or as difficult, as winning a million dollars in a lottery. You buy a ticket, wait a few months, and here you are, a millionaire. A hurt pause, invariably followed by 'Oh, I see,' would confirm that I was no longer in Vnukovo, where a guest's alien truth did not need to be simple to be believed. We had sold the house in Vnukovo, and gambled. Three months later a policeman rang the doorbell of our Moscow flat, saluted smartly, and handed over a brown envelope with our destiny's winnings. To occupy ourselves with the future of our earthly possessions would have been as incongruous as loading a funeral barge with an alarm clock and spare shoe horns. We left just hours after the policeman's visit to catch the first available flight operated by a Western airline, abandoning everything that could be abandoned in Moscow. Money or even books, they were now irrelevant. 'Naked we came to paradise,' my father said, 'naked we leave.' Had the flight not been available until the following day, we would have happily considered making a human sacrifice, perhaps in the form of the first of our blood relations to call into doubt 'the wisdom of our precipitous decision' in the same cautionary monotone in which they droned that 'the boy should go to school'. A week later, in Rome, I watched *Nicholas and Alexandra*, Robert Massie's story of the last Russian tsar made into a film. Installed at a cheap hotel operated by an international relief organization, my father began writing a book destined for obscurity, although as I now look at its jacket flap I see that according to Mr Massie it was 'destined to become a twentieth-century classic'. I went to the cinema. Vaudeville and fur-hatted, peasants on the screen, coquettishly draped with a velvet curtain of the colour acerb Muscovites used to call socialist bordeaux, kept muttering '*rivoluzione*'. *Rivoluzione!* Artfully made-up princesses swooned. Why had I never before imagined the shadow theatre which I was too jaded to build as a child from the point of view of my disappointed visitors? 'The West, the West.' This was the West, and a warm evening besides, but in the Piazza del Popolo, improbable, cinematic, floodlit crowds of Miss Eagle's husband's extras marched about and sang:

> Avanti popolo, tuona il cannone,
> Rivoluzione, rivoluzione!

A rally, the hotel's owner explained, his espresso machine roaring and whining like an artillery shell. He himself preferred the fascist *Giovinezza*, but anyway the original words were 'about the red banner of communism':

> Avanti popolo, alla riscossa,
> Bandiera rossa, bandiera rossa!
> Bandiera rossa la trionferà,
> Evviva il comunismo e la libertà!

His mother, a widow from Lombardy, objected that neither of these was the original, which went as follows:

> Ven chì Nineta sota l'ombrellin,
> Ven chì Nineta te darò un basin.

'Come here, little girl with the parasol, come here and I'll give you a kiss.' Here as in Vnukovo, apparently, bourgeois reality was only a generation away from totalitarian artifice. But I was no longer in Vnukovo. The curtain would soon rise as promised. Then again, I was in the West, and doubt was no longer tantamount to suicide.

16

It was ironic that the Vnukovo guest who took the Polaroid picture, Daniel Rose, should have presented his Russian hosts with an encyclopedia, a gift at once so naïve and so pragmatic. This was reason enough to regard the gesture as quintessentially American. It also highlighted America's historical link with the French tradition of Enlightenment: we were a people in the dark, as it were, and the *Encyclopaedia Britannica* was a lantern that would enlighten us. Admittedly, at the time, the lantern was still a product of British, not American, civilization, yet since we believed that in Mr Rose's house there were many mansions, it was perfectly plausible that he himself should live in New York, whence his gift came by ordinary post. We loaded it, volume by beautifully boxed volume, on to my sledge to take it home. One of our weekend guests, a brilliant raconteur who used his prominence as a poet to simulate loyalism, could hardly believe that something so physically bulky and morally explosive had actually arrived in the post, since he never dared receive so much as Christmas cards from abroad. 'You see, Zhenya,' my father laughed, 'relationships with power are not always reciprocal. You may love the wield, but it does not return your affections. I hate the wield, but apparently it loves me in return.' The boxes were opened and the cardboard discarded. I remember stamping on it, and as I write this in another enclave which at times seems no farther from Moscow than Vnukovo, I wish with a heavy heart that our gnostic faith in the reality of the godhead as an earthly power, so tragic in its extremes of hope and despair, had been shaken by all that ritual jumping up and down. For the truth, bitter as the wormwood of Hamlet's voice, is that the divine pleroma whose existence was ontologically proven in Vnukovo now has no continent, no country even, to call its own. At best it is a ghetto, whose blind inmates believe in the patent falsehood that it encompasses the earth, that this will never change, that the West is the world. There was nothing in the boxes but an encyclopedia, I may now reflect. Yet we, former inmates of Vnukovo and other enclaves of mock liberty within the totalitarian maze, cannot stomach passive reflection. We recognize the validity of a specimen, and the set of *Britannica* is undeniably a specimen of civilization, as Crimson's lines or Danube's music are a specimen of militarization and its omnipotent wield. The complicating factor is that the wield has been a culture unto itself, and one syncretic enough to have absorbed and assimilated the heritage of aristocratic individualism, along with its Pasternaks and Prokofievs. Grist to the mill, I concede, but so long as there was a mill it needed such grist. Yet what of Western civilization and its modern culture, presumed as it is to be the world's? Individual inmates of the ghetto may only know Pasternak as a novelist because *Doctor Zhivago* was once made into a film, while of Prokofiev they may only know 'Lieutenant Kizhé' because the suite was used as the soundtrack to another film. But *Britannica* is a specimen of their collective cultural persona, their common consciousness. Even when we read it in Vnukovo, we remarked with surprise that it knew nothing of Pasternak and never mentioned Mandelstam or Tsvetaeva, while our Vnukovo neighbours figured prominently, including the writer at No. 3 Mayakovsky Street, the one whose claim to fame was a mystery even to us at No. 4. We never dared to think that *Britannica* had blatantly lifted these entries from our school textbooks, which I never read because I did not go to school and was not obliged to read textbooks. For this reason, as I now open Mr Rose's magic lantern, I take the precaution of assuming that Russian poetry is too rarefied, totalitarian propaganda too powerful, for any encyclopedia to shed light on them, even one which arrives in such beautiful, beautiful boxes. Concentrate on the known, I murmur. Here is an article on the evolution of music, which gives a concise summary of the subject without aiming at completeness for its own sake. Thus Monteverdi, for instance, is mentioned not merely because an educated man must know his name, but because *L'incoronazione di Poppea* broke with the earlier practice of basing opera plots on Greek mythology. Similarly, in the section covering the music of the eighteenth and nineteenth centuries, the article mentions the names of seventeen composers, omitting many famous names like Schumann, Grieg, Mendelssohn, Berlioz or Tchaikovsky because its aim is to name only those names without which an overview of the evolution it describes would be demonstrably inaccurate. Although *Britannica's* editors are British, not one of the seventeen composers it identifies as having made such unique contributions to the evolution of music is an Englishman. Nor would a Frenchman or a Russian have reason to feel proud of his nation's impact on Western culture: of the seventeen, fourteen were German or Austrian, two were Italian and one was a Pole resident in France. Thus considered, the list, with its sobering ratio of 8.5 composers per 100 years of civilization for all the nations of Europe and the world, illustrates the capricious rarity of genius. But ask an inmate of the ghetto, and you will hear that it illustrates no more than the deplorable élitism of a bygone age, when poverty was law and enlightenment the province of a chosen few. The aristocracy of Vienna gathered to hear Beethoven, and those who did not belong could not participate in or partake of the miracle of cultural evolution which the *Britannica* article outlines so succinctly. 'The West, the West!' In my own and my father's lifetime, it has succeeded in fostering the sort of optimal conditions under which that evolution might be expected to continue. It is now quite unencumbered by the weight of brute monarchy, and it has never felt the yoke of tsarist autocracy or known the century-long decades of totalitarian oppression. It boasts universal literacy and suffrage. A vast majority of its population enjoy the blessings of indoor plumbing, and in many other respects are no worse off than the aristocracy of a bygone age. Its young have a practically unlimited access to musical education, if only because recordings are widely available and public libraries common, so that a cook's son, if he so chooses, can hear more Beethoven in one week than Count Waldstein had in his whole life. The result? Germany and Austria, which gave the world fourteen-seventeenths of what makes music music, have not produced a single composer under the optimal conditions of democracy and prosperity, when the evolution of music could be expected to continue. And only two modern composers are performed, there as elsewhere in the ghetto, with the reverence reserved for Beethoven: Prokofiev and his peer Shostakovich, both humble subjects of the totalitarian *pseudotsargod*, as my father called him. Admittedly, Prokofiev escaped from Russia when it fell under the wield, and wished desperately to transplant himself to the West. What he found in America was tolerable hotel rooms, superb pianos, exquisite music paper and no secret police. But there was no Count Waldstein, only 'critics who never tired of uttering platitudes like "Beethoven is a great composer"'. A composer, he patiently explained to a New York magazine interviewer, is a madman who composes music which is by definition incomprehensible: 'Only after some time the paths he has charted, provided they are genuine, will become clear to everyone else.' With that he returned to Russia, giving himself up to the totalitarian demiurge as if he were Count Waldstein. Why? his son has been asking ever since. 'Because culture is not wilfulness,' my father told him in New York half a century later. 'It is not the shaking off and the letting go, but the ruthless autarchy of genius. Remember, Oleg, rhyme was being abandoned. What need of rhyme? Forward march, avant-garde! Down with the classics! But Pasternak never wrote a stanza without rhyme. Remember what he told Mandelstam? It was after Mandelstam's last public reading, when it suddenly occurred to Pasternak that his peer sounded like a Futurist: "I envy your freedom," he said. "For me you are a new Khlebnikov, and as alien to me as he is. *I need unfreedom.*" And Khlebnikov *was* a Futurist and Mandelstam a *classicist*, for God's sake! In the West, Prokofiev and Shostakovich would have let go, lost their moorings, put on the faceless modernism which is one of the masks of timeless banality. Russia's culture flowered centuries later than the West's, with the result that when our pseudotsargod put it under glass it had not been philistinized as thoroughly. He saved it, as fruit is saved up in syrup, and allowed the genius under his patronage to go on rhyming. It is sometimes said that he forced composers to create music for the masses. This is absurd, because only charlatans, nowadays bouncing billiard balls against piano strings even as they used to prattle that Beethoven is a great composer, create music for the masses. Our pseudotsargod isolated Prokofiev and Shostakovich from philistine twaddle, allowing them not to let go of the divine discipline which alone accounts for evolutionary advances in art, forbidding them to shake off the infernal yoke of creative individualism which Russian culture still bears. He, who may be said to have forcibly ended our culture, has also forestalled its death of natural causes, its dissolution in Western banality, its universal philistinization. He was the saviour of all there still is.' So the rule of Jehovah over the civilization we call Western has been, for some, a millennial tyranny which even blood has not washed white, particularly because the blood was not Jehovah's. Many parents or grandparents, after all, routinely abandon their offspring to a cruel fate. One can easily cast Abraham, for instance, as an American industrialist, Isaac as his prodigal son, Jehovah-jireh as Santa Barbara, the knife as a financial instrument, and the angel of Genesis as a California magistrate who unexpectedly overturns the old geezer's last will and testament whereby all the money was left to the Abraham Memorial Foundation for Cosmic Harmony Research. Equally, that 'God so loved the world' is an assertion – not unlike the familiar claims of powerful businessmen concerning their factories and employees – while as a matter of historical fact the actual sacrifice was made by another, whose altruism was wholly and unmistakably human. Power breeds such ambiguities. Is it surprising, then, that to some Jehovah is a petty tyrant, while to others he is the moving force of civilization?

17

I very much doubt that this was the kind of enlightenment Mr Rose had hoped would gush from his magic lantern. Our latent reaction was similar to that of a university acquaintance of mine, many years later, who turned to what he described as 'that monument of Enlightenment reasonableness, the *Encyclopédie*' to find that 'les Nègres sont grands, gros, bien faits, mais niais & sans génie'. He was Kwame

Anthony Appiah, nephew of Otumfuo Nana Opoku Ware, King of the Asante. He was quite slim. And what would the Western man, an intellectual product of *Britannica* manufactured under the optimal conditions of democracy and prosperity, make of the reader's letter handed to me one January afternoon by the literary editor of a London newspaper for which I was then writing? 'A shamefully long time ago,' went the letter, 'I read out to my wife who is a former Muscovite something from a piece you had written. She said something to the effect: "At last, someone who makes sense about Russia – who wrote that?" I read out your name. And of course she said: "But I know him, we used to be neighbours at the dacha!" My wife, Katya, maiden name —— and granddaughter of ——, the Soviet poet, then told me that there was a family with a son called Andrei who bought a dacha near theirs in the writers' settlement at Vnukovo and that the family later emigrated. Anyway, I said she ought to try to get in touch if, as seems likely, you really are acquaintances from that other world, but nothing got done about it. I am afraid that this was for my part because of laziness and for my wife's part because one of the few traits she retains after more than ten years here is a Pavlovian reflex distrust of current or former fellow citizens. However, I have remained curious as to whether two former neighbours have both found themselves here in England. So if you are that Andrei Navrozov and if you feel like it, please do write . . .' 'What can I say,' I wrote to him in reply. 'It is I, I mean it is she.' I did not remind him that Marmot was Pasternak's murderer because by then I knew this not to be true, but I had to say that he drove my father to attempt suicide in Vnukovo. What had begun as a dispute between neighbours developed into a case of libel in defence of my father's good name, and Marmot was preparing to instigate criminal proceedings. The imperial Pieria buzzed like a beehive when the Prosecutor General, Rudenko, arrived in an armoured limousine with motorcycle escort to deliver in person his symbolic gift for Marmot's seventieth birthday, an ornamental dagger. Father took the hint, and decided he would save us from himself. It was not until we reached Rome that we learnt that the legal case argued in our absence, by a lawyer in a land without law before the judges of an epoch without justice, was decided in my father's favour. As he liked to say in Vnukovo, relationships with power are not always reciprocal. He survived by a miracle, wrought by the hands of the same family physician who had impressed him as an adept of Mill a few years before. 'He survived by a miracle,' I wrote. 'On the other hand, my own wife's grandfather would not hesitate before driving her to suicide, though he is only a Californian businessman. This does not keep me from loving her. Life is like that, as the English say, proving yet again they are straight out of Chekhov. The only thing I remember is that Katya was very thin, while I was, to translate from the Russian, "inclined to fullness". Perhaps for that reason I hated her intensely (spiritually I was already a writer then, and a writer, by contrast with the world he inhabits, is feminine and hence vain). To imagine Katya in the West is frankly inconceivable. Something out of Heisenberg's lectures on physics: planes cut for demonstration purposes from clear laboratory plastic, at odd angles. When will I learn to expect anything of an ending world.' Then came the Red Queen's neatly typed reply. 'Your letter oozed matchless charm – this does not worry me, as you are supposed to be a writer. You were, in addition, exceptionally prompt in your response to a strange letter out of the blue – therefore my own tardiness does not worry me, seeing as it was my husband who decided that it was a good idea to get in touch with you. He did so because my own recollections of you and our for a time friendly relationship at the dachas are very vivid. I think it probably means that in some way they are important to me – and that goes further than my undying gratitude to you for teaching me to ride a bicycle. Me in the West – yes, it is inconceivable, from the point of view of those long-gone years and everything that came with them. Yet it is just as inconceivable to me now that life could have gone any other way. I now feel "more British than the British", which is probably a very frequent thing. But even though I lived there much longer than you, lucky chap, and arrived to live in London at twenty-five, my whole existence in Russia seems to be no more than a story told to me by somebody else, in great detail, on numerous occasions and therefore very well known, but a story nevertheless. I have not been to Moscow once since leaving, and I have never felt like returning. My English is probably fairly pathetic compared to yours, but my Russian is pathetic full stop. I hate speaking it, and I do not feel comfortable and muddle my words when I have to. My mother, visiting me for the first time, was horrified by my accent and hesitancy. Parents – it is not clear from your letter whether yours are alive. If they are, please give them my sincere best regards, terrible phrase but in this case genuine. The two luckiest, cleverest and overall best things I ever did apart from marrying my husband were to learn English and to learn to type, both wilful decisions pursued with total dedication. While learning English

45

was OK, learning to type was considered weird by almost everyone. Even though they have probably forgotten all about me and my very existence, I have to tell you that your father was responsible for the first, and your mother for the second.' There was a handwritten postscript: 'Thinness is a condition affecting people who fail to develop proper muscular structure, whereas I have small bones and limited amounts of fat.' God bless you Katya, I thought, God bless your small bones and limited amounts of fat, you exist, I did not invent you, we bicycled, Vnukovo is not my private fiction. No, it is a world of things between heaven and earth, things which you cannot look up in *Britannica*.

18

My first impression of the West was a dream I had in Vnukovo. There must have been a logical reason for having it on an October night full of rain, after the day's excursion to Moscow. The components which made it so dramatic and detailed must have had a specific source. Perhaps it was the stream of advertisements in the back issues of American magazines and newspapers which we hoarded so diligently, with their colour photographs or black-and-white line drawings of the season's fashions. Anyway, in the dream I was walking the length of Madison Avenue, on the right-hand side of the street, going north. I know it was north, although at the time I could not have known that this meant 'uptown', because the first time I found myself walking uptown on Madison I recognized everything in the dream and realized that it had been a vision. I recognized the shops, the curve of the pavement, the clothes on the women. I have never stopped watching them, these women blown past like oak leaves, rushed and rushing toward some mysteriously fashionable destination, a glass of white wine, an assignation, a seamstress. I have not stopped watching them since that dream came true, and in all these years I have not seen two of them wear the same clothes. Sometimes there is a superficial resemblance, even the occasional hint of an occupational uniform, in the cut of a secretary's jacket, in the shape of a poodle-walker's mink, in a Negro maid's naïve coat buttons. But in the moment between the first glance and the last, the differences overpower the similarities. *Civis, civilis*. Rudimentary Latin, enough for the amateur etymologist. I shut my eyes and try to imagine civilization, to trace its inner reaches with a single inspired guess, as totalitarian militarization would be glimpsed in the course of our dinner conversations. Millions of women in New York, millions more in Los Angeles, Dallas, Pittsburgh. Blouses, dresses, stockings, each with a different pattern, a different texture, a different price. Shoes, gloves, scarves in Paris, Brussels and Oslo. Everything invisible and unmentionable, secretly embroidered and clandestinely spun from this dragonfly wing or that gossamer, in Milan, in Paris, in the millions, for the millions. For the hair there are combs, pins, bands, clips and a hundred other devices, no two alike, in Venetian velvet, in lace, in black-pearl satin, in space-age plastic. These are civilization's women, with such hair. What's to become of all the gold? No two alike, however alike God made them, because such is the power of civilization, an unembraceable infinity of whims satisfied with massage and lipstick, diets and magazines, Krug and Cartier, cosmetic surgery and depilatory treatments, gyms and saunas, evening taffeta and afternoon crêpe, bracelet-length sleeves and noise-less zippers. It expands like a universe, with glimpses of decoration and interior design, colour schemes and soft furnishings, table and bed linen, curtains with pencil pleats and goblet headings, pelmets and blinds, valances and cushions. This beautiful, irresistible infinity absorbs millions into a teeming void of human ingenuity, resourceful-ness, talent and ambition. It reverberates with innovation and discov-ery. *Eureka*, a new synthetic material has been found, which, woven into any fabric and even the coarsest tweed, will give a revolutionary curve to the midriff, a curve simply unimaginable just a few years ago. *Eureka*, a radical solution to the problem of attaching metal-stem buttons, once so unwieldy, to the most delicate silks will give designers a new freedom. *Eureka*, it was discovered that consumers of mass-market fragrances invariably prefer French names, like Le Jardin or even Le Jardin d'Amour, while the nomenclature of fine perfume is less susceptible to the francophone illusion. Top scientists, business meetings, market research, advertising campaigns, corporate intrigue, commercial espionage, millions of lives and words have figured in all this, and as the leaf in the colours of autumn is rushed by, a pattern of green veins intruding on a field of suede so becoming that red-maned disdain of Mandelstam's poem, civilization is as divine as it appeared in the Vnukovo dream. *Civis, civilis*, just like the Latin lesson, and here the ornate infinity of civilian concerns, its organic circle of seasonable change, its feminine wiles and stratagems, is so intricate it becomes a lesson in theology, like the real autumn leaf that one is invited to contemplate in order to glimpse, in the unpredictable yet unswervingly logical variety of God's universe, the work of a great designer. That Vnukovo dream grew out of streets that were black and grainy with autumn rain, where all colour, even the colour of women's hair, had been suppressed long ago, where the capital city unfolded like a militarized Versailles of cell blocks masquerading as vistas, and men as women, with one brand of perfume named Red Moscow and a single fashion called clothes to counterfeit what was known of civilization, and where Pasternak asked:

> O city, city! Miserable miser,
> What did you save on flax and kerosene?

I recalled how the economics editors of *Britannica* described what I saw in the dream as 'artificially generated wants', and how Greta Garbo, playing the role of 'commissar' in the Ernest Lubitsch film I later saw on television in the West, succumbed to their power and laughed. GARBO LAUGHS, even my father who never went to the pictures remembered that. When Melchior Lengyel's story was adapted for Broadway by Cole Porter in the 1950s, the power of those artificially generated wants was symbolized by the silk stockings of the title. *Britannica* contrasted them with 'actual necessities', although from my father I knew that, as the social scientist Strumilin had shown in research which became the ethical foundation of the economics of militarization, the actual necessities of life, called 'optimal norms of consumption', were 1,250 calories a day derived mainly from 1.54lb of rye flour and 0.25lb of groats, such as porridge, with an admixture of animal or vegetable fats. The old Garbo film, like everything destined to last in Hollywood, was based on ideas bandied about in the theatres of Berlin, where Russian *émigrés* had brought the news of a different world in the making. Perhaps for that reason the heroine's first impression of the West, a hotel lobby with a display of improbable hats, rang true. How can a civilization that produces such hats survive, she asked. Contempt in form, pity in content. Walking the length of the avenue was an ordeal, waves of unreflecting, piercing, almost hormonal pity washing over me with every unsteady step, because biologically a man lives for women and sees the future of mankind in their destiny. Because in peasant Russian, 'pity' has the dialectal meaning of 'love', and Jesus pitied the harlot. Because in every beautifully painted, radiant face I saw the totalitarian future, and absolute weakness in every sign of God's abundance and wealth. How can civilization, which produces them, withstand the wield, with resources just as vast, with power just as great, and not squandered on manicures and buttons but concentrated on the single task of subjugating civilization? Resilience, resilience the synonym and substance of the soul, where was it, where would it come from? *What of soul was left, I wonder, when the kissing had to stop.* How strange that Browning is the name of a gun. Shadow theatre! The lights go out, then come back on again, but everything is different. *Dust and ashes.* And, from loudspeakers in Central Park, Crimson's

> Broad is my native land,
> With forests, rivers, fields aplenty.

19

'The West, the West!' was how my father's book began. He started writing it in Rome, never leaving our subsidized *pensione* as he never left the cabin aboard the SS *Leonardo da Vinci* which ferried us across the Atlantic, not even when the passengers, to a soul, gathered on deck to cheer the Statue of Liberty crawling into view. I have seen enough credal symbols, he said. It was the Polaroid and *Britannica* man, Mr Rose, who welcomed us to New York. A flat in one of the many buildings owned by his family's real-estate development firm, in a New York suburb which my father would persist in describing as 'leafy' despite readily available botanical evidence to the contrary, was waiting for the refugees from paradise. It was furnished, down to the refrigerator filled with food. With thinly veiled animosity, once the bane of relatives, my mother had the furniture removed at once, expressing as mistress of the house her view that cane, not to mention plastic imitation cane of a particularly sickly hue, was unsuited to civilized existence, and that she would rather have no furniture at all than spend another evening admiring the ingeniously caned back of a modern American version of a nineteenth-century settee in the style of Louis XVI. Only the beds remained, shorn of their bedsteads, as intricate as anything ever imagined at the head of a bed by a downtrodden paterfamilias anywhere in Europe a century ago and now rendered in plastic to facilitate mass production. The food was edible. Perhaps because my father was absorbed in his writing, it was eaten without comment. The refrigerator had to be restocked and the immigrants were duly ushered into the supermarket, an American institution we had been told. Systematic analysis revealed that only products unique to the institution, such as wholly artificial 'beverages' and 'cereals', were in any way remarkable. They represented civilization and, in so far as they were entirely frivolous in both function and design, demilitarization. Unless he was a deserter looting the supermarket, it was downright impossible to imagine a soldier eating Rice Krispies. Television commercials confirmed this. In one, a man apparently heartbroken because he had run out of the Krispies in question, sang of his sorrow to the music of Leoncavallo, and what could be more civilian than grand opera? Coca-Cola was equally pacific in intent, its commercials showing people of draft age, who looked suspiciously like conscientious objectors, apparently celebrating a victory no more dear than that of their own youth. Apart from such products of the gloriously demilitarized psyche, the goods on display resembled the produce at the Central Market in Moscow, where a single tomato out of season cost the equivalent of a labourer's weekly wages. That tomato, however, tasted the way a tomato tastes when it is in season. Here seasons seemed not to exist, and everything was equally cheap, plentiful and tasteless the whole year round. Melons tasted like cucumbers, cucumbers were covered in film, apples tasted like the film used to cover cucumbers, pears tasted like strawberries, which tasted like apples, and though the logical inference, that apples tasted like melons, was not borne out empirically, it was none the less clear that the Russian labourer's American counterpart, whoever he was, could not get tomatoes out of season either. He could only spend his weekly earnings on a ticket to wherever they were in season. None did, of course. Ecclesiastes was defeated only symbolically, at the level of commercial presentation, institutional deception and social myth. The electric portals of the supermarket opened on to an organized religion as mercilessly rationalist as nineteenth-century science and as shamelessly authoritarian as the clerical Christendom which stood in its way. 'Man is descended from an ape!' was what could be read in the sign advertising Shopper's Special: Tomatoes, 99¢. Excommunication awaited those who would deny that the shopper's special was made in the tomato's image – with the tomato's gnarled, flaming and vulnerable flesh, its greenish-yellow seeds, its squirting juice – those who would proclaim that what lay before the shopper was in reality a descendant of the tennis ball. Once felt, the sway of this unanswerable creed was everywhere in evidence. In the life we had left behind, the process of delineation between private truth and public religion (which, in my own and my father's lifetime, variously blended communism, chauvinism, socialism, nationalism, xenophobia, Marxism, internationalism, Russian Orthodox Christianity, utilitarianism, pragmatism, paganism, demonism, trades-unionism, state capitalism, as well as just about everything else except the freedom to openly disbelieve it) was instinctive, automatic. Public religion went with the power of the wield, private truth was for us and our guests, and a fence freshly painted forest green divided the two like an iron curtain. There, the sway of public religion was theoretical, like gravity. Once, as a child, you had learnt to take it into account, it ceased to be a practical impediment to intellection. Here, by contrast, its precise nature and composition were unclear at any given moment. It worked not as a calculable physical force, but as a gaseous substance of variable composition and origin secretly released into the air you breathed. At times it produced the effect of laughing gas, at other times of tear gas, it might smell like ozone or chloroform, detergent or perfume. You could not guard against its toxins and its tonics, although in retrospect I realize that we might at least have forewarned ourselves of their existence by extrapolating the contradictions of *Britannica*, such as the unexpectedly hilarious, chaotic absurdity of its idea of Russian poetry on the one hand and the impartial, austere, categorical reasonableness of its exposition of Western music on the other. You turned on the television to watch the news and saw documentary footage of the war in Vietnam. It was not a fraud, if only because the film had not been shot in a Pentagon studio. You opened a newspaper, and saw a photograph of a group of politicians. It was not a hoax, if only because the head of one had not been cropped by a censor or replaced with a large vase of flowers. You switched on the radio. A coloratura soprano, whose name you had never heard before, was better than Galli-Curci. It was not a fiction. The voice was real, and when the announcer came on to say that it belonged to the winner of a regional music competition in Atlanta, Georgia, or somewhere equally implausible, you believed it almost in spite of yourself. Yet when that same television programme presented fresh evidence of Moscow's struggle for peace in South-east Asia,

51

when that same newspaper published a leading article which read as if it had been lifted verbatim from the previous week's *Soviet Life*, when that same announcer explained how Prokofiev suffered, or to the contrary flourished, sharing the destiny of his people, you were alerted to the presence of something alien in the oxygen. But where the breathing gas ended or the others began was impossible to tell, and no quantitative analysis, no van der Waals equation would stand up to the impenetrable mystery.

20

I went into a bookshop on Madison Avenue. Chunky and portable, a paperback *Portable Nietzsche* stared back from the shelf. Once, at the age of twelve, I ventured into the Lenin Library on my own to see if I could get anything of Nietzsche's, as no trace of him remained even in the home libraries of our friends. I only knew of Nietzsche because in 1903 Rozanov, preserved in my grandfather's library, compared him to Leontyev, who also vanished, and only the occasional nasty reference to the three of them, 'pessimist thinkers', could still be found, here and there, in an article or a footnote. The librarian, a woman whose face I shall never forget, responded as though she were the headmistress of a boarding school for girls and a local businessman had asked her if it would be all right to borrow three or four of them for the evening as a friend of his would be in town and might want to party. Basically she said she was going to call the police. And here he was, the pessimist, with his laughing *Zarathustra*, complete and un-abridged yet eminently portable. A whiff of the alien gas in that 'portable', of course, printed in big letters across the purple cover. Still, you opened the book at random and had to admit that this was no fraud. It was him all right. But then you turned the book over and read on the back cover that '*The Portable Nietzsche* is an extraordinary buy. We urge a reading of this *Portable*' – it flashed through my mind that the writer of the *New York Times* blurb intended this as an intellectual qualification, like 'pessimist', or perhaps even assumed it was the thinker's nickname – 'if for no other reason than to remedy the vague notions we have of the superman thing.' More than a whiff, near asphyxiation. But this was him all right: 'Down there everyone talks and no one listens. You could ring in your wisdom with bells, and shopkeepers in the market place would outjingle it with pennies.' It was true, then, I had stumbled on the beginnings of something, a science with its own van der Waals equation and its own Gay-Lussac. It was only a matter of effort. Eventually I would come to know the composition of this public religion, graph its pressures, analyse the toxins and the tonics, predict the effects, test the hypothesis and, having understood the behaviour of the gases, conclude that the promise of the West had been fulfilled. Did not our 'art' live on in their 'attempt'? Was not the freedom of the individual, which we had hoped to find under conditions of political pluralism, akin to the scientist's freedom of experiment? I looked round the bookshop. With some revulsion I noticed that, as in my broad native land, the prices of books, printed on their covers, were all the same. It seemed preposterous that in the economically free West, where a pair of trousers, as I had already learnt in Rome, could be bought for a thousand lire or for a hundred times that amount, the price of a book, whether the volume of Nietzsche which I held in my hands and once would have given anything to possess for an evening, or some inconsequential drivel, was fixed as firmly as that of a volume of Marx in a Moscow bookshop visited by the occasional Zambian tourist. The only difference between books was that paperbacks were cheaper than hardcovers, several times more dear but just as uniformly priced. The revulsion I felt was instinctive, automatic. It was as if, at a fancy dinner party, I had witnessed the host diluting wine with water in the kitchen. Should I say something? And to whom? I had not yet developed the scientific detachment necessary to reflect on the significance of what I was seeing, or to contrast it with the economic 'arrangement' which had given Russia's writers their freedom in the days before my father and I were born. When books all cost the same, it may not mean that the spiritual values they contain are widely presumed to be commensurate. It certainly does mean, however, that only those authors who are expected to sell a certain number of copies of their books will be published. But *Zarathustra* was published in forty copies, and few of Nietzsche's other works sold more than a few hundred in his lifetime. Father, apparently, belonged to a lucky few. He had his book contract, and magazines were already publishing excerpts from his book. I had pocket money to spare. I shelled out the two bucks and, a hundred years after the pessimist's gospels first saw the light of day, safely transported him, now portable and unthreatening, to the family enclave in the suburb Father insisted was leafy. A nickel and a dime, my fifteen cents change, jingled on the bookshop counter.

21

'The West, the West!' Soon the unthinkable happened. I went to school. The idea of organized education did not ruffle the family feathers because, after all, in the life we left behind I had not attended school for fear of being collectivized, of growing up with divided loyalties, of losing the freethinker's freedom of the enclave. Here, presumably, such pressures were unknown. Besides, there was curiosity. The kind Mr Rose was on the governing board of an expensive and famous school not far from our leafy suburb. I agreed. He arranged a scholarship. Horace Mann was a boys' school, presided over by a youngish headmaster who arrived every morning in a pink Cadillac convertible, was often seen in the corridors dribbling a basketball, and otherwise lent the school the unmistakable aura of a progressive institution. He had put an end to the dress code, the required jacket and tie, with the consequence that nearly every pupil, from the first-form tot to the fifth-form gay blade, used the psychological pretext of choosing his own attire to 'choose' the uniform of blue jeans and a sweater or, in warmer weather, a cotton shirt of the sort called 'May shirt' in Russia, the sort of shirt one imagines an unemployed lout would wear while beating his wife for a transgression which he knows she has not committed. A group of some eight or nine boys, however, persisted in wearing jackets and neckties. They had short haircuts, and one even sported a crewcut of the military type, while I, like nearly everyone else in the school, had shoulder-length hair. This commodity I had imported from my past along with the pair of American jeans given to me by Oleg Prokofiev for my birthday, symbols of nonconformism the both of them because military haircuts were mandatory for schoolboys while jeans, even at Versailles, were procurable only in a Bulgarian imitation denim. The comfortably determinist conceit of good and evil took a battering when I noticed that the neat boys, the ones who looked like clerks anxious to keep their ten bob a week in an English novel, never seemed to ask me how

I got out of Russia and whether it was true that nobody had jeans over there. The natives of an East African tribe, I read somewhere, are eager to learn three things on acquaintance with a Western visitor: whether or not he is circumcised, whether or not his family own cattle, and whether or not he knows how corrugated iron is made. Such were roughly the questions which the messy boys, the ones who looked like Beethoven, angry eyes stabbing a darkened sky in the famous Beethovenhaus portrait, never tired of asking. The two types shared a political view of the world, however, crystallized by the presidential election campaign in which every boy in the school with the single exception of myself supported George McGovern, the Democrat running against Nixon. My own views, freshly imported from Vnukovo, gnostic in that I had experienced first hand the reality of the totalitarian wield and was now one with the pleroma of freedom, made me defend Nixon because the power of the West was all I had left. Grandfather had lost his life, Father a part of his. My people had lost their country, as had the Georgians and the Armenians, the Estonians and the Lithuanians, the Poles and the Czechs, the Chinese and the Cubans. Nixon's opponent now thought that the Vietnamese should lose theirs. My schoolmates called me 'fascist', of course, but what made me call them, rather than myself, 'fascist' was that not a single boy in the school dissented from his teachers and headmaster, all of whom openly proclaimed that the incumbent president represented absolute evil. I had come from a world where verbal conformity outside the enclave, symbolized by the credal abstraction of 'election results', seemed total. In fact, my schoolmates' credal acceptance of authority within their enclave was even more absolute, extending as it did to behaviour, and the fact that they rejected the external authority of the nation's leader proved only that his authority was in actual fact an abstraction. Naturally they did not want to be drafted, which made my wearing a Nixon campaign stickpin to school particularly tactless. But what puzzled me most, I remember, was why adolescents in the thrall of McGovern's pacifism should show such interest in sports. Even the most jaded Beethoven types, critical of McGovern for selling out to the military and industrial complex – which in the school's microcosm I alone apparently represented, I, son and grandson of Russian intellectuals, I, without a penny to my name, in a school for the children of industrialists and financiers – even these Beethoven types, I marvelled, cheerfully donned sports uniforms to chase balls and jump barriers. In Vnukovo, going to the lake meant 'bathing', not 'swimming'. The only physical exercise countenanced without sarcasm was skiing, 'because you can just walk', or walking, 'as in the Lyceum', or badminton and cycling, 'for fun'. Anything more strenuous, such as downhill skiing, was considered militaristic. Brawn was cannon fodder by another name, muscles had been rippling on every totalitarian poster the world over for as long as people could remember, everyone knew in advance whose broad native land would win all the medals at the Olympics. Besides, as Father would remark, peering absentmindedly into the currant bushes: 'No matter how much he exercises or trains, man will never develop the muscles of an ape, the speed of an antelope, the eyesight of an eagle, or the stamina of a cockroach. On the other hand, no ape, no antelope, no eagle and no cockroach, however perfect, will ever do what individual men have done, that is, invent fire, jet propulsion, radar or pesticides. Whether or not civilization endures depends on its ability to keep this in mind, an ability called history.' But here, with perfect freedom to grow no muscles whatever and Nietzsche to read, youthful pacifist Beethovens played tackle and read the sports pages. In fairness it must be noted that the clerks, who tolerated me despite my fascist warmongering, shirked the gym as much as I did. We all signed up for track, and fulfilled the school's sport requirements by walking round it until dusk, when time came to take the bus home or to go listen to someone practising in the music rooms. Both types, incidentally, played musical instruments and listened to music. The Beethovens tended to favour drums and something called 'acid rock', which they were visibly pleased to tell me I did not have in Russia, while my friends the neat clerks, usually children of poorer parents than the billionaire Mr Rose – whose son played the drums and artistically banged on any resonant surface such as the door of every gym locker he happened to saunter past – the anxious clerks played the piano and the violin. They often asked me what I thought of Prokofiev and Shostakovich, and one of them, in corduroy jacket and big polyester tie, once brought a pair of sheep's hearts to the senior common room, plopped them on the table and said 'Let's play hearts!' with that genuinely mad, calm intonation which I never discerned in the games of the louder boys, despite their assurances that acid rock was all but 'illegal even in this country'. Michael, whose father had been a mathematician with the Manhattan Project and now owned America's largest privately held market research firm, was studying Russian in order to read *Lolita* in the original. Despite the fact that the novel was American, and in English, this was a generational *salto mortale* worthy of Thomas Mann's Buddenbrooks. He wrote a song for me that had this refrain:

> Life ain't a bowl of roses,
> I've got tuberculosis:
> Dah-stah-yev-sky blue-u-ues!

His favourite pastime was passing round cryptic messages in class, neo-Maoist slogans as he called them, 'The whiskers of rat are wiser than this horse's instruction' or 'Fate knocks on the door just once, but homosexuality keeps sticking notes underneath it'. Even more spectacularly unpredictable was the drift of the clerks, with the sulky exception of Michael who maintained that it was all a load of boloney, to two of the school's English masters whom I remember as Mr Ermine and Mr Fallen. At once antithetical and synthetic, the pair pretty much ran what there was in the way of intellectual life at the school, a sparsely populated province of the curriculum cheerfully abandoned by the other teachers when they embraced their leader's vision of progress and peace embodied in the pink Cadillac convertible. Mr Ermine was a wizened little man, with a shaved head and dark medical glasses which he never removed. His first class of the term, as one of my new friends had warned me, invariably passed in total silence, with Mr Ermine eyeing his students, rarely more than eight in number, through the impenetrable spectacles. Whatever he taught, Shakespeare or Russian Literature, he assumed the poise of predator preparing to claw or sting some mindlessly boisterous food, and took good care to sustain the simile in his pronouncements. 'Gentlemen,' he would hiss, 'in this class you will write things *down*. You will write them down until your little *boyish* fingers grow numb, and begin to *bleed*.' It was obvious that this exercise of authority thrilled him to bits, and I realized that the anachronism of jacket and tie survived among my new friends largely as a byproduct of his tyranny, since those who would not uphold the old dress code were not accepted into his class. In a tiny gap within a centralized institution, Mr Ermine had carved out a private fief of power for himself and his coeval, Mr Fallen, a highbrow eyrie balanced over the valley of May shirts and acid rock whence potential acolytes could rise and offer themselves up to the two of them as willing victims. I promptly procured the required jacket and tie because it was immediately clear to me that Mr Ermine's fiefdom was an enclave, while his tyranny, however perverse, was in reality sanctuary from the insti-

tution, however benign. He held up his end of the bargain. When the
school's fire alarm sounded, as it did every so often, set off by a couple
of Beethovens in a fit of impetuous rage against parental indifference
or the tedium of school life, Mr Ermine remained in his swivel chair
for the duration, hissing, to the accompaniment of hundreds of young
feet in the stairwell: 'Run, children, run. Run for your little *lives*.'
Nobody moved, of course. Even Mr Fallen felt obliged to evacuate his
students, although on such occasions he shuffled his feet more than
usual and did not leave the classroom until he had bundled together
all the books on his desk into a kind of spiritual parcel for what the
fire engines outside intoned might be the last journey down the back
staircase. Mr Fallen gave everyone top marks because, he said, life
was a dream and his marking, if it aimed at fairness, had to reflect
this. 'When you wake up in the morning,' he would often say, the
tobacco stain of his cavernous face to the window and the tired tweed
of his sloping back to the class, 'don't say — .' Here he would quietly
spit out the butt end of an unprintable verb that naughty children
incise into tree bark on summer evenings, then pause, spin round to
face the sniggers, and roar: 'Say *bless*!' Mr Ermine rarely gave top
marks, or ethical advice of any kind, to his students, whose intellectual
inadequacy he impressed upon himself once a term by means of
special tests. These were conceived as an overview of the history of
Western culture from Agamemnon to Zadig, with questions like 'What
is Gogol's Dead Souls?' 'Poem' was the answer that counted. 'Which
of Chopin's piano concertos is the first?' Since Chopin wrote only two
and these were trick questions, 'Second' was the easy answer, though
not if a boy was paralysed with fear at the thought of hearing an
unlucky guess ridiculed the next day along these lines: 'Mr Sachs is a
numerologist. He believes in the power of numbers to deliver him from
the *woes* of knowledge. His father, if I am not mistaken, is a banker, is
he not, Mr Sachs? Perhaps it *would* be best if you followed in the
footsteps of Sachs-*père* and left the woes of *knowledge* to others. What
does it matter to the *banker*, gentlemen, when a piano concerto was
composed? The *pianoforte* is not a cash register, not a pocket calculator.
It is insignificant – *een-see-gnee-fee* . . .' and so on with that mosquito-
pitched emphasis of his, a cross between Ionesco's homicidal professor
and the Baba Yaga of Russian fairy tales. It goes without saying that
Mr Ermine thought of himself as a misunderstood Matthew Arnold,
or a neglected Walter Pater. He reminded me of Zina's Kolya, though
he lacked Kolya's kindness. Our bright faces, reflected in his dark

television-screen spectacles, acted as a kind of universal irritant. Like America's newly portable Nietzsche, he was the hundred-year echo of a genuine utterance, objectively harmless if not vaguely absurd so long after it had been silenced, yet still engaging and at times almost frightening to the adolescents he lorded over. In addition to the tests, there were also 'Mr Ermine's lists' of the thousand greatest people who ever lived, grouped into ten phalanxes of one hundred in the order of their cultural and historic significance. We pored over the first of these, which was distributed to the whole class, unlike the subsequent lists with which only the two or three most devoted 'Erminites' were rewarded, looking for errors, omissions and contradictions. No clues to the mystery could be found without the other nine chapters, of course, since the absence of Spinoza, Florence Nightingale or Matisse might well be accidental unless it was deliberate, and those nine chapters were jealously guarded by the Erminite inner core. Amid such investigations another year of life had found the chance to slip by 'like night to the sound of a dilapidated hansom', as Pasternak said.

22

The *raison d'être* of the 'best school' is to ensure that it is followed by the 'best university'. In America, I soon knew, this meant the Ivy League, which grouped together a dozen of the most prestigious 'colleges', that is to say the undergraduate components of what comprises the university in the European sense. To be sure, it was immediately clear even to a neophyte like myself that once raised, the issue of prestige would recede into infinity rather like Mr Ermine's lists, and indeed everyone believed openly that Harvard, Yale and Princeton were the patriarchal seed of the lot, while University of Pennsylvania and even Columbia were no more than poor relations at the table, treated kindly but without warmth. So the many mansions of this particular promise dwindled, on closer inspection, to no more than three. In their final year, schoolboys sat a variety of examinations, the 'college boards' and 'achievement tests' which were, paradoxically, not unlike Mr Ermine's only far easier and, as befits the practice of mass education standardized to gauge the commonest high denominator, embarrassingly trivial. There was, consequently, no question of even the least faithful Erminite having a less than perfect score in the Literature or European History examinations, with their computerized groping for the author of *The Education of Henry Adams*, Adams, and the site of the Battle of Waterloo, Waterloo. Unfortunately it transpired that little, if anything, would be gained by a perfect examination result where entry into what seemed to my classmates the kingdom of heaven was concerned. The petty god of the Ivy League was capricious, vindictive and unpredictable. He accepted the face of none, and took not the person of man (Wyclif, I seem to remember, made it into Mr Ermine's first hundred). So untraceable and mysterious were his ways that we suspected his vicar, our school's 'college placement officer', of shamanistic bluffing even when he merely delivered himself of vague generalities like 'So, it's Yale for you, is it? Yale is a hard nut to crack.' The sad fact, as my fellow Ivy League aspirants explained it, was that there were other factors. They spent their waking hours tabulating these factors with the zeal of medieval scholiasts. Faith or good works? Editorship of the school paper or a summer job at Rizzoli? The petty god would not be second-guessed, it seemed, and offered no clues. 'Too many other factors.' Sport, it turned out, mattered because colleges had teams whose success against other college teams boosted college morale and, with it, alumni donations to the colleges. Poor Columbia was always losing out, but at least I knew why everybody played games when they could be reading, or smoking corncobs like Tom Sawyer. Birth mattered because no college wanted to anger its alumni by rejecting their children, and of course it was also a way of getting to prominent families not previously associated with the college by taking their offspring into the fold. Geography mattered because colleges wanted to be perceived as national institutions, which prevented them from accepting too many applicants from areas like New York, which had too many. Any shrewd New York parent with a second residence, say in Bermuda, would encourage the child to apply as a Bermudian. Interests, under the scientific designation of 'extracurricular activities', were said to matter a great deal, and here hopeful parents spared no effort in acquiring the necessary equipment, credentials and connections to enable the hopeful scion to claim that he had run an oil rig in Texas, worked with the sick in Calcutta or covered a Brooklyn fire for the *New York Times*. It would naturally be overlooked, in the dense flowering of civically responsible sentiment, that the applicant was the son of a Texaco executive, a consular official in India or an editor of the *New York Times*. But what mattered most, it seemed, was the twin ordeal of 'the college interview' and 'the college essay'. Its aim was to encourage the applicant to reveal himself, but in such a way as to reveal nothing unpredictable, and to present himself as unpredictable, but in such a way as to reveal nothing. There was something oriental in the exercise, something stylized, Byzantine or even Japanese, something that belonged to a world of whispered asides and the kabuki theatre. Without contradiction, it also evoked the little speeches of contestants in a beauty pageant I watched on television soon after our arrival in New York, rather more avidly than I cared to admit to myself at the time, where shameless conformity was wrapped in the veil of paradox just thick enough to be endearing. It also reminded me of the tactics of a courtier in a Russian play by one of my grandfather's contemporaries, who always began by telling the king that although he was only a humble courtier he was no flatterer or timeserver, that he knew he would suffer punishment and disgrace for the simple, homespun word of truth he was about to utter, that men like him were always getting the short end of the stick, and so on, concluding: 'You are the greatest statesman on earth, Your Majesty.' In short, the college engaged in what in Russia is known as provocation while the applicants engaged in what is universally known as bum-kissing. The college's aim was to flush out, and reject as unsuitable, those who were truly unpredictable, uncooperative, or stubborn, as well as those who, by revealing their inability to clothe predictable, conformist platitudes in paradoxes of appropriate thickness, showed themselves to be future failures. As I observed these proceedings, a feeling grew that somebody was behind it all, that the god of college prestige was not as inscrutable as everyone seemed to believe, and that as in *The Wizard of Oz*, which I had read in Russia under the title *The Magician of the Emerald City*, careful attention was to be paid to the man behind the curtain. The results of any such speculation could only be treated by me as highly preliminary, bound up as these were at the time with my own predicament. Still, some things seemed clear enough even then, if only because the man behind the curtain at Horace Mann was none other than the kind Mr Rose. The official admissions policy pursued by the Ivy League was 'diversity'. Yale was the original architect of that policy. Encouraged by Mr Rose, a distinguished Yale alumnus, our headmaster, R. Inslee Clark, had done a long stint as Yale's director of

61

admissions, until Mr Rose brought him back to Horace Mann 'to now ruin this place', as Mr Ermine once told a loyal Erminite. It did, in fact, seem plausible that, since diversity could obviously mean diverse things to diverse people, an insider like Mr Rose might have seen the many advantages arising from having a hand in its definition. Public influence is at once the end and the means of business, and members of Mr Rose's business dynasty knew perfectly well that where money is convertible into public influence, it is philanthropy, education and politics which act as converters. To Mr Rose's dynastic eye, Yale was a hub of the American establishment. The achievement of having placed his protégé at its main traffic chokepoint was legendary. I think I was offered a place by Yale because the admissions office there had so entangled itself in the rhetoric of diversity that it felt obliged to accept a student with a biography as odd as mine. Later I recalled the lessons of American history, taught at Horace Mann by the corpulent Mr Tops, who had the odd habit of resting his hand on the nearest boy's shoulder while lecturing, and since by the Friday of each week he would have leaned on no more than a third of his pupils – because to move about any faster would have been frankly disruptive – come Monday he would usually have to start leaning on the same boys all over again. Mr Tops was uncompromising in his condemnation of the Tammany conspiracy, which effectively ran New York politics from the 1830s to the 1950s, when Averell Harriman became Governor of the state. The Tammany 'society', divided into thirteen 'tribes' with names and ceremonies based on mock Indian ritual, became the secret force behind Democratic party politics, suppressing or surviving the revolts of the Logofocos and the Whigs. Mr Tops explained how the new immigrants to America, in particular, were helped to obtain jobs, then quickly naturalized and persuaded to vote for their benefactors, overlooking the corrupt labour practices and fraudulent electioneering of the Tammany bosses. It was quite apparent, in short, that Ivy League 'diversity' had a wealth of historical precedent. As it happened, Harvard and Princeton accepted me as well. There, at least as far as I knew, Mr Rose had no special influence, although the admissions brochures, following Yale's lead, were just as full of photographs of Rastafarian youths recumbent on lawns of emerald green, and tiny oriental maidens, giant cello cases in tow, with smiles to camera worthy of a *Soviet Life* cover girl. Verily, in Mr Rose's house were many mansions.

23

Quite apart from the portable Nietzsche, now that I was abroad there was my grandfather's generation to catch up with some more. The émigré diaspora, which numbered in the millions, had over the years preserved or exhumed much of that generation's heritage, lost and buried in Russia. The diaspora had libraries, archives and publishing houses all its own. There was Mandelstam's prose and Tsvetaeva's correspondence, Klyuev and those silenced poets that never circulated posthumously even in typescript, Zamyatin's *Faces*, Olga Forsh's *The Mad Ship* and other memoirs of the epoch, Lev Shestov's *The Scales of Job*, more Rozanov than I ever knew existed. All this had to be ingested and understood. Reminiscences and chronicles of the period were naturally followed by the diaspora's forgotten Cassandras, and sometimes its equally inaudible Gibbons, scribes like Melgunov, Solonevich, Bazhanov, Souvarine, Nicolaevsky, Orlov and the rest. Their writings, and the response these received from a uniformly apathetic, indifferent or hostile West, led on to the writings of Western exceptions who dissented, welcoming those early fugitives from paradise as peers, or as martyrs in a cause which only posterity would appreciate as universal. Into my hands came *Assignment in Utopia* by Eugene Lyons, *Artists in Uniform* by Max Eastman, *The Thirties* by Malcolm Muggeridge. For the first time I read André Gide's historic *Retour de l'URSS*. *The Triumph of Provocation*, by the Polish exile Jozef Mackiewicz, had not yet been translated. On the mind's bookshelf, next to Zamyatin's *We* and Platonov's *The Foundation Pit*, now stood Orwell's novels and essays, *When William Came* by the improbably prescient Saki, Huxley's *Brave New World* and Wyndham Lewis's cryptic *Self-Condemned*, and it was easy to see how all their rage and sorrow presaged or variated upon the theme of the individual as the last free man in unfreedom. What Nietzsche had discerned, intuitively, in the twilight of Europe, lived on in its nightmare as the creeping flesh of universal enslavement which these writers felt as their own. How few of them have existed, I marvelled. How many, I wondered, existed still. After school, in the afternoons, I often took the subway to the Fifth Avenue library where Father, harvesting published or archival material for the book he was writing, could always use another pair of hands. When there was time to spare, I looked to magazines and newspapers for the answer. But in the stream of information about the place and the people we had left behind there was rarely anything of value. The scandal of the expulsion abroad by our erstwhile masters of a subject of theirs, who had disobediently compiled a documentary history of the concentration camps, was making headlines, an echo of the earlier scandal involving this writer which I remembered wafting through warm summer air along Mayakovsky Street from Zina's guest cottage. But there was nothing in his books, as far as my father and I could tell, that would have been news at the dinner table in Vnukovo, nothing that either added to the facts uncovered long ago by Melgunov, Solonevich and others or illuminated, any better than Mr Rose's *Britannica* did, the uniquely modern darkness of the individual in unfreedom. Yet that shrill-voiced writer had already been awarded the Nobel Prize, and was now dominating both the foreign news and the literary pages where he was being compared to Pasternak. At first I thought that the comparison was an accident or a prank, a freak analogy hazily concocted at presstime. Yet before my very eyes it became common coinage. You could not open a magazine or a newspaper without seeing the two laureates linked together, one a forerunner and the other the saviour. Father used to say that the Nobel Prize adorned Pasternak as a frock-coat button would the *Aphrodite* of Praxiteles. But then I remembered Mr Rose's *Britannica*, with its wild, blind-drunk fantasy of Russian literature. What had seemed a curious anomaly, especially when contrasted with the measured sobriety of its articles on the history of music, now, against the background of the press coverage that the new laureate was receiving, seemed mendacious and menacing. It was as though a maiden aunt whom once, in childhood, you had seen slightly tipsy, was suddenly dancing in the nude on her front lawn, a bottle of peach schnapps in one hand and a shotgun in the other. The bacchanalia of sudden 'interest' in all things totalitarian, which followed the laureate's expulsion, was equally sudden and unpredictable. It was a daily ordeal to observe, in the newspapers, magazines and even on television, the proliferation of 'experts' on Russian history and culture, each of whom was every bit as ignorant or obtuse as the *Britannica* microcosm of Russian literature which once puzzled us. Now, like the Chinese dragon that springs up from a ball of paper in warm water, that microcosm grew to monumental size, obliterating the sun and the stars and the very horizon of civilization. The dragon spoke with a thousand jaws, and its philistine prattle was heard by the millions. Suddenly, at school, my classmates had new questions for me. These were no more incisive than the old ones, about jeans and corrugated iron, but that was enough to make me realize that I was witnessing one of those waves of mass hysteria which, in civilization, are spontaneous and triggered by a media sensation, while in militarization they are deliberate and set off by the rulers at will. The hysteria was gratifying in one respect. My classmates, their worldview invaded by the media's discovery, or rediscovery, of totalitarianism's inhumanity, stopped calling me a fascist. But, needless to say, they still played sports. They still ate two soggy hamburgers and drank four glasses of milk at lunch, they still hated their parents and hoped to escape to college. They still were the same Beethovens, still the same clerks, and my conversations with them were still conducted on the same plane. They still saw me as a social invalid, even as I saw myself for what I was, a child of my parents' paradise. And if unlike childhood, I reflected, paradise is a world without beginning or end, if, unlike Vnukovo, it is not limited by thoughts of suicide or a fence freshly painted forest green, then what need of a culture? Perhaps mere demilitarization is enough, and everybody can now grow hair like Beethoven or the Rastafarian youth in the college admissions brochure. Forward march! Avant-garde! Down with Matthew Arnold! Take your bony *index dei* out of life's dyke, Mr Ermine, and put it where it belongs. 'In America', a Beethoven from the village of Scarsdale who was bound for Harvard as a lacrosse player of intercollegiate promise once told me, with a smirk rather too didactic for my taste even then, 'we have something called the pursuit of happiness.' But in Russia, I meekly rejoined, they have something called the hydrogen bomb.

24

Not that Vnukovo's inarticulate rejoinder, as I now recall it, expressed an eschatology any less cosmic than Scarsdale's smug invocation of the famous constitutional principle. But I was missing the point all the same. On more than one occasion, in essays written before and shortly after the start of the world war, Orwell challenged the ability of 'private capitalism' to survive the coming onslaught on the simple grounds that 'a bombing plane is equivalent in price to eight hundred pairs of silk stockings'. Hindsight – a faculty upon which, if only out of respect for the Scarsdale point of view, I bestow both a Ph.D. in political science and a history professorship – objects that the greatest of all realists did not take into account the wild card of science, which he believed would end up in the hands of the 'planned system geared to a definite purpose, world conquest, and not allowing any private interest to stand in its way'. For science, Dr Hindsight explains, cleaved to freedom, with the inevitable result that the most militarily significant advance since the invention of gunpowder was made in and for civilization, thus ensuring that militarization everywhere, however purposeful its 'state capitalism', would be deterred, contained and ultimately defeated. Professor Hindsight is right in so far as several Jewish refugees who happened to be scientists of genius did flee Hitler's Europe and did develop the atom bomb in the United States. But was this inevitable? If not, *Herr Professor* is only right in the short term, while Orwell is 'only wrong about the date' as his pupils would have it, now that 1984 is behind them. A conditional argument in favour of such inevitability, a qualified attempt to show that civilization's margin is slim yet real, was made by my father in Vnukovo, in the following imaginary scenario. The crux of the matter, he reasoned, is the subjunctive. If the pseudotsargod had known the military value of what Einstein and others were thinking or doing, he would have had the atom bomb developed ahead of the United States. If only he had known! He would have come in person to chat with Einstein, and probably would have struck the new Newton as a simple, modest, charming man, deeply devoted to science, Jews, and Einstein personally. Does Albert Germanovich need anything for his work, comfort, happiness? Let him name it, and it will be. Because this is not the West, where Albert Germanovich would have to depend on handouts from some academic bureaucrats. He *is* the new Newton, and the academia is for him, not he for the blasted academia. But how could anyone have known? Einstein had been regarded as a dunce at university, was unable to get an academic post on leaving, and finally ended up with an irrelevant minor job at a patent office. Nevertheless, in 1905, in the nontotalitarian Europe, he could, despite his irrelevant minor job, readily publish his studies. This 'nevertheless' may strike a citizen of a civic society as odd, because to have a hundred copies of a letter-size page printed offset in New York a man needs only a few dollars. In a totalitarian society, however, this seems as anarchic, wasteful and criminal as would the liberty of every inhabitant to print money, take pictures off the walls of museums, or sell poisons or medicines to all comers without licence or prescription. The only possible career of a yet unrecognized Einstein is as follows. First, it is necessary to determine what benefit will accrue, some three or four decades later, to the owner called State from the individual called Einstein. For if no benefit can be anticipated, and the man is a quack or a madman, how can State paper, State typographic ink and State labour be wasted on his studies? On the other hand, if some benefit can be anticipated, he should be made a salaried research associate of the SISNOTASIGAS (State Institute of Studies of Nonexistence of Time and Space in the Generally Accepted Sense) founded for the purpose, with State allocations from the State budget, State premises and State janitors, which will in due course entitle him to a State apartment, State trips abroad, and finally the publication of his studies on State presses, unless of course SISNOTASIGAS is a 'closed' institute. But the conversation between Einstein and the relevant bureaucrat of the day is only too easy to imagine:

EINSTEIN: . . . I repeat once again that these studies of mine are more important to space-time physics than any since Newton. Perhaps no one can evaluate them adequately today. This is *new* physics.

BUREAUCRAT [*thinking during this monologue about a highly sophisticated intrigue centred on a newly established departmental Chair, and hearing only the phrase 'new physics' which makes him instantly hostile*]: New physics? What new physics? So we all are *old* physics? Who are you, sir?

EINSTEIN: As I told you, I have found that time and space do not exist in the generally accepted sense.

BUREAUCRAT [*turning pale and now only wishing to get rid of the maniac without provoking him*]: I am asking you what institution you are with.

EINSTEIN [*drily*]: I am a clerk at a patent office. I have been unable to get an academic post. This has nothing to do with my discoveries upsetting Newtonian physics.

BUREAUCRAT [*having got rid of Einstein, to the secretary, both excited*]: I saw it just as he entered. That gleam in the eyes.

SECRETARY [*scolding*]: You are always giving appointments right and left, Mr B. Anybody can just waltz in here.

The thrust of my father's imaginary scenario was that in so far as a civic society permits a minor employee at a patent office to publish his studies of the nonexistence of time and space in the generally accepted sense *before* he is made a salaried research associate of a prestigious SISNOTASIGAS – actually established in Moscow in the 1940s as NIIYAFANSSSR – such a society has an advantage over its totalitarian adversary which, however narrow it may seem in the light of Orwell's intuition, is none the less real.

25

In the twenty years that have passed since I first heard the scenario aired, our perceptions have evolved. There still seems to be something indomitably true about the scenario and its underlying premiss, though to say that Orwell has been defeated by hindsight would be to miss the point as I missed it back then. It was not until recently, here in London, that a strange contrapuntal exchange, between two historical moments I had come across within a few months of each other, supplied the missing logical element and resolved the fundamental issue of inevitability. Cardboard-flat categorical hindsight and the subtly lifelike scenario on the one hand were reconciled with Orwell's intuition and my own experience of totalitarian reality on the other. The first moment was recorded in a Russian novel freshly exhumed from oblivion, Vasily Grossman's *Life and Fate*. The hero, Viktor Shtrum, a Jewish theoretical physicist modelled on Lev Landau, receives a telephone call identical to the one which changed Pasternak's life and fate ten years earlier: ' "Good day, Iosif Vissarionovich," he said, astonished to hear himself pronouncing such unimaginable words on the telephone.' The conversation is brief. 'I think you are working in a very interesting field,' says Shtrum's interlocutor. The physicist's first reaction after putting down the receiver is psychologically flawless: 'For a moment he felt almost embarrassed at his sudden feeling of happiness.' He then turns to his wife, like Zinaida Pasternak a Russian Orthodox Christian: ' "Lyuda, Lyuda," he said. "Just think! I didn't repent. I didn't bow down. I didn't write to him. He phoned me himself." ' Grossman writes: 'The air was still full of the fire and smoke of battle, the rumble of tanks and the trampling of boots, but a new, still silent tension had appeared in the world. The most powerful of all hands had picked up a telephone receiver. A theoretical physicist had heard a slow voice say: "I wish you success in your work."' As the curtain comes down on the historical moment, Grossman has time to mention the physicist's apprehension that all his time would now be taken up with administrative matters. 'But the cars he travelled in were fast, the meetings he attended began punctually and moved swiftly to a conclusion, and all his wishes were immediately granted', Grossman writes. '"I really am absolutely free," Shtrum said to himself with surprise.' But the other historical moment – which provides a counterpoint to the grant of absolute freedom that Gross-man's Shtrum, unlike my father's hypothetical Albert Germanovich, received from the pseudotsargod – has been documented in *The Making of the Atom Bomb* by Richard Rhodes. In the spring of 1939, Enrico Fermi arrived in Washington to report on neutron physics to the Department of the Navy. The theoretical physicist, an Italian married to a Jewess, had already won the Nobel Prize. Rhodes records that Fermi limited himself 'to a conservative presentation. The contempt of the desk officer who went to announce him to the admiral encouraged that approach. "There's a wop outside," Fermi overheard the man say.' What took place during the presentation itself was my father's Vnukovo scenario come to life, although the Albert Germano-vich standing before the bureaucrat was not a minor clerk at a patent office but a scientist with an international reputation, albeit a filthy wop. For while in militarization there may be absolute freedom and a SISNOTASIGAS-NIIYAFANSSSR for Grossman's Shtrum, that is to say for Lev Landau and others like him, in civilization there may only be xenophobic contempt for the likes of Albert Germanovich. Thus it is he, in the end, who must write to the President of the United States in order to convince civilization, which he believes this exalted office represents that he, a kike named Einstein, is working 'in a very interesting field' whose development will save civilization from the Nazi peril. But what if the letter is mislaid? And what if his studies of 1905, even more obscure than his friend the wop's, do not impress anybody in Washington? Dr Hindsight, put on your specs! 'I need unfreedom', Pasternak said, implying that the absolute freedom a poet needs can only come from on high. And, in due course, from on high it came: in the summer of 1934, in Moscow, the poet received the same grant of absolute freedom that the physicist would receive a decade later. Like poetry, physics had been synonymous with freedom ever since the young Niels Bohr wrote of the atom as an 'individual' possessed of 'free will' in a paper inspired by Søren Kierkegaard, when totalitarian unfreedom was only a morbid premonition and the young Pasternak was a philosophy student at the University of Marburg. 'His paper', comments Richard Rhodes, 'was not only an examination of the physical world but also a political document', because physics itself, which an individualist like Bohr felt had become an authoritarian discipline, stifled him as 'a similar authoritarianism in philosophy and in bourgeois Christianity had stifled Kierkegaard'. In short, if Hitler had had the foresight to grant Bohr's peers, many of whom were Jews from Central European villages who had risen to the Nietzschean summit of their discipline as Russia's poets had risen to the summit of theirs, the 'honorary Aryan' status and the unlimited creative freedom that is a totalitarian ruler's to bestow, history as we know it would have soon ended. Hitler happened to lack the foresight. That time round, history did not end. But Nazi Germany was not the only vehicle of militarization. Another ruler might be wiser. Hence the telephone call to Shtrum. Hence the fact that Pasternak was granted such a status and such a freedom. Hence the miracle of Prokofiev and Shostakovich. Just a few grants, *et voilà*! Militarization would have its *logos*, so powerful that civilization could only envy, emulate and ponder it in encyclopedias. And if, as in the case of Landau and others at NIIYAFANSSSR, these grants happened to come a few months or years too late to ensure that militarization could outsmart civilization, and not only overpower it by brute force, surely that outcome was not more inevitable than the success of a bizarre attempt by a group of wops and kikes, who happened to be physicists of genius, to persuade Washington bureaucrats that they were neither quacks nor madmen.

26

Regarded as I can now regard it, some distance though hardly at a safe remove from the two species of social organization I have observed, the difference in their ability to survive in a strict Darwinian sense, with the victor displacing the vanquished from the face of the earth, is a matter of historical nuance. As Orwell perceived, one of the two species is all brawn and is likely to become dominant. As we believed in Vnukovo, the other is all brain and is full of unpleasant surprises for its antagonist. In the light of the two historical moments I have now described, however, it seems that the brawn is capable of growing a brain, while the brain may grow weak and atrophy. In the abstract, as my father's imaginary scenario demonstrated, brain has a slim yet real advantage over brawn, as primitive man able to master fire has a slim yet real advantage over larger and fiercer animals without that ability. But in reality, as I say, this largely subjunctive difference is a matter of historical nuance, and nothing about the struggle for survival between the two species is inevitable. The common name of that nuance is 'culture', a word etymologically allied with 'cult' because it characterizes the overall direction of the exertions, physical as well as spiritual, in evidence within a community. Thus the culture of militarization into which I was born had one public religion, while the culture of civilization, which I pondered in the Madison Avenue bookshop, had another – its unpredictable, gaseous blend of toxins and tonics so unlike the solid monolith of official cult beyond the fence freshly painted forest green. But culture, whether of bombing planes or of silk stockings, is not only the official cult: it is also the stuff of individual motivations and ambitions, of conversations and private thoughts, of small lives and vast circumstances. The encyclopedia, a valid sample of the collective consciousness of civilization, may say one thing. Privately and even publicly, denizens of civilization may believe another, or nothing at all. Hence what on paper is civilization may in reality, given the unpredictable play of historical nuance, turn out to be merely demilitarization, whose brain had atrophied along with its survival instinct to make man the eternal civilian cultivating his own garden. Progressive demilitarization, such as Orwell, Greta Garbo and I saw in the West, relies on hindsight to explain its continued survival. Like Kolobok, the round bun of Russian folklore, it believes that it will escape the wolf because it has escaped the hare, that it will escape the bear because it has escaped the wolf, on and on through time without end. There is an English variant of the archetype:

> Run, run, as fast as you can,
> You can't catch me,
> I'm the gingerbread man!

'*Kolob*', the Russian word which gives the lucky bun its name, has been derived by etymologists from the same Indo-European source as the Old English '*hweol*', wheel, a semantic pedigree that might have lent the bun's tale universal validity comparable to that of time itself had it not been for one small snag, namely, that after the bear came the fox, whereupon history as the lucky bun had known it, ended. Yet Kolobok's timeless movement, in what the lacrosse champion of Scarsdale so poignantly described as the pursuit of happiness, is called the progress of civilization, or simply progress. The cult and culture of total demilitarization is total optimism, because this gives every denizen of civilization the excuse to pursue his individual happiness without having to worry about collective survival, which is pre-established and pre-ordained to continue even as Kolobok was destined to roll on and on. It is hardly surprising that the literary counterpart of the doughboyish antihero should be called 'Candide', or that the full title of Voltaire's satire was *Candide, or Optimism*:

> Run, run, as fast as you can,
> You can't catch me,
> I'm the gingerbread man!

The freethinker's target was the German scientist Leibniz, who proposed that the pre-established universe mathematically progresses, or rolls, towards the 'optimum'. Voltaire was hardly an unbalanced misanthrope who thrived on apocalyptic prognostication, although were he alive today his assault on the very soul of modern demilitarization would certainly be dismissed as so much paranoid raving. In his day it was banned by the Church, because God in heaven and realism on earth rarely make good bedfellows. In the subsequent two centuries, however, even as Christendom has become increasingly perceived as a reactionary force, the doctrine of progress toward the optimum has filled the vacuum left by organized religion. It is only because the sway of optimism, central as it is to the cult and culture of demilitarization, is now stronger and more universal than that of the Church in Voltaire's day, that Voltaire can be ignored under the safe name of 'literature', not banned as an apostate for ridiculing the belief that all is for the best in this best of all possible worlds. (So *Zarathustra* is published in portable form. So Orwell's *Nineteen Eighty-Four*, with its eye-opening truth of universal provocation and its message that no eye-opening truth, including Orwell's, can matter under totalitarianism, is published under totalitarianism, and only a few years behind schedule. In this best of all possible worlds, does it matter?) Candide's tutor Pangloss, modelled on Leibniz, is the spirit of demilitarization and the eternal embodiment of its culture. His pupil, who blindly follows him to the four corners of the earth, is civilization, which, in the absence of a more realistic Virgil, may be said to be 'progressing' only in the sense that the proverbial monkeys with typewriters can be said to be 'progressing' in their task of writing another *Divine Comedy*. We are living out the victorious days of this new religion. Never before, in the post-Enlightenment history of European thought, has the effect of its Panglossian chant been so hypnotic, reactionary and oppressive. Not since the Dark Ages have free men given such wholehearted credence to postulates which they cannot prove by experiment, or openly espoused doctrines which they are powerless to oppose. The omnipotent cult has eroded the margin of safety that was Europe's inheritance, essential to its autarchic survival in an age of global predators. That treasure was accumulated by an aristocratic culture which allowed Voltaire to survive as an individual despite such powerful opposition as the established Church. Could a realist as controversial as Voltaire survive today in the teeth of such opposition from the media, the courts, the tax authorities? Could he survive a publisher's routine expectation that his immortal satire must compete, copy for copy, with penny dreadfuls if it is to see the light of day, or else that he must secure the approval of some academic Pangloss, potentially the very object of his ridicule, and be published as a lapdog is brushed by an idle spinster? The publisher's routine expectation, the principle of narrowly commercial competition, and the alternative of academic approval are all recognizable components of what comprises the culture of modern civilization. 'We have no conviction', wrote an editor to an author, 'that this is the right point of view from which to criticize the political situation at the present time.' He was T. S. Eliot, in the employ of the publishers Faber & Faber, and the book he was rejecting, Orwell's *Animal Farm*, was as direct a descendant of Voltaire's *Candide* as anything his civilization had produced. Certainly Eliot was no more a cockeyed optimist than Voltaire was a misanthropic boor. But how could he, even he, have laid his career on the line if he lived in a culture whose poets, even poets like Eliot, have careers? When he was thirty-five years of age, eight years after he had produced 'Prufrock', perhaps the last poetic statement of everlasting significance engendered by his culture, he received an offer of private patronage under the terms of which the salary he was receiving as a bank employee would be matched for the next five years. He replied that he could not leave his bank, to which he referred as the Bank, because by terminating his employment he would jeopardize the pension to which he was entitled on reaching the age of sixty. By contrast, a provincial notary's son, showered as he was by the King with honours and privileges, could say to his mistress, Mme du Châtelet, who was playing cards with the Queen: 'You are playing with cardsharps.' Voltaire's culture gave him the protection a freethinker needs to think freely, since the very act of thinking, essentially insubordinate, is an act offending the great. Without that protection, even an Eliot is doomed to behave like a timeserver at Geoffrey Faber's court, and it is only the telescope of intuition that enables the poet in him to see things as they are:

> No! I am not Prince Hamlet, nor was meant to be;
> Am an attendant lord.

Without that protection, would Galileo, enabled by Fleming's tele-scope, have dared to look the moon in the face, a *scandalum magnatum* beyond the imagination of kings and princes? Eager for the knowledge which only a freethinker's insight into the nature of things can procure, Galileo's aristocratic milieu nourished his intellectual arrogance. It did so irrespective of where individual patrons, grandees like Cosimo de Medici and Maffeo Barberini, stood politically or philosophically at any given moment, as shown by the fact that Galileo continued to publish after his notorious trial and enforced seclusion in bucolic Tuscany. 'The Englishwoman's red-maned disdain'. Without that protection, could Mandelstam, in the second decade of totalitarian decimation of the aristocratic milieu which provided it, have written these words on a piece of paper? Let me put them in context. I have already referred to the thought that literature is the creation of novel inequalities and unforeseen hierarchies. In the spring of 1931, as the optimal norms of consumption made way for the terror by famine, what could be more novel or unforeseen?

> I toast to the asters of wartime
>   and everything held up to shame:
> To the nobleman's furs, to asthma,
>   to the gall of a Petersburg day.
> The pines of Savoy and their music,
>   petrol fumes in the Champs-Elysées,

> I toast a Rolls-Royce bearing roses,
>> the oils of a Paris landscape.
> The Bay of Biscay with its ebbing refrain,
>> an Alpine jug full of cream,
> The Englishwoman's red-maned disdain . . .

E pur si muove, Mandelstam is saying, because his culture is still Galileo's. Without the contrariness inherent in such a culture, civilization can never have the conviction that this is the right point of view from which to criticize the political situation at the present time, or anything else for that matter. Only demilitarization remains, where the earth is at the head of the universe, the ruler at the head of the earth, and Geoffrey Faber at the head of Faber & Faber, all rolling inexorably, like the lucky bun Kolobok, through time without end. Effeminate as a courtier, its timelessly optimistic psyche wears the silk stockings of Orwell's wrath and the hat of Greta Garbo's dreams as she glides aboard the Orient Express, rolling through an unreal world where Browning is only the name of a poet.

> As for Venice and her people,
>> merely born to bloom and drop,
> Here on earth they bore their fruitage,
>> mirth and folly were the crop:
> What of soul was left, I wonder,
>> when the kissing had to stop?

Soul, zest, vital force, resilience, resistance. 'Mary, Mary, quite contrary.' The zest is gone, as Anna Karenina thinks to herself in Count Tolstoy's idiomatic English. That red-maned disdain is gone, along with the quinine of distant colonies in the next line. Women, where are your husbands, lovers and sons? Dear dead women, with such hair, how does your world end? Not with a Turkish bang, I dare say, but with a philistine whimper. In the language to which I was born, 'philistine' means simply resident, inhabitant, civilian, a man who cultivates his own garden. And I say 'man' because in Russian the word does not exist in the feminine gender.

27

'Damn philistines', Father used to yell. At issue was not so much our abiding distaste for their furniture and furnishings as the sanctity of a freethinker's caprices. The freethinker is conscious of his isolation. His inability to think like others is a disability, an almost physical handicap, which he leaves off trying to overcome early in life. A compensatory awareness is the sense of class, of belonging to the aristocracy of the spirit, with the result that for a hundred years Russian culture classified those who would intrude on its enclave under the rubric of 'philistine'. The handicapped freethinker was isolated, at times as a madman or a quack, most often because he was simply inaccessible. But while physically sound, the outsider was isolated spiritually, in a garden of his own cultivation, in a ghetto which he was free to imagine was the whole wide world. No use rising from a humble cot with a lone apple tree to the palatial splendour of the metropolis, with a private park, a gilt carriage and liveried footmen. Other people's thoughts are other people's thoughts, no matter how large or ornate your garden. Conversely, like an orphanage or a monastic refuge, the enclave was open to anyone with that peculiar disability, whether his earthly dwelling had been the obscure hut in a Siberian village or the mansion in St Petersburg, not 'par le droit de naissance', as Herzen put it, but 'par le droit de milieu'. Indeed, the word translated here as philistine has been inherited by the language from those earliest days, when Russia's culture first defined itself in relation to the bourgeois *liberté, egalité, fraternité*. Unlike the English equivalent, the word does not describe one who shuns, avoids or mistrusts high culture, but one who embraces high culture without belonging to it, as one might to a social class. England, where social antagonism has never existed to the degree it has on the Continent, borrows its vocabulary of class gradation from France: *parvenu, arriviste*. A philistine, in Russian, is the intellectual analogue of a *bourgeois gentilhomme*. The reference is not haphazard: no less than Eliot was Prufrock, Molière was himself a *bourgeois gentilhomme*, whose disability had enabled him to ennoble himself into the class governing his culture. Centuries later in Russia, Mandelstam's genius similarly ennobled him, and one cannot understand how this son of a Baltic Jew in the tanning trade could have penned, at the cost of his own life, a poem mocking a Georgian cobbler's son – by a twist of fate, omnipotence incarnate – for his 'fat fingers', without having felt the weight of cultural authority that comes with such ennoblement like an orb of state or a mantle of ermine. Nor is it possible to understand how an Odessa Jew called Leonid Pasternak, whose father was little more than a rag-picker, could have become, without having so much as contemplated Orthodox baptism, an artist whom Tolstoy described as 'more Christian than I' and to whom he entrusted the illustration of his *Resurrection*, nor why the rag-picker's grandson was in the end free to become the least 'Christian' of poets since Shakespeare. To curse the philistines, for my father, was to proclaim the supremacy of a lost culture as we understood, remembered and revered it, the noble culture of our precursors which, we had no spiritual alternative but to feel, was alive so long as a single freethinker had thoughts that were uniquely his. But to hear the philistines cursed, for me, was also to be reminded that the world outside the fence freshly painted forest green had no claim to universality, and that, in the capriciously inverted hierarchy at the very heart of my ancestral culture, common knowledge was ignorance or deceit, ordinary thoughts were far more shameful than bleating, and any claim of an earthly power that fell short of the apocalyptic *eskhaton* of totalitarian omnipotence was so much boastful impudence, provincial pretension and laughable insularity. Reminded, in short, of what distinguishes the *bourgeois gentilhomme* from the ordinary poor slobs whom their creator does not ridicule: unlike them, Molière's hero thinks he is central to the universe. Which is another way of saying that he thinks he thinks.

28

In Paris after the war, a young American shivered in an illegally heated room reading a Russian writer's impressions of the West published some eighty or ninety years earlier. For Dostoevsky, a commoner by birth, France was the birthplace of the bourgeois, busily gnawing at the tree of hereditary privilege the deeper to bury his nose in its fruit's sweet flesh. The usurper's supper, however, was not the issue so much as his table manners, which, even to a commoner like Dostoevsky, appeared to be as abominable as any previously recorded by history: *'après moi le déluge'*. Accordingly, it was not so much the writer's politics as his portrayal of the Frenchman's behaviour that struck the American as the vivid and vital element of the book he was reading. 'Why does he put all the poor people away somewhere and insist that they do not exist? Why is he satisfied with banal literature? Why does he have a furious desire to convince himself that his journals are incorruptible?' Dostoevsky wondered. 'Why are husbands portrayed on the stage as noble and wealthy, while lovers are always ragamuffins without position and without protection, clerks or artists, rotten through and through? Why does he dream that every last wife is faithful to the utmost degree, that home life is beautiful, that the *pot au feu* is boiled on the fire of virtue, and that her coiffure is in the best style imaginable? This question of the coiffure has been resolved once and for all; it is no longer open to dispute; it has found its own solution. And in spite of the fact that cabs continually pass by on the boulevard with drawn shades, in spite of the fact that there are plenty of refuges for all the interesting needs, in spite of the fact that the wives' dresses are frequently much more costly than one would imagine possible on the basis of their husbands' means, it has been so decided, it has been signed and sealed, and what more do you want?' The American was Saul Bellow. He walked the same boulevard. He saw the same world. 'To a Frenchman, this world is *the* world', he wrote. 'Do you want to see an Eskimo? Turn to the *Encyclopédie Larousse*. There you may see him *as he is*. He cannot be otherwise. On a fiercely hot day in Paris a storekeeper told me, "La chaleur est plus brutale chez vous." He had never been *chez moi*, but he had no need to leave Paris in order to know this.' Naturally, in this best of all possible worlds, all is ever for the best. Louis XVI, for whom the cane-back settee was designed, thought he was central to the universe because his father had been. Subsequent events proved the monarch wrong. The French bourgeois, who commissioned an imitation of the cane-back settee a century later, thought *he* was central to the universe because Leibniz promised him that the universe is pre-established and progresses towards the optimum. The American businessman, whom Bellow may have met, furnished a mass-produced flat with a mass-produced version of the bourgeois imitation for the same reason, because *he* was now central to the universe. Besides, hindsight told him that the glory that was France progressed and became America, and hence Voltaire, whom he never read in college, was wrong, while Leibniz, whom he never read either, was right. In aesthetic terms, the monarch's solipsism was the least offensive, since an imitation, to say nothing of the imitation of an imitation that so galled my mother, necessarily represents a more barbarous culture than does the original. As I said, for a freethinker in the days before the totalitarian deluge it was largely a question of table manners. But for a freethinker like my father, who had looked the immanent *eskhaton* of totalitarian power in the face, it was not that the modern culture of the West could be construed as barbarous which mattered. What mattered was that it was not realistic, its solipsism far more naïve than the proverbial offer of brioche that signalled the end of history as Louis XVI knew it.

29

Educated opinion in the West, muses the protagonist of Bellow's novel *More Die of Heartbreak*, 'envies the East its opportunities for cultivation and development because *there* they suffer more deeply. Here suffering is trivial. Nobody gets hacked to pieces for his ideas. This means you might as well be playing backgammon. Well, maybe so. But *Homo sovieticus* is a boring entity. Through no fault of his own, I grant you. It's mainly a question of how the human spirit was defeated by the so-called Revolution. However, there is a special Russian asset, which is the belief that Russia is the homeland of the deeper and sincerer emotions. Dostoevsky among others promoted this reputation for unlimited passion. The West was nothing but a hospital for emotional-frostbite amputees and other cripples. Well, there *are* Russians who tell us we have been sold a bill of goods. Lev Navrozov, who is nobody's fool, says that for irrational and purely emotional behaviour, America is in the twentieth century what Russia was in the nine-teenth.' Bellow adds: 'He even accuses Dostoevsky of being an ideologist who was personally a cold and calculating rationalist, ninety per cent spleen.' The Russian freethinker who had looked the totali-tarian *eskhaton* in the face and now found himself in the West could scarcely worry about manners, mores or morals. True, American enlighteners like Mr Rose seemed to us indistinguishable from Russian liberals in Chekhov. True, a schoolboy like Michael, odd, sulking, in love with *Lolita*, obsessed with the soul, a morbid prankster playing with sheep's hearts, was straight out of Kuprin. You could imagine him on a window sill stained with tobacco juice and potassium permanganate, talking excitedly to the woman in the room struggling to conceal her yawns. You could see a provincial Russian schoolmaster of the last century, infinitely kind and under the shadow of consumption, in Mr Fallen. Mr Ermine could be transported to Petersburg, terrorizing the fashionable *gymnasium* Mandelstam attended, where children 'played football dressed in the Cambridge style' and the biology teacher forced pupils to listen for his heartbeat under a thick embroidered waistcoat. You could attest to the universality of these types, no more 'Western' than any in Russian literature, without recourse to anything more precise than the sense of smell, from the luxurious newness of carriage leather in Mr Rose's limousine to the monastic, bachelor poverty exuded by Mr Ermine, with its hints and promises of a box full of yellowed-ivory collar stays, a piano long out of tune, of wrinkled, desiccated fruit in a bowl on the kitchen table. But even if all this was only a mirage, a figment of the excitable foreigner's generous imagination, even if the West was in reality the grim and soulless nightmare recorded by Dostoevsky, could we, fugitives from the immanent *eskhaton*, say simply that the show was over and life was no longer worth living? Hence Bellow's portrayal of my father's intellectual disposition, free as this disposition was from the start of even a microscopic trace of moral didacticism. He had no more of a bill of goods to sell than did Einstein in his letter to Roosevelt. Other people have bad table manners? But surely noticing other people's bad table manners is a sign of the worst table manners imaginable. These people are philistines? So long as they do not intrude on the freethinker while he is thinking, he need not intrude on the unexamined life they are living. It is not worth living? Nonsense. All life, in civilization, is worth living, since civilization is life *a priori*, just as militarization is death or a provocation unto death, stumbled into out of stupidity, cowardice or habit. All its earthly hypostases, from Rastafarian pothead to doctrinaire schoolmaster, businessman to civil servant, must be assumed *a priori* to have infinite, unpredictable meaning. These people want to cavort like spring lambs on a verdant hillside, or leap into the abyss like so many Gadarene swine? Not only is this their right and privilege, it is the transcendental aesthetics of freedom, which is to say of the picnic, the carnival and the masque. They want to pursue happiness by accumulating wealth, not by reading books? Who but the writer, with a suspect motive, is to gainsay them? Besides, their acquisitiveness may have laws of its own, its own patterns of evolution, and what the writer bemoans today may be lauded tomorrow by the architect, the painter and the musician, not to mention the hosier and the milliner. Anyway, even if that too is an illusion, surely life can be lived without art or thought at least to the extent it is lived without rice, or alcohol, or goat's milk, or insect grubs, or tulips, or religion, or motorcars, however inconceivable this might seem to certain people at certain times in certain places. Infinite freedom is what life has always been, the freedom to rise and to fall, to be or not to be, to live like an animal or to die like a god, to have the choice of beverage and mode of transport, to buy, sell, and otherwise contract, to eat lotus blossoms and to collect French furniture, to have plastic surgery and to choose one's gender, to listen to acid rock or to nobody, to write books or to burn them, to wear silk stockings and breathtaking hats, or blue jeans, or hair shirts. It is the freedom of delusion and self-delusion. It embodies the aesthetics of peace like a children's picture book in which the lion lies with the lamb, and like these Arcadian animals, men are above morals and without culture because they do not need them. If such freedom is the essence of life, and the very heart of civilization, it has all the millenarian appeal of paradise. Imagine, a paradise as big as the world, unbounded by any fence, and only space and nothingness all around. There is a small snag, however. The vision is not realistic. Paradise is a walled garden. Delusions and self-delusions, as the words suggest, are not everlasting. Outside lies power, epidemic in the etymological sense of the term, power over people. And when civilization rolls into a golden age, so aesthetically perfect, so like the verdant slope of a Cornish hill, so like Madison Avenue at the shopping hour, so like Venice in Browning, there is a predator waiting somewhere beyond the horizon. It is militarization. It is neither above morals nor without culture, because it needs them both in so far as it aims to encompass civilization and thereby impose itself upon paradise. Imagine, a boundless hell as big as the world, and only space and nothingness all around. It is this predator, with its culture of waiting and its morals of mimicry, that turns the millenarian dream into a totalitarian nightmare. Otherwise, what can be more appealing than civilization's delusions and self-delusions? If only these could be eternal! But only the predator has the motivation to see them for what they are, and the organization to place them in the wider context of time and probability. Without this context, Adam and Eve could have tasted the fruit with equanimity, Kolobok would still be pursuing happiness, Marie Antoinette's offer of brioche would have been as charming as it sounded, and no beast of the forest or fowl of the air would ever take the trouble of raising its young. A visionary free-thinker like Dostoevsky could only guess at the context's literal existence, and hence his critique of the emerging West was largely directed at modern civilization's manners, its morals and mores. So many in our century have followed in his footsteps, tinpot moralists and reactionary aesthetes one and all, seeing in America the ugly face of European civilization grown larger than the gilt rococo frame intended to contain its reflection. To our minds, by contrast, nothing could be more pleasing than this spectacle, with its abundance of infinitely receding delusions and self-delusions. If only these could be everlasting! There, and only there, was the small snag. Unlike Dostoevsky, we saw in civilization not only the bourgeois morals and mores of a West shorn of its aristocratic cultural antecedents, but the future itself, a West rolling into the maw of totalitarian militarization beyond the horizon, a progress which its culture, solipsistic and geocentred, was not realistic enough to view in a wider context and hence powerless to stop or even to retard.

30

So Bellow was right. Father was no Dostoevsky, born as he was of a time in which *le déluge*, shrugged off by blue-blooded philistines the world over for centuries, finally inundated 'one country, separately considered' and was licking the outer wall of civilization's garden. A year after Father's book was published, Bellow travelled to Jerusalem. His intellectual motives had nothing whatever to do with his being a Jew, although genetic categorization did help, perhaps, when it came to his travelogue's American reviewers having to swallow some of the harder insights of *To Jerusalem and Back*. Bellow's motive was the desire to experience a civilization in one of those historically rare moments when it is conscious of the weakness within and of the strength without, a microcosm of its actual predicament which, in the macro-cosm of democracy in America and Western Europe, is ordinarily distended by the delusions and self-delusions that have all but displaced the Promethean culture of armed realism. Bellow quotes an aged Tolstoy confessing to a pianist his inability to comprehend the bloody barbarism of the world around them, adding a confession of his own: 'As an American, I can decide on any given day whether or not I wish to think of these abominations. I need not consider them. I can simply refuse to open the morning paper. In Israel, one has no such choice. There the violent total is added up every day. And nothing can be omitted. The Jerusalemite hooked by world politics cannot forget Gerald Ford and China, Ronald Reagan and California; he is obliged to know that Harold Wilson has just asserted in a speech that England is still a force to be reckoned with. He cannot afford to overlook the latest changes in the strategy of the French Communist Party nor the crisis in Portugal and Angola; he must remember the mental character of the Muslim world, the Jews of the Diaspora.' It is this awareness of the predator without, this willingness to take up arms in defence of a perceived truth, that makes the rare microcosm what it is. Thousands of years of Jewish history are no more a part of the equation than Dostoevsky's indictment of bourgeois manners. Have not the Egyptians thousands of years of history to look back on? Have not the Persians? It is the realism inherent in seeing one's defenceless self, one's own fenced garden, in the larger context of time and probability, that makes for the living culture which enables a civilization to survive. For individuality, the predator without may be society, whether 'democratic' or 'aristocratic' or 'theocratic', or organized according to some other principle. For civilization, the predator without is always militarization, waiting until delusions and self-delusions have lulled the demilitarized victim into spiritual and cultural torpor. Small wonder Bellow had this to say of the microcosm he had observed: 'It is both a garrison state and a cultivated society, both Spartan and Athenian. It tries to do everything, to understand everything, to make provision for everything. All resources, all facilities are strained. Unremitting thought about the world situation parallels the defence effort. These people are actively, individually involved in universal history. I don't see how they can bear it.' Small wonder, too, that *To Jerusalem and Back* contained this passage about the book Father had just had published. 'What disturbs is whether Americans understand the world at all,' wrote Bellow. 'To dissident Russian writers like Lev Navrozov, the Americans can never be a match for the Russians. He quotes from Dostoevsky's *The House of the Dead* a conversation between the writer and a brutal murderer, one of those criminals who fascinated him. I haven't the book handy, so I paraphrase. "Why are you so kind to me?" Dostoevsky asks. And the murderer, speaking to one of the geniuses of the nineteenth century, answers, "Because you are so simple that one cannot help feeling sorry for you." Even when he robbed Dostoevsky, he pitied him as one might "a cherub-like child." Navrozov, exceedingly intelligent but, to a Westerner, curiously deformed (how could an independent intellectual in the Soviet Union escape deformity?), sees us, the Americans, as children at whom the Stalins smile through their mustachios. Perhaps there is a certain Vautrin-admiring romanticism in this. Dostoevsky, no mean judge of such matters, thought there was much to be said for the murderer's point of view. Navrozov extends the position. Liberal democracy is as brief as a bubble. Now and then history treats us to an interval of freedom and civilization and we make much of it. We forget, he seems to think, that as a species we are generally close to the "state of nature", as Thomas Hobbes described it – a nasty, brutish, pitiless condition in which men are too fearful of death to give much thought to freedom. If Hobbes is too nifty an authority, let us think of the social views of Jimmy Hoffa. Or of the Godfather. Or of Lenin, as Navrozov accurately characterizes him. And this is what America, bubbling with political illusions, is up against. So, at least, Navrozov thinks.' No, Father was not Dostoevsky, nor was meant to be. Rather he was the hardened criminal out of Dostoevsky, or Balzac's Vautrin, a freethinker with experience of the totalitarian wield thrust into the midst of all the philistine delusions and self-delusions of a civilization disarmed. And I was by his side, watching civilization's response to his account of that criminal under-world, of militarization, a response that would have been fascinating even a century earlier, when that underworld was still confined to dens or prisons, not feared by whole nations or honoured by them, resplendent in Labrador marble, glossy magazine page and the common consciousness of mankind.

31

A century earlier such fascination might grip the readers of Mill's *On Liberty*. Like Dostoevsky, whose contemporary he was, Mill could not possibly anticipate the quotidian of totalitarianism as recorded by Zamyatin and Orwell, nor its metaphysics. Dostoevsky and Mill could only extrapolate their experience as freethinkers to determine how the societies they were observing might evolve in the future. Bellow argued that Father was closer in philosophical outlook to one of Dostoevsky's criminals than to Dostoevsky. I would say that both Father and I were even closer to Mill, not only in philosophical outlook but in temperament as well. There is another parallel here. In the enclave of my childhood, Dostoevsky, 'one of the geniuses of the nineteenth century', was admired as a freethinker for his Promethean, which is to say civilized, individualism. But like Prometheus he was not a good family man, and in the totalitarian wield the last refuge of individualism is the family, first stumbled into through the accident of birth, but later chosen like a homeland, a vocation, a bride. Hence the cultural model of civilized individualism to which we inclined ever since Vnukovo was that of the Mill family. The model, like almost everything else in our life since those Vnukovo days, had its own eschatology. Would the deluge engulf the earth in the father's lifetime, or in the son's? Dostoevsky, living as he did in a Russia nearly as free as the rest of Europe was in the century-long summer of 1815, could treat the family, and filial links in particular, as little more than a parody. His eschatology, after all, was that of a Christian born within a few years of Queen Victoria. The end of the world was nigh, but not so nigh that a father could imagine a microelectronic identity tag surgically implanted in the corpus callosum of his son's brain. Yet Feodor Jnr., Dostoevsky's son, lived to witness the early days of the totalitarian deluge, which not only made hell on earth a viable prospect until the end of time but for ever altered the tragic truth of Christianity's foundational metaphor. He died in the year Zamyatin wrote *We* and Orwell left Eton.

32

To read a freethinker's thoughts on liberty is to become aware of the dynamics of the soul. Whether or not they are equated with the mind – as they can and ought to be in a utilitarian and rationalist perspective – soul, zest, vital force, resilience, resistance all figure in the hyponoia of Mill's ostensibly political discourse. Goethe's now hackneyed admonition at the end of *Faust*, that he alone deserves life and freedom who fights for them each day, underlies, like the very etymology of the Germanic 'soul', this English freethinker's polemic. And a polemic is what it is, fittingly, in the noblest sense, because the soul is, in the noblest sense, polemical. Each day the gramophone needle would follow the groove and, after a few rasps and scratches, an invisible mouth that I knew belonged to civilization would remind me of this with princely disdain in syllables bitter as wormwood, asking whether 'tis nobler in the mind to suffer the slings and arrows of outrageous fortune or to take arms against a sea of troubles and, by opposing, end them. Whether the opposition is internal or external, private or public, contemplative or active, is the only alternative. The first is secret dissent, internal immigration, writing for the desk drawer, Hamlet's soliloquies, monastic scholarship, private thoughts. The second is public dissent, politics, Socrates on trial, publishing, rebellion, war. Either way, the soul exists, and defines itself as living, in so far as it opposes. In the Indo-European spiritual cosmos, there is not nor has there ever been a third way. And since the irrepressible soul, or indeed the rebellious mind, of civilization is the selfsame Promethean culture which, in order to survive, civilization needs – far more so than, given its brawn, does militarization ('He is fat and scant of breath', Queen Gertrude says of Hamlet) – any civilization whose culture is not based on the polemic, on the principle of external and internal opposition, on rebellion and dissent, will not survive. The global aim of militarization is totalitarian peace on earth. The aim of civilization, accordingly, must be to produce the culture capable of bearing forth superior truths such as those of Galileo and Einstein, Voltaire and Orwell, one in which the soul of the individual thinker is free to dissent, to rebel, to wage war. A living truth cannot emerge but from the war of thoughts which Mill identified with 'individual spontaneity'. Peace is falsehood and death, whose spiritual desert Mill, following de Tocqueville, called 'conglomerated mediocrity'. This vital dichotomy is even more self-evidently true in my mother tongue, because in Russian 'spontaneity' is, literally, 'nonmediocrity'. Pacified by mediocrity, civilization loses the culture it needs in order to survive, as an individual forfeits his soul when he stops fighting to save it. 'And thus is kept up', writes Mill, 'a state of things very satisfactory to some minds, because, without the unpleasant process of fining or imprisoning anybody, it maintains all prevailing opinions outwardly undisturbed, while it does not absolutely interdict the exercise of reason by dissentients afflicted with the malady of thought.

A convenient plan for having peace in the intellectual world, and keeping all things going on therein very much as they do already. But the price paid for this sort of intellectual pacification, is the sacrifice of the entire moral courage of the human mind.' It only remains to add that Mill wrote this of Palmerston's England, acknowledged by the visiting Herzen as the freest nation on earth, and one whose military prowess had recently been reaffirmed in the Crimea, an imperial nation with mastery over the seas 'and the quinine of distant colonies'. To stress, in short, that civilization's survival, or sovereignty, was not then the crucial issue and that, like Dostoevsky, writing when the totalitarian wield could not be anticipated in its technologically infinite, bewilderingly sophisticated quotidian, Mill was still largely concerned with civilization's mores and their effect upon the survival, or sovereignty, of the individual. Culture, to him, was an internal matter for civilization, because, either conceptually or as a matter of practical reality, civilization as yet had no external adversaries to contend with, or at any rate none powerful enough to be taken into consideration. All nations in Europe had long traced their common ancestry to the birth of Christ; Napoleon, or even Alaric or Genghiz Khan, could still be viewed from a perspective of the eternal return, of cyclical enfeeblement and rejuvenation; and Kolobok's absolute smugness was not yet absolutely laughable. Who would dare to encroach upon the sovereignty of Victorian England, separately considered, or upon that of Europe as a whole? Mill's Europe, as he himself realized, was the Europe of the Reformation, of revolutionary thought spanning the latter half of the eighteenth century and the Germany of Goethe. 'The impulse given at these three periods has made Europe what it is', he wrote, keen-eyed enough even then to perceive that this impulse had been nearly spent, 'and we can expect no fresh start, until we again assert our mental freedom.' Yet Mill's desired and stated aim was no more than improvement of the spiritual wellbeing of mankind, impossible without the truth he imagined as 'a struggle between combatants fighting under hostile banners'. With the coming of the deluge in 1917, however, the freethinkers of Europe, and later of the world, began to measure their common history in years of the totalitarian era. The stakes were raised, commensurately with the adversary's power. Not mere wellbeing, but the very survival of civilization in the age of totalitarian predators became the crucial issue. It is as if Mill's reflections on liberty begun in 1854 paralleled Einstein's studies of relativity begun in 1905, in that at the moment of their conception both appeared as spontaneous abstractions, which only the wider context of time and probability would make truly relevant or useful. My father and I aimed, in Bellow's phrase, to extend the position of the Dostoevskian criminal by acting as the Mills of civilization in the year 67 of our common, totalitarian era. 'The West, the West!' A Christian moralist might have said that we wanted to save its soul, but he would have been speaking with us at cross purposes. To father and son alike, uprooted, curiously deformed freethinkers in the obscurity of a New York suburb, the salvation under discussion was the means to an end. Civilization had to be polemicized, its soul 'saved' only in so far as this would ensure its physical safety and preserve its human, corporeal aesthetics, its life, its teeming Madison Avenue and those petrol fumes in the Champs-Elysées. Otherwise we had nothing against its hosiers, with their silk stockings, or its milliners with their delicious hats, nothing even against acid rock. We had nothing against gardening. Nothing against the philistines.

33

It was with good reason that Father habitually referred to the totalitarian demiurge of his childhood as 'pseudotsargod'. A learned bore once insulted the demiurge by calling him an outstanding mediocrity. Outstanding . . . mediocrity! Get it? Like all bores he thought that nothing wounds like wit, and one can only imagine his disappointment when the demiurge wounded him back by having his cranium pulped with an icepick. This shows that mediocrity is only an ambiguous concept when conflated with others. The demiurge had never claimed that he was a wit, only that he was the best there was when it came to totalitarian militarization, with its sophisticated culture of power and its morality of eliminating everything that stands in the way. The bore, by contrast, had not only opined that he was perfectly suited for demiurgy, but believed that he was a nonpareil wit as well. When it came to laughing, however, the joke was obviously on him. Years earlier, when the bore still regarded the future pseudotsargod as a junior comrade, hopelessly uneducated and with-out a sense of humour, he once said that in the society they were busy creating man would become 'immeasurably stronger, wiser and subtler, and his voice more musical'. Like all learned bores, he loved culture and knew that the music called classical was a part of it. 'The average human type', he went on to say, 'will rise to the heights of an Aristotle, a Goethe, or a Marx. And above this ridge, new peaks will rise.' The public religion of totalitarian militarization incorporated his optimism into its syncretic, mercurial whole, and echoes of it sounded on old 78s left over from the previous owner of No. 4 Mayakovsky Street:

> 'Cuz we got the chicken and we got the oven,
> And everybody is a Be-e-e-t-hoven!

But it would be infinitely naïve to suppose that the demiurge, who was the best there was when it came to totalitarian militarization, actually relied in his acts of creation and destruction on the belief that he was surrounded by Aristotles and Goethes, or at least by Marxes. Instead, he rightly believed that he was surrounded by mediocrities, many of whom were learned bores, and he acted accordingly. Pasternak's treatment at the hands of the demiurge rivalled Napoleon's flattery of Goethe at Erfurt ('*Voilà un homme!*' said the temporal master of Europe), and it is no exaggeration to say that Landau got everything Aristotle Nicomakhovich himself might have wished for, including swift motorcars and punctual meetings. Characteristically, the demiurge never sought out a Marx. What, another learned bore? He had so many that his apparatus of destruction worked overtime pruning and weeding just to keep them under, those universal geniuses of all fields and masters of none, indifferent Red Army generals meddling in politics, Bolshevik apothecaries with a penchant for public speaking, balding leather-jacketed RAPPers who thought they knew a thing or two about poetry. The demiurge needed nonmediocrity. He realized only too well that totalitarianism reduced, not increased, the potential for spontaneity, where all creation, that is to say all production of strategically vital scientific and cultural truths, originates, and created artificial enclaves to protect that spontaneity from the onslaught of mediocrity. The learned bores, his erstwhile associates, had never understood this. How could they? They thought they were the masters of culture, with their love of Beethoven. But as an exasperated Prokofiev had to explain, in the age of Prokofiev the lovers of Beethoven were a dime a dozen. The lovers of Beethoven, mediocre in everything, knew less about what makes music music than did the totalitarian demiurge, who was the best there was at something, however unrelated that something was to music. In short, the demiurge showed himself to be a thinker and a realist, while they proved themselves to be philistines whose claim to being something other than mediocre was that they thought they thought. The more optimistic the public religion of totalitarian militarization grew, the more realistic the demiurge became, often having to feign irrationality and, in the final years of life, even madness, to deceive those whom he had not conquered into believing that his creation was at once invincible and laughable. How much printer's ink, and blood, has been shed in the West since then to prove that man under totalitarianism would never rise to the heights of an Aristotle, a Goethe, or a Marx – to prove that, in what had been advertised as a paradise, there were not only no Beethovens, but no chickens and hardly an oven! It was conveniently overlooked that the contemporary Western civilization had even fewer Beethovens, and that the initial imbalance of the nuclear scales in its favour was the subtle play of historical nuance. Civilization was collectively responding to the demiurge's creation just as that learned bore, his erstwhile senior comrade, had responded, assuming all the while that it, civilization, was where the mastery of culture was lodged for the simple reason that it had been always lodged there, and that anyone doing what it, civilization, could not comprehend was an outstanding mediocrity. But, to evoke Prokofiev again, the lovers of culture knew less about what makes culture culture than did the totalitarian demiurge, who was the best there was at something, however unrelated that something was to what is so grandly called culture. And thus civilization began to lose its collective mind, intermittently terrified by acts of destruction and amused by acts of creation neither of which it could fully comprehend. There is a famous Russian fable about a peasant driving his geese to market. 'The ignoramus does not seem to know,' complain the geese to a passing traveller,

> 'He owes us great consideration,
> For we our high descent from those same geese can show,
> To whom the town of Rome stood debtor for salvation.
> Why, there a special feast is honoured with their name.'
> 'But you,' the traveller asked, 'have you a special claim?'
> 'Of course, Our ancestors . . .' 'Yes, yes, I've read it too,'
> I know all that. But tell me, do,

What good from you yourselves has come?'
'Why, yes, our ancestors in Rome . . .'
'But was there some one whom you did the same to?'
'We've not done anything.' 'Then what's the good of you?
Do leave your ancestors alone!
To them was due the honour shown,
But apple sauce is all you have a claim to.'

Apple sauce, said the totalitarian demiurge to the learned bore after the global apparatus of destruction had pulped that mediocre cranium of his in distant Mexico, apple sauce is all you have a claim to, because Aristotle, Goethe, Marx are no more, and culture, by any definition save that proffered by learned bores for reasons too obvious to enumerate, is not about memorizing the names of the dead from whom descent by the living can be claimed. Apple sauce, militarization will say to civilization when its intellectual demilitarization has progressed far enough for the gaggle of conglomerated mediocrity to drown out the last discord of militant individualism:

'Cuz we got the chicken and we got the oven,
And everybody is a Be-e-e-t-hoven!

Back in Vnukovo, it was strictly the public religion of the world which lay beyond the fence freshly painted forest green. Now the public and the private were one, at least in theory. Here the toxins blended with the tonics. I feared it might take a lifetime to analyse them all, and with these dissentient thoughts, in the year 67 of our common totalitarian era, I finally arrived in New Haven, Connecticut, United States of America.

34

What was I, then? An obscure young *émigré*, son of a curiously deformed dissident, grandson of a forgotten playwright. I recited my genealogy to any that asked. My paternal ancestors, I said, apparently called Nav-Ruzi, came to Russia from Persia during the reign of Ivan IV, known as the Terrible. They first came as traders, but later adopted Orthodox Christianity, were ennobled by the Tsar and settled in Muscovy. Whereupon Russia, as well as my family, witnessed four centuries of civic evolution dimly reflecting Western progress towards constitutional government, individual liberty and universal suffrage. Then my grandfather, the playwright Andrei Navrozov, a hereditary Muscovite and a drunkard, married my grandmother, a Jewess who knew Blok's every line by heart. But what are you, they would press on. I am a hereditary freethinker, I would reply, looking for the excitement of public dissent denied my family for three generations, the excitement for which private dissent is no substitute and one which no culture can do without, certainly not your own. I come from a society that nurtures the culture it needs to subjugate you in special enclaves, restricting it to the private domain of the laboratory and the study. My father and I left the comfort of such enclaves behind to come among you and stir up dissent in the public realm, because dissent is culture and culture is salvation, your salvation. By this juncture I rarely had an audience, despite my best efforts to intersperse the monologue with sincere offers of brandy and what I hoped was engaging laughter. Who the hell do you think you are, the rare listener who stayed behind would finally blurt out. Had I made a last attempt to buttonhole him or, as is the usual course at eighteen, her, look, I would have gone on to say, look, you are missing the point. Nearly a century ago Remy de Gourmont could proclaim in the *Mercure de France*, publicly and without hindrance, that Waterloo was good for the whole world and for France first of all. Nobody asked him who the hell did he think he was. Yet despite all the economic, political and military undertakings or upheavals of the century, it is clear that this truth is still a paradox in the ears of the French, who prefer to think of themselves as the invincible nation of Napoleon. Human folly, in Renan's words, is still the only thing that gives an idea of infinity. The English do not often like to think of themselves as the nation of Neville Chamberlain, do they? The Germans prefer to recall Beethoven who, after all, was a German. But human folly aside, it is quite clear that a free society's capacity for cultural insularity is infinite. Listen to this family anecdote. When my father was born, on the centenary of Lev Tolstoy's birth in 1928, he was named Lev. My grandfather wanted to name him Ivan, and although she knew Blok's every line by heart, my Jewish grandmother laughed hysterically whenever she remembered her husband's absurd request. 'Ivan, light the stove!' To her, culture was a supranational universal, and Count Tolstoy embodied her vision of Russian culture to the extent he embodied that universal. Yet there you have it, laughter which could be construed as hysterically Russophobic, especially because 'Ivan', like 'John', is only the modern version of an ancient Hebrew name. Years later, I would proffer another anecdote to my buttonholed yet quite possibly still imaginary listener. A Russian *émigré* engineer I know told a New York editor that the twentieth-century battle for control of the cosmos is not unlike the fifteenth-century battle for control of the seas, and that the permanent space station Mir has now been operational for a decade while its American analogue is still on the drawing board. The editor, a young woman of Irish descent, replied proudly: 'Crap!' Although this scientifically illiterate New Yorker might be hard pressed to tell her rear axle from her L-beam, her synthetic judgement *a priori* was that the nation of Ivans is scientifically backward. For the Maginot Line is ourselves, Neville Chamberlain really was Britain's Prime Minister, and Adolf Hitler did win ten times more votes in Beethoven's Germany than the Bolsheviks ever had in a barbarous land once called Russia. On the other hand, please note that the once and future masters of that barbarous land, in the person of Yuri Andropov, made the Briton I mentioned earlier as my father's English examiner their personal adviser with the rank of general. Can anyone rule out that there were certain private thoughts, far more grave than the 'Ivan, light the stove!' variety of my grandmother's bemused Russophobia, that associated in Andropov's mind with the name Harold 'Kim' Philby? A nation of phlegmatic shopkeepers? Of effete pederasts? Of Cambridge communists? They are all alike, Andropov might have reflected, apple sauce is all they are good for. 'Kim' indeed! Who the hell does he think he is, Kipling? But the omnipotent ruler, unlike the obscure editor of the anecdote, did not act upon his xenophobic impulse any more than his predecessor ever relied on the public belief that naturally he would be surrounded by Aristotles or Goethes, or at least by Marxes. Instead, dutifully and attentively, he listened to Philby's weekly briefings until the day he died because he knew that to understand a nation like Athens one must listen to a native like Alcibiades. Every insularity has a share of interstices, every xenophobia has its exemptions. Some are strategic, of course, while others are random. Whether or not it is widely perceived in the West, today, or when I first came to Yale, or a decade hence, that totalitarian militarization cannot but triumph over demilitarized civilization, one generously inclusive notion about the nation of Ivans remains widespread. Russian literature, even for *Britannica*, has been exempt from xenophobic scepticism and has become a fixture in the Western mind, alongside French viniculture and Italian singing. Thanks to the pseudotsargod's subsequent conservation effort, this warmly inclusive notion survived Russia's totalitarian abduction in 1917, perhaps by analogy with the Route de Champagne under the Vichy or La Scala under Mussolini and despite Zamyatin's foreboding that the only future for Russian culture would be its past. Anyway, that was the reason I wrote 'literature' in the blank space provided by the Yale matriculation form. Subsequently, the above disquisition was greatly abridged, until only the androgynous question, 'Hi, what are you majoring in?' remained, and the hermaphroditic answer 'Literature'.

35

Variations existed, such as 'Where are you from, by the way?' – which the gruff, Hemingwayan reply 'New York' invariably failed to parry with quite the coyness desired, New York not being a fashionable place to come from anyway – or 'What college are you in?', angelically transparent in so far as it was actually a demand to produce superficial proof of belonging, like a rations card or a gas bill with a home address. To the presumed outsider, it transpired, 'college' meant 'university', and the insider of yesterday began to savour today's hermeneutic pleasures as soon as he learnt that, here and nowhere else in America, every undergraduate belonged to a college. For reasons of propriety, and out of consideration for the exotic traveller who might have seen the Cam and the Isis flow, a figleaf qualification like 'residential' was sometimes prefixed, a sly admission on the university administration's part that the colleges were, after all, no more than dormitories, whose separate identities were a fiction, a placebo to calm the intellectual jitters of a doubting Thomas from Nebraska whose father, a Yale man himself, had promised him the diversity that goes with a liberal education, a really good liberal education. Curiously, my own first impression of Yale, which, then as now, would do credit to any of the University's admissions brochures, was likewise one of diversity. In retrospect I realize that I was looking upon diversity as a savage might into a fragment of a cheap shaving mirror, discovering within such depths of verisimilitude as would make a civilized man, well used to shaving in the morning, simply shrug and occupy himself with a blemish on his freshly denuded chin. Physically much of the University is Gothic, the architectural style whose original exponents inspired awe in generations of my countrymen travelling abroad. As the Byzantine whorls of Russian churches have for centuries served the West as a ready symbol of Eastern mystery, no Russian can think of civilization, that is to say of Europe and the West, without imagining a Gothic dirigible in flight, propelled by the power of Christendom. Yale built its Gothic structures in the 1930s. The official line was that they replicated the colleges of Oxford and Cambridge, with the implication that the spirit of Europe was now happily resident in the United States generally and the city of New Haven, population 137,000, in particular. This is why I call the structures 'Gothic', not 'neo-Gothic' as a superficial observer, an outsider, might describe them. They are fakes, not imitations. The distinction has been made by an Italian writer visiting New York who saw in Lower Manhattan a 'masterpiece of living architecture' whose 'skyscrapers, neo-Gothic cathedrals, neoclassical Parthenons and primary cubelike structures' come together for 'a jam session in stone', an architecture that is living because it illustrates the revivalist awareness of the time when it was practised. Wall Street's neo-Gothic follies are not fake, 'at least no more than the Madeleine is, in Paris, and they are not incredible, any more than the Victor Emmanuel monument is, in Rome. Everything is integrated in a now homogenous urban landscape, because real cities redeem, in their context, even what is architectonically ugly.' But New Haven is not a real city, if only because a good half of its inhabitants are caught up in university life. Yale's Gothic buildings are fakes, and intended to deceive. Given my earlier experience of the French settee, laminated cane and all, I wonder why the whole idea did not immediately strike me as barbarous. I had lived in Rome. I had seen illustrated books on architecture. And still I fell for it, no doubt about that. I swallowed it hook, line and sinker. I bought it, because laminated settees notwithstanding, America was the great citadel. No sceptic can disbelieve everything he is told or shown, no freethinker can for ever sustain his mistrust of received ideas or images with the full intensity of that brand of paranoia which Mill called the malady of thought. Sooner or later the immigrant buys the Brooklyn Bridge, even if in his native country he was a hardened criminal or a compulsive nonconformist of some other, less practical kind. America was the Atlas of civilization because it alone had the power to hold civilization aloft, like a Gothic dirigible, above the rising flood. That it also possessed the power to achieve what the Italian writer has described as 'furious hyperreality' in its displays of itself, corroborated the view and reassured the viewer. As the immigrant of old once gaped at the Brooklyn Bridge before buying it, as the foreign investor sizes up the skyscrapers of Manhattan before losing his money to the fast-talking operator of a pyramid scheme, so at the sight of such cultural audacity the newcomer to Yale was disarmed and found himself inclining to the pleasantly unrealistic. Was it Oxford? Marburg? Wittenberg? 'I pray thee, stay with us, go not to Wittenberg.' It was autumn. A Bach prelude tinkled charmingly from the belltower dominating the Old Campus and nearby colleges. The morning sun played on the lead used to repair window glass that time had never cracked. Undergraduates, arm in arm, were crossing the quad of a Gothic college, all shafts and stairwells and gargoyles. The Italian writer is a native of civilization, who may prove hopelessly trusting when political ideas which I instantly recognize as received are put before him, and he has certainly never looked to the West for miracles as I have. On his grand tour of American hyperreality, Umberto Eco finds in California a café in the seaside style of Brighton, with lifelike figures of 'Mozart and Caruso at the same table, with Hemingway standing behind them, while Shakespeare, at the next table, is conversing with Beethoven, coffee cup in hand'. He finds a three-dimensional representation of Leonardo, painting La Gioconda in the two dimensions of a canvas while the artist's three-dimensional subject, 'complete with chair, feet and back', is there for all to touch. Never fully sated with all the harebrained Xanadus, pharaonic monuments, absurdly incoherent palazzos and unnaturally ancient villas, stretching like a street fair of heritage fetishes from Atlantic City to New Orleans, he finds a whole United States 'filled with cities that imitate a city, just as wax museums imitate painting and the Venetian palazzos or Pompeiian villas imitate architecture', Disneyland only the best known among these. I have never visited any of them, save New Haven. Yet Eco has never visited the Versailles that was the Moscow of my childhood, the greatest Hollywood set of them all, the rubber dummy artificially inflated to befuddle outsiders, the Potemkin village for foreigners to deceive themselves by observing understandable forms of life, when natives know all the while that a hundred paces due north there begins a different country, with tens of thousands of underground cities called bases, installations called closed towns and secret factories called postboxes. Can any native of civilization understand why a former subject of the totalitarian wield would tremble with joy at the sight of Disneyland, with its regular flights to Mars 'experienced from inside the spacecraft'? He trembles with joy because a simulated flight to Mars is a sign that civilization may yet win the battle for control of the cosmos, and that the dimwitted Irishwoman, who argued that it would, may yet be proven right. Although a simulated flight to Mars is as innocuous as a new hat or a pair of silk stockings, he trembles with joy because visible complexity, even when it appears to exist solely for the entertainment of children, is a sign that some invisible, inner, hidden complexity is at work somewhere, and that smoking hashish and growing hair like Beethoven is not what civilization is all about, however aesthetically perfect the spectacle may appear to the lover of liberty. He trembles with joy, in short, because he knows that power is a culture, wheels within wheels and enclaves within enclaves receding into infinity, and as he gazes into this antique looking-glass for the first time with the excitement of someone who has only seen cheap modern mirrors, he reflects that time, after all, may not end with him or his son. So it is no exaggeration to say that as the autumn sun illuminated my first days at Yale, a Bach prelude tinkling down on the incredible and fake Gothic world beneath, I trembled with joy.

PART TWO

MICROCOSM

1

'The trick of being tiresome', said Voltaire, 'is to tell all.' The great
historic upheavals that are the reference points of my childhood and
adolescence may all be looked up in *Britannica*, which can equally be
relied upon to furnish a superficial history of Yale, or of American
universities generally. Abstractions like cultural diversity, liberal
education and academic freedom have lost none of their popularity
since the day I first encountered them in the admissions brochures.
What no encyclopedia can be expected to suggest, however, is what
paranoid misfits like Mill and Orwell have always known to be true,
namely that when, for one reason or another, a society lets go of the
adversarial principle I have compared with the human soul, it
develops therapeutic myths of itself which present its weaknesses as
strengths, myths that displace truths in the pages of encyclopedias
and allow the many to diagnose the few as paranoid misfits. The
popular abstractions I place among the constituent myths of modern
civilization's public religion are not outright lies, of course. They are
what Mill called half-truths, noting that 'not the violent conflict
between parts of the truth, but the quiet suppression of half of it, is
the formidable evil'. By absorbing the violent shock of dissent once
represented by such abstractions into its placidly gaseous whole, the
religion quietly dissolves potential opposition, with the consequence
that, in Mill's words, 'truth itself ceases to have the effect of truth by
being exaggerated into falsehood'. But as the Bach prelude, gently
pealing from the chapel's Gothic tower, stilled my paranoid aspira-
tions, I had no time for formulations of this kind. Courses had to be
chosen, and under the influence of the visible environment, which I
obediently interpreted as the university had intended, I chose a course
of lectures on Hegel. The first paper assigned by Professor Rockmore
was an analysis of a famous chapter in *The Phenomenology of Mind* in
which Hegel examines the relationship between master and slave. I
hoped to approach Hegel, and indeed all my studies in those early

weeks of my first term, exactly the way such matters had been treated at the Vnukovo dinner table. Obviously none of our guests liked to be thought of as a learned bore, and consequently it was unimaginable that in the course of a conversation bubbling into the small hours, somebody would summarize a chapter from a book everyone else had read. I viewed the professor as my host, and the essay I submitted was intended to divert him by presenting Hegel as a slave to platitude, an antihero of thought, a man so wanting existential imagination that in a Napoleonic Europe steeped in serfdom he was unable to recognize serfdom as a reality transcending the insular concerns of an ambitious *Privatdozent*. Hegel's idea that the slave enslaves the master, I reasoned, is not a paradox because in the broad historical context of universal servility it is sycophantic, as Proudhon's idea that property is theft would not be a paradox in a society of thieves. As I wrote, I imagined Father and our guests, eviscerating an academician's conceit here, taking a stab at a bureaucrat's witticism there, Tsinandali flowing amid roars of laughter. I read the essay to Father over the telephone, adding news of this new university life of mine, which I imagined as a continuation of and perhaps even an improvement on the lost life of the Vnukovo enclave, a paradise perfected. The following week I came to class, expecting the thrill of violent conflict between parts of the truth, the thesis being that Georg Wilhelm Friedrich Hegel was a celebrated philosopher and the antithesis, that this son of a Stuttgart government clerk led an intellectually sheltered existence. The dialectic, however, did not work out as I expected. 'May I see you for a moment?' said Professor Rockmore. I noticed red blotches on his face. He told me that he could not give my essay a mark, and that if I wanted to stay in his course I would have to rewrite it. 'But, Mr Rockmore, this is what I think,' I protested, 'these are my thoughts on Hegel's treatment of the subject.' He referred me to my college Dean, who received me in the Gothic grandeur of his study. The Dean advised me to withdraw from the course, explaining that it was for advanced students and closed to freshmen anyway. I have been strictly reared, as Mark Twain used to joke, but if it had not been so dark and solemn and awful there in that vast room, I do believe I should have said something which could not be put into a Sunday-school book without injuring the sale of it. With a sinking heart I realized that the *faux pas* I had made was not unlike that of a tramp barging in on a ladies' circle evening devoted to problems of the homeless. This Shavian dramatization aside, suppose philosophy were a science, like mathematics or chemistry, and a drunken beggar barged in to disrupt a university lecture on metal ethoxides with his ideas about ethanol and its applications. On the other hand, it would never have occurred to me to disrupt Professor Rockmore's course in this way if the subject discussed was symbolic logic, or any branch of philosophy that borders on mathematics. I remembered that Mill, in his discussions of intellectual freedom, specifically used mathematics as the example of an exact science 'where there is nothing at all to be said on the wrong side of the question' in contrast to 'every subject on which difference of opinion is possible' and, in Mill's view, essential to what makes a freethinker's life worth living. Yet the subject under discussion was not Hegel's logic but his view of slavery, a subject upon the stark reality of which Mill began reflecting while the Jena timeserver was still alive. Besides, Hegel's dialectical vision of the world process added a new dimension to Leibniz's optimistic myopia, and while I considered myself no more competent to discuss Hegel's logic than Leibniz's mathematics, I failed to see why discussion of a subject like slavery by the former should be closed to literary intrusion when, in the case of the latter, such an intrusion had produced *Candide*. I then approached several of the students attending the unfortunate course of lectures, none of them, admittedly, a callow freshman. Many were even bearded, after the Young Hegelian fashion of Professor Rockmore himself. One student essay from the unfortunate week was finally produced, complete with a top mark and the professor's comments, whereupon, with the pain that I can only compare to that of a forcibly extracted illusion, I discovered that the bearded essayist had done what schoolchildren do the world over, namely, repeated Hegel's argument paraphrastically, just as if it had been the proof of a Euclidean theorem or the tale of a big bad wolf called *Sein*. The tramp had not quite expected, perhaps, that he would be given crumpets with tea and asked to tell the ladies what the homeless need. He might not have expected that his audience's kindness would outlast the short speech he planned to wind up by demanding a shilling from everyone present. But least of all he expected to find the good ladies naked, or mute, or dead. Yet this was precisely what I, in the role of tramp, admitted to university for reasons that had less to do with diversity than with the homogenizing of diversity, found there.

2

Once a social misfit has let the grit of paradise get in under the shell of his scepticism, only a cataclysm of inductive reasoning can keep illusions from growing apace. As the grit kept crunching its way inside I welcomed the insinuation grain after grain. The Hegel episode soon seemed like a minor flap, and the provisional hypothesis was that the classroom is simply not a good place for conceiving pearls. Experimentally this was confirmed by sporadic attendance at required lectures and bouts of auditing courses that, like Professor Rockmore's, were restricted to upperclassmen. In the whole of the university faculty, I discovered, there was not a single conspicuous eccentric, not even along the familiar lines of Messrs Ermine and Fallen, a mad professor who could serve as a point of departure, a dot on the graph of public dissent from which a coordinate system of one's own might be extrapolated. There were a few exotic butterflies, like the Kantian Stephan Körner, but these existed in a postgraduate world of their own far from the collegiate crowd, a cocoon whose precious silk the university spun into international prestige. Anyway, my 'major' was literature. For the freshmen there were introductory courses, lectures packing giant auditoriums with two or three hundred newcomers to academia, to refresh their schoolboy memory of classic puzzles like the authorship of *The Education of Henry Adams*. For the upperclassmen there were small seminars, twenty to thirty souls in each, where discussions only slightly more heterodox than a routine conversation with a librarian took place between the students and the presiding professor. Here the roles had been distributed in advance, it was obvious, according to a set of unwritten rules governing deployment of the diversity incarnate in the student body. The professor impersonated earnest scholarship as he entered the room and made his way towards the chair at the head of the table, exchanging this for the easy, bantering persona of a man who makes a vocation out of familiarity, a tour guide perhaps, or a lifeguard, as soon as he was seated. The boy nearest to him, with dark curly hair, usually called Jeff and sometimes Josh, was invariably from New York and affected an attitude of energetic nonconformism by interjecting comments prefaced with 'I totally disagree'. Next to him was the perverse girl who never added the name of a state to the geographically remote part of America whence she came, Wichita Falls or South Bend, who

104

never missed class and never said a word except 'Would you open a window, please?', with a presumptive twin in a white cashmere sweater seated all the way in the back, near the door, who made herself known a few minutes later by asking that the window be closed. They were the blondes. A third girl, a brunette, was there to argue with the curly New Yorker, steering the discussion in the general direction of 'Freud in Europe' and 'fascism in America', or maybe it was Freud in America and fascism in Europe. It hardly matters. The two of them were typically the nucleus of controversy, and the only ones in the room who effortlessly referred to a Henry James story as the 'text', brandishing words like 'protagonist' – when just about everyone else in the room would have said 'dude' or, upon reflection, 'guy' – and then pricking each other with 'fictionality of narrative'. An optional addition to this quartet of stock characters was a mumbling young Republican from New Jersey or Maryland, who would mumble, as it were, straight from the heart. Here the erstwhile antagonists would join forces and their victim's naïve utterance would be torn to shreds like a leaf of Bethany lettuce, because they were the professor's pets, boarding-school children of prominent bankers or publishers, and they knew it, while he was an uncouth provincial nobody, a child of the faceless middle class, a pimply protofascist who had never even seen a psychiatrist, and in the end he knew it too. And the rest? The rest played football. I exaggerate, of course. There were only about forty of them on the university football team, out of some four thousand undergraduates. Even with all the substitutes and hangers-on, they made up no more than two per cent of the student population. But that was merely the apex of the pyramid. A substantial minority, at least in every class I ever attended, was made up of boys and girls called jocks, for whom the mental effort of saying 'guy' instead of 'dude' was all but unthinkable. The light jocks, many of them alumni children, went in for squash, lacrosse, crew, field hockey, soccer and almost every other conceivable kind of competitive sport, with the possible exception of spitting, that had an established alumni following, however small. They were the specialized instruments of the university fundraising effort. Real jocks played football, if not on the team then as an intramural sport. These were the fundraising generalists, and each of them mattered more to the university than all the scholars of the next twenty years put together. Each was the apple of the administration's covetous eye, because the promotional campaign of every academic year found both consummation and justification in the football season, a series of matches played against Ivy League opponents that reached its climax with the Harvard–Yale game, known as The Game.

3

The Game is a sporting event for which Royal Ascot is the only convincing social analogue. The Oxford–Cambridge boat race is a narrowly undergraduate affair by comparison with this nationally televised clash of titans in the groves of academe, a splendidly turned-out crowd of a hundred thousand captains of industry and commerce in flag-waving attendance. Red for John Harvard, blue for Elihu Yale:

> When the sons of Eli break through the line,
> Our team will never fail!
> Bulldog! Bulldog! Bow, wow, wow!
> Eli Yale!

Here the thoroughbreds, huge, carnivorous, fed on special rations 'from the Kremlin canteen', are usually black, or else Italians and Irishmen from old immigrant stock, proles, cannon fodder, gladiators selling their muscle for the promise of a top job in sales or insurance. The social prominence thrust upon them has a history, which, like the Coliseum in Rome, may one day puzzle the onlooker. At the turn of the century, American football caught on as a quaint public expression of the collegiate ethos, following Harvard's historic decision to play the game by Rugby rules and its subsequent evolution in the hands of one Walter Camp, 'Father of American Football', an 1880 graduate of Yale who became his university's director of athletics. An educational myth of conflict, of combat, was needed to fill the vacuum of peace, so artfully filled both before and after the Civil War by the victimization of the native population of North America under the mythopoetic misnomer of 'Indian Wars'. This merits a digression within the digression, because to understand Walter Camp's success one must understand George Crook's. In the beginning, there were the cowboys and the Injuns. Then there were only the victors, playing the theatrical role of cowboys and using the vanquished as a didactic illustration of the just fate that is never escaped by the morally inferior, although in reality such a fate is never escaped by the technologically inferior. Yet even when it was still the real cowboys and the real 'Red Indians', one convenient thing about the Indians was that the cowboys always knew that in the end they would win:

> Whatever happens we have got
> The Maxim gun, and they have not.

General Crook, fighting the Apaches in Arizona, won his stripes at the precise moment in the evolution of small arms when smokeless powder, magazine loading and bolt action were introduced. The machine-gun had been invented by Gatling some decades earlier, and the innovations of Maxim and Hotchkiss were coming into their own. The reputation for tolerance and patience acquired by Crook as he chased the befeathered Geronimo over the plains was one consequence of these technological advances. The Indian reservation – in the terminology of the next century, a ghetto – was another. But if the eventual aim of this pacification campaign had been known from the start, by the time the Bureau of Indian Affairs was established the campaign's success could not be doubted. That was some sixty years before Crook's triumphs. Which is to say that if the generation of Walter Camp's grandfather shot fish in a barrel, while that of his father used a small jug, by the time the Father of American Football graduated from Yale, Crook was acquiring his reputation for tolerance and patience by occasionally holding himself back from blasting away at a thimble. The next two or three generations of Americans would live through two world wars and witness the quantum leap from Maxim's workshop to a technological future which we call the present. The heritage of nearly a century of pacification, meanwhile, rapidly mythologized as the drama of the frontier, became the one mainstream of American culture which was wholly aboriginal and not a *sui generis* continuation of a European tradition. While Emerson and Emily Dickinson are but reluctant descendants of Coleridge and Blake, this mainstream originated at Yale – albeit in the mind of a failed imitator of the English novel of manners. It was on the wave of sentiment following the establishment of the Bureau of Indian Affairs that James Fenimore Cooper rose to fame as the 'First American Novelist', with tales of the frontier which could now be safely romanticized. To recall how dramatizing the power of the vanquished enhances the value of his scalp in the eyes of the victor, one need only think of Proust's cook, crying 'You filthy brute!' every time she wrung the neck of a chicken.

Cooper came to Yale as an undergraduate at the beginning of the last century from Cooperstown, New York, which his father had founded. Although he never got his degree, his later popularity endeared him to future generations of graduates, who could proudly preface the famous novelist's name with the honorific 'Yale's own'. It was for this reason that Mark Twain prefaced his famous savaging of Cooper with an encomium from a Professor of English Literature at Yale. 'Cooper's art has some defects,' Twain murmured in disagreement. 'In one place in *Deerslayer*, and in the restricted space of two-thirds of a page, Cooper has scored 114 offenses against literary art out of a possible 115.' What most offended the outsider in the writings of Yale's favourite son, called by Wilkie Collins 'the greatest artist in the domain of romantic fiction yet produced by America', I would describe in modern parlance as surrealism. 'He saw nearly all things as through a glass eye, darkly,' Twain explained. Indeed, what I would describe, by analogy with 'socialist realism', as 'capitalist surrealism' may be said to have originated in Cooper's tales of the American frontier. Much of Twain's essay is taken up by the outsider's intrusion into this surrealist world, where anything is not only possible but likely, as in the account of a shooting match during which Cooper's 'Deerslayer-Hawkeye-Long-Rifle-Leather-Stocking-Path-finder-Bumppo' sees the chipped paint on a nail head a hundred yards away and, with a mysterious cry of 'Be ready to clench!', drives it into the wood of the target with his bullet:

> The recorded feat is certainly surprising, just as it stands; but it is not surprising enough for Cooper. Cooper adds a touch. He has made Pathfinder do this miracle with another man's rifle, and not only that, but Pathfinder did not have even the advantage of loading it himself. He had everything against him, and yet he made that impossible shot, and not only made it, but did it with absolute confidence, saying 'Be ready to clench.' Now a person like that would have undertaken the same feat with a brickbat, and with Cooper to help he would have achieved it, too.

The outsider is a sceptic, a realist awakened in a surreal world. What would Twain have made of James Bond? Of the 'magic bullet theory' proffered by the United States Commission to Report upon the Assassination of President John F. Kennedy, with James Fenimore Cooper's descendant, Yale's own John Sherman Cooper, among its seven distinguished members? Prophetically, Cooper's earliest patriotic tale was called 'The Spy'. By the time Harold Philby, spying for the Russians and against the British in Britain, would assume the name of Kipling's child hero, Kim – spying for the British and against the Russians in India – he would be unconsciously romanticizing the power of a vanquished West in exactly the same way Cooper romanticized Red Indians. Thus, a whole century before Philby's Cambridge of the 1930s, long before the boulevard surrealism of Arthur Conan Doyle and Ian Fleming found its consummate expression in the medium of film, Cooper had invented The Game. Its rules were simple. General Crook's opponents were not equipotent adversaries, as the Russian and the British colonial powers vying for India were to Kipling's Kim, but defenceless victims, mythologized by the mainstream of American culture to avoid the appearance of what the twentieth century would call a holocaust. Similarly, in our own day, although Kim Philby was real and James Bond a fiction, in the same mainstream of American culture they figure as equipotent adversaries. This is the ethos that Walter Camp objectified when he fathered American football, with its dramatized simulation of a contest, a combat, between two adversarial and equipotent forces. All that the simple rules required was that society's control over these forces be unchallenged and absolute, as in a dream. No outsiders, please, to disturb the microcosm. No reality lurking beyond the visible horizon, to sneak up on Deerslayer-Yale-Quarterback-James-Bond-George-Crook-Sherlock-Holmes-Earl-Warren-Bumppo and pulp the surrealist's cranium with a tomahawk quicker than you can say Geronimo. And when the sons of Eli break through that line, let their victory mean no more than their defeat. Because when Nero's gladiators fight, the gladiators they fight against must also be Nero's.

4

Gregor Samsa, a North American cockroach, woke up one morning to find himself transformed. Once an ordinary, brown *Blattella germanica*, suborder Blattaria, order Orthoptera, class Insecta, tribe Arthropoda, kingdom Animalia, he was now a dashing bachelor, rich and famous, with a red Ferrari and as many women as the beaches of southern

California could provide. Alternatively, he was a journalist, committed to printing the truth without fear or favour. Or a private eye on the prowl, a New York cop on the beat, a cowboy fighting Indians, a team captain calling the plays, an intelligence agent outwitting the secret police in Moscow, a Jew hunting former Nazis, a nuclear scientist secretly working for peace, and all of them, with that characteristically hysterical insistence I knew so well from childhood, drove the spectator on to the inevitable conclusion that all is for the best in this best of all possible worlds:

> 'Cuz we got the chicken and we got the oven,
> And everybody is a Be-e-e-t-hoven!

Here in America, our broad native land occupying one-fiftieth of the globe's surface that is not water, every cockroach is free to become a handsome bachelor in a red Ferrari or a prize-winning journalist, to say nothing of a nuclear scientist or a composer of genius. Whenever I watched American television, or went to the movies, I found myself shaking with Kolya's reactionary cackle, with the difference that here the object of Kolya's fury was no longer a marginal evening pastime for old men and children, but the bricks and mortar of civilization's broadest church. Seeing *Nicholas and Alexandra* in Rome was surreal enough. Seeing *Hamlet* at Yale, with Laurence Olivier in the title role, only to realize that the most sacred totem of my childhood was a fragment of the film's soundtrack, was unbearable, from the moment words appeared on the screen to the effect that this was the story of a man who could not make up his mind. But even these rude artifacts were not of the mainstream that was Hollywood, which at length I learnt to recognize by its inanely Kafkaesque twists. With the same collapsible hat of history turned inside out to reveal a happy ending, with the same rabbit of Hegelian dialectic to provide for any unforeseen exigencies of plot and action, Hollywood surrealism lent Cooper's invention, The Game, the kind of universal significance initially bestowed by Moscow upon Marx's game of class struggle. Admittedly the credit for inventing the game of progress in which the good guys cannot lose could just as easily go to Kolobok or the Gingerbread Man as to Leibniz or Cooper. But unlike its early exponents, who suffered the iniquity of being bitten by such wily foxes as Voltaire and Twain, optimism in its modern Hollywood incarnation as capitalist surrealism was impervious to ridicule because it already contained all the features of parody, as the slogans parodied by Orwell were no more absurd than the real thing plastered all over Moscow. The slogans withstood ridicule because what made them real was the reality of totalitarian power, the same power which endured ridicule from the learned bore, whom Orwell for a time admired or pitied, and then cracked his head open as easily as one breaks the eggs without which, as the unfortunate egghead himself had sagely remarked, one cannot make an omelette. Here, too, at least for a freethinking outsider, it was a case of power to be resisted rather than of mediocrity to be decried. A culture introduced for the purposes of inoculation and a culture causing disease may only differ in that the human body resists one and succumbs to the other. Here the social organism was striving with every cell, with all the power of modern civilization, to accept and develop the progressive toxin of Hollywood optimism rather than to limit or localize its growth. The result was a cultural mainstream that, although originally a rivulet with a source in the frontier mythopoesis of the most outstanding mediocrity in American literature, could now sweep all opposition in its path, washing over the newspapers and the organs of government, universities and town halls, domestic and foreign policy, academic scholarship and trade publishing, economics and business. At this juncture, my mother telephoned me at Yale. She was in tears. Mr Rose's block of flats, like all of New York from the mansions of Fifth Avenue and Mr Rose's own duplex on Park to the slums of South Bronx, was infested with cockroaches. Without red Ferraris, without California blondes, these were ordinary cockroaches, brown, fast and numerous. 'Your father keeps joking,' Mother wailed, 'that the cockroach has been immortalized by Kafka and is in the twentieth century what the nightingale was to the nineteenth. But I haven't seen anything like it since the lice in that hospital, where you and I almost died.' The combined civic powers of the great metropolis, apparently, liberals and conservatives, intellectuals and men of action, politicians and businessmen, optimists and pessimists, could do nothing to stem the tide of reality irrupting from the gloom of the Carboniferous Period, not even Mr Rose himself, as it had been decided long ago, by an unspoken consensus, to pretend that the cockroaches did not exist. The rich had maids to sustain the consensus, the poor had themselves to sustain. That winter, Mr Rose presented us with a book dedicated to him and Mrs Rose, George Steiner's *In Bluebeard's Castle: Some Notes Towards the Re-*

Definition of Culture, based on a series of T. S. Eliot Lectures at Canterbury and published by Eliot's old firm, Faber. Here is the passage that caught my eye:

> The urban inferno, with its hordes of faceless inhabitants, haunts the nineteenth-century imagination. Sometimes the metropolis is a jungle, the crazed tropical growth of *Hard Times* and Brecht's *Im Dickicht der Stadt*. A man must make his mark on its indifferent immensity, or he will be cast off like rags, the dawn flotsam which obsessed Baudelaire. In his invention of Rastignac, looking down on Paris, challenging the city to mortal combat, Balzac dramatized one of the focal points of the modern crisis.

That challenge to mortal combat, Mr Rose's pen-friend ought to have reflected, is the very reason why the nineteenth century was what it was, the century which, in a self-flattering mood, we like to believe we are still living in. The focal point of the modern crisis is a metropolis where no man can so much as challenge the cockroaches, not to mention leave a mark on their indifferent immensity. The focal point is modern civilization's collective reluctance to allow any debate that might confirm the existence of these nightingales at least to the extent the existence of unfaithful wives in France in the 1860s, or of concentration camps in Germany in the 1930s, could be debated by a Russian or an Englishman. The focal point is that, while playing freethinker to his patron, Professor Steiner was never free to dispense the kind of frank advice on household matters which Voltaire, protected by an aristocratic milieu, might have proffered to the good Mr Rose: 'Use boric acid.' By contrast, I was free to give this advice to Mother, and a day later the cockroaches were gone, our flat on the twenty-first floor of Mr Rose's block alone in New York to have progressed beyond the Carboniferous Period. My dear fellow, I might have pressed myself to concede even then, what was it you said about the aesthetics of freedom? Cockroaches! Think of it. What could be more real, more conspicuous? Reality is staring you in the face, it is scampering across the dinner table. Do you still turn on the television, intrigued by Gregor Samsa's newest trick? Do you still gaze admiringly at the women who stroll down Madison Avenue, and believe that the eternal return of these fashions is life itself, life with its changing seasons, its cycles of decomposition and metamorphosis, its mysteriously veined leaves and invisible roots? There is no life here, there is only demilitarization, that is to say, progressive inundation of reality by unreflecting optimism. No, life *is* here, I would have persisted as I persist today, and my sole concern is its fragility. By the oath of my tranquil childhood enclave I am bound to John Stuart Mill. A doctor marvels at the human body and fights to ensure its survival whether or not his patient is a literary mediocrity or even an indicted gangster. He is bound by the oath of Hippocrates. Neither optimism nor pessimism has a place in his scientific culture, which, like all genuine culture, is born of debate with outsiders like Vesalius, the sceptic from the free commune of Padua who overturned the myths that had gone undebated since Galen, the physician to the gladiators of imperial Rome. The optimist in me, and the immigrant is by definition an optimist, has already been squashed by the threat posed by optimism to the survival of civilization. The pessimist is squashed just as easily with a sample of pessimism:

> Show me first an America which has successfully coped with the problem of crime, drugs, deteriorating educational standards, urban decay, pornography, and decadence of one sort or another; show me an America that has pulled itself together and is what it ought to be, then I will tell you how we are going to defend ourselves from the Russians. But as things are, I can see very little merit in organising ourselves to defend from the Russians the porno-shops in central Washington. In fact, the Russians are much better in holding pornography at bay than we are.

Thus George Kennan, a Galen to the gladiators of the American foreign-policy establishment, Washington's most famous witch doctor. He is not bound by any oath to uphold the principles of any science. He does not want to debate, only to tell of his undying belief that *'mens sana in corpore sano'*. To him, 'pornography' is America, as surely as the technological successes of the nation of Ivans are 'crap' to the New York editor. The truth is that the optimist does not want to fight because all is well in his garden, and always will be in this best of all possible worlds, while the pessimist does not want to fight because everything is for the best elsewhere, while in his garden everything is going to seed anyway. They march side by side. They are the rank and file of peace. A few years before I was nearly stillborn among the lice, when the pseudotsargod was ordering a public hanging in Red Square to convince the West that he too had the bomb, Dr Kennan,

113

United States Ambassador to my broad native land, had this vision, so pacific that to this day I cannot decide whether the Arcady he describes is an optimist's or a pessimist's:

> Everything takes place in a genial intimacy and informality; hammers ring; roosters crow, goats tug at their tethers, barefoot women hoe vigorously at the potato patches, small boys play excitedly in the little streams and ponds, family parties sit at crude wooden tables in the gardens under the young fruit trees. The great good earth of Mother Russia, long ignored in favour of childish industrial fetishes of the earlier Communist period, seems once more to exude her benevolent and maternal warmth over man and beast.

A sign in a road near my house in Chelsea commands soldiers from a nearby barracks to break step when crossing the Albert Bridge. When I first saw it I thought it a hopeful sign. Perhaps it ought to go on to say, I reflected, that a civilization worthy of survival must guard all its civilian structures against soldier-like uniformity. Because soldier-like uniformity, not porno-shop decadence, is the demilitarization by which civilizations fall. That winter, in New York, my father's book was finally brought out by a descendant of Harper and Brothers – Mark Twain's publishers, which I also thought was a hopeful sign.

5

One may feel that what emerges as my central juxtaposition, of 'civilization' and 'militarization', is merely fanciful, that it is a conceit, a play on words, a rhetorical affectation. Still more wearying is the imaginable suspicion that by cleaving the universe in two with a single stroke of the pen, I wish to get at what has been mocked in science as a 'theory of everything', donning the imperious monism that looks dapper on theologians and metaphysicians yet tawdry and homespun when worn by a political savant like Marx or Klemm, not to mention an impressionistic storyteller without a field of study to call his own and only the freethinker's cap for epistemological cover. The forgotten Gustav Klemm, Marx's contemporary, held in his influential and voluminous *Allgemeine Kultur-Geschichte der Menschheit* that 'humanity in its entirety is, like man, one being which is divided into two parts', namely, 'the active and the passive part, the male and the female', with the incontrovertible conclusion that the Russians and other Slavic scum, what with their 'ample cheek-bones, their eyes which are small and slanting, their thick flat noses and their dark or livid complexion', belong to the passive and female part. As for the Latins, whom Klemm begrudgingly considered active and male, the Germans 'had always vanquished them, thus demonstrating their moral and intellectual superiority'. Today one may laugh, though I should say rather prematurely. One need look no further than Marx, or Freud, or any number of presences still as eminent as they are familiar, to realize that the spirit of that laughable age, with its tirelessly categorizing pseudoscience of everything under the sun, abides with us still. And so it comes to pass that there are in this world many perfectly practical people who, without counting themselves adepts of Marx, believe in the political reality of class and see in class struggle a fundamental social conflict, despite the plain fact that the trucker next door is pulling a hundred grand a year, which the banker down the street can barely match and the tenured university professor upstairs only curse and envy. There are, similarly, many who would see a fundamental organizing principle of the human psyche, with all the social and political implications gleaned by Marx from the dynamics of class warfare or by Klemm from the theory of racial determinants, in the sexual impulse, without considering themselves Freudians or giving a moment's thought to the plain fact that the impulse in question, at least as they and the Viennese charlatan have known it, is as unknown to at least nine-tenths of the earth's population as potted plants, lace doilies and cane-back settees. Still others, only slightly less monistic in outlook, would insist that the fundamental, all-clarifying distinction is between what they call 'communism' or, less confidently, 'socialism' on the one hand, and 'freedom' or, less confidently, 'democracy' on the other, and by the latter essence, Aryan or angelic in contrast to the dark, Asiatic one, they usually mean the free market where, *mirabile dictu*, individual liberty is engendered and resides. Here, too, they are unruffled by the plain fact that Adam Smith and even the wise author of *Reflections on the Revolution in France*, in the context of our totalitarian era, are mere relics, because even in a prosperous, tranquil Western democracy like Japan a lone grocer is as powerless against supermarket chains, and a lone freethinker against the mass media, as a citizen of Paris ever was against the

115

raging iniquity of Robespierre's terror. Individual liberty does not grow on trees even in paradise, and to believe that it is immaculately conceived by democracy is to parrot Pope on Newton:

> Hell and Hell's laws lay hid in night,
> We said *Let Jefferson be* and all was light.

In contrast to these and other mass ratiocinations of the last two centuries, the antithesis of civilization which I apostrophize here, 'militarization', is a universal and palpable reality that belongs to our totalitarian era as firmly as Jefferson's democracy, Smith's free market, or Burke's tradition belong to the time when civilization was Europe and Europe was Christendom. The conceptual opacity of my chosen term – 'militarization' – is the result of its contamination by associations from those olden times, by images of spiked Prussian helmets and memories of soldiers goose-stepping out of a more recent past, when totalitarianism still emulated the imperial grandeur of a Europe long lost. The Western imagination is to blame for these anachronisms, since at the close of the twentieth century every totalitarian demiurge of the twenty-first already knows that people who step like geese will end up like geese. Militarization is organic and flexible, because totalitarianism imbues it with a culture all its own, one which flawlessly mimics the lost European culture of aristocratic individualism and may even continue it, at least as much as modern civilization does in practice. In other words, there is more to totalitarianism than militarization in its routine sense of focused technological progress and centralized social control, as there ought to be more to civilization than demilitarization. Yet the modern denizen of any Western democracy, reared on the Eskimos of his *Larousse* and the Russians of his *Britannica*, is unhappy unless he finds, under the notional entry headed 'Civilization', the antonym 'Barbarism'. Insensible to the truth that was once so plain for Orwell, he would be even more unhappy to find, in the text of the entry, any reference to the rude contradiction of which 'the aeroplane, which was looked forward to as a civilizing influence but in practice has hardly been used except for dropping bombs, is the symbol'. Despite his unhappiness the contradiction endures, tormenting enough for George Steiner to observe, in the book dedicated to the *Britannica* man, Mr Rose, that although civilized men like himself used to believe that 'where culture flourished, barbarism was, by definition, a nightmare from the past', this is no longer true. In fact, the libraries, museums, theatres, universities, research centres, in and through which the transmission of the humanities and of the sciences mainly takes place, can prosper next to the concentration camps. The discriminations and freshness of their enterprise may well suffer under the surrounding impress of violence and regimentation. But they suffer surprisingly little.

So much, then, for barbarism as the alleged antonym of civilization in the common domain of the humanities and the sciences. Steiner sounds equally sad, almost funereal, when he realizes, as he must,

> that obvious qualities of literate response, of aesthetic feeling, can coexist with barbaric, politically sadistic behaviour in the same individual. Men such as Hans Frank who administered the 'final solution' in eastern Europe were avid connoisseurs and, in some instances, performers of Bach and Mozart. We know of personnel in the bureaucracy of the torturers and of the ovens who cultivated a knowledge of Goethe, a love of Rilke. The facile evasion 'such men did not understand the poems they read or the music they knew and seemed to play so well' will not do. There is simply no evidence that they were more obtuse than anyone else to the humane genius, to the enacted moral energies of great literature and art.

Barbarism, in short, is civilization's favourite bugaboo and straw-man. How untraceable, by contrast, are totalitarianism's ways, how elusive its theoretical limitations! So vast is the unrealized potential of militarization that even Orwell, endowed as he was with an imagination more powerful than any of his contemporaries, East or West, failed to assess it realistically. In January 1941, in an *Evening Standard* article on the future of the Home Guard after the war, he limited this potential as follows, in words capitalized to solemn effect:

> The totalitarian states can do great things, but there is one thing they cannot do: they cannot give the factory-worker a rifle and tell him to take it home and keep it in his bedroom. THAT RIFLE HANGING ON THE WALL OF THE WORKING-CLASS FLAT OR LABOURER'S COTTAGE IS THE SYMBOL OF DEMOCRACY. IT IS OUR JOB TO SEE THAT IT STAYS THERE.

I am in sympathy with the spirit of Orwell's anxious insight, of course, and the progressive demilitarizing of civilization of which I write here is an extended gloss on his wartime anxiety. But fifty years later, in peacetime, it should be clear that it is not the 'totalitarian states' that deny their citizens the right to bear arms. Totalitarianism, on the other hand, may soon be in a perfect position to arm all human insects on earth with pikes, knives, chains, clubs, swords, shotguns or even rifles, because even its modest routine of focused technological progress and centralized social control, to say nothing of its yet unrealized potential, is sophisticated enough to reduce the rifle to what Orwell could not imagine it might one day become, an *empty* symbol of democracy.

6

A further paradox is that the totalitarian end, to which militarization is the enduring means, is peace on earth, as peace was once the enduring aim of every monarch seeking to impose his absolute dominion upon the rival principalities of his domain. In this narrow sense, militarization is not unlike the historical tendency to absolutism, while totalitarianism's intended victim, civilization, exhibits the textbook characteristics of feudalism. But here again the reader must beware the sort of literal-mindedness that brings spiked helmets out of the mothballs and on to the parade ground. London houses are often fenced with ornate iron railings, which are quite useless against trespassers yet functional as symbols of property and the rule of law. Like other European countries with the notable exception of Switzerland, Britain may not allow its citizens the right to bear arms, yet some of its citizens possess ancestral escutcheons which affirm that right and are legally meaningful as symbols of an undisarmed liberty. To ignore these realities, or to presume that feudalism is all about knights in shining armour smashing into each other, shaving basins agleam, with the crash of dropped cutlery, is Quixotic in reverse. In the narrow sense just mentioned, as a historical tendency to resist pacification, modern feudalism has long proven itself as an obstacle to totalitarianism. Accordingly, totalitarian culture has always striven to mimic its salient features, along with all other forms of individual, regional and national opposition. One need look no further than the proliferation of emblems and flags, epaulettes and sashes, ornate seals and parchment scrolls, charters of alliance and declarations of independence, native alphabets and local costumes which adorned and complicated the routine of centralized control from Kamchatka to Berlin even when totalitarianism was in a position of relative weakness. In civilization, by contrast, whether in the name of popular democracy, or of civic progress, or of the social equality ridiculed by Dostoevsky after that summer in Paris more than a century ago, demilitarization works to dismantle the existing feudal structures even before totalitarian militarization can get near enough to supplant them with tactical facsimiles of its own. There are times, of course, especially in its infancy, when totalitarianism lapses, implodes, and must rely on informers and missiles, on militarization's most primitive tools – just as in practice civilization's culture, shrivelled by progressive pacification from within, may leave no room for anything but demilitarization, that is, silk stockings and wondrous hats, football and dreams of a lasting imperium. Here is the crux of the matter, and the reason my central juxtaposition is so fundamentally convincing. Taken at their most mediocre, with totalitarianism reduced to militarization at its most primitive and with civilization utterly demilitarized – that is to say, with one antagonist deprived of strengths that it must laboriously cultivate and the other deprived of strengths that are its birthright – the outcome is a foregone conclusion. Why that is so can be illustrated as follows. Civilization had produced Fischer, militarization had produced Spassky, and the two chess champions battled it out at Reykjavik when I first arrived in New York. Such battles, it was clear to me even at sixteen, are not what shapes world history, for if they were, all would be well and Voltaire would be remembered as a knee-jerk reactionary. I would be free to write poetry, or grow hair like Beethoven. But the fact was that in addition to Spassky, whom Fischer easily vanquished in open combat, militarization could field a hundred thousand mediocrities only slightly less mentally agile, while in civilization after genius came a yawning abyss of total ignorance. Thus if the combat between civilization and militarization were taking place 'in an ideal world', as plumbers baffled by stopped-up drains like to say to bewildered home-owners, with an Einstein turning up on the side of peace every time the enemy captures a Berlin, civilization would invariably win, Dr Hindsight would still be right as always, and Kolobok would now be spotted by astronomers rolling

across the face of Saturn with visible glee. Unfortunately world history
unfolds in this, the real world. Taken at the flood, the continuum of
antagonism, limited only by one side's will to pacify the other and by
the will of the other to resist pacification, is a continuum of mediocrity,
where minds a hundred times less agile than Spassky's contend with
minds a hundred times less agile than Fischer's in every field. And the
conclusion is that unless civilization follows Mill's command to
'reassert our mental freedom', curbing its progressive pacificators as
decisively as it once curbed its absolutist monarchs, and forces the
battle onto a battlefield where its genius is given free rein, totalitarian
militarization will be the stronger adversary now and ever and to the
end of time. That battlefield is, of course, culture, with the attendant
paradox that as it demilitarizes, civilization makes the terrain increasingly uncomfortable for the individual to fight on against the beliefs of
the mediocre multitude, while totalitarianism, even of the routine kind
that lay beyond our fence in Vnukovo, uses its power to establish and
foster enclaves where individuals like Pasternak and Landau are
protected against the multitude, as well as against the public religion
organized for the multitude's benefit. The only conceivable alternative
to the prospect of such a reformation, which, should it ever occur,
may be called neo-feudal, has been depicted by Mill in merciless
detail:

> As the various social eminences which enabled persons entrenched
> on them to disregard the opinion of the multitude, gradually become
> levelled; as the very idea of resisting the will of the public, when it is
> positively known that they have a will, disappears more and more
> from the minds of practical politicians; there ceases to be any social
> support for nonconformity – any substantive power in society,
> which, itself opposed to the ascendancy of numbers, is interested in
> taking under its protection opinions and tendencies at variance with
> those of the public.

Where this would leave the individual freethinker, and a thinker like
Einstein is no different from a thinker like Fischer at least in the sense
that neither is democratically elected to represent science or sport, is
equally clear:

> The combination of all these causes forms so great a mass of
> influences hostile to individuality, that it is not easy to see how it can

stand its ground. It will do so with increasing difficulty, unless the intelligent part of the public can be made to feel its value – to see that it is good there should be differences, even though not for the better, even though, as it may appear to them, some should be for the worse. If the claims of individuality are ever to be asserted, the time is now, while much is still wanting to complete the enforced assimilation. It is only in the earlier stages that any stand can be successfully made against the encroachment.

When my father and I disembarked in New York, how were we to know if the time of which Mill wrote had already passed? How was I, surrounded by the Gothic pseudorealia of the American university, to know this? A copy of my father's book finally reached me in New Haven and notices of it began to appear in the press. I had every reason for optimism. Yet this is how Mill's thought concludes:

> The demand that all other people shall resemble ourselves, grows by what it feeds on. If resistance waits till life is reduced *nearly* to one uniform type, all deviations from that type will come to be considered impious, immoral, even monstrous and contrary to nature. Mankind speedily become unable to conceive diversity, when they have been for some time unaccustomed to see it.

7

Unaware of its murky past and still murkier future, yet perceiving that the collegiate ethos I loathed instinctively was present in the classroom as much as on the playing field, I stayed away. The professor was Walter Camp. He was Nero. The spectacle of Jeff the Thracian, with his dagger and round shield, slaying the pimply Retiarius from New Jersey, naked, with only a net and a trident for weapons, or else running circles round the heavily armed Samnite brunette, was a far cry from the free and open contest I had come to the West to fight in. I stayed away, and a pleasant routine soon developed. I slept until lunchtime, then loafed about the library, sifting through its Russian collection until dinner. I had a scholarship, which meant that unless I flunked more than one course a term, my room and board for the next four years were secure. To avoid failing by accident, or through the kind of misunderstanding I had had with Professor Rockmore over Hegel's peculiar view of slavery, I adopted two strict rules that would serve me to the end of my student career. I never turned up at more than three classes in any one course, usually including the first lecture and the lecture before the midterm examination, and I was never late with an essay. In any one course, anywhere between one and eight 'papers' might be required, totalling some fifty typewritten pages of verbiage. At first I found it difficult to platitudinize. Then I realized that mainstream American culture saw platitudes, and intellectual banality generally, in educational terms, in keeping with its definition of the 'philistine' as one who rejects culture or is unable to scale its heights. To the educated Russian ear a Muscovite equivalent of 'Cor, I could murder a lager!' or 'Hey Jackson, wass goin' down?' is not a banality, while any didactic exposition of the essential banality of uncouth phrases, or even of the essential banality of didactic expositions possibly including the sentence I have now written, is. This is why Oswald Spengler, were he to write *The Decline of the West* in Russian, would read like Mark Twain, and why Nabokov's attempt to define *'poshlust'* for his Western audience is a hilarious flop by the standards of his native milieu. It is also the reason why Russia has not produced a single systemic philosopher on the German model. In the sacred mainstream priested over by the faculty of Yale, I soon learnt, even Mark Twain would write the German of Spengler. Small wonder that the professor's pets gleefully joined forces to suppress the young Republican from New Jersey. His platitudes, which he recited slowly and solemnly, like a blind man reading something set in Braille, were out of bounds. They were the artlessly commonsense platitudes of the everyday and the everyman. Theirs, by contrast, aspired to rival the professor's own in fragmented obscurity. They were the small-print platitudes of the initiated. Provided the professor did not have the opportunity to observe me in class and to provoke me into joining the discussion, all that was needed for a paper of mine to get a passing mark was to feign a mastery of that small print. Jocks, in a position not unlike my own in that they too needed passing marks to keep from flunking out, called this highly formalized ritual 'BS', which of course it was. A quote from Spengler in an essay on Mark Twain meant you passed, a quote from Mark Twain in an essay on Spengler meant you failed, it was as simple as that. Their problem was that they had not heard of Spengler, unless he was a tackle for the Chicago Bears. Mine was avoiding the professors. Besides, those who did not cut the lectures and kept up with the reading had no time to write the papers, often falling behind. Since classroom attendance was not strictly required, and I would rather spend a whole term reading the unabridged *Biographia Literaria* than four days reading the complete works of Coleridge as the television-quiz pace of the introductory courses often required, the trick of the thing was to find out the essay topics as soon as these were assigned, and then drop the finished paper into the communal pile before the lecture on the day it was due. This technique had the added advantage of keeping my young brain entirely unpolluted by the critical writings produced, under the university's 'publish or perish' policy requiring a professor seeking tenure to garner the recognition of his peers, by the professor and his peers. But more of that later. In the evenings, after dinner, bottles of Guinness stacked under my bed, the prospect of four whole years of unencumbered loafing about seemed especially sweet. How disarming, I thought. The aesthetics of freedom! Their sport, a rigged contest and a travesty of the adversarial principle of human existence, may be childish, but nobody makes me participate. Their industrial-scale effort to mass-produce academic platitudes, a school for learned bores run by humourless pedants, may be foolish, but nobody makes me attend. So here I am, cool as a cucumber, smoking Virginia tobacco in a bunk bed with a reasonably soft mattress, drinking Irish stout fit for the Politburo and looking out on a college quad in the Gothic style, not the real thing of course, but on the other hand nobody makes me admire it and what is the difference anyway? Paradise perfected. Vnukovo on the Quinnipiac. One wintry night, as if to round out the illusion, some guests even turned up at my door.

8

At the door stood two upperclassmen, a sophomore and a junior, who explained that they were out recruiting. It was the established practice of the various undergraduate organizations, unless like some publications and clubs they used posters or leaflets to avail themselves of the next generation of hacks, to canvass the freshman populace swarming the cavernous dorms of the Old Campus and meet prospective recruits face to face. By the time the freshmen became upperclassmen, it was assumed, and swapped the Old Campus nooks for proper college rooms or disappeared to private lodgings in town, it would be too late to mould their impressionable minds into the servile shape suited to the tasks ahead. I had already got rid of a few uncongenial embassies with vague promises of participation or attendance, but Rick and Gene arrived with the air of invited guests, obviously expecting entertainment where others had expected mere results. They had heard of me, they said, through somebody who had met me at dinner, somebody whom, apparently, I had managed to buttonhole for a few minutes longer than usual. Their organization was called the Party of the Right, and it was one of the parties within the Yale Political Union, along with the Liberals, the Progressives, the Independents and the Conservatives. Richard Brookhiser was tall, eloquent, showy, effortlessly successful in his studies, from a small town in upstate New York, a contributor to William Buckley's *National Review* since boyhood. He was the very model of 'the thinking conservative', as he described himself, his origins, as unfashionable at Yale as those of any pimply young Republican from the boondocks, elegantly draped in the best manners imaginable. He was wearing a bow-tie, and had an ebony walking stick in hand. 'We do not care what you think,' he unveiled with an engaging smile the slogan by which his party distinguished itself from the narrowly political parties within the Union, 'so long as you do think.' Eugene was the son of Frank Meyer, one of the founders of *National Review*. Thin, quirky and introspective, he was the more intriguing of the two, the only American I ever met, before or since, who entered university without having been to school. Ensconced in their house in the country, a few hours from New York, his late father allowed him and his elder brother to educate themselves by reading and thinking. Gene and I stayed up talking until morning, whereupon I solemnly promised to turn up at the next 'toasting session' at Mory's, where these symposia, I was told, were held in weeks when there was no scheduled debate. The following Thursday evening, the doors of a private room at Mory's, part faculty clubhouse, part undergraduate watering hole, opened to reveal a long table packed with three dozen steaming faces, an ornate silver cup making its rounds. Passed to the right, of course, it held a mixture of champagne and *crème de menthe* until drained by the reveller, obliged to pay for the next one if even a droplet of green showed on the starched

napkin beneath when the overturned cup was brought down. The
session began with the chairman, a gold medal with the image of
Charles I on his neck, rising to give the chairman's toast, reputedly
the last words spoken by the King in the episode which the school
textbooks of my childhood friends called the English Bourgeois
Revolution. Everyone stood. 'To the people,' intoned the chairman.

> Truly I desire their liberty and freedom as much as anybody
> whomsoever; but I must tell you their liberty and freedom consists
> in having of government, those laws by which their life and their
> goods may be most their own. It is not for having a share in
> government, Sir, that is nothing pertaining to them. A subject and a
> sovereign are clear different things . . . Sirs, it was for this that now
> I am come here. If I would have given way to an arbitrary way, for
> to have all laws changed according to the power of the sword, I
> needed not to have come here; and therefore I tell you and I pray
> God it be not laid to your charge, that I am the Martyr of the people.

I was stunned. The cup passed from the chairman to the secretary, a
girl in white who rose to say: 'Ladies and gentlemen, the Kings and
Queens of England. Egbert . . .' Out flew the Æthelreds, the Edmunds
and the Canutes. She went on: 'William, William, Henry, Stephen,
Henry, Richard, John, Henry, Edward, Edward, Edward . . .' Lancas-
ter and York rushed past like yellow cabs at daybreak. 'Henry, Henry,
Edward, Mary, Elizabeth, James.' She took a deep breath. 'Charles.'
About a third of the standing company tumbled into their seats, the
hardliners, I realized. The girl went on with her recital, ending with
'Elizabeth, long may she reign.' The rest crashed down, and the
drinking began. I was stunned. What could be the meaning of this?
Were they monarchists? One thing was clear. If Mr Ermine had been
at Yale, this was the sort of social function he would have arranged. I
almost felt that the party secretary in white polyester lace was an
Erminite in Shakespearean disguise, for it was inconceivable that a
Yale professor, much less a student, should know by heart the dynastic
history of Britain from Egbert onward. Copies of a mimeographed
'party songbook' had meanwhile been distributed:

> Deck the halls with commie corpses,
> Fa-la-la-la-la
> La-la-la-la!

> 'Tis the time to be remorseless,
> Fa-la-la-la-la
> La-la-la-la!
> Draw we now our sharp stiletti,
> Cut the pinks into confetti . . .

I love Christmas, said one of my neighbours with a hiccup. Pinks means communist sympathizers, soberly explained another, as in Adlai Stephenson:

> Adlai the baldheaded comsymp
> Had a very shiny head,
> And if you ever saw it,
> Saw it,
> You would have to say
> 'It's red.'

Some four hours later, well after midnight, after many more bouts of hoarse vocalizing and a few dozen toasts of equally plucky sentiment, the revellers broke up with the singing of the party anthem, to the tune of 'Deutschland, Deutschland, über alles', the last word rhyming, fortuitously, with 'chalice' and even 'solace'. I walked unsteadily the twenty yards separating Mory's from Yorkside Pizza. Another thing became clear. These people, for reasons that hardly concerned me for the present, were out to make trouble for themselves, to stir things up. It was an impulse I appreciated, and in weeks that followed I came to understand the motive. They were hungry for public attention, attention which Yale, being what it was, denied them at every turn, in the dormitory, in the classroom, in the debate chamber. They did not want to play The Game of set topics like 'Resolved, That American Presence in Vietnam is Criminal' or of class discussions where an open expression of heterodox sentiment meant academic martyrdom. They felt outnumbered a hundred to one, trapped by the choice between conforming and quitting. To the pimply young Republican from New Jersey, though by no means to him alone, they were the oxygen of a living culture, a rare tonic among his civilization's toxins. In their toasts on abstruse or taboo subjects, offensive or merely silly to anyone but a social misfit, he, in his mumbling, intuitive way, discerned what his Yale professors and classmates refused to acknowledge, that a viable culture is born of antagonism and is an iconoclasm before it is anything else. He would follow them anywhere, as his

126

adult predecessors, in a Weimar Republic homogenized by bourgeois pieties of that historical moment, had followed leaders whose only lure was the one truth they were clever enough to voice, the scandalous, suppressed, unprintable truth that The Game is rigged. That private room at Mory's was their beer hall. They had been hungry for attention as individuals and now, banded together, they were determined to get it at any social cost to themselves, despite the fact that most were children of poor parents struggling to make the middle-class ends meet, parents who had sent them to Yale in the hope that here they would succeed, get ahead, make influential friends, land important jobs.

> Oh, father and mother pay all the bills,
> And we have all the fun.
> That's the way we do in college life,
> Hooray!

So, at least, Yale boys sang in the good old days. Only one or two among these, however, came from alumni families or went through boarding schools on the way here. Only one or two were rich swells, or had an 'intellectual' background like Meyer's. Yet united by what they called politics, united, in fact, by their defiance of something they only dimly perceived as the social rules of The Game, all wore expensive suits with embroidered waistcoats, carried canes or Briggs umbrellas, hardly ever studied, and made flamboyant *épatement* of the bejeaned collegiate multitude their common task. What astonished was the sheer scope of their success, or failure. Thanks to a whipping system that was the envy of the Union and a knowledge of the minutiae of debating protocol that would not be out of place in Westminster, they hijacked debates, derailed amendments and detonated intrigues that flared for months on end, terrorizing Union hacks and general membership alike. They were universally despised, though as with all lepers it was never clear where revulsion gave way to fear. Whenever I mentioned to a classmate my attendance at a toasting session or a party debate, he would flinch, roll his eyes and say, 'Yeah, yeah, I know: "Resolved, That the Earth is Flat".' The better informed, usually girls, would say: 'I can't believe you've been, don't you know that song they sing, what are you, some kind of Nazi?' This last point might have struck me as curious even if I had not been called a fascist before for wearing the Nixon pin at Horace Mann. The fact is that although the Yale motto is 'Lux et Veritas', which no

doubt made the enlightenment-minded Mr Rose proud of his leadership role in alumni affairs, the Yale anthem is sung to the tune of '*Die
Wacht am Rhein*', with

> Bright college years,
> With pleasure rife . . .

where the original has '*Die Vaterland, die Vaterland . . .*' It was with this
tune, bellowed by a hundred thousand throats including Mr Rose's,
that the crowded stands exploded every football season. Yet, as no
eager beaver from the *Yale Daily News* had ever contrived to make an
issue out of this, to my ears perfectly ordinary, act of musical
brigandage during the previous fifty years, no student or alumnus I
ever spoke with had the faintest idea that Yale as a whole was no less
Nazi than the gang of miscreants in whose clutches I now found
myself. 'It was written by Haydn,' was all I could say in their defence.

9

Could I have said more? The public stirring of an intellectual
opposition, any intellectual opposition, was what I had hoped to find,
to learn from, to aid and abet. And here it was. Yet could a political
minority, within a certain narrow context, be equated with such an
opposition, especially if its views were held, outside that context, by
the majority? Nixon had, after all, defeated McGovern in a landslide
win. It all came down once more to the question of what constitutes a
platitude. Plainly, to take an example from the Hegel mishap, the
opinion that the slave enslaves the master is a coquettish platitude
among slave owners, with only mint juleps on the veranda to refresh
them after a hard day's worrying about their property's fate. In the
context of a society where slavery in the literal sense is only a memory,
it becomes a philosophical paradox deserving of academic study. But
viewed in the broader context, whether of history or, if the society in
question is unique in its rejection of the concept of human property,
of geography, it again becomes a sycophantic platitude. Similarly, the
contention that Jews, communists or masons have sold Russia down
the river may strike a man who has never read a book in his life as
original and convincing, while being spurned by the overwhelming

majority of educated people who may comprise a political minority.
Yet an educated man, finding himself, for whatever reason, in a
position of humiliating powerlessness among his fellows, may seize on
the platitude and use it as a weapon against them, lethal because all
of a sudden he, alone among them, speaks for the broad political
majority. Mill's great discovery, in his reflections on the relationship
between truth and liberty, is what I would call the calculus of context.
If every contention tends to the platitudinous, losing the essentially
antagonistic character of truth with public acceptance, then the value
of a contention can only be expressed by the freethinker as a function
of its public acceptance, with the number of column inches used to
uphold it in the national press, for instance, as the variable criterion.
Identical contentions published in a typewritten journal, disseminated
among thirty persons at considerable risk to their lives and careers,
and in a mass-circulation newspaper, published to uphold the existing
order, may have diametrically opposite meanings, one a whispered,
dangerous revelation, the other a roaring commonplace and a lie. A
logician would say that the substance of truth is 'indexical' and
inalienable from the accidents of intent, medium and circumstance, so
that the statement 'Hans Frank is a mass murderer' means one thing
when uttered by a Resistance partisan in occupied Poland and another
on the lips of our neighbour Ponomarenko, one thing when believed
in secret by a Wehrmacht officer in 1939 and another when mouthed
by a Cambridge undergraduate in 1989. If a rule of conduct for the
freethinker were to be derived from Mill's calculus, it would probably
resemble G. K. Chesterton's declaration that he liked to be in hot
water because hot water kept him clean. In practical terms, such a
rule required dissent from minority as well as majority opinions. To
my mind, the contentions implicit in the political stance of the revellers
at Mory's, including their fervent identification of 'communism' and
'socialism' with totalitarianism, had all the hallmarks of a lukewarm
platitude. Anyone with a native's eye for the culture of militarization,
a native's ear for the mercurial and syncretic public religion of
totalitarianism, could, I assumed, instantly recognize the identification as childish, primitive and false. Totalitarianism, by definition,
had total power to integrate and to absorb, an iron stomach that could
digest loyalty to monarchs, freedom of scientific enquiry and worship
of the muses, not to mention trifles like commerce or conventional
Christianity. It could almost digest individualism, provided a sufficient number of people in the world, happy to regard themselves as

129

individuals in their own gardens within the confines of a fence painted forest green, had forgotten what the word means. Yet it was equally clear that at Yale, among educated Americans, in the circumscribed context in which I then found myself and had every expectation of remaining, the lukewarm platitude had all the hallmarks of an iconoclasm. Provided I never forgot that freethinking individualism lives and dies by the larger context, I was intellectually justified in aligning myself with these theatrical heretics of liberal education. They were my propylaea. With them my America formally began.

10

I was back in New York for the summer holidays. As the train pulled into Grand Central station, I was still engrossed in the batch of cuttings Father had sent me, reviews of his book in the American press. 'The West, the West!' Its response was mixed. Oldtimers who remembered the pseudotsargod, whom Father never mentioned by name in the book for fear of platitude, came nearest in recognizing the first volume of *The Education of Lev Navrozov* for what I believed it was intended to be, literature's only description of a hell on earth written without the didactic presumption which stultified European thinking on the subject since Dante. Eugene Lyons, whose *Assignment in Utopia* gave Western intellectuals a first glimpse of their paradise on earth in the 1930s, wrote of 'startling insights that were new to me, and which I recognized at once as true and profoundly significant'. Another oldtimer, Max Geltman, wrote that it was 'the single most important work of literature to have come out of the Soviet Union in almost sixty years'. The aged Marxist philosopher Sidney Hook wrote that 'as an autobiography, despite its Gothic dimensions and bizarre components, it bids fair to take its place beside the works of Laurence Sterne and Henry Adams, whose styles it suggests, but it is far richer in scope and more gripping in content'. It was upon the antique worldview of these people, and of their younger contemporaries who came on the scene in the 1940s, that the edifice of American 'conservatism' once rested. Many were European by birth and education. Most had been socialists in their youth, as if still following Bismarck's advice to have a heart. Like Orwell, they were horrified by what happened to the learned bore's cranium because, like Vnukovo's genuinely kind, genuinely powerless Zina, they found many things terribly unfair, and certainly if one closed one's eyes and imagined that the learned bore had not had the blood of innocent millions on his head, its forcible transformation into an omelette ordered by his former lackey was more than unfair, it was ugly and barbarous. 'Who ever knew such cruelty existed?' was the great political revelation of that epoch. By 1940, Orwell could already stand back and mourn such innocence, observing that Western intellectuals, considered as a caste, 'can swallow totalitarianism *because* they have no experience of anything but liberalism', illustrating the point with a quotation from Auden in which the poet had used the phrase 'necessary murder'. The phrase, Orwell insisted, 'could only be written by a person to whom murder is at most a *word*'. Outside the domain of Orwell's intuition, however, the revelation remained a revelation for the entire caste to which he belonged, affecting a tiny or sizeable minority, or a small majority, or at times even an absolute majority of its members, depending on the 'international situation' as it was quaintly called. When totalitarianism's fortunes seemed to revive, these early prototypes of future American 'conservatives' increased in number, when they seemed to dim, doubt would cast a pall over the revelation once more, although, needless to say, whether optimistic or pessimistic, their reactions to world events were as seldom based upon any substantive reality shaping contemporary history as those of the rest of the caste's members. It was as though some of Mr Rose's friends would argue that cockroaches in New York disappear in really hot weather, while others would maintain that they only disappear on weekends. They were the only ones willing to acknowledge that something was out there, in short, and invariably they missed the point of what it was. 'When one looks back at the twenties, nothing is queerer than the way in which every important event in Europe escaped the notice of the English intelligentsia', Orwell wrote of the general caste attitude against which these early prototypes were reacting. 'The Russian Revolution, for instance, all but vanishes from the English consciousness between the death of Lenin and the Ukraine famine – about ten years. Throughout these years Russia means Tolstoy, Dostoevsky and exiled counts driving taxi-cabs.' Yet totalitarianism, in its routinely militarized form which was the only form they knew how to recognize, would suffer only one setback in their lifetime, and that was the migration of theoretical physicists from Europe to the United States.

Everything else, from Hitler's perfidy to Mao's elopement and from Teheran to Yalta, from the renaming of central Europe 'Eastern' to the renaming of the pseudotsargod 'Uncle Joe' and from Korea to Vietnam, was merely a never-ending loop of the newsreel, a zero-sum game like thimblerig, an alchemist's fantasy of metamorphosis. By the early 1950s, when as a matter of historical reality, totalitarianism, due to the setback just mentioned, was at its weakest, playing for time and bluffing its way out of the nuclear imbalance, the 'conservatives', as they now called themselves in America, failed to call the bluff because their understanding of totalitarianism was even more rudimentary than that of their prototypes had been in their day, and just as outdated. Instead they grew more vociferous and influential than ever, uniting in the face of what they believed was a clear and present danger yet remaining as ignorant as ever of the precise nature of that danger, seeking no illumination outside themselves and their own political motives, taking advice only from the 'conservative' oldtimers whose names they had learnt in their youth. Men of new and historically relevant insight, like the Polish refugee Jozef Mackiewicz, were ignored and doomed to obscurity. Hopelessly entangled in the rhetoric of 'communism', which a whole generation earlier had become second nature to Orwell's caste and its American counterpart, the newly united 'conservatives' used all their intellectual and political energies to hunt those whom they regarded as enemy agents in their midst, or simply as dangerous pests infesting their otherwise beautiful kitchens and bathrooms, human beings who chose to cling to the selfsame ideological sympathies which had been so commonplace a generation ago but which the united 'conservative' front now saw as perverse, repulsive and evil. Totalitarianism's investment in culture was paying off, if only because, like a trained seal, civilization had been educated by it to follow the bouncing ball of ideology. As a result, instead of facing reality during the one and only moment in history when they so easily could, even those who were willing to cry cockroach did no more than their predecessors had done when the cockroaches had first arrived, posing such questions in their scholastic disputes on the subject as 'Are cockroaches godless and motherless?', 'Is there a cockroach god, and if so, is he the same for the red and the black ones?' or 'Do cockroaches sincerely believe that they shall inherit the earth?' Out of such debates grew the sole organ of 'conservative' opinion in America, *National Review*, founded by William F. Buckley, Jr., then still a recent graduate of Yale, with the encouragement of several oldtimers like Frank Meyer. It is easy to see why, twenty years later, by the time I got off the New Haven train with the sheaf of cuttings under my arm, our erstwhile summer neighbour, already compared to Pasternak by every literary critic from Stockholm to Timbuktu, had become the idol of the 'conservatives' united around the figure of Buckley. What could be more satisfying than seeing their worldview resoundingly corroborated for the first time since their unification, and sheepishly shared by those who had been ignoring them? Who ever knew such cruelty existed! No chickens and hardly an oven. No Beethovens either. A bunch of godless and motherless reds. Torture straight out of Dante. It was all just like they always said, and worse. What nobody realized, of course, was that time had passed, that their optimistic joys and pessimistic sorrows were as obsolete as ever, and as ineffectual, because by the time our erstwhile neighbour squealed on his former masters and exposed their cruelty, totalitarianism had successfully bluffed its way out of the nuclear imbalance to catch up with its once and future prey. The one and only opportunity to face reality without adverse consequences had been missed. The era of the totalitarian routine, which the earlier generation of 'conservatives' understood decades too late, was drawing to a close. The dreaded routine was now goose-stepping aside to make way for a new era in which militarization would be invisible save for the occasional nuclear test, for that long-awaited era of universal provocation and deception on a global scale. As I stepped off the train and began walking to the subway, my mind still reeling, I became aware of an old man pushing against me, drunk or ill or both. Unshaven, in a tattered overcoat. He was motioning with one hand to a plastic envelope he clutched in the other. 'Call the doctor,' he stammered, 'give you a reward.' He seemed ready to collapse. I looked. In the envelope, divided into compartments, lay a dozen gold coins of different sizes. On top was a stapled sheet of notepaper with the owner's name and telephone number, a doctor with a Fifth Avenue address. 'Call the doctor, for Christ's sake,' said the man, 'he left this on the train, there'll be a reward.' We walked over to a pay phone in the station. While the bum swayed back and forth, holding unsteadily to a railing, I dialled. A woman's voice answered: 'What? I can't hear you! Sorry, I can't hear you!' I tried once more, with the same result. The line was obviously out of order. I needed to get home. The gold coins gleamed in my hand. 'Look here,' I said brightly to the bum, now bunched up on the stone floor like a tattered parcel, 'I'll give you the reward, and get in touch with the owner later.' I gave him all the cash I had, thirty-five dollars. He vanished. The next day there was no reply at the doctor's, nor the day after that, nor the next. I grew attached to the coins, and often thought of them as the nest egg of my virtue. Many months later I went to a Washington numismatist to have them valued. They were not gold, of course, and totally worthless. I had been had. 'Got took', as my university classmates liked to say when they wanted to show they were streetwise. The whole incident in Grand Central was a complex psychological swindle from the first moment to the last. The woman on the phone was the bum's witting or unwitting accomplice, and he was neither drunk, nor ill, nor a bum, just old, unshaven and a conman. Whenever I later recalled the incident, I could not help thinking that the intellectual caste to which I belonged was even less familiar with the reality of the swindle than with the experience of murder. To just about everyone I have ever known as a journalist or met socially, 'swindle' is at most a word, as predictably as Browning is the name of a poet. To this day civilized men cannot foresee what barbarians like my father saw decades ago as the dawn of a global swindle. They were equally surprised that cockroaches refused to stay in the kitchen, where the maid was. Like their philistine ancestors, astonished to hear from a freethinker who specialized in general truths that peasant girls have feelings too, they were still unable to grasp that power, and not only time, music, hosiery or democracy, is a culture. Perhaps only a trained psychologist can see through the conman's trick, and it may be that only a specialist in entomology can explain what the cockroach is doing in the marble bathroom. One thing was certain, however. Buckley's 'conservatives' did not have a freethinker like Mill or Orwell among them.

11

Mankind speedily become unable to conceive diversity, when they have been for some time unaccustomed to see it. Months later, on another visit to the leafy neighbourhood of my father's stubborn imaginings, there was new opportunity to check how that infernal insight worked in practice. Father told me of a conversation he had

had, with a man who was not quite a literary agent, nor did he quite own a publishing house, and in general nobody knew exactly what he did, but he was somebody, our New York friends had sworn, who was a power to be reckoned with in the business. It turned out that the man left Russia, where he had had a glorious career as an army sergeant, some thirty years earlier and made money in 'book distribution', whatever that was. Father said he was puzzled to discover that the man had not read anything in Russian or English besides book titles and review quotations. 'What could I tell him about myself?' Father rhetorized. 'A ballet prima who absconds to the West is often automatically assumed, perhaps falsely, to be better than any American dancer. But while ballet is allowed and encouraged in Russia, for ever since the eighteenth century it has never been thought dangerous to any regime, a Russian underground writer or thinker can only cite as his credentials some hearsay whisperings of some equally obscure underground connoisseurs. My voice laboriously forced, as though I had already grown hoarse speaking with a half-wit at a noisy marketplace, I told the former army sergeant that *American* reviewers compared me – in alphabetical order! – to Dostoevsky, Milton, Orwell, Proust, Sterne, and Twain. "More than a hundred reviews!" I shouted like a marketplace crier as I waved the sheaf. "*New York Times?*" he asked. "No." "*New York Review of Books?*" "No." "Then forget it," he said. People like Saul Bellow or Sidney Hook are outsiders. Their attention to me is like the clandestine attention of those editors and writers who privately valued my underground manuscripts in Moscow.' Father went on to say that the army sergeant was quite right, and that none of the reviews I had read was going to make the slightest bit of difference. I had wasted my time thinking about what the various oldtimers said about the book because what they, or any 'conservatives' or 'liberals', said did not matter unless it was said in the *New York Times* or the *New York Review*. Buckley's weekly magazine, *National Review*, had some 50,000 subscribers, but this pitiable statistic was beside the point. The monthly *Commentary*, which had recently embraced 'the conservative cause' albeit after a show of Pentateuchal squeamishness, was published under the auspices of the American Jewish Committee and edited by Norman Podhoretz. Mr Rose's brother was chairman of its executive board, and it was through him that the editor had heard of Father's book and excerpted it in advance of publication. *Commentary* had *half* the *National Review* circulation, but again the statistic was simply beside the point. *Time* and *Newsweek* measured their circulation in millions, but no one had ever seen them contradict the *New York Times* or strike an attitude that would not be contiguous to the newspaper's. Only one thing mattered politically, the *New York Times*, and in a full-page review the *New York Times* snorted that while 'the so-called Soviet dissenters' in Russia are nonconformists, 'Mr Navrozov, who has recently arrived in the United States, is a nonconformist among nonconformists'. According to my father's publishers, Mark Twain was dead and this quote from Harrison Salisbury's review was not the 'quotable quote' they needed. Only one thing mattered culturally apart from the *New York Times Book Review*, the *New York Review of Books*, edited by Barbara Epstein, which was a kind of highbrow crutch for the larger, and therefore less manoeuvrable, Sunday book supplement of the one and only influential organ of opinion in America. The *New York Review's* circulation was not much larger than that of Buckley's pitiful weekly, but, in the august shade of its political and cultural ally, its influence was immeasurable. Father explained how the *New York Review* had disposed of his book 'with a series of inverse theorems: (1) Navrozov is *not* Gogol, (2) Navrozov is *not* Orwell, (3) Navrozov is *not* Pasternak. Why am I not Gogol and Orwell? Because I "failed to emulate the seriousness that underlies their work". And why am I not Pasternak? Because my writing is not such as "in Pasternak's words, can 'make the heart stop beating'". This dreary pop-song elegancy attributed to Pasternak was the reviewer's ironclad proof that I am *not* Pasternak.' Anyway, the army sergeant knew what he was talking about. The book was doomed. Father had fallen afoul of the only people who mattered, the powers that be, the élite, the establishment, the Mafia, call it what you will. The *New York Times* was Versailles, the *New York Review* one of its finest grottoes, and there the academic aristocracy of Harvard and Yale strolled, changed costumes, watched fireworks, made love or duelled as fancy took them. 'The lefties!' grumbled the downtrodden Republican multitude outside the gates. 'Nattering nabobs of negativism!' whispered their party's speechwriters, affecting the effortlessly highfalutin' *Sprachgeist* of those whom they envied as much as derided. 'The liberal establishment!' intoned the debonair Buckley. Yet not one Republican tycoon, not a single one of those numberless money-bags of American business, industry and commerce whose pictures appeared in the *New York Times* amid torrents of personal abuse presented as investigative journalism, had ever started a newspaper that would defend *his* interests, articulate *his* views or promote *his* political party. Since the late 1960s, when the *New York Tribune*, the last national organ of opinion independent of and equipotent to the *New York Times*, closed down, its once glorious name divvied up between the *New York Times* and the *Washington Post* as co-publishers of the *International Herald Tribune*, only the *Wall Street Journal* represented 'conservative' interests outside the ghetto into which Buckley had corralled his fellow dissentients. To see the *Journal* going up against the *New York Times* on a cultural issue was to see old Kolya flinging an apple core at the Picasso etching all over again. The *New York Times* published a daily *encyclopédie*, so full of weighty issues that a Sunday edition delivered by newsboy in the wilds of a suburb of Columbus, Ohio, was once reported to have killed the family dog. In Washington, where the local paper also mattered and the *Journal* was read as a matter of course, all nineteen thousand Congressional aides, whether Democrat or Republican, began the day with the *New York Times*. At Yale and Harvard, students and professors alike studied its pages with Talmudic zeal. In the provinces, far from the cultural metropolis of New York, editors of local newspapers not already owned by the *New York Times* looked to those same pages for guidance as a nervous boy on a first date looks up, blinking, at the sommelier towering over their corner table for two. In the metropolis itself, editors and researchers at the three national television networks waited for the *New York Times* to tell them what had happened in the morning so crews could be despatched and newscasts prepared for the evening. In my broad native land of old, news and opinion composed in the capital and approved by the centre were transmitted to the local press as part of what the American 'conservatives' were always quick to point out was totalitarian control of the media. In fact this was one of the more obsolescent cultural traditions of militarization, which also required the local newspapers to print the transmitted items verbatim so everybody always knew where they had come from. Everyone at our dinner table in Vnukovo understood that one day the tradition would be jettisoned as so much cultural ballast, with the consequence that the centre's official wisdom, colourfully paraphrased and inventively re-punctuated at the local level, would become more insidious and irresistible. That, of course, was exactly how the cultural monopoly of the *New York Times* controlled the rest of the American media, while the Humanities faculty of Yale and a thousand lesser institutions churned out its annual quotas of qualified paraphrasts to fill the social order placed in Times Square. But the amazing fact was that even the 'conservatives', confined to their ghetto of opposition, never seemed to understand or acknowledge that the formidable evil lay in the unchallenged supremacy of a single political and cultural trend, set daily by a privately owned corporation with monopoly powers over the educated opinion of the nation. Instead they believed that the evil lay in the trendsetters themselves, who were as congenitally 'liberal' as the Russians were motherless, the Jews scheming and the Eskimos the way *Larousse* depicted them. If only they could get back from the usurpers the power that was rightly theirs! However horrific I found the totalitarian spectre of the media monopoly, I had to surmise that were its power ever to fall into the hands of the united 'conservatives' the results would be even more chilling. This was never to happen, but here I must jump ahead. My surmise lay fallow for a few years, until the populist triumph of the Republican Party's presidential candidate, a former Hollywood actor. His was a landslide victory, which the 'conservatives' were quick to claim as their own although it was unlikely that more than one per cent of the American electorate had ever heard the names William F. Buckley, Jr. or Norman Podhoretz before casting a majority of their votes for Ronald Reagan, since even the *New York Times*, despite its total monopoly over educated opinion, has no influence over the man in the street. It was then, in 1980, that Times Books published a memoir entitled *Without Fear or Favor: An Uncompromising Look at the New York Times*. Its flyleaf was decorated with a quotation from the patriarch of the ruling dynasty, Adolph Ochs: 'To Give the News Impartially without Fear or Favour Regardless of any Party, Sect or Interest Involved'. It was written by Harrison Salisbury, the expert on Russia who had reviewed Father's book five years earlier. 'By every objective criterion', wrote Salisbury, the *New York Times* was

> the most thorough, most complete, most responsible newspaper that time, money, talent and technology in the second half of the twentieth century had been able to produce.

'The very title of the book would have delighted many a royal court', Father laughed. 'A courtier of Elizabeth I of England entitled his book *The Historie of the Most Renowned and Victorious Princesse Elizabeth* and declared that he wrote it "without prejudice or affectation, whilst writing with an undistempered and even mind". Of course it would have been much cleverer of him to entitle his eulogy *Without Prejudice or Affectation: An Even-minded Look at Elizabeth I.*' But the great revelation of the book was that, according to the author, the 'top echelon of the *Times*' had never been anything but 'true blue conservatives'. Six hundred pages of Salisbury's memoir were used to assign to his employer 'anti-communist' or 'conservative' virtues by contiguity – as mendaciously as some thirty years earlier 'communist' or 'liberal' vices had been assigned by contiguity in yard upon yard of his employer's newsprint, and as effortlessly as 'liberal' virtues and 'conservative' vices had been assigned in the intervening decades. Turner Catledge, managing editor? His classmate 'had been John Stennis, as stalwart a hawk and military proponent as was to be found in the US Senate'. Clifton Daniel, Catledge's successor? 'His political persuasions were close to those of his father-in-law', none other than the tough cold warrior President Truman. The legendary journalist 'Scotty' Reston? 'An essentially conservative man who grew more conservative as the years passed'. The rising star Max Frankel? Why, this true blue 'consciously modelled himself on Reston'. Abe Rosenthal? He 'had emerged as the most conservative editor on the paper', and even 'Rosenthal's close friend, William F. Buckley, Jr.' spoke of him 'with awe as a terrific anti-communist'. One passage of Salisbury's testimony, inviting as it did the rhetorical question, 'Who was a better anti-communist, Joe McCarthy or the *New York Times*?', was particularly instructive. Citing a letter written in the late 1940s by the newspaper's publisher, in which Arthur Sulzberger averred that in the hour of national emergency 'all of those persons' known as 'communists' – 'plus those who were even suspect' – 'would be out', Salisbury concluded that while 'McCarthy sought to sow general distrust and hatred of the press, Arthur Sulzberger was fighting to preserve the press and to protect it against contamination. He expected his editors to guard vigilantly against tainting of the news.' Moreover,

> Sulzberger's fear of the Soviet Union and of Communism was not to diminish. He argued for several years over an editorial that had been drafted – but not published – in the mid-1950s by Otto Tolischus, an extremely conservative member of the editorial board, about Russia's broken promises. The editorial was so long it would have occupied the whole *Times* editorial space, very harsh and listing every pledge which, in Tolischus' opinion, had been broken by

Stalin. As late as 1960 Arthur Sulzberger was proposing that the editorial be exhumed and published.

In short it was obvious that what Salisbury meant by the unique ability of the *New York Times* to tell the truth impartially, without fear or favour, regardless of any party, sect, or interest involved, was its unique ability to take on the coloration of whatever political or cultural forces were in the ascendant, and in so doing to maintain and augment the monopoly power over educated opinion which was itself the source of this unique ability. Yet still the 'conservatives' saw evil not in the principle of tyranny but in the personality of the tyrant, and specifically in the fact that despite the Republican populist triumph which they announced was theirs, the 'liberal' usurpers still ruled educated opinion. What cheek, those usurpers! Calling themselves 'true blue conservatives'! Yes, this was Kolya's impotent fury on a political scale. It was the blind rage of all those who are unable to comprehend the reality of power, for whether that power chooses to crack a man's head with an alpine axe or, without fear or favour, monopolizes opinion, it is the real existence of such a power and not the verbal representations of those who happen to wield it that serves to abridge individual liberty. But this clear and present danger to liberty was never something for the 'conservatives' to diagnose or to lose sleep over. They could not even see that, for decades, the *New York Times* had been the royal court of their beloved American democracy, a fact which another sycophantic courtier worth mentioning did not take care to conceal when he entitled his book, every inch as uncompromising as Salisbury's, *The Kingdom and the Power*. This is how Gay Talese described a man who was, after all, only the managing editor of a newspaper:

> His style of cool elegance, the courtly way in which he conducts corporate matters at the *New York Times*, the ease with which he occasionally rejects a bottle of vintage wine at the Oak Room of the Plaza, all suggest that he is a man bred from the very beginning into a world of privilege and power.

Was it not right that the hero of this passage, Clifton Daniel, who had shown his mettle as a 'true blue conservative' by sharing the tough opinions of his father-in-law, should in time become a duke, a marquess or at least an earl? Except that, since Talese's book was published a decade before Salisbury's, the true test of nobility in its pages was the courtiers' 'communist' rather than 'anti-communist' connections. What, then, of Harrison de Evans, Fourth Earl of Salisbury? Here he was,

> calmly at his desk against the south wall of the newsroom composing
> a letter to a Communist friend who might be able to help him obtain
> a visa for North Vietnam.

Aristocratic friendships paid off and the Earl became the only American correspondent in Hanoi, whence he reported the sensational estimates of civilian casualties in the war which happened to coincide with those of North Vietnamese propaganda. Several days later the noble Earl admitted that the information had come from North Vietnamese officials, but this is how Talese described his return home:

> Had he been riding a chariot behind three white horses, his entrance
> would not have been more conspicuous. The *Times'* editors behind
> their desks stood. They walked over to shake his hand. His stories
> had gotten a fantastic reaction around the nation and the world, and
> the criticism of his reporting, so very trivial in view of the achieve-
> ment, was now forgotten.

'Although it would take historians to evaluate the impact of Salisbury's reporting on the peace movement in America', Talese concluded with the detachment that so becomes a timeserver, 'the Salisbury stories were considered by the *Times'* editors to be worthy of a Pulitzer, and thus he was nominated.' But what of Marquis Clifton de Daniel, with whom the gentle Earl would so magnanimously share the title of 'true blue conservative' a decade later? His reporting, according to Talese, 'captured not only the political rumblings, but also the mood of the people', as witness this startling glimpse of Arcady in winter:

> This was Christmas morning in Russia, and a cruel snow-laden wind
> blowing straight out of the pages of Russian history and literature
> whipped across roofs and through the frozen streets of Moscow. At
> midnight the bells . . .

'But I suppose I have no reverence for the aristocracy', Father would say and choke with laughter as he read. Yet as far as our own future in America was concerned, this was hardly a thing to laugh about. At our own peril, we got close to identifying and analysing one of the toxins whose effects I had felt in the Madison Avenue bookshop years earlier. The *New York Times* was the royal court of American democracy, and woe betide the freethinker who would dare to speak revolution. Had *anyone* ever stood up to the *New York Times?* In *Without Fear or Favor*, Salisbury surveyed the field in this way:

> Not one critical work of magnitude or seriousness has ever been undertaken and only one book about the *New York Times* has been written in more than a quarter century, Gay Tálese's *The Kingdom and the Power*, a wonderfully readable account.

A search of the libraries, however, revealed that indeed there had been such a revolutionary. His fate left no doubt as to what our own was likely to be. Several years before we arrived in the United States, Herman Dinsmore, who had been with the *New York Times* for thirty-four years and was the editor of its international edition, which the *International Herald Tribune* superseded, dared to mark his retirement with a book whose title, *All the News That Fits*, was an irreverent pun on the newspaper's motto. Like the learned bore to whose violent end history and I keep returning, Dinsmore assumed that the past of the institution to which he formerly belonged was glorious, yet the institution had swerved from it into an ignominious present. Despite so timid a critical premise, the catalogue of the New York Public Library revealed no trace of the apostate, and we learned of the book by hearsay only because it was still within the living memory. Eventually a copy was found, and a search for the contemporary reviews began. The *New York Times* Review Index: 1896–1970, five volumes in quarto totalling more than five thousand pages, contained no mention of the traitorous egghead. Another index, registering book reviews in two hundred and twenty-five other periodicals, revealed that Dinsmore's book, published in the same year as Talese's, did get *one* review. Writing in a magazine of no influence, the one reviewer bold enough to mention the apostate by name in a three-paragraph notice of the book concluded by saying that 'you don't have to read Dinsmore at all'. Initially the reviewer

> was delighted to pick up a book with the title *All the News That Fits* by Herman Dinsmore that promised 'a critical analysis of the news

and editorial comment' of the *New York Times*. Here surely was a fitting companion to Gay Talese's *The Kingdom and the Power*.

But he was in for 'a sad disappointment'. Instead of tales of life at the royal court, complete with cavorting dukes, irresistible marquesses or at least honest, plain-speaking earls, he found a book that

> wanders about discussing the wrongheadedness of our attitudes toward Communism, the balance of power in the postwar world, the East European peoples, Castro, Lee Harvey Oswald, Korea, and Vietnam.

In addition we found *one* other, unindexed review, in a publishing trade journal affiliated with the *New York Review of Books*. In the first two sentences, out of a total of nine, the reviewer described the book as a 'conservative diatribe':

> For years the *New York Times* has calmly withstood criticism from both the Right and the Left. Certainly it will not be ruffled by Dinsmore's conservative diatribe.

Father said the majestic rhythm was unmistakable:

> For years both Right-wing and 'left-wing' criticasters have been trying again and again to 'disprove Marx'. But the great Marxist-Leninist teaching stands like a granite rock.

In the remaining seven sentences the reviewer intimated that the *New York Times* was 'liberal', which, a decade before Salisbury was authorized to confess that it had always been 'conservative', amounted to the same thing: neither Left nor Right, seeking and telling the truth without fear or favour, brilliantly, with intelligence and wit. But now that a former courtier had disgraced himself by doubting this in public, he was a traitor, an enemy, a 'conservative', and everything he had to say was lies, lies, lies. Dinsmore charged, for instance, that to initiate the self-deception of 'détente', the *New York Times* had been screening out the successes of totalitarian militarization. A decade before Salisbury's confession, this showed Dinsmore to be a lunatic cold warrior. Salisbury's confession, by contrast, was intended to show that nothing called 'détente' had ever existed, and the term itself was unmentioned in the exhaustive index to *Without Fear or Favor*. Does anything ever change at court save the names of timeservers and the semantics of adulation? It was a rhetorical question, the answer to which we forgot when leaving behind that broad native land of ours. Not before they were authorized to be repeated, word for word, by the global power of totalitarianism in the 1950s, did the insults which the learned bore cast into the whirlwind of obscurity in the 1930s become known as the truths of history worthy of a Nobel Prize. Because whatever an apostate says is lies, lies, lies, until power touches these lies of his and turns them into bright shining truths told without fear or favour, brilliantly, with intelligence and wit. Dinsmore, by our standards the meekest of bureaucratic dissenters, had vanished without a trace, pulped, pulverized. What chance had I, or my poor freethinking father, cooped up in a miserable little flat in a godforsaken corner of New York? 'The West, the West!' Here, in the metropolis that no longer knew what a freethinker was because so long accustomed to the monopoly on opinion, a reviewer actually thought that to call a writer a nonconformist among nonconformists was to bury him alive. Equally amazing was that like the improbable army sergeant in the book trade, the reviewer was right. It was a rather dispirited admirer of Mill that returned to New Haven the following autumn.

12

In the sophomore and junior years my infatuation with the Party of the Right dissolved, leaving behind the characteristic detrital sediment of a few friends and many enemies, as all socially imprudent fascinations tend to do. Academically, my plan for survival now included courses in subjects so obscure that it was in the professor's interest to lift the tax of possessive supervision from his students, without whom his own academic career would be headed for bankruptcy. I soon found Bentley Layton, offering a course of lectures in Gnosticism and the history of early Christian dissent. Professor Layton was quick to draft me into a postgraduate course he wanted to offer in an even more rarefied discipline, the Coptic language, an extinct form of demotic, Hellenized Egyptian in which many of the Gnostic writings were preserved. Armed with mimeographed copies of Layton's type-written *Coptic Grammar*, three, or on good days four, desperadoes from the faculty of Religious Studies pored over the sacred papyri, originals in the possession of the university's Beinecke Library of rare books and manuscripts, in a room next door to the Ezra Pound archive. As the poet said, with the paranoid intensity that belonged at Nag Hammadi,

> I am homesick after mine own kind,
> Oh I know that there are folk about me, friendly faces,
> But I am homesick after mine own kind.

For the first time since Vnukovo I was learning something that was demonstrably new from something that could not be bought in a bookshop for a tenner and change. I was fascinated by the cosmic audacity, and often the sheer madness, of these second-century writers in the desert enclaves of northern Africa, far removed from the unifying pacification of what would eventually emerge as the syncretic orthodoxy of Christendom. I had enrolled in the course hoping to escape, to find refuge from the opulent round of academic councils which I saw linking the university, the media and the government in a single philistine chain, binding the freethinker to silence. I found an excitement that was almost paternal. Leaning over the cradle of dissent, I watched Gnostic juxtapositions teething in the milky texts of the Pistis Sophia and the Gospel of Truth, juxtapositions of temporal, worldly power represented by the evil archons, among whom the omnipotent deity of the Old Testament was frequently included, with the divine inner being of individual man. They were the abandoned children of early Christian thought, untutored, irreverent, wild. So much more unpredictable and complex than the worldview I had often heard contemptuously dismissed in educated parlance as 'Manichaean', these images of the universal evil as an intrinsically hylic, material substance, in contrast to the otherworldly, pneumatic good, expressed radical truths which the Christian orthodoxy excluded, sometimes because its founders were the better writers, but often because they were the weaker thinkers, eager for peace and inclined to compromise. I had glimpsed these images before, I realized, not only in the political banter at the Vnukovo dinner table, but in the whole of Russian literature, where they found sanctuary in the wake of the ecclesiastical reforms that had driven the imaginative heterodoxies of the Russian Church underground in the seventeenth century. The schism was never to heal, and because no orthodoxy was ever to succeed in unifying Russia's religious thinking, a submerged volcano of sectarian dissent continuing to send shocks of scepticism through the nation's culture, Russian literature persisted in portraying the human spirit with diversity and depth unmatched in the West. Even in the West, however, culture seems to have lived to the extent it was not unified or homogenized, and it is well remembered that the discord of the early Fathers contributed more to the development of thought than any of their accords, sealed and made ecumenical law by the opulent round of councils that consigned Gnostic heresies to oblivion at Nicaea, Constantinople, Ephesus and Chalcedon. Still, despite more than a millennium of concerted pacification by orthodoxy, the ruling élites of Christendom remained no less combative than they were permeable, and all along they continued to cling to the principle of debate with opponents where many in their place might have opted for simple suppression. The very term 'heresy', from the Greek *hairesis*, meaning 'choice', 'course of action', 'system of values', was originally looser, and closer to the vital notion of argument, than the turgid, blindly presumptive certitude of the modern word. Hence, at least semantically, at a time when no orthodoxy is any longer meant to exist even in matters of faith, everyone seems to know what constitutes a heresy, in stark contrast to the earlier times when religious orthodoxy had palpable political significance yet heresies seemed to flourish. Turning from such uncharacteristic episodes as the Inquisition to what he saw as the polemical side of Catholicism, which alone ensured its survival, Mill noted that the Catholic élites, 'such at least as can be fully confided in, may admissably and meritoriously make themselves acquainted with the arguments of opponents, in order to answer them, and may, therefore, read heretical books'. He went on:

> This discipline recognizes a knowledge of the enemy's case as beneficial to the teachers, but finds means, consistent with this, of denying it to the rest of the world; thus giving to the élite more mental culture, though not more mental freedom, than it allows to the mass. By this device it succeeds in obtaining the kind of mental superiority which its purposes require.

This advantage, Mill maintained, is denied to the ruling élites in countries professing Protestantism, 'since Protestants hold, at least in

146

theory, that the responsibility for the choice of a religion must be borne by each for himself, and cannot be thrown off upon teachers'. Were Mill writing today, an unpublished, embittered, eccentric scribbler by night and a college bedder by day, he would have seen that whereas at the heart of the former orthodoxy lay the arguments against heresy, instead of transferring the responsibility for those arguments to the individual, the modern culture of democratic plural- ism, a political outgrowth of the Protestant Reformation, has done away with them altogether. Beneath the sway of an ostensibly oppressive religious orthodoxy, diverse theological disputes bubbled into the small hours, but where the freedom of conscience was ostensibly won by Luther, all was still, and the same pacific silence has since been extended to every other domain of Western culture, including political thought. The polemical caste has been supplanted by a deaf, apathetic conformity, affecting each individual separately with exactly the same cultural and political results, so that where the ruling élites once had the advantage of being 'mentally superior' to the mass, the Western élites of today are no more capable of defending even their own position in society, to say nothing of their society as a whole, than was the raw mass of humanity in the Middle Ages. Yale, in whose deceptively Gothic playgrounds the American élite received its training and accreditation, was the logical place to gape at this paradoxical conundrum. Its inescapable implications spilled over into every aspect of cultural and political life, so that attending a popular lecture, or opening the *New York Times*, I was each time confronted with a conformity far more crushing, it seemed on reflection, than the one which scuttled the Gnostic sects I was studying. Professor Layton's obscure enclave saved me from a total rejection of everything the University had to offer, and in the end I pulled through to graduate with my class. It was spring in New Haven. For the twenty- second time in my life I saw nature impersonating the weather, with shrubs and birds for inanimate props and Pasternak for a monologue:

> The buds burnt to butts their unctuous essence
> To lighten and lessen the burden of kindling
> April. The parks grew redolent of adolescence
> And forest replies redounded, dwindling.

13

Initially for the diversion of the few friends I had made, and later to satisfy the dissertation requirement of my university degree, I began translating Pasternak into English. Like much of his contemporary culture in Russia and elsewhere in Europe, the poetry that made Pasternak's name synonymous with the prodigality of genius that Emerson celebrated in the Elizabethans, was rooted in paganism, in polytheism, in nature. One need not stray further east of Schopenhauer, perhaps, than Wagner and Stravinsky, Nietzsche and Scriabin, Symbolism in France, Blok, the resurgence in Russia of the cults of Flagellants and Castrates, Diaghilev's aesthetics, the invasion of painting by primary colours and the revival of interest in myth and the fairy tale, Tsvetaeva's dissonance or Klyuev's ritualism, to be reminded that the cultural landscape of Pasternak's milieu cannot be seen through his later, barren or misbegotten, largely irrelevant reputation as a Christian moralist. My brush with the desert schismatics had been useful in that their thought ran parallel to many of the currents that nourished this milieu. Similarly, my childhood hearing of language as a kind of gnostic fantasy, an ideal world of secret paroles devised by an ancient conspiracy of the intellect, an enchanted circle drawn round the enlightened few against hylic intrusion by the power of the deaf-mute many, was well attuned to Pasternak's cabalist incantations. How sharp my childhood hearing was is difficult to say, but I would not underestimate those intuitions. Indo-European etymology is still a young discipline, and even linguistics as a whole is formally dated from the publication, merely two hundred years ago, of Sir William Jones's paper at Calcutta which revealed for the first time the historical kinship of Sanskrit with Latin, Greek and the Germanic languages. The discipline has never had the chance to act upon philosophy, nor has it ever pollinated any of the social sciences with the possible exception of cultural anthropology. It always seemed bewildering to me that the culture of Europe, during a seminal period like the Renaissance, had not had the benefit of Jones's revelation, or that the French *philosophes* arrived at universal truths of human existence knowing next to nothing about the universal language of man. It is like imagining Newton inventing calculus while utterly ignorant of the multiplication tables. To imagine this is to understand the role of intuition in the play of creativity, or the role of nature in springtime and other, less well-known plays. When, in 1913, Pasternak rhymed the Russian word for 'pear' with the verb 'to crush', he had only that intuition to guide him. Not until some seventy years later would etymologists discover that the Russian word 'pear' is actually a variant of the Russian, and incidentally of the English, verb 'to crush', a reference to the fruit's granular texture intended to distinguish it from the apple. The title of Pasternak's 1924 epic, *High Illness*, anticipating his prose autobiography, *Safe Conduct*, is another example. Not until the 1970s was it conclusively shown by etymologists that the Russian word for 'illness' is a taboo meaning 'to be in power', a deception intended to ward off the evil masters of cosmic matter. This sense, of course, is amplified by the title of the autobiography, with its innumerable other connotations, at first glance all equally inscrutable. As I began unravelling Pasternak's early verse, and weaving it back again into the language of Elizabethan paganism, revivified in the nineteenth century in the patriarchal enclaves of New England by Emily Dickinson and the Transcendentalists, naturally I knew that English translations of Pasternak already existed. I gathered them all, and realized for the first time just what sort of milieu had engendered them. Since I now write this book on the assumption that the reader has no Russian, in the absence of an original to judge these translations it is impossible to convey the depth of their vulgarity and idiocy except by the following stratagem. Mark Twain, an innocent abroad who had been charmed by 'Die Lorelei', translated the poem for his American readers. Twain's German was rudimentary, by his own admission execrable. As a translator he relied on his intuition, as Heine must have relied on his:

> Ich weiss nicht, was soll es bedeuten,
> > Dass ich so traurig bin,
> Ein Märchen aus alten Zeiten,
> > Das kommt mir nicht aus dem Sinn.

A country bumpkin from Hannibal, Missouri, with only a musical ear to guide him, Twain translates:

> I cannot divine what it meaneth,
> > This haunting nameless pain.
> A tale of the bygone ages
> > Keeps brooding through my brain.

One can like these lines or dislike them. Then again, one can like or dislike Heine. But a Yale savant named L. W. Garnham had translated 'Die Lorelei' before Twain, and the country bumpkin from Hannibal, Missouri, who insisted that Franz Silcher's musical score must be bound into all editions of his European travelogue, was amazed to find that 'it don't fit the tune', explaining that 'in places it hangs over at the ends too far, and in other places one runs out of words before he gets to the end of a bar. Still,' Twain went on, suddenly smelling the blood of a Yale man, 'Garnham's translation has high merits, and I am not dreaming of leaving it out of my book. I believe this poet is wholly unknown in America and England. I take peculiar pleasure in bringing him forward because I consider that I discovered him.' Garnham translates:

> I do not know what it signifies
> That I am so sorrowful:
> A fable of old times so terrifies
> Leaves my heart so thoughtful.

After another gush of praise, Twain pretends to have calmed down: 'Mr Garnham's reproduction has other merits – a hundred of them, but it is not necessary to point them out. They will be detected.' Then he is back again with a vengeance, introducing Garnham's 'rival', the author of a catalogue of pictures in Munich's Alte Pinakothek:

> It is not permitted to make use of the work in question to a publication of the same contents as well as to the pirated edition of it.
> An evening landscape. In the foreground near a pond and a group of white beeches is leading a footpath animated by travellers.
> A learned man in a cynical and torn dress holding an open book in his hand.
> St Bartholomew and the Executioner with the knife to fulfil the martyr.

It is no exaggeration to say that Pasternak's translators, and as I soon discovered American translators of modern Russian poetry or prose generally, were likewise Garnham's rivals. This made me understand anew why *Britannica*, that Anglo-American monument to universal reasonableness, collapsed into insanity only slightly tempered by platitude when it came to the overview of Russian literature. These masters of arts and, by extension, of the universe simply did not know Russian, at least to the extent they knew the history of music, or to the extent, let us say, that Fenimore Cooper could be expected to hit a tree at ten paces with his rifle. At Yale I attended postgraduate lectures in Russian literature. The professors avoided my eye. Recognized by the *New York Times* and the *New York Review* as the leading experts in their field, they could scarcely construct a simple Russian sentence without three elementary errors. Nabokov's anecdotal elephant could not have done more to disrupt a zoology lesson. When my dissertation on translation was finally submitted, it was one of the readers from the English faculty, a medievalist, who ensured that it received a good mark. At about the same time, trivial as it now seems to recall the episode, the head interpreter of the United States Department of State who accompanied President Carter on an official visit to Poland turned out not to know the country's language. Probably, like Molière's nincompoop, he had assumed that the prose he spoke all his life was actually Polish prose. Although his ignorance came near to causing an international incident he received a handwritten note from the American president, saying in part: 'You helped to make my visit to Poland very enjoyable and successful.' The president was a fool, but that did not matter, because an elected representative of a democracy may be a fool without damaging its political fabric beyond repair, any more than a blockhead of a juror necessarily undermines due process of law. What mattered was that the president's top expert, certified as competent in a discipline where a man's qualifications are presumed to be as verifiable as any scholar's, was an ignoramus. This discipline, which I had already glimpsed in *Britannica* and the *New York Times*, and now experienced first hand at Yale, was born of the promise that not only can a fool become president as easily as a nameless cockroach can wake up as Gregor Samsa and drive a red Ferrari, but that any ignoramus can be educated into a *magister* – insolent enough when rendered as 'master' but actually the double comparative form of *magnus* meaning 'greater than the greater' – or even, miracle of miracles, into a *doctor*, from the Latin *docere*, 'to teach', teaching others how to become great, and greater than the greater, without so much as asking them if perchance they are nincompoops who belong in Molière. Father used to say that the discipline's optimism is only partly medieval, calling to mind as it does the scholastic conception of intelligence, knowledge or wisdom as folios of bookish lore that a man must commit to memory, preferably by rote, before his petition to write such folios of his own can be granted. Partly it stems from the perception of any occupation as a craft or a trade, so that poets or thinkers, to say nothing of translators, can be trained like tap dancers or plumbers. Partly it is philistine or egalitarian, so that little Sammy is either a Beethoven because he has a master's degree that says so, or not a Beethoven because Beethoven's folks had access to a quality liberal arts education and Sammy's didn't. Partly it is mechanistic, in so far as life is a kind of machine, like a riverboat engine, which can be operated if the machinist receives proper schooling. And partly it is fraudulently commercial. 'Step up here, young man in the hat, you from Texas? Hannibal, Missouri! You don't say. Step up to this here lectern, Sam. Now, give us your or your parents' money and we will educate you into a humorist or a thinker, to say nothing of a doctor of cockroach philosophy or a top expert on Poland and Slavic culture generally, whatever your Dad wanted to be or your Mom wishes you to become. We will teach you how to live, we will show you how to become the most intelligent, witty and handsome person on earth, we will train you in anything from the art of winning the prettiest girl at the college prom to the science of knowing Jesus Christ our Lord. Step right up, don't be shy now, here's your chance to convert some of that filthy provincial lucre into the blue-blooded nobility that everybody will respect you and even your children will thank you for, yes sirree they will. Because what I am offering you here, young fellow, is the hereditary peerage of our great American democracy.'

14

It was to this milieu that my Pasternak was to be transported, a pagan solipsist from the lost Atlantis of cultural universalism thrust among thoroughly civilized men, big babies for whom the pagan solipsism represented by the pronoun 'I' was a cultural universe, and whom only the tribal plural 'we', so feared by Zamyatin, elevated to nominal adulthood. It was not so much a case of scattering pearls before swine as of carrying coals to Newcastle, or samovars to Tula. An audience convinced that it consists of droll wits will sour at the sight of anyone genuinely funny, and only an inexperienced hostess will seat two raconteurs, or two celebrated beauties, together at dinner. Here, just to listen to another man think was to sanction his galling presumption socially. Everyone voted, worked, paid taxes, and ultimately believed that he could do anything as well as any man alive so long as he put his mind to it. Why would an American university graduate care to know a Russian poet, or for that matter any poet at all? Poetry is a kind of consommé, emphatically proscribed from the diet of sanguine optimism. The optimism is calcified in his veins, in the semantics of education, progressing from the Latin *ducere*, 'to lead', as in 'duke', to the fascist *duce*. He, democracy's nobleman, its Medici and its Mussolini, with a pedigree of liberal arts education going back to the geese of ancient Rome, could have written these poems and composed this music. Was he not Gregor Samsa? Did not fate, society and the laws of nature prove powerless to deny him the red Ferrari? Had he not become, thanks to the Protestant Reformation, master of his own conscience and, thanks to the Pilgrim Fathers, master of his money, his vote, his culture? To savour another's solipsism or marvel at another's thoughts would be inconsistent with these achievements of modern civilization. Why, the very process of reading seems to have been devised to humiliate. '*I* shall write', says the individual thinker, unashamed of the incongruous élitism of his position, 'and you, all of you, *you* shall read!' where the logical thing, the decent thing, would be to transfer the responsibility for what he is about to write to a democratically elected committee and in the end, should this prove technically feasible, to enable each citizen in a democracy to contribute a sentence to every book, every magazine and every newspaper by pulling appropriate levers, all in the privacy of a cosy little flat with a marvellous view of the communal gardens. Nowhere is such élitism more offensive than in the attempt to describe an alien culture, to induce the necessary attitude of humility for the sake of conveying an alien idea, to impart an alien worldview by means of violent, open confrontation with its intellectual product. One tries to imagine how unpleasant that is, being subjected to an attempt of this sort, for the denizen of a Western democracy who has already qualified as a *magister* or a *doctor*. It is fine for schoolboys – who must stick to the curriculum of their educators, that is to say, their leaders – before becoming leaders themselves, whereupon Hank Adams becomes, if not the president, at least a president's grandson. It is certainly *not* fine for mature, important, busy Americans living in the real world, a world where, even in the valleys, Yale men are supermen and not only has death been vanquished by superscience but ripe tomatoes are available at supermarkets the whole year round. The prospect of a benevolent reader autographing the books of grateful writers, clamouring for his approval like a barnful of hungry hens, is much more plausible in a world so adult, so uncompromisingly realistic. I went into bookshops. For hours on end I browsed through books of poetry written by my educators. I was told that it was not uncommon for any one of the major American publishers to reject fifteen thousand unsolicited manuscripts a year, which meant that some five thousand books of prose or verse were finished, typed, photocopied, packed and posted every day of the year excluding Sundays. I was told that there were three thousand 'published poets' in America, and two thousand 'buyers of poetry'. Yale alone accounted for about a tenth of each, while the eighty thousand college and university libraries scattered throughout North America accounted for the fact that any poetry was published at all, although it was equally plain that most of it was none the less printed at a loss – in order to give the *New York Times* something to review, or not to review – by the New York publishing moguls too timid to abandon the pretence of being something other than hirelings of Hollywood. I met these 'published poets', these bearded babies in blue jeans, these wheyfaced bureaucrats with jowls sagging from the unbearable sameness of academic life, these noblest of mandarins suffering from sterility, cunning and gout, these helpless conformists, these professors of cabbage soup as we called them in Vnukovo, scarcely expecting that in the West they would be our leaders, teachers and friends. The omniscient pseudotsargod had preserved the Apollonian forms of the culture whose content he had replicated in facsimile, and if his travesty had brought death, at least it had done no dishonour. Those who lived the simulacrum did not need to be reminded that death, especially death under torture, was the only form of oblivion worth fretting over. So long as they were living, kindred souls could find one another in the infernal gloom of that paradise, and Eurydice would always make the son of Calliope a nice cup of ersatz tea. Here, in the culture of deathless optimism, oblivion, for the first time in our lives, my father's and mine, became a morbidly tangible possibility, and it was ridiculous to reflect, of a winter morning, bills paid, the telephone connected, hot water running into the bath, that something called the *New York Times* was able to achieve what the omnipotent pseudotsargod had thought imprudent to attempt. All right, perhaps the *New York Times* was more a symbol than the root cause, but this did not change the truth of the matter. In that paradise, oblivion was death. In this, death was oblivion.

15

Logically, the only way of survival open to a poet or a thinker in the West was the creation of an extra-literary, for instance political, sensation or scandal, of the kind that made *Lolita* and *Zhivago* ubiquitous and duty-free, like Chanel No. 5, with *Ulysses* and *Lady Chatterley*, for similar reasons, available alongside them in airport gift shops. A scandal packed with such ingredients as improbability or immorality, and the photogenic realia to impress these upon the general public, might now and again make a poet or a thinker into a household word, his books bought as souvenirs of the media excitement as decorative mugs are bought to commemorate a monarch's jubilee, an athletic event, or the anniversary of a technological triumph like the flight of the Wright Brothers. The nature of the ingredients mattered less than the quantity, and it was better for the man of the hour to bite more dogs in the hour, in order to translate his experience into souvenir doggerel, than to bite just one very hard. So James Joyce had everything against him, and yet he made that impossible shot, and not only made it, but did it with absolute confidence, saying, 'Be ready to clench!' So in the wake of the *Zhivago* scandal it hardly mattered that in his youth Pasternak had been the poet God sends to a language once in a millennium, the poet that Joyce might have become if he had been sustained by the culture that sustained Pasternak in his youth. Few of those who bought the souvenir were ever to realize that Pasternak was a poet at all, and even fewer bothered to discover why the author of *Ulysses* had failed as one. What mattered was that Zhivago's creator was alleged to have bitten so many running dogs of communism that the experience made him unwell, and there he collapsed, with a cry of 'Be ready to clench!', all photogenic and anti-communist, onto his Nobel Prize-winning deathbed. If the culture in which Pasternak was reared had resembled the culture which observed his passing, Tolstoy's last flight on the heath of madness which Orwell later mercilessly compared to King Lear's would have been similarly interpreted. Instead, Rozanov wrote:

> When our simple Russia got to love him, for his *War and Peace*, with simple and glorious love, he said: 'It isn't enough. I want to be Buddha and Schopenhauer.' But instead of 'Buddha and Schopenhauer', there appeared some forty-two photographs, in which he is pictured three-quarters length, half-length, full face, in profile and, I believe, 'from the legs' – seated, standing, resting, in a blouse, in a smock, and in something else, at the plough, on horseback, in a cap, in a hat, and 'just so'. 'Which postcard shall we choose?' say two schoolgirls and a schoolboy. But they buy three at once, paying threepence.

In the spring of my graduation, amid unprecedented publicity, Harvard awarded an honorary doctorate to our shrill summer neighbour, the Nobel laureate, while Yale bestowed similar honours upon another Russian exile, Joseph Brodsky, setting him on course for the Nobel Prize he would later receive. We never met the poet in Russia, although we knew of him through mutual acquaintances and by his work, which circulated in typescript. Although a collection of Brodsky's poems had been printed by an *émigré* publisher, needless to say, this had been utterly unknown in the West until his arrival which he shrewdly portrayed as involuntary exile. Exile was exciting, sensational, newsworthy: 'Totalitarianism Bites Dissident'. A second shrewd step was taken to the door of Auden's house, where he turned up to commune with the prophet of necessary murder just before his death of natural causes, evoking Yevtushenko's private and widely publicized communion with Eliot a decade earlier: 'Patriarch of the West Meets Patriarch of the East'. I mention Yevtushenko, with whom we had planned to buy and share the house in Mayakovsky Street before deciding to go it alone, because Mr Rose's *Britannica*, to hoots of laughter and disbelief from our Vnukovo guests, described him as the greatest Russian poet living. If such a thing can be imagined, this was even more hilarious, or puzzling, than not mentioning Mandelstam and Tsvetaeva in a survey of Russian poetry. Anyway, by the time Brodsky bagged his *honoris causa*, Yevtushenko, despite his historic tête-à-tête with Eliot whose full significance can never be appreciated because neither spoke the other's language, had been forgotten, though obviously his methodology of public relations

endured. Another reason to recall our almost-housemate in Mayakovsky Street was the phrase itself, the greatest poet living, epitomiz-
ing the kind of extra-literary sensationalism which I had come to
think of as uniquely Western. Yet it was in roughly these terms that
the pseudotsargod ranked the achievement of Mayakovsky, as in the
name of the street, when he resurrected him for posterity by scribbling
the words 'was and remains the best and most talented poet of our
epoch' on a tearful petition from the suicide's mistress. In *Safe Conduct*,
Pasternak described the resurrection as the poet's second death.
Adjusted for the differences in attitude to death and oblivion, the
similarities of the extra-literary approach to literature on the part of a
Byzantine tyrant on the one hand and the culture of a liberal
democracy on the other, were striking. Even more remarkable was the
speed with which a migrant from one paradise to the other adapted to
these similarities, exploiting them as naturally as a bird exploits the
air. The third shrewd step taken by Brodsky was to court Tatyana
Yakovleva, not so much because Mayakovsky had courted her, even
proposing marriage, some fifty years earlier, but rather because her
present husband had long been lionized by the *New York Times* in his
official capacity as the artistic director of the Condé Nast magazine-
publishing conglomerate: 'Greatest Russian Poet in *Vogue*'. In all, the
three shrewd steps took the Russian exile to the brink of stardom,
despite the fact that the English translations of his verse were, every
line of them, as meaningless as Yevtushenko's celebrated meeting with
Eliot. By chance I ran into Brodsky at Yale. We spoke of the extinction
of rhyme in English poetry, and I bragged a little about the success I
had had with finding English equivalents for Pasternak's rhymes.
Rather naïvely, I explained to the greatest Russian poet living that
since I admired some of his poems, I could probably do them justice
in English. Rather grudgingly, I thought, he assented. Some months
later, I decided to try my luck by sending a couple of finished versions
to the *New York Review* when the editor's son, Jacob Epstein, a
university contemporary of mine, suggested that I let his mother see
them. Jake's father was the Random House publisher, Jason Epstein.
I first understood what this meant when I saw a fattish mandarin,
Edward Mendelson, who had become Auden's literary executor, greet
the twenty-two-year-old leather-jacketed Jake in a New Haven street.
To say that the professor's demeanour, handshake and hello brought
to mind an ancient Chinese custom is to do the political influence of
the Epstein family an injustice. His facial expression, as in the famous

story by Chekhov, was so sweet that I, a mere bystander, nearly vomited. Jake's tragedy, it later became clear, was his inability, bordering on defiant unwillingness, to convert the influence his parents wielded into personal capital. He had one interest, watching television, which he did from dawn to dusk instead of working on the novel which his parents were forcing him to write the way parents force children to mow lawns, to babysit and to go to school. Eventually he had the last laugh, by filling the novel with passages from other writers, including Turgenev and Martin Amis, which did not prevent the *New York Review* from praising it to the skies as we all knew it would, until Amis complained and poor Jake was exposed as a plagiarist. This was absurdly unfair, because his only literary crime was to have copied the passages whole rather than pellmell, as anyone else at Yale would have done, and to have borrowed from an unpublished manuscript of a living writer where a true Yale man would have robbed a grave. In these terms, Jake was a total failure. But that spring the scandal was yet to come, Jake had fled to California to get away from his parents' harshness and from his professors' tenderness, and was sending me letters encouraging me to persevere with his omnipotent mother. This I did, and in the end got a reply:

> We were immensely impressed by your translation of Brodsky's 'A Grand Elegy for John Donne'. Our problem is largely one of space: the poem is just too long for our pages. Also, we did find the last part of the poem obscure: who is the speaker? Or perhaps we are being dim?
>
> In any case, although we can't use the elegy, we thought your translation was excellent, and would like very much to see other, shorter translations you may have done. Can you send me some for us to consider? I look forward to hearing from you.

Were my mind now to speak to the mind of then, I would have explained that the problem of space meant that despite the theatrical exile, the tête-à-tête with Auden and the favour of Mayakovsky's old flame, the greatest Russian poet living had not, to use the American phrase, made it. That is why Jake's omnipotent mother was being dim in thinking Brodsky's poem obscure. Obscure! I might have recalled the unfortunate Dinsmore, whose sad disappointment of a book its one disappointed reviewer thought 'woolly'. It had been woolly for the three decades Dinsmore spent as the man of the kingdom and the power, of course, and guess what? Nobody noticed. When a fabulously rich dowager puts salt in the guest's coffee instead of sugar, how charming, inimitable and eccentric she seems, and how senile the guest's own stupid mother, who forgets to turn off the bathroom light, simply crazy, she would really be better off in a home but you know what that costs nowadays? When power would finally touch Brodsky with its wings, when future editions of *Britannica* would drop any mention of Yevtushenko and replace him with Brodsky, when the *New York Times* would print photographs of him three-quarters length, half-length and full face, then Mrs Epstein would see that nothing he wrote was obscure, or if it was, then obscure it was meant to be, as clearly as she would see that her son was a plagiarist who did not deserve to have any spending money. Years later, after the shrill Vnukovo neighbour of ours, the greatest Russian writer living, was forgotten – as Yevtushenko, the greatest Russian poet living, had been forgotten before him – Father would say to me: 'Remember when the *New York Times* called Solzhenitsyn an *extraordinary genius*? I wrote a jocular letter to the editor, complaining that this was redundant. They did not print it: "How Russians envy one another!" Then they published Gore Vidal's discovery that Solzhenitsyn is not a writer at all, and again I sent off a letter. Who *is* a writer, then? Gore Vidal?! Again they did not print it: "How intolerant Russians are of other people's opinions!"' But that was later. That spring I was still too young to know any better and Brodsky had not yet made it as the greatest Russian poet living. So I tried again, this time with some of his shorter poems. I received this reply:

> I'm very sorry to be returning these poems, even though we were much impressed by your translations. Yet something didn't quite work for us in them. They seemed a bit intractable, abstract, hard to get a grip on. Though there were so many brilliant places, at many other points, there were also many places that mystified us.

What should I have told the omnipotent Mrs Epstein? That Russia was a mystery wrapped in an enigma? That the grand elegy for Donne, to say nothing of the short poems, was so transparent it was almost a parody of English clarity, and that it was in this 'almost' that Brodsky's originality lay?

> All is asleep. In their coffins lie
> the dead. They rest in peace. Embedded and adjacent,
> over a sea of sheets the living fly.
> Sometimes alone. And sound asleep. Embracing.

To hell with you, Mrs Epstein, I said to myself instead, because I was still too young to know any better and Brodsky was still a poet. It never occurred to me that the *New York Review* and I had been discussing poetry at cross purposes, as in the old *émigré* joke. Two Russians meet in a Paris night club and drink until closing time. 'What should we do now, smash the mirrors?' says one. The other sobs and says, 'They won't *understand*.'

16

Hope having been spotted earlier as a dot in the landscape of springtime, it is necessary to prefix a specific reference, quoting chapter and verse, and then watch the dot advance to the foreground, watch it fatten itself on distance, watch it swell to the size of a moving truth. Again it happened in a bookshop, a second-hand bookshop on the Upper West Side. There was a bin of battered old things at fifty cents apiece, *Elements of Calculus II*, *The Black Stallion*, *Who's Who in America 1970*, and this thick anthology with a cream paper cover. I opened it at random as one opens the eyes to a mortal hangover, bleary, reluctant, in a room full of sunlight and crumpled sheets. 'The trees are coming into leaf', it began, 'like something almost being said'. A poet called *Larkin*. Sounds Russian, I thought, but no, he was English, and living. Impossible, this was ours, this was Russian, this was what poetry was and was meant to be:

> Yet still the unresting castles thresh
> In fullgrown thickness every May.
> Last year is dead, they seem to say,
> Begin afresh, afresh, afresh.

It was Russian in the sense that it was lyric poetry written at a time of compelling, incontrovertible, eyewitness evidence to the contrary, Russian in the sense in which one can legitimately speak of a Japanese pianist as the new Liszt, Russian in the sense that my grandmother regarded Tolstoy as 'Russian' to the extent he embodied a universal. But apart from all that, it really did sound Russian, down to the Pasternakian anaphora:

> Let us free words anew,
> As our garden lets – its amber rind,
> Both careless and kind,
> A few, a few, a few.

This is exactly how it happened. How hope, like an outrider from an ancient chronicle, again appeared on the horizon that spring. It was not enough that George Orwell could *understand* everything, or that an American teenager, Michael of the sheep hearts, could show an *émigré* how to brood with the saddest of them. If Philip Larkin was able to write this, somewhere here, somewhere near, in the West, then verily all was not lost, at least not yet. Extrapolation is the opium of the thinker, and in springtime, when the stuff of ecstasy and miracle comes out of the flowerbed as if it were a grimy mattress, even an unbending rationalist may be overcome. My duty here is to record the incident.

17

As for luck, meanwhile, that socialist creature with a perpetually changing face and a commitment to the redistribution of resources seemed to smile on my father at last, although no one I knew at Yale understood why I said so, not even my friends. Indeed it is unlikely that in retrospect I would describe the movement of the creature's facial muscles as a smile, because it was more like a leer, or join in the jubilation, as I did then, at the strange news. But this time the news should not come unannounced. The human voice, produced by the vibration of the vocal cords in the larynx by the air from the lungs, is not necessarily audible. It can sound in the mind before the production of sound, called phonation, takes place. As any voice coach knows, the vocal impulse itself is indescribable. So it is with all forms of human expression, which are quantifiable only in practice, as a *fait accompli*, while so long as they exist merely in the mind it is anybody's guess what their real effect will be in the end. The idea of individual liberty breaks on this utterly human, almost physiological fact. A denizen of New York, such as my freethinking father, had every freedom to project his voice by having a printing press, or a mimeographing machine, installed in his flat overlooking the leafy suburb, setting his opinions up in type and disseminating them as Voltaire, some two centuries earlier, and even the denizen of Moscow my freethinking father had been some two years earlier, might disseminate them. Fair enough, but on the same principle it could be argued that a thinker need not say or write anything at all, since under all but the most inhuman conditions an individual has the total freedom to think what he likes, and this is what defines a 'thinker'. It is not so. Thoughts undergo a change when they become audible, words are transformed on paper, writing evolves into literature. The printed word is inextricably linked with its practical destiny, and to imagine that all a novelist needs is a pen, or that all a polemicist needs is a Xerox machine, is as brutal and ignorant as believing that a captive Mandelstam, destination Kolyma, ought to content himself with the freedom of thinking up new rhymes by the fire. But even if one were to assume that art is accidental to the articulation of thought, and ultimately at least as inessential to civilization as tulips have proven to be to the culture of modern Holland, it ought to be admitted that articulated thought is what civilization cannot survive without. Articulated thought means something audible, in contrast to something secretly or privately conceived at one's typewriter or in one's mind. My father and our Vnukovo guests could have spent a lifetime exposing in private the public deceptions of *Pravda*. Father could have bought a printing press in New York to challenge the *New York Times*. But in Moscow, *Pravda*'s six pages affected the course of events, and the survival of civilization, far less directly than did the *New York Times*, one Sunday edition of which contained 946 pages and weighed nearly eight pounds. How could even Voltaire, or Mill, out-argue an opponent in debate when for every word they whispered at their own expense the opponent would come back with a million, and at a profit? The obvious conclusion was that in civilization the growth of corporate institutions, which now held the eminences formerly occupied by individuals, paralleled the development of the weapons of mass coercion in militarization. For individualism, and if culture is defined as the individual's psychotic compulsion to defy authority then for culture as well, this was the rock and the hard place. The American media for my father and the American university for me were simply first experiences of this, civilization's rocky underside. We came to the West knowing that the cardinal pathos of civilization lay in its history of struggle against centralism, against the pacification by despotism and tyranny which we, in our own lives, observed in its penultimate totalitarian form. But in the West we found it became obvious that the blessed weakness of executive government, when combined with the virtually unlimited freedoms extended to powerful corporate institutions like the *New York Times* or Yale, not only does not increase individual liberty, but to the contrary allows it to be reinterpreted and devalued for the benefit of these institutions until the very notion of the audible freethinker becomes unrecognizable and remote. The purely physical protection from pacification by central authority, meanwhile, still enjoyed by denizens of civilization even as the law still stands between a dissenter and his straitjacket, is mistakenly equated with individual liberty, although by the same reasoning a soprano need not actually sing out loud, only lock herself in a practice cubicle and think coloratura. Small wonder that Mussolini's regime, which like Hitler's had been lauded by the *New York Times* until its reality could no longer be ignored, bore the name of 'corporate socialism', nor is it surprising in retrospect that these regimes came to power, more effortlessly than their counterpart in Russia, by building on the edifice of corporate authority already in place. The freethinkers in despotic France whose names are now synonymous with intellection, Montaigne, Pascal, de Sévigné, La Rochefoucauld, Saint-Simon, La Bruyère, Rousseau, Montesquieu, Diderot, d'Alembert, enjoyed the freedom of phonation and projection, as well as of thought and expression, while directing their voices against centralizing and pacifying authority. In the America we discovered, being an intellectual meant being free to attack the weak, including a weak central government, while heaping sycophantic praise on powerful corporate institutions, such as the media and the academy. America's Constitution, as everyone knows, arose from the minds of freethinkers under French Absolutism. But no one seemed to realize that its corporate adaptation was a culture in which the central myth of the cockroach who rose to become Gregor Samsa did little to temper the harsh truth that here, in democratic America, not one of the freethinkers in question could have risen from obscurity to claim for his voice the freedom of phonation he enjoyed in despotic France. Here the only way up, for all of them, would lie through institutions, whose corporate platitudes they would have had to learn to animate and diversify at university before being permitted to make them nationally audible as masters of arts or servants of the *New York Times*. The only roundabout way, at least a few yards from the beaten path of any such career, was the media sensation, one that did not directly threaten the corporate peace and which could be reinterpreted in the institutional interest before being profitably presented to the public at large. Thus Brodsky, our runaway success, and Solzhenitsyn, our momentary neighbour, became sensationalized and were able to achieve a small measure of independence thanks to the persecution they had suffered, or alleged to have suffered, at the hands of a regime which the corporate institutions of American democracy, at least in so far as the regime threatened them, saw fit to condemn. Conversely, it is difficult to name a single thinker born and bred in the West in the latter half of the twentieth century who managed to attain even this small measure of independence, and this is not surprising. Because for a man to oppose, and to be persecuted, in the West, means to oppose corporate institutions and to be persecuted by them, denying himself in the process the independent public existence that only their champions can attain. The result is that it is the foreign victims of alien despotisms, whatever their merits as freethinkers, who have supplanted the native strain which prophets with honour in their own land, like Voltaire in France or Mill in England, once comprised. Neither Mill's nor Voltaire's intellectual independence, vulgarly known as fame, was earned by anything other than their writings, incidentally, and neither the Englishman's arrest for pamphleteering nor the Frenchman's incessant persecution by the state contributed anything to make that independence more real. Here, by contrast, even the one remaining source of oxygen, apparently the last unobstructed artery running through the corporate heart of American culture, was bricked up by the ubiquitous equation of fame with notoriety, of intellectual independence with public scandal. For a person whose name had not already been made for him abroad by the vagaries of political or cultural climate in distant places of which the West's institutional establishment knew no more than it needed to disapprove, public scandal, then, was the only option. Public scandal began in court, and one can only imagine my father's elation at the news that following the publication in *Commentary* of his article 'Notes on American Innocence', Golda Meir, Prime Minister of

Israel, had filed a lawsuit for defamation of character against him and the magazine in the State of New York. The brick wall was about to give.

18

Filed when I first came to Yale, the lawsuit percolated for several years after Golda Meir left office. Israel's prime minister claimed $3 million in damages for the harm done to her reputation as a statesman by Father's article, in which he distinguished between stupidity and naïvety in the West's 'dialogue' with totalitarianism, using the examples of Golda Meir and Winston Churchill to illustrate the latter, more rare quality of mind. Father described in passing how the formidable lady, when Ambassador to Moscow, collaborated with the pseudotsargod in drafting lists of Jewish volunteers for the war in Palestine, whereupon a hundred thousand victims of their joint provocation were rounded up and exterminated. The story was still well known in Moscow and as a child I met several of the survivors, disfigured by frostbite and torture. It was a minor episode in the history of the universal provocation in the making, and to dwell on that episode in a way different from the way Father mentioned it, to illustrate a point, would be as incongruous as arraigning Pol Pot on a charge of trapping endangered butterflies for export. None the less she sued. On the face of it, Father's would have been an open-and-shut case even if the First Amendment did not exist and the Prime Minister of Israel were not a public figure. Israeli government archives still contained all the relevant documents, which an Israeli official had indexed in a book. Questioned about these, the plaintiff would either have to deny their existence, in which case perjury could be proven, or refuse the court access to them, in which case her claim would be thrown out. 'The West, the West!' This was no Vnukovo, ladies and gentlemen of the jury, where Marmot's pal, the prosecutor general, could drive a man to suicide by brandishing an ornamental dagger. The plaintiff hired the most prestigious law firm in New York, where $300 bought a single hour of a lawyer's attention. Every morning the doorbell rang and the postman delivered several pounds of impeccably typed legal papers for the defendant to answer. No, this was no 'Broad Native Land'. It was only *Bleak House*, where, fortuitously, Father happened to be at home. *Commentary*, published by the American Jewish Committee, had bolted like a man scalded. Mr Rose had bolted, finally realizing that his Vnukovo host was more of a Dostoevskian criminal than the *New York Times* would ever deem decorous. Friends bolted, foes gloated, and sympathetic bystanders whispered that they could recommend a good lawyer. A good lawyer! There is no greater insult to the obsessive individualist than the mention of a good lawyer. Did Socrates have a good lawyer? Did Christ? Father bought every textbook of law he could find and got himself a part-time typist, which was not inconsistent because in Athens as in Galilee he would have had at least one full-time disciple, and every morning several pounds of legal papers impeccably typed by the broad-shouldered temp would go off in the post for the plaintiff's lawyers to ponder. For in the edifice of this particular corporate cartel, the legal profession, was a tiny loophole called '*pro se*'. Since the defendant's case involved only himself, rather than a member of his family, a friend, or a business, he was entitled to conduct his own defence without spending $300 an hour, roughly the amount my parents spent each month in their leafy suburb's supermarket on food, toothpaste and the rest of life's little luxuries. The tiny loophole saved the freethinker from having to pay for his freethinking with hundreds of thousands of dollars he happened not to have, and one shuddered to ask what his fate might be once the loophole was plugged by the legal profession, as it easily could be. What judge wants to have a nut with the Socrates complex in his courtroom? What lawyer wants to weaken the power of his cartel? What citizen puts dignity before prudence, principle before success, right before peace of mind? In Hollywood myth, the American. In Vnukovo myth, the Russian. In reality, only a misfit, a paranoiac, an introverted oddball, a member of a statistically negligible minority, a deracinated, anti-social, strange character who hides Jews from the pursuing Nazis muttering that he would hide them if they were Nazis and their pursuers Jews. Father marched into the loophole, filing a $4 million counterclaim against the plaintiff for malicious abuse of judicial process. The first hearing was not what he had expected. 'Are you Meir?' demanded the judge in the tired voice of W. S. Gilbert's Lord Chancellor. The plaintiff's lawyers jumped to their feet and delivered thunderous orations at $300 an hour to the effect that their client, and not my father, was the former prime minister. 'The West, the West!' Here justice was blind, or at least it liked its martinis very dry. The second hearing was even more Kafkaesque. This time the judge knew who Meir was, and he bade Father to approach the bench. 'Mr Navrozov,' said Judge Kaufman without taking the trouble to lower his voice, 'tell me, is what you are doing good for the cause?' 'I beg your pardon, Your Honour,' said the *pro se* defendant in Meir *v.* Navrozov, 'what cause?' 'Well, the Jewish cause,' said the judge sternly. None of this made any difference, however. What mattered, in this as in any other case where something other than money was at stake, was the institutional bureaucracy of the legal profession which passed for jurisprudence and gave giant corporations like the *New York Times*, with huge law firms at their disposal, unlimited opportunity for forcing the individual to conform or perish. Not every thinker, after all, models himself on Socrates, and some prefer Buddha. It was simply an accident that Father's temperament enabled him to mount his own defence. What if the victim were weak-voiced, like Demosthenes, without having the Greek's gift for oratory? What if he is a stammerer? A poet? In Father's case it was fortunate that executive government, whether American or Israeli, does not wield the corporate power of the universities or the media. What if the victim happened to be not only weak-voiced, like Demosthenes, but also a government employee, like Dreyfus? He might not start out as a character in Zamyatin and Orwell, but surely he would end up 'like a dog' in Kafka's *Trial*. Anyway, several years thereafter Father's mad paperwork tipped the scales. The most prestigious law firm in New York was forced to drop Golda Meir's suit, leaving him to pursue his case against the former prime minister. A modest six-figure sum was named by the law firm, still billing the poor housewife she had by then become at $300 an hour, to settle out of court. Father gleefully accepted, but here he made a blunder. Friends, who had come back to the fold once the case against him had been dropped, convinced him to hire a lawyer for this final phase of the proceedings, a proposition which he did not find insulting because by now it was only a matter of trusting Crito to deliver the proverbial cock to Asclepius. The Crito in question, besides, was no less wily a lawyer than Roy Cohn, the erstwhile counsel to Senator Joe McCarthy and still the darling of Mr Buckley's 'conservatives'. He never came back with the money, but this was not the miserable conclusion to the cases of Meir *v.* Navrozov and Navrozov *v.* Meir. The miserable conclusion was that the brick wall did not budge. Apart from a paragraph when the cases were filed and another when they were dropped, not a line about them appeared in the only place that mattered. If Israel suddenly became a province of Syria, editors of the *New York Times*, along with Judge Kaufman, would have shrugged and reasoned that the whole thing was a bad idea from the start. Why, *they* were Americans. *They* did not even have to know where Syria was. *They* were right here in New York, lunching at the Oak Room of the Plaza. Depending on what they had had for lunch, and on the weather, they would have gone on to muse that lunatic socialist lefties or lunatic cold warriors was what the Israelis had always been, and that living in peace with Syria would now be the best thing for them in this best of all possible worlds. But as it was, to ask a New York court to decide whether an Israeli prime minister had maliciously abused the judicial process in order to suppress a penniless writer who had called her naïve was simply not good for the cause. What cause? Well, the Jewish cause. 'The West, the West!' Father began writing a sequel to *The Education of Lev Navrozov*, which he proposed to entitle *What the New York Times Knows About the World. Commentary* was now publishing him again, and in my last spring at Yale they printed 'What the CIA Knows About Russia', a preview of what he perceived as the larger and more colourful subject. His point, if I remember correctly, was that if the CIA had been staffed entirely by foreign agents it would never have dared to become the incompetent, insular and ignorant bureaucracy that it was, for fear of exposure. But when, one evening, I saw William Colby, the CIA's director, tucking into a ham, cheese and lettuce grinder at Yorkside Pizza, a few doors down from Mory's, and asked him what he thought of Father's article, all he said was: 'Yeah, your Dad really gave it to us.' Then I knew that the brick wall would never budge unless a battering ram, bigger than any single act of reckless individualism, could be found.

19

Pre-Raphaelite faces are often alleged to exist in real life because the effortless precisionism of the cliché flatters the observer, making him feel as though after merely glancing at the racecard he has won the Derby and all that needs doing now is to get a drink, but Lizzie, a friend of Jake's, really did have such a face. If only because they did not wish to refuse themselves the pleasure of feeling discerning, her friends, myself included, liked to look at that face of hers and do whatever favours she might require in recompense. I was waiting to graduate, with nothing much left to think about under the Gothic arches, when Lizzie asked me to help her put together the spring number of an undergraduate magazine she was cursing herself for having agreed to edit. This always happened all around me at Yale to people who did not have a single overpowering passion, such as the one that glued Jake to the television, as they got entangled in university 'activities' from which they could not later extricate themselves without losing face, seldom Pre-Raphaelite to begin with, and usually I felt little sympathy. But of course I agreed to give Lizzie a hand. I had seen the magazine once or twice before, scattered all over the campus at irregular intervals, a giveaway collegiate rag like any other, crooked line drawings and a staple through the tubercular spine. It was looked at as an envelope lying on the ground might be looked at by the passerby, provided it is not too dirty or wet, to see if by some odd chance the addressee is known to him, and on the one or two occasions I had picked it up I remembered recognizing the names of several students, and even one or two professors, conned by an editor into participation. To dismiss it as awful, pretentious and ugly would be incomplete, because, while retaining the peculiarly school-boyish flavour of amateur hackwork, it exhibited many of the pro-fessional traits that characterized intellectual life in the great world beyond, including smugness, provinciality and all the associated attributes of cultural pacifism. To observe the student editors of the University newspaper, the *Yale Daily News*, mouthing the political platitudes of yesterday in anticipation of tomorrow's edition of the *New York Times*, was not disturbing when one realized that grown men and women, whose ranks these undergraduates would soon swell, were doing the same from Alaska to Miami. But to watch students volunteering to go through the same conformist drill in the obscurity of literature, where to rise meant to march, single file, up the corporate ladder of academic ranks and posts until, at thirty-four, you and your books of verse were singled out as worthy of being subsidized by the sales of Hollywood pulp, was every bit as disturbing as, in retrospect, a square full of men shouting *Sieg Heil!* appears disturbing to many conformists nowadays. It was a matter of belonging to a class, in this case the corporate guild of licensed practitioners of the free arts rather than the priestly caste of Aryan socialism, and Father, to whom I turned for elucidation, told this story. 'We know an American lady', he said, 'who used to be married to a composer and now married a millionaire. The millionaire, to borrow a phrase from the lexicon of mothers-in-law, brings her coffee in bed. And the composer used to wake up in the middle of the night – and this is no longer just a phrase but the stark truth – to demand that she bring *him* coffee in bed because, *ma chérie*, he just had a musical idea destined to live for centuries. You don't get him his coffee, and who knows, for centuries you will be the laughing stock of every biographer. So in many ways it is not only easier for people to become artists than millionaires, but more useful as well. Nor is it surprising that when a society supports the aspirants in sufficient numbers, they develop their own class interests. A literary magazine, for them, is probably what a party cell used to be in the days of Marx and Dickens.' But by now it was too late. I had agreed to join Lizzie in the class struggle by helping her to produce the next number of the *Lit*, which in collegiate shorthand meant *The Yale Literary Magazine*.

20

Accordingly, one morning I dragged myself out of bed and made my way to Woolsey Hall. Under its ornate dome, up several flights of narrowing marble stairs, nestled the offices of the University yearbook, the *Yale Banner*, which had taken over the financial responsibility for publishing the magazine several years earlier. That was all I knew about the *Lit* when Lizzie opened the door, and what I found inside did not make me curious enough to ask questions. It was the usual paraphernalia of the undergraduate publishing effort, a camera tripod, a cracked light-box, a phototypesetting machine. For the next few days we valiantly cut and pasted, laughing at the preposterousness of the whole thing. A mutual friend of ours, not coincidentally the Teutonic beauty I had been courting, also came to help, and placidly I watched Lizzie, who, like me, was about to graduate, persuade Mary to accept the editorship of the magazine for the following year, although it was said that the *Banner* was itself on the brink of bankruptcy and would no longer sustain the rag even at its shabbiest. This finally explained why, in what I had supposed to be a party cell for practitioners of the free arts, there were no members, no intrigues, no party strife. After the issue we were producing the *Lit* would be no more, which would be a relief, and hence Mary's acceptance of the editorship was wholly symbolic, which was even more of a relief. On our last evening under the Woolsey dome we sat on piles of old yearbooks and student directories, drinking coffee from Styrofoam cups, when my hand found itself resting on an evil-smelling storage container where bulky volumes, of what I thought were more year-books and directories, lay quietly rotting. But that old library hand of mine felt that the books it was touching had once had leather bindings, and so I pulled one out to have a look. It was a bound volume of the original, *The Yale Literary Magazine*, and when I opened it lazily, as I always open a book, to a random page, sudden bewilderment, and also something like sudden shame, bulged my eyes and turned my jowls to wet plaster. How stupid I'd been! Of course this magazine didn't just hatch, a fledgeling fighter in the class struggle for insti-tutional preferment, with the mouthful of a name like *The* — boom! — *Yale* — wheeze! — *Literary* — gurgle! — *Magazine* — gurgle! If it did, it would have been called *Zip*, or *Meta4's*, or *GoGoGay*. In homage to the discovery which would change my life I reproduce in full what I saw on the crumbling yellow page.

> Attind ye lasses at Swate Parnasses
> > An' wipe me burnin' tears away
> For I'm declinin' a chanst av dinin'
> > Wid the bhoys at Yale on the foorteenth May.
> The leadin' fayture will be liter-ature,
> > (Av a moral nature as is just an' right)
> For their light an' leadin' are engaged in readin'
> > Me immortal worruks from dawn till night.
> They've made a club there an' staked out grub there
> > Wid plates an' napkins in a joyous row,
> An' they'd think it splendid if I attindid
> > An' so would I – but I cannot go.
> The honust fact is that daily practise
> > Av rowlin' inkpots, the same as me
> Conshumes me hours in the Muses' bowers
> > An' laves me divil a day to spree.

Whin you grow oulder an' skin your shoulder
    At the World's great wheel in your chosen line,
Ye'll find your chances as time advances
    For takin' a lark are as slim as mine.
But I'm digressin', accept my blessin',
    An' remember what ould King Solomon said,
That youth is ructious an' whiskey's fluxious
    An' there's nothin' certain but the mornin' 'head'.

It was signed 'Rudyard Kipling'. KIPLING. Kipling! *Kipling*, and not a dog's horseradish as we say in Russian, not a pompous professorial mug, not a clerk of the damn corporation, not some class-struggling practitioner of the free arts. I turned the cardboard box upside-down, feverishly grabbing at the decomposed ruins, my hands, face and clothes already covered in the ochre dust of dry leather. Here was a parody of Nietzsche, apparently written when he was still alive:

Thou art going among critics? 'Remember thy whip!'
    What is a critic? A self-seeker? What is a self-seeker? One who seeketh in behalf of himself, or his brother, or his sister, or his aunt.
    In what manner seeketh the self-seeker to encompass? By the sting of stings, and the scratching of nails. Sometimes it is long before the hide yields to the scratching of the self-seeker.
    The critic is a little animal, and running about he biteth lions. One day the lion will roll upon him. Let the lion be heavy and good at rolling.
    Let us stand by our lions, for pleasant is the sight of them rolling.

That in portable form the original was an extraordinary buy the *New York Times* would discover later. *Much* later. 'To remedy the vague notions we have of the superman thing', remember? And here was an issue from a still earlier volume, with an essay on Turgenev. 'In reading Ivan Turgenev's novels we fall into the mood of one studying a great painting by a master hand', this began. All right, perhaps no bolder than something one would find in an issue of the *New York Review*, but for crying out loud, at least this admirer of Turgenev was writing in Turgenev's own century! More than a hundred years after Turgenev's 'First Love' they still could not easily identify it as the source of poor Jake's plagiarism. It would have gone unnoticed but for Martin Amis's wounded *amour propre*, which yelled stop thief. More than fifty years after Prince Mirsky's *Russian Poetry from Lomonosov to Pasternak* and his *History of Russian Literature*, both published in England in the 1920s, *Britannica* still did not mention Mandelstam or Tsvetaeva who had been dead more than thirty years! This despite a 1949 American reprint of the *History*, in which Mirsky devoted chapters to Tsvetaeva's 'staccato' and Mandelstam's 'Latin sonorities', a reprint to which Professor Whitfield, its editor, contributed the following dim footnote:

> It is an interesting fact that Mirsky eventually returned to Russia, where for a time he took active part in Soviet literary life. He has long since disappeared from the scene, and the Soviet Embassy in Washington has been unable to give me any recent information concerning him.

Professor Whitfield, Professor Whitfield! Are you still there, teaching the young 'uns? Have you heard of Mayakovsky, as in the street? Then do what the poet said and get off the bicycle of your spectacles. In 1949 Mirsky had been dead for ten years, rotting at the bottom of a Siberian swamp. One hundred, fifty, thirty, ten years, all this flashed through my mind with the weird praeternatural speed of three, seven, ace in Pushkin's *Queen of Spades*. This was Yale. This was America. Were they not already the Yale, and the America, of Fenimore Cooper and Walter Camp? To be sure, they were. But apparently they still played by the original rules, when Rugby or craps were only amusements and those who did not wish to play could brood, read Turgenev or study German. Seven-eleven wins a promotion, two-three-and-twelve loses a pension, you mean this game was not always played like this? You mean there was a time when the fake imitation settee that Mother threw away in disgust was just a plain old imitation, and before that there had been an original? You mean, before all the Gothic façades, and all the sallow faces, and the class-struggling practitioners of the free arts in their uncounted millions, think of it, five thousand book manuscripts a day, there was once a time when an American, and a student to boot, could pick up a copy of a magazine that parodied Nietzsche when Nietzsche was alive? That knew Turgenev? That published little billets-doux from Kipling? Yes, this is what the old lady meant.

21

Pushkin's Herman, out for the big score, was just how I felt. 'The Old Lady in Brown', as the magazine had been called for a century by those who basked in its permanence, held all the cards I needed. Even if dated from its first numbered volume, published in 1836, this was the oldest literary review in America, older than *Harper's* and the *Atlantic Monthly*, which still published, and older than innumerable other titles that had ceased long ago. Actually, 1836 was already the fifteenth year of its existence as the circular of a literary society modelled on those of England and the Continent. It was a time when the New World was universally looked down upon as a barbarous land, often with the same conformist conviction that much of Europe now looks up to all things American, superstitiously linked as they are in the popular imagination with intellectual excitement, artistic inno-vation and cultural freedom. It was a time when Emerson met Carlyle and Coleridge, his visit to England as significant an episode in the history of Western thought as Milton's Italian journey two hundred years earlier. It was a time when America still resisted the compulsory mythologies of Fenimore Cooper and Walter Camp, when a small educated class, mindful of the links between religious dissent and intellectual tolerance, still valued diversity above correctness, admir-ing Europe in so far as it was, like America, an original. Out of this milieu, which had already absorbed the pamphleteers and the pol-emicists of the Revolution, came Poe and Dickinson, Hawthorne and Whitman. Into it came the Adamses and the Jameses, and, in some ways no less noteworthy, O. Henry and Jack London. By this time the *Lit* had already become the Old Lady in Brown and the *New York Times* was under its present ownership. The Yale ethos of Cooper and Camp was beginning to shape the nation's polity in the image of Deerslayer-Quarterback-Crook-Holmes-Bond-Bumppo, and not even Twain's iconoclasm could impede such progress. Pound, Eliot, Stein's lost generation of Paris expatriates, Henry 'Inside the Whale' Miller, Hemingway, Wolfe, all this was already milk on the run from the cauldron of Flaubert's dictionary of received ideas that American culture was becoming, spilt milk that only Europe would occasionally cry over as Dickens cried over the prostrate South and Swinburne over the martyred Poe. Like soft limestone the magazine recorded the conflagration, as the nation's flora and fauna grew thinner, more feeble, with every pacifying, centralizing, platitudinizing decade that passed. Sinclair Lewis, Thornton Wilder and Stephen Vincent Benét were among the *Lit* editors before 1920. However small their bearers' contribution to letters, these names represented an autarchy of talent. They still stood on their own, with no more propping up by the academic and media bureaucracies than those of O. Henry or Jack London. In the decades following the Great War, these originals were supplanted by simulant writers like Brendan Gill and John Hersey, whose future existence was wholly determined by and enmeshed in the *New York Times*, or by unashamedly institutional men like Henry Luce and Maynard Mack, who would devote their lives to making the catch-all mesh stronger and narrower. Gill went on to the *New Yorker*. Hersey became a pillar of the *New York Times* establishment. Luce founded Time-Life. Professor Mack topped the hierarchy of literary studies at Yale. But the further along in the forest, as the Russians say, the more firewood. Until the late 1950s, *Lit* editors who did not make it as writers would dissolve in the professional pool of university graduates, still clearheaded enough to become not the eternal prac-titioners of the free arts but bankers, doctors or lawyers. It was a mark of this residual realism, about themselves and the implosion of their increasingly insular academic microcosm, that volumes of the *Lit* in the 1950s were filled with writers who had never set foot in New Haven. Contributors to the Dylan Thomas issue from Volume 122 included Richard Eberhart, William Carlos Williams and Marianne Moore, while Volume 123 had an issue with a cover by Henri Matisse, with Jacques Lipschitz, Darius Milhaud and Leonid Massine among the contributors. By the time I joined Lizzie in the class struggle, however, most of the key editorial positions on the 'culture side' of the *New York Times* were held by *Lit* alumni, including architecture, film, science and poetry, which meant that since the early 1960s, when practitioners of the free arts had started on their long march, the magazine had been supplying the institutional rank and file with foot soldiers. By now the academic world offered more direct, more brutally unambiguous opportunities to those who wished to enlist. Not *Lit* editors but Yale professors writing in the *New York Review* were now the BMOCs, the Big Men on Campus, and everyone knew that getting on Maynard Mack's good side was worth more than having a hundred poems in the *Lit*. In 1969 the magazine went bankrupt, and it was only in its subsequent shadowy appearance, as a giveaway adjunct of the University yearbook, that it became a party cell for those practitioners of the free arts who were not nimble enough to make the necessary connections in the normal course of an undergraduate career. All of them dropped out, naturally, when it became known that the *Banner* was about to stop subsidizing the magazine altogether, and Lizzie was left holding the bag. And there, in Woolsey Hall, sat I, an immigrant who had just held in his hands a priceless relic of America, hearing Lizzie tell me that if I liked the magazine so much the *Banner* would probably sell it to me for a dollar. For sale, the Brooklyn Bridge. Price, one dollar.

22

In October 1978 an article in the *Yale Daily News Magazine* entitled 'Selling Off the "Lit"' began with the sort of playful flourish of journalistic suspense that, once securely paperclipped alongside the rest of the applicant's cuttings to an impressive curriculum vitae, would surely soften the heart of the most uncompromising employer in New York, to say nothing of Peoria, Illinois.

> Ron Pollack, editor-in-chief of the *Yale Banner*, was in New Haven during the summer of 1978 to work on the forthcoming issue of the *Old Campus*. One day in mid-July, he was surprised by a telephone call from Mary Schwarz. Schwarz, a former staff member of the Yale *Lit*, inquired after its status. When she discovered that it was temporarily dormant, she offered to take it off Pollack's hands. Within two weeks, the *Lit*'s copyright had been legally transferred.

The author of the article was a student 'investigative reporter' named Jennifer Davis. Although I had graduated that spring and the two friends who had agreed to buy the magazine with me were still undergraduates, the reporter seemed certain that a dark conspiracy of foreign interlopers with greaseballs for names was in the offing, and of course in a certain historical sense Miss Davis was right:

> Pollack said that at the time he 'couldn't see why not' to accept the offer; it seemed a good alternative to letting the *Lit* shut down. He met Schwarz, Navrozov and Liberman in the New York law

office of Lee Liberman's father, James B. Liberman. During the meeting, they drafted an agreement to transfer the *Lit* from the *Banner* to the three students; the agreement was held in escrow while Pollack considered it. Later that week he decided to go ahead with the transfer, and by July 25th the *Lit* had changed hands.

Even now I remember every last cigarette stubbed out in midsmoke at my kitchen table by the swarthy criminals and their trusty molls during that sweltering week in July, to prayers of 'Sign it, sign it!' Then finally it happened. The phone rang. The *Banner*'s lawyers had cleared the sale, for the sum of one dollar, of the *Lit*'s copyright, subscription lists, books, records and history. It was with an outline of the latter that Miss Davis concluded her article, and I remember Lee, who had read all of Dostoevsky's novels in French translations, murmuring charitably that the opening sentence sounded like something dictated to a stenographer after a disastrous gambling tour of the French Riviera:

> The *Lit*'s history – while stormy – is long. In fact, the magazine is America's oldest, established in 1836, under the more dignified title *The Yale Literary Magazine*. Its longevity earned it the nickname of the Old Lady in Brown. Over the years it has published the literary work of Yale undergraduates like Archibald MacLeish, Stephen Vincent Benét, Thornton Wilder, Paul Mellon, Brendan Gill, Maynard Mack and Mark Strand.
> 'Like other human institutions,' the editors wrote in the centennial issue of 1936, 'it has had its shifting periods of prosperity and decay.' The last few years can definitely be classified as a period of decay. In 1969, the *Lit* went bankrupt. The *Banner*, which was then prospering, took it over in order to keep it alive. Despite the *Banner*'s ownership though, the *Lit* remained beset by financial problems.

A year later the following item appeared in the Class Notes section of the *Yale Alumni Magazine* under the rubric '1925'. The author was John Chamberlain, a journalist who, like Frank Meyer, was one of the elders advising the young Buckley in the early days of *National Review*.

> Memo to the 1925 board of *The Yale Literary Magazine* editors, Bill Bissell, Frank Ashburn, Dick Crenshaw and, self-addressed, Your Corresponding Secretary. The *Lit*, which has not appeared regularly

in recent years, is about to have a rebirth as a quarterly which editor Mary Schwarz, a Yale junior, hopes to make a national publication. It will print articles, reviews, poems, and fiction by good writers wherever they may be found, whether they are Yale undergraduates or not. The criterion will be talent. Your Corresponding Secretary had lunch at Mory's with Miss Schwarz and her adviser, Andrei Navrozov, and was impressed by their enthusiasm and the scope of their plans.

Apart from these two notices and the inevitable rumours, nothing betrayed the furious activity at the grim two-storey house on Edwards Street, in a remote part of the campus called Science Hill. As if to suggest that the history of the American university might not be clear enough, for the worker ants that we now were, to learn from, our new offices came with a *memento mori*, a disused, boarded-up basement full of dusty marble slabs bearing Roman inscriptions. Some fifty years earlier the house had been the headquarters of the Dura-Europos archaeological excavation project, organized by my compatriot M. I. Rostovtzeff, which uncovered the progressive demilitarization of the great Roman city on the Euphrates from Hellenistic times to the day when the Persians invaded and it became just another sand dune in the desert called peace.

23

'Southwestern' is the name of an American publishing company that recruits thousands of university students during the summer holidays to sell its products, usually Bibles and encyclopedias, in the often inaccessible towns and villages of the Southwestern states. With every justification, those who have 'done Southwestern', mostly boys aged nineteen to twenty-one, think of themselves as survivors, as honours graduates of the school of commercial daring with nothing to fear from the corporate world. A Southwestern student finds himself in a training camp. Awakened at dawn to begin his search for 'motivation', he is taught to look in the bathroom mirror and recite the company mantra at the top of his lungs: 'I feel happy, I feel healthy, I feel ter-r-r-ific!' Whereupon he goes out to work his territory, calling on a thousand homes in a month and applying secret methods of persuasion like Selling Through the Screen Door. 'Mrs Jones', he asks with the practised sympathy that flatters the old spinster, 'is your husband in?' 'Mrs Jones', he lets loose, with a straight face, a time-tested one-liner, 'not only does this here 'cyclopedia contain over one million words, but they are all in the right order.' 'Mrs Jones', he closes on a small point, 'can you give me the cash now or would it be more convenient for you to write a post-dated cheque?' He revels in the routine of being arrested for trespassing, of being shot at from the back porch by women in gum boots. The company has an instant-bail scheme, as well as medical insurance. He works sixteen-hour days and at the end of the summer comes back East with more money than his genteel classmates with office jobs on Wall Street would make in a year, but that, he realizes, is not the point. The point is to make the Century Club, to go down in the history of Southwestern as one of the year's hundred best salesmen, and John F. S. Laing, 'F. S. for Frankly Speaking', made the Century in the summer of his sophomore year. He was born in Brussels, son of a British diplomat who later moved to New York. An Abercrombie leather pig that had lost an ear to time or tide was the only souvenir of the Empire that John had brought to the New World. The great salesman had finished Harrow, ended up at Yale, and was about to leave New Haven when a chance conversation with a Russian classmate, during which he let drop some of the vital Southwestern particulars, sealed his fate. Nothing I ever heard from him about his adolescence, not even the story, told with as tight and stiff a lip as the Admirable Crichton's, of trekking through the Australian desert with Prince Charles, made as much of an impression on me as those Southwestern tales of his, frontier tales in which the world of commerce, of nickels and dimes, resounded, as I had never before imagined it could, with the echo of individual achievement from America's forgotten past. 'When I came back to New Haven in the autumn,' John remembered, 'and the people I knew would see me in the street and smile, "Hi, John, how are you? How was your summer?", I started crying, because I could not understand them. They were so bloody calm.' Only once more would I hear of an episode in a man's life throbbing with such intensity of action, and the analogy that presently suggested itself did not seem either spurious or frivolous. The man was a Russian whom I met in London to interview for the *Spectator*, a military intelligence officer who had defected to Britain. The episode was his induction into

179

Spetsnaz in the days of his youth. That summer Viktor was a lowly tank company commander, a junior officer, to be precise, in command of ten tanks attached to a tank battalion of the 910th motorized infantry regiment of the 318th motorized infantry division of the 13th Army of the Carpathian Military District, when the regiment went on unscheduled manoeuvres and he ordered the crews of his tanks to ram the enclosing wall of the tank park. His was the first company to get out. A court-martial followed, but it was already too late for colonels to pass judgement on a man whose initiative had been noted by generals. He had made it into Spetsnaz, militarization's Century Club. Viktor was short, shaped like a bean that could easily be imagined popping from the pod of a tank, with closely cropped hair and ill-fitting clothes, civilian clothes that he had not seen until he was fourteen, brought up as he was in one of the innumerable installations, called closed towns, scattered from the Sea of Okhotsk to the Baltic. In England the defector became a writer, and when my father read his books he said that nothing like it had been written since Chekhov. John was tall, at once beefy and gangly, almost bald at twenty, conversant since childhood with the shirtmakers of Jermyn Street and the tailors of Milan. The expatriate Englishman had never read any Dickens, never looked at newspapers, mocked Yale and Harrow alike. Girls chased after him like mad, not only because he looked twenty years older than his goody-two-shoes, politically-conscious contemporaries, and unlike them was a born raconteur who made his audience weak with laughter, but also because they felt that the unfamiliar strength underlying this flow of irreverence could some day be harnessed to great advantage. Intuitively they understood that mavericks, in civilization as in militarization, are rare, and that under the circumstances of real life, in contrast to those of the Yale game, insubordination distinguishes the likely winner. Incidissidentally, as John took to saying with a wink, I too understood this. I sensed that the adventurist acquisition of what I envisioned as a base on America's cultural mainland would sooner or later be interpreted as an act of aggression, and that on the commercial terrain of modern civilization the ensuing war of words would be unwinnable by purely literary means. Besides, my original partners did not want to stay in New Haven for ever. John would replace them.

24

'Henry Ford? This is John Laing. How are you this morning, sir?'
John said he was out to poach every old boy in America. We did not
limit ourselves to the Yale preserve, though anyone who had ever had
his name appear on the *Lit* masthead for any reason whatsoever
between 1914 and 1969 received a fundraising letter followed by at
least one telephone call. The campaign, successful in part because
those donating money to an institution recognized as a charity by
Internal Revenue could deduct the contribution from their tax bill,
netted the magazine $10,000. The takings were then used to mail a
subscription brochure to each of the one hundred thousand graduates
of the University. The printing was done on credit. This moment in
the life of a publishing venture, when such credit is gouged from the
indifference of the business world, has an analogue in the struggling
actor's first break: nothing that happens thereafter is ever again as
unexpected or intoxicating. Suddenly, something or someone real,
calculator in hand, has judged this coloured air, this product of
drunken dreams and celestial illusions, a viable business proposition,
and not only was Van Dyck Printing real, it was one of the finest
printers in America. I had met the owner through a Russian friend of
ours, Igor Galanin, a fiercely original painter in the tradition of
Douanier Rousseau who used to rent Crimson's summer cottage and
was now a great success in New York. Igor had been asked by his
gallery to find a suitable printer for his exhibition catalogue, and of
the man he had found he said laconically: 'Leonard grows orchids.'
Verbum sapienti. A printer who grows orchids in his spare time is likely
to want to print a literary magazine, especially the sort of literary
magazine I had in mind. I wanted to translate everything I knew
about the golden age of publishing in Russia into a modern idiom,
and to hypnotize my provincial bourgeois audience with this shimmer-
ing phoenix. I wanted the quarterly magazine to look mysterious,
unclassifiable, like something from another planet. I wanted a special
binding which, once a copy was opened to a page, would keep it open
to that page. I wanted colour reproduction of paintings that would
put American 'art book' publishers to shame. I wanted paper that
looked and felt like lily petals. I wanted no more than one poem, and
no more than fifty lines of prose, to a page. I wanted it to be expensive,
not just more expensive than any of the American 'literary' magazines,

but more expensive than anything one could buy at the newsagent's. Leonard understood everything. It must be like your rarest orchid, I said. Our brochure, meanwhile, had brought in nearly two thousand subscribers, who were now waiting for the first of their four issues. In the bank sat some $50,000 of their money, enough to pay Leonard's bill for producing both the brochure and the first issue. But not the next three. It was at this point that my feminine intuition told me how John's talent might be harnessed, because the answer to the eternal dilemma was advertising. This answer struck everyone, including John, as preposterous, rather like the great business idea from an old Moscow joke, because who in hell would want to advertise in boom, wheeze, gurgle, gurgle? 'Darling, I made out like a bandit,' says the Muscovite to his wife after a night at cards. 'You remember that coat I bought for a hundred roubles? I just lost it for a hundred and fifty.' But from the start, and for reasons that had nothing to do with the inevitable deficit, I wanted advertising in the magazine as much as I wanted it printed on petals of seventy-pound Quintessence, milled in Canada, normally hard to obtain 'but let me see if I can', as Leonard would purr with a faraway look in his eyes, the look that meant he was thinking of the capricious thermostats and humidity regulators at home. The equilibrium between low commerce and high culture, which made the golden age of publishing in Russia what it was, had to be re-established and adapted to the second half of the bourgeois century. The public had to be reminded that literature was not an old-age home, a hospice for the indigent, a grubby charity that was supported so long as it flaunted its poverty. If nobody will believe a magazine's publisher that its readers matter, why should anybody believe the magazine's editor that its writers matter? Advertising, at least of the sort that I wanted John to land, would be the requisite reminder, linking for the first time a rarefied and otherworldly journal of ideas with the Madison Avenue of my Vnukovo dream. The *New Yorker*, I said not entirely in jest, was the Old Lady's only competition. On the face of it, they had some advantages, a circulation in the hundreds of thousands, a paper mill of their own and twenty million smackers sweating in the bank, for starters. But the Old Lady had been around for a hundred years before they got going, and at least *we* never ran ads for instant coffee or costume jewellery. Most important, we had John 'Frankly Speaking' Laing, where the *New Yorker* had, as he would now tell himself with Southwestern zeal in front of the mirror each morning, 'wombats in Gucci loafers'. Besides, a page in the *New Yorker* might cost as much as $20,000, which no art dealer in his right mind, for instance, would spend even if the painting he wanted to advertise was priced in the millions. That was our market niche, then. We set the rate at $2,000 a colour page, announced that only full-page displays would conform to our format, and concentrated on businesses which might benefit from the sale of a single item, an item that was, however, expensive enough to justify the long shot. The cold logic of our reasoning, which distinguished it from Mayakovsky Street revery and Jermyn Street snobbery alike, was borne out by the realization that a company producing instant coffee or costume jewellery would never want to buy the attention of magazine readers, no matter who they were, at a dollar a head. They did not want us, we did not want them, it was as simple as that, and this is why from morning to dusk that clipped Harrovian voice in the next room would fold itself into the telephone receiver like a metal tape-measure, inching its way towards those few who were called and even fewer who would call back. There was, needless to say, no magazine at that juncture, not a poem, not an article, nothing at all but a room with a telephone. According to my childhood prejudice this was shadow theatre on a commercial scale, which is to say common fraud. But according to the Southwestern apophthegm that had made John the Chrysostom of the Century, this was just what it ought to have been. 'Don't sell the steak, sell the sizzle.' The voice was selling the sizzle through the screen door. 'Mrs Jones,' it undulated, 'America's oldest review *is* the Rolls-Royce of magazines, and may I say frankly that nothing would please us more than seeing Rolls-Royce Motors in our pages. Circulation? Mrs Jones, perhaps I haven't mentioned that the combined wealth of our readership, small though this may seem when compared to the mass circulation of the *New Yorker*, is equivalent to three per cent of America's Gross National Product.' An exquisitely printed folder had been produced to illustrate the latter claim, complete with the profiles of a hundred most prominent patrons of the magazine, household names like Paul Mellon, Henry Heinz and John Hay Whitney. 'Mrs Jones,' warbled the voice on the street side of the screen door, 'when it's a pricey – that is to say, when you are marketing something of great value, is it not rather meaningless to speak of demographics? We ought to speak of oligraphics, of pluto-graphics if you wish. May I send you our folder then? You have? I did not realize our people here were so efficient. Well, shall I come and see you next week, or would it be more convenient for you to let me have an insertion order this afternoon?' Soon a laudatory article about our shadow theatre appeared in the town daily, the *New Haven Register*, under the banner headline: 'Oldest Literary Magazine Combines Arts, Hard Sell'. John felt happy, he felt healthy, he felt ter-r-r-rific, and this despite the fact that neither of us had anywhere to live or anything to eat. By May 1979, when Van Dyck delivered five thousand copies of the first issue, Volume 148 Number 1 of *The Yale Literary Magazine*, cover price $6, we were at the end of our rope. Penny after penny dropped into the phoenix, whose unladylike stomach with a piggybank slot in the middle had already digested, apart from John's beloved Saab Turbo, his Turnbull & Asser shirts and his wild nights at La Boîte, every hope of a landfall I had had since finding Kipling's billet-doux in the Old Lady's attic. One morning I put on my only tie and went with John to New York, to beg Bill Buckley for help. We were taken to lunch in his famous double-length stretch limousine. Some landfall.

25

When so much is staked on chances so slim by those who have so little, inevitably every new decision opens a fresh wound of anxiety, every new choice uncovers an agony so novel it can be patented. My editorial choices were no exception, if only because of the knowledge that a single petal-smooth page of the issue represented $1,000 in production costs alone, not counting payments to contributors. These were set at $6, symbolic of the cover price of an issue, per line of verse, a fabulously generous fee for a country where the only commercially viable magazine with highbrow pretensions, the *New Yorker*, paid considerably less, while most paid their poets nothing at all. The rate for prose was less spectacular, because obviously we could not outdo the mass-circulation *New Yorker*, not to mention *Vogue* or *Playboy*, but we did make sure that it would be more generous than that of *Commentary*, *National Review*, *New Republic* and other subsidized journals of serious opinion of whatever stripe. To collect material for the magazine I did the naïve thing no editor I was ever to meet boasted of having done. I went to the library. There I read through three or four bulky reference books, each a kind of 'Who's Who in Poetry', on the presumption of my own absolute ignorance of who, in actual fact, was who in Anglo-American poetry since the days when, as C. H. Sisson once put it, 'there were still drawing rooms in Mayfair'. Apart from Philip Larkin, that is. The unique advantage of my declared ignorance was that it made me utterly indifferent to the power of names, encouraging me to rely exclusively on quotations from the poets under scrutiny, merchandise samples that the fair-minded authors of these critical entries nearly always included. To my socially naked eye already exasperated by the small print of those entries, a famous American poet like W. S. Merwin was a conformist hack with all the talent of a doornail, while a complete unknown like G. S. Fraser, who, when I wrote to him in mysterious 'Stoneygate, Leicester', turned out to have been dead for some time, was obviously a living poet. 'Like Larkin', as I now identified the emergent phenomenon in conversation, while still thinking to myself: 'Damn it, this fellow sounds Russian!' As for Larkin, he wrote back on eggshell-blue paper to say that 'poetry seems to have given me up, whether temporarily or permanently I don't know', though consenting to have 'The Trees' reprinted in the launch issue. In later issues Larkin would be joined by Charles Causley, Douglas Dunn, John Heath-Stubbs, Leslie Norris, Michael Schmidt, Anne Ridler, Vernon Scannell, Christopher Fry, Charles Tomlinson, all chosen by my reputation-blind 'Hamburg' method. In the 1920s, a well-known littérateur who was an acquaintance of my grandfather's joked that while the public knows the world's greatest boxers by their rankings, the boxers themselves evaluate one another at a secret meet at Hamburg, and that a similar tradition cannot but exist in literature. Strangely, all the poets ranked highly enough to merit critical entries and Russian enough for me to admire were, with one or two exceptions, British. To find a known American poet worthy of our $1,000 petal-smooth page, plus $6 a line, was proving impossible, which had a good side. Every unsolicited submission from an unknown was read hopefully. Once the unknown turned out to be a Yale undergraduate named Margaret Cohen, and the poem followed Larkin's in the first issue:

> Look out, I thought, to read how time will be,
> To point to clearness in a midnight sky,
> But looking out is only looking back.
> Like reading, it turns left around to right.
> A stare that reaches out to grasp a star

Finds only shadows representing forms
That fade with lightning swiftness out of sight,
As passages retraced return to night.
Though they seem cold, these stars are other suns,
And by resemblance take on strength to light
Old wood long dead to warmth and tongues of life,
Illuminating worlds with formal sparks
In blackened passages. Look, now the sky
Hangs framed between the shadow and the shade.

Another time a plain manila envelope, postmarked 'Santa Barbara', yielded a harvest of nine poems:

Now it's in sheaves and the moon is full,
Contributing tractors, oiled, asleep.
Goodbye to that crop, sweet dreams to the soil;
The spoil and the scent shall keep.

I met Rudolph Schirmer months later, in winter, in the ornate library of the Knickerbocker Club in New York. He was the last scion of the G. Schirmer music publishing family, which introduced Tchaikovsky and Scriabin to America. His mother's *nom de théâtre*, taken from an equally lyrical ancestor, was Swinburne. He had been sending poems to the *New Yorker* for decades, and innocently he showed to me his collection of 'terribly kind' rejections. The American composer Samuel Barber, a lifelong friend of his, bought a copy of our launch issue shortly before his death. Maybe it was Larkin, maybe it was Margaret Cohen, but that evening he phoned Rudolph: 'You must send them your poems!' The Hamburg method was obviously working, at least where musical sensibilities were concerned. The prose section of the first issue included 'a mixture of diary and I don't know what' by the Rumanian-born philosopher living in Paris, E. M. Cioran. Then there was the cover article, with six flawless reproductions of new Galanin paintings: 'Much, much better than the originals, khe-khe!' as the artist, whom Father had taught his first English words, 'art' and 'money', approvingly commented, guffawing his way to a final, Muscovite street-smart snort. There was also an essay on Bruno Schulz, another on Hector Berlioz, and a suitably incendiary piece by my father entitled 'Mediocrity and the Rescue of the West'. It soon transpired, however, that the editorial content of the magazine was, for the time being at any rate, the least criminal aspect of the whole undertaking. No sooner did the phoenix spread its firebird wings over the academic wasteland than the following assessment of our triumph, in one of the freebie undergraduate sheets modelled on the *Lit* as Lizzie and I had known it, suggested that if controversy was what we were after, John's effort had been far more successful than mine. I quote a section of the article in its entirety, so unexpected was its thrust, and I remember thinking, Wait, am *I*, or are *they*, still in Moscow?

As is always the case, a magazine's advertisers indicate whom it is directed at and, therefore, much about its nature and conception. As with the production of the *Lit*, opulent is the key word to describe its advertisers and their ads, each of which covers at least one entire page.

In the first issue of Volume 148 there is an advertisement for Christie's fine art auctioneers which incorporates a lovely oil painting by George Henry Durrie. Christie's announce their upcoming auction at 502 Park Avenue and mention their catalogue which can be purchased for $14.

A number of art galleries are represented, too. The James Maroney ad includes a color reproduction of an oil panel by Raphaelle Peale entitled 'Still Life with Strawberries and Ostrich Egg.' An 'impressive portrait', in color, painted by John Singleton Copley dominates the Vose Galleries of Boston ad. And the back cover announces the upcoming display at the Kennedy Galleries, replete with yet another color reproduction and offering their catalogue for $10.

Passing over the Mellon Bank ad (Mr. Mellon is on the *Lit*'s Board of Patrons, along with Henry J. Heinz II and a host of other wealthy businessmen), and the Rizzoli International Publications page, which reads, 'For Connoisseurs, Magnificent Art Books from Rizzoli', the most striking is the Hermès page. It shows a well-dressed man and a beautiful chestnut horse against a blurred, bright green background. 'Bring us your horse. We'll do the rest,' announces this equestrian accessory manufacturer. The man is kissing the horse.

The second issue contains more of the same, including a page dedicated to the around-the-world tour of the Queen Elizabeth II (which left January 17th from New York and is probably passing through the Panama Canal about now) and a two-page advertisement for Rolls-Royce Motors, featuring a photograph of the Silver Shadow of 1979 emerging from the archway of what appears to be a neo-Gothic palace, but for some inexplicable reason bears the Princeton coat of arms. The other noteworthy additions are two color pages devoted to jewelry ads: Buccelati and Bulgari, which 'takes pleasure in announcing the opening of showrooms at the Hotel Plaza-Athenée, 27 Avenue Montaigne, Paris,' presumably intended for those who cannot reach their Rome, New York, Geneva or Monte Carlo showrooms. We may now safely add to our description of the intended *Lit* reader that he takes great delight in expensive material objects and that extreme comfort, to the point of rare luxury, is something to which he realistically aspires.

If wealthy people choose to spend their money on luxury items, it is their privilege; I see no reason for condemning the *Lit* simply for appealing to wealthy clientele. However, when the contents of the magazine are considered along with the design and intended reader-ship, then it appears to be a publication founded upon an inherent contradiction and a false sense of art and the artist.

The rest of the article, logically enough, set out to prove that the new magazine was founded upon an inherent contradiction and a false sense of art and the artist. As if the feverish didacticism of *Pravda* were not sufficient to make me spasm with *déjà vu*, the author ended with this exhortation:

> Now, when it is time for our art to be proud and inspirational, it is a shame that the *Lit* has chosen the road of decadence and falsehood. It is still more of a shame that its wealthy and influential readers are being seduced into believing that art is designed to dissipate hope and alienate men from each other. We all deserve better air to breathe.

'Well, *that's* good,' said John, ruefully fingering some old cheque book stubs, his face in the lamplight rather like something Jerome K. Jerome might have liked to depict. 'I *told* Mrs Jones our readers were wealthy and influential.'

26

The third issue was being set at Van Dyck. Antique hot-metal machines, lovingly looked after by an old Scotsman, dropped slug after slug into position. The galleys were pulled as in the days of Mark Twain, before phototypesetting. Then the intervening century made itself known, as the pages were photographed and plated. Leonard walked about with a printer's loupe in his eye, no doubt thinking of his orchids as he checked the colour of an early Chagall we had found in a private collection, *Vitebsk from Zadunov Mountain*. Reams of printed signatures sat on pinewood skids waiting to be folded. With mortified hearts and weak knees we scanned the sheets for misprints, by now as uncorrectable as anything in history. Roy Fuller's 'Bedside Notebook', this must be the second sig. 'Nasturtium leaves – badly-drawn wheels, as by child.' Is this how you spell 'nasturtium'? Why no article before 'child'? 'The man who cannot see the wonder of a rabbit must spend large sums of money to discover its presence in a hat', that must be Lewis Lapham's piece on conspiracies. Ah, there is Navrozov *père* in the last sig, wreaking vengeance on the *New York Review*:

> However, since no physical destruction of myself has so far been entailed by my exposé of the provincial ignorance and sterility of the Central Intelligence Agency (and that is what makes it all so refreshing after the mafia of *Pravda*), I think I can challenge the *New York Review* as well: surely there must finally be an outsider who would review *its* reviews, evaluate *its* evaluations, test *its* genius. Anyway, I am that outsider, and after Stalin even Mrs Barbara Epstein seems to me not so frightening.

Elsewhere at the plant, that last signature is being printed again, on airmail paper. This is our most reckless gamble to date because our credit at Van Dyck is at an end, though all the same Leonard agreed to give it a whirl. The unsuspecting publisher of the *New York Review* has rented to us, on a single-use basis, their subscription list. The plan is to mail to each of the 67,487 addresses on the list a copy of the *Lit*'s 'Review of the *New York Review*', along with an invitation to subscribe to our magazine and a freepost 'business reply' envelope. This is a nation of commerce, is it not? Of door-to-door sales? Of junk mail? Of name-brand comparisons? All right, two can play the game.

189

America's intellectuals! Stay away from bargain brands like the *New York Review*. Shop and compare, as in 'Tide gets your whites whiter!', 'And now I use Pepsodent!', or 'In taste tests, most cats choose Purina!' You want a brand name you can trust? Well, how about Mr Kipling?

27

Review of reviews is a genre of journalism familiar to every educated Russian, and no British or French reader would find the idea particularly startling or disconcerting. But with that scurrilous mailing, unprecedented in the placid frog pond of the bureaucracy of literary criticism, our real troubles began. In the interests of continued peace the *New York Review* set out to mobilize the Yale faculty, insisting that somebody punish the insolent interloper on the prowl in what they had regarded as their own back yard, so much so, apparently, that they had rented their subscription list to the *Lit* at a special discount rate. Recriminations and rumours flew long before the response to the mailing started coming in at the Yale Station post office. When it finally gushed, for the first time in his life John was scared. Business-reply envelope after business-reply envelope was opened, disgorging hundreds of 'hate letters', inarticulate groans of class rage, hand-written curses, tightly folded wads of lavatory paper, pieces of brick. Occasionally a polemical letter arrived, neatly typed, a first-class stamp on the envelope hinting that the author did not wish to be indebted to us for the postage. Occasionally, a subscription. A week later John said that he could not take it any more. He was broke, we were stuck, I was crazy. Perhaps because I saw the truth of all three contentions, in the end we parted amicably. But now I was all alone. We had a student staff, but none of them would have been able to sell the Star of India to a Saudi prince for ten roubles. To escape the ever larger ghost of Dura-Europos, I trudged down Science Hill every morning to collect more bricks, more lavatory paper, more *National Geographic* covers. Oddly enough, after a few more days of humiliation, the other response began to trickle in. Apparently it is a known feature of direct-mail campaigning, one of which neither John nor I had been aware, that negative response of the kind we were receiving, bricks and all, anticipates any positive response, hate being less capricious and more absolute an emotion than love. By the end of the month I had nearly a thousand new subscribers, who had sent in enough cheques to cover the cost of the scandalous escapade, but it was too late, John was gone, and the accounts payable ledger for May 1980 showed liabilities totalling $74,039.53. It was at this juncture that, mixed with the last of the blue envelopes, spoils of my editorial success in the fight for market share against the *New York Review*, I found a letter headed 'Yale College, Office of the Dean' and addressed to 'Mr Andrei Navrozov, Editor, The Yale Literary Magazine', which began:

> Dear Andrei,
>   It seems clear that we should have a discussion about the current and future relationships, both budgetary and legal, between *The Yale Literary Magazine* and the University.

Initially I thought that this was Stalin's, I mean Mrs Barbara Epstein's, revenge. The frog pond had long been alive with croaking of every kind, to the effect that sooner or later the university 'would have to get involved'. So-and-so has called Galbraith, Styron had been on the phone with so-and-so, 'and these aren't even Yale people, you know', Shapiro from the *New York Times* is just furious, 'I know for a fact that Hollander had lunch with them on Tuesday', MacLeish himself used to edit the *Lit* and said it's an outrage. Every Yale professor with whom we had some friendly contact would bring me news of the mudslide moving towards the administrative centre of the university, where the offended academic community expected justice to be done. Would Yale countenance the outrage? Several years later, describing this moment of uncertainty in a magazine article, my old chum Brookhiser would write:

> Navrozov's only brush with officialdom occurred in 1980. That February he ran into A. Bartlett Giamatti on the train to New York. Giamatti, a professor of English and Comparative Literature, had become president of Yale the same summer Navrozov bought the *Lit*. The two of them, Giamatti recalls, had a 'nice chat'.

Emboldened by the fortuitous meeting – why is it, I ought to have wondered instead, that trains and railway stations attract swindlers and patsies – I arrived at the Dean's Office. I found a Dean, like Giamatti a professor in the English Department, who was all sweetness and light, with only an incidental concern, our outstanding liabilities, ever so slightly wrinkling his brow. One or two of our creditors, he said, had approached him to find out whether the university would pay up in the event of the magazine's failure. I was only too happy to assuage his concern. I owned the magazine, and fortunately for the university my ownership was legally unassailable. Our partnership did not borrow the *Lit* from Yale, which, as he knew perfectly well, never spared a penny to save it from collapse either in 1969 or in 1978, but bought it in good faith from an independent corporation called Yale Banner Publications, Inc. The magazine was now mine alone, but if the university, perhaps under pressure from those who did not like the way I was running it, chose to dispute this legal certainty, then the university was welcome to it. Along with the magazine's debts, that is. 'How much is that?' asked the good Dean, suddenly sensing that his whole career might well depend on my answer. 'Current liabilities $74,039.53, to be precise, not counting the subscription obligations themselves, of course, about four thousand individuals and five hundred libraries waiting for the next issue. And not counting, of course, our two years of work without pay, which would go down the drain if . . .' I trailed off, pointing to the abyss. The explanation had a simplicity about it that was Solomonic, and the skilful bureaucrat withdrew to ponder the bureaucratically unwieldy situation. At our next meeting the Dean intimated that although the Solomonic simplicity of my explanation might satisfy the Office of the Dean, the Office of the General Counsel was insistent that the university be formally indemnified against any adverse consequences of our present and future actions, drawing my attention to a clause in the *Banner* contract which expressed the intention to incorporate our partnership as a limited-liability Connecticut corporation with independent charitable status. If I were to incorporate, the university would not be liable for the *Lit*'s debts, and neither would there be any reason for Yale to interfere in our affairs beyond ensuring that every year, in accordance with another clause in the same contract, we continued to 'register' our staff as an 'undergraduate organization' with the Office of the Dean. There was nothing threatening about the proviso, but to reassure me on this score the Dean handed me a copy of the University Report of the Committee on Undergraduate Organizations, wherein I read that

The Committee spent many hours in an attempt to agree upon a definition of an 'undergraduate organization'. No definition seemed as inclusive as we wished it to be. The effort was finally abandoned, since the diverse nature of student organizations and the student body in Yale College seemed to suggest that no single definition would fit every organization on campus, nor could it anticipate new organizations which might be formed.

Good old diversity! Yet the Dean obviously had his mind set on having that umbilical cord, that vague symbol of the Alma Mater, retained even after our incorporation. This, according to the General Counsel, was necessary because the university was duty-bound to exercise a measure of responsibility over our use of the name 'Yale' in the *Lit*'s title, formal protection against the unlikely eventuality that the future corporation should fall into the wrong hands 'and decide, for example', said the Dean solemnly, 'to sell the title to *Hustler*'. 'I am not against pornography,' sufficiently amused by the prospect to philosophize a little, I replied. 'I am only against pornography, or anything else for that matter, masquerading as literature.' The skilful bureaucrat knew that unless I agreed to incorporate he would be out of a job, and to this day I remember his understanding chuckle.

28

It was no coincidence that the English professor who rescued my Pasternak was a medievalist. The Anglo-Saxonists, by the time I got to Yale, were roughly in the same position within their department as the Party of the Right was among the parties of the Union, or Buckley's 'conservatives' were within the bipartisan political establishment nationally. They were outcasts, tolerated, as Professor Layton with his Gnostic *idée fixe* was tolerated and even tenured, because as a nuisance they were tolerable. The faculties of English and Literature, by dint of their consanguinity with the national media, were far and away the most visible and influential of Yale's academic departments, especially since my last spring as an undergraduate when Giamatti, a forty-year-old professor of English, became Yale's nineteenth president. The cabal was run by the adepts of a new scholasticism, known in polite discourse as 'deconstruction'. Since, like 'diversity', the term was intentionally meaningless, by the time I graduated vigorous departmental intrigue had already succeeded in inflating it to encompass, under the name 'poststructuralism', anything under the sun that the professors thought useful to their careers, including 'structuralism', 'referentiality', 'feminism', 'psychoanalysis', 'gender theory', 'Marxism' and so on. If any had been interested in reading pigeon entrails, no doubt a corresponding cult would have been resuscitated, to respectful plaudits from the learned journals and the national media alike. In short, like any ideology touched by collective power, theirs was syncretic in the extreme, which did not mean, needless to say, that it was any the less rigid as an orthodoxy. At first glance, literary critics like Harold 'The Walrus' Bloom, Geoffrey 'The Rabbi' Hartman, Hillis 'The Nihilist' Miller or Paul 'The Nazi' de Man had little in common with one another, and even less with authors like John Hersey, James Merrill or John Hollander, except prestigious names and oedematous faces. Yet so elastic was their common ideology, so synoptic its doctrinal exterior, that to an outsider like myself their views and methods of enquiry could not but seem as predictably uniform as peas in a pod, vipers in a nest, happy critters in an ark of inanity afloat on the waters of intellectual peace. Whatever their intrigues among themselves, against the outside world they stood, or rather slouched, united, bonded by the kind of insatiable appetite for collective power that might well have struck old Ponomarenko as uncouth. Their aim was to appropriate, or rather to expropriate, European culture by raising themselves, as critics, above the laws of creation, which in practical terms enabled them to attain collectively the eminence which, in that culture, had belonged to the individual utterance. As 'diversity' came to mean uniformity on Mr Rose's terms, so 'deconstruction' came to mean the construction of a Babel under their bespectacled supervision. Any man who finds some women unquestionably attractive, and others for some reason repellent, may find the following analogy convincing. Such a man is likely to have discovered that the attractive ones are frustratingly moral, while the unattractive ones view the whole world, hopefully, as a good place for an orgy. So it was with the Yale professors. The Anglo-Saxonists, who had in their heads something worth knowing if only because the ability to read an ancient manuscript in the original is as rare among human beings as the ability to perform open-heart surgery, regarded Europe's cultural past with the scrupulous morality of a Cinderella.

The rest wanted to revolutionize it, to the tune of '*Ven chì Nineta*', in order to make room for themselves. Thus, among my friends at university, Mary alone seemed to me unattainably beautiful. Others, like Lizzie, were engaging, and I could see how another might fall in love with them. And invariably it was the ugly ones, in whose lives that hypothetical 'another' did not seem plausible, who were unashamedly vociferous in their demands that human affections be reorganized or redistributed. They were against the past in so far as they were against the present, and whatever they saw as the lingering vestiges of the past, love or war, furs or jewels, rules of grammar or summer parasols, was loathsome in their eyes because it gave the Cinderellas among them an advantage they considered unfair. Because if life was, as the Camp ethos had been signalling for generations, a Yale game, it was as logical for them as for their professors to argue that the playing field must be level, and if necessary levelled, to eliminate the unfair advantage which Dante had over John Hollander, or a girl courted by a prince over her ugly sisters. On this, essentially a family brawl, I barged in with my glass slipper, not as the prince of the fairy tale, of course, but as the editor of the court circular where the tale would first appear.

29

Even if I were to yield to the Dean's entreaties, I reasoned while the summer ebbed, by signing the papers the university had drawn up and incorporating the magazine, as I had all along intended, into 'American Literary Society, Inc.' with myself as managing director, this would do little to avert the looming disaster. It hardly made a difference to Leonard, for one, whether the autumn would find me bankrupt as an individual or as a Connecticut non-profit corporation under the provisions of Section 501(c) (3) of the Internal Revenue Code. The magazine had grown, prematurely, into a *Wunderkind* with an overpublicized persona and an undercapitalized structure. But money, I sensed, was out there somewhere, and because a 'conservative', Ronald Reagan, had just captured the White House in an unforeseen landslide, it was in politics that I decided to have a looksee. As any oaf could tell, then as now, elected representatives in a democracy came and went, while the unelected political establishment stayed in place. It was somewhat less obvious, but none the less equally true, that the nourishing medium of this élite, the titanic *Ersatzkultur* of the *New York Times*, of Yale, of great corporate institutions and their institutional individuals, was what made the élite so Olympian, elevating its intellectual consensus above the contest of the democratic process. Those who partook of this corporate food of the gods could expect to follow them into the heaven of power, where no one is called to account by the *Untermenschen* below who cannot even spell 'Hegel', much less explain why the master's burden is heavier than that of the slave. Interestingly, the political landscape of America on the eve of the Reagan landslide had been painted three decades earlier, by a freethinker named C. Wright Mills whom the Left, as the Communist Party then was, thought a crank, and the Right, as the *New York Times* then was, thought a commie. 'Publics, like free associations', wrote the commie crank in a book entitled *The Causes of World War Three*, 'can be deliberately and suddenly smashed, or they can more slowly wither away. But whether smashed in a week or withered in a generation, the demise of the public must be seen in connection with the rise of centralized organizations, with all their new means of power, including those of the mass media.' The commie crank went on:

> Today we cannot merely assume that in the last resort men must always be governed by their own consent. For among the means of power that now prevail is the power to manage and to manipulate the consent of men. We do not know the limits of such power and we hope it does have limits, but these considerations do not remove the fact that much power today is successfully employed without the sanction of the reason or the conscience of the obedient.

On the residual, by then almost entirely withered, public awareness of the accuracy of this picture, Ronald 'Mr Smith' Reagan went to Washington. But even a populist mandate as massive as the one now brandished by his administration would influence the consensus, and affect the course of human events, only superficially. As I already knew, an institutional courtier like Harrison Salisbury of the *New York Times* could change his political *modus operandi* overnight without ever changing his intellectual *modus vivendi*. And Salisbury, after all, was a writer, even as the institution to which he belonged was a newspaper of record. What was true of them was doubly, no, a hundred times more true of Washington 'think-tanks' and 'policy-research' organizations, of civil bureaucrats and appointed functionaries, of 'advisers' like George Kennan and 'officials' like Henry Kissinger, of 'wise men' and learned bores of every colour ever found in the great rainbow that stretched across the establishmentarian heaven of the *New York Times* as a radiant sign of their immanence. It was necessary, I decided, to identify the forces which had brought about Reagan's populist success and now, upon its assimilation by the unelected establishment, stood to lose influence. My first excursion into politics took me to the New Hampshire villa of William Loeb, editor and owner of the *Manchester Union Leader*. By a trick of geography, New Hampshire being the first state in America to hold a presidential primary, Loeb's little newspaper held extraordinary sway over the outcome of every presidential election in memory. It was the *Union Leader*'s doing that Edmund Muskie, the Democrat grandee whom Mr Rose was backing when the SS *Leonardo da Vinci* brought his troublesome Russian guests to New York, stood atop the campaign lorry and cried like a baby before the cameras. Unfortunately Loeb's veto did not extend beyond New Hampshire, and the Republican whom he mistrusted as much as he despised Muskie, Richard Nixon, went on to capture the White House. It was now the *Union Leader*'s doing that Reagan emerged victorious from the New Hampshire gaggle of presidential contenders, a blue-collar populist unafraid to grab the microphone away from them just to have his grandfatherly say, and was bound for Washington in the autumn. But again, what neither Loeb nor anyone else could foresee was that this plain-talking California proletarian would recapture the White House not for Roosevelt-style populism, but for the same ineluctable élitism which Loeb mistrusted. A sworn enemy of the Republican establishment and, to the Democrats, evil incarnate, old Loeb had a naturally subversive mind that instantly grasped the myriad scandalous possibilities that would open for the *Lit* once our finances were sound. On my behalf he promptly wrote a series of personal letters to the moneybags who had backed Reagan, careful to bury his private insight into my aims in orthodox 'conservative' prose. Here is one of them, written ten days after the election and addressed to a Maecenas in Palm Beach:

Andrei Navrozov, the son of the Russian dissident, Lev
Navrozov, is editor and publisher of *The Yale Literary Magazine*.

What he is trying to do with this publication is, I think, very effective.

Instead of going after the liberals with a meat axe, such as is used by *National Review* and other publications, he is attempting to infiltrate the opposition culture with a very refined magazine which nevertheless subtly brings around the conservative viewpoint. This is a little too indirect for some of our conservative friends whom he approached for support for the magazine.

It occurred to me that with your own background as a renaissance man you would understand what young Navrozov is up to and might be able to suggest a source of funds for him. I am sending him a copy of this letter, so he will be writing you directly. In the meantime you can be thinking about people who would be interested in his conservative approach. I would appreciate it.

I have my fingers crossed as to who Reagan is going to pick for his Cabinet officers, and I am sure you have, too.

A very different admirer of the magazine, Eugene Rostow, for a decade the Dean of the Yale Law School and later a member of President Johnson's cabinet, was a Democrat. He set out to sell the idea to Reagan's backers without misleading them into thinking that to support the magazine was to support their own 'cause' as they, at any rate, were likely to interpret it:

> I understand that your foundation is considering a grant of $50,000 to support the brilliant, dazzling, improbable, and very important effort of the group led by young Andrei Navrozov to convert the dear old *Yale Literary Magazine* into a powerful highbrow review of real influence – an organ of the *intelligent* intelligentsia. It would be popular but misleading to label the new *Lit* editors as 'conservative'. It is more accurate, I think, to describe them as sophisticated; intellectual; passionately committed to the ideals of liberty; and capable of using the weapons of wit and eloquence in behalf of their principles.
>
> The first issues of the new *Lit* have been lively and original, both in form and substance. There is every reason to have faith that the experiment will succeed, and that the cultural alliance between St Petersburg and Yale will prove to be creative and fruitful as well as stimulating.

The above letter was addressed to the private foundation of Richard Scaife, like Paul Mellon an heir to the Andrew Mellon fortune that gave America, among other trifles, the National Gallery in Washington. Unlike his famous relative, however, who sent us a cheque in memory of his bright college years with pleasure rife on the *Lit*'s editorial board, Scaife had dropped out of Yale and had the reputation of a gruff maverick. Over the next few years his foundation along with forty or fifty other patrons targeted for the *Lit* by the likes of William Loeb and Eugene Rostow would pour $1 million into the cultural alliance between St Petersburg and Van Dyck Printing: not Yale, because by September 1980 the university had got its way and the magazine had been incorporated. My friend Leonard, whose bill had been miraculously paid once more, thought this a just denouement. 'If they wouldn't have you when you had the debts', he reflected, *in loco parentis*, looking anxiously at the veins of a purple protuberance in the tiny pot he was holding at nose level, 'now that you don't, you should be happy they are . . .' He hesitated, spraying. 'History.'

30

But history would not be fooled. In the autumn of Reagan's first year as president, Yale was in the news more than ever before, and not only because an old blue was now Reagan's vice-president. It was President Giamatti, who, in September 1981, delivered an address to the freshman class that was more widely publicized than anything President Reagan would ever say to the nation, with the possible exception of his speech about 'the evil empire'. The title of the address which made the front page of every newspaper, to cheers from the English professor's departmental colleagues from sea to shining sea, was 'A Liberal Education and the New Coercion'. I shall cite but a handful of expletives from a single paragraph of this long and memorable address: 'satellite and client groups', 'old intimidation and new technology', 'angry at change', 'chauvinistic slogans', 'absolutistic in morality', 'political pressure', 'authoritarian positions', 'voices of coercion', 'license to divide', 'meanness of spirit', 'resurgent bigotry', 'political retaliation', 'injunctions to censorship'. The evil empire of this president's imagination, on the face of it, was the 'Middle America' coalition of grass-roots organizations lobbying under the name of the Moral Majority, in contrast, presumably, to the minority of elderly gentlemen with waxed whiskers who speak French and ogle dancing-girls at the *café chantant* that is not 'Middle America'. But since scarcely anyone at Yale, not to mention the smooth-chinned and open-mouthed freshmen receiving the address in Woolsey Hall, had ever seen anything of the evil empire that so troubled the English Department, all this invective was loosely interpreted to mean that Giamatti, and by implication all thinking people, had told Reagan, and by implication all 'conservatives', to take a long walk off a short pier. But to say that Giamatti was brave to stand up to the evil empire would be unnecessarily morbid. As befitted a great helmsman of the intellectual establishment, he was optimistic. The delicious subtext of his fearless remarks was that since Vice-President Bush was himself no redneck, every boy and every gal in the Class of 1985 – which Private Willis in *Iolanthe* would have rhymed with 'either a little Liberal or else a little Conserva-tive' – could take Giamatti to have meant that the evil empire would not outlast Reagan's term in office. To fortify this subtext, Giamatti made a great show of palling around with Yale's favourite son in Washington. Such was the background of the cultural alliance between St Petersburg and Van Dyck Printing, which continued to be creative and fruitful as well as stimulating. A week or so after Giamatti's address to the freshmen, posters went up all over the campus announcing that

The Yale Literary Magazine
will be awarding its annual

FRANCIS BERGEN MEMORIAL PRIZE
FOR POETRY

The sum of two hundred and fifty dollars is offered to the person who submits the best original short poem or cycle of poems for publication in *The Yale Literary Magazine*. Longer poems will be considered if their length is warranted by their quality. Translations will be judged on the same principles as original poems. The deadline for submissions, which should be sent to Box 243-A Yale Station, is Friday, Oct. 16.

The following kinds of verse have the poorest chance of being published: blank verse in the manner of Valéry produced to show how beautifully incomprehensible its writers' inner lives are; verse imitating the moderns because it would give itself away by imitating the classics; prose written as verse to sound significant; and verse scenes of horror or sex assumed to be profound by virtue of mere repugnance.

It now seems like a shameless lie, but in the next few weeks, from a student body of some four thousand undergraduates, the magazine received nearly three hundred submissions. Apart from this, if the purpose of the experiment was to find a poem worth publishing, it was not a success, although a young woman by the name of Naomi Wolf did eventually collect the purse for a poem entitled 'Jeanne d'Arc'. It was a success in the sense that it made the magazine the talk of the town, along these lines:

This is not ordinary snobbery: it is snobbery of a peculiarly reaction- ary sort. The *Lit* is not simply condemning bad verse. What the *Lit* really objects to is bad verse in the modern idiom.

The little Liber-al touched on other matters in his *Yale Daily News* column:

A week ago, President Reagan informed us of his belief that, should the Soviet Union launch a tactical nuclear strike in Western Europe, the United States might react in kind without risk of escalation. Leonid Brezhnev responded yesterday, saying that any nuclear exchange between the two countries would be 'dangerous madness and suicide.' Now, who appears to be a saner man, Reagan or Brezhnev?

The *Lit* responded with a letter to the Editor:

The word 'snob' still means 'shoemaker' in some British counties, and 'snobs' is what English aristocrats called shoemakers and other plebeians striving for refinement, distinction, or whatever else not befitting their humble origin. If Mr. Levich assumes the role of such an aristocrat, we accept the role of snobs in that sense. We are not aristocrats by birth. But we do strive for refinement, distinction, and other qualities which were once thought to be the exclusive privilege of aristocracy.

As for our snobbery being reactionary, we can only pity . . .

The next day a little Conserva-tive joined the fray in *his* own *Yale Daily News* column:

> The preciousness and complacency which are the favorite styles of the *Lit* are neatly epitomized in the letter by its editors which appeared in yesterday's *News*: '. . . we can only pity Mr. Levich's Marxist (or any other Young Hegelian) worldview, according to which life is a single progressive cosmic process – which reactionaries seek to arrest and will arrest, unless they are properly condemned and eliminated.' I happen to know Mr. Levich pretty well, and so just for the record I'd like to assure the readers of the *News* that he is not now, nor has he ever been, a Hegelian.
>
> Nevertheless, I do wish that he had abstained from calling the *Lit* reactionary. As a reactionary in good standing, I consider this a bum rap. T. S. Eliot was a reactionary. William Butler Yeats was a reactionary. S. T. Coleridge was a reactionary. Dr. Johnson was a reactionary. Jonathan Swift was a reactionary. The *Lit* is not reactionary – it is merely bad.

The *Lit* responded with a letter to the Editor:

> Mr. Frum claims that we called his friend Mr. Levich a Hegelian and swears to God Mr. Levich is not. We claimed nothing of the kind. We simply suggested that the Hegelian worldview had permeated the cheaper varieties of metropolitan journalism and still lingers in the writings of those unfamiliar with Hegel.
>
> Usually we are accused of being conservatives and hence beyond the pale of the civilized community. Since Mr. Frum seems to consider himself a conservative, he assures the public that we are *not* conservatives and hence beyond the pale of civilized community.

At this point Connecticut's metropolitan newspaper, the *Hartford Courant*, stepped in with forty-seven closely set paragraphs of a front-page 'News Focus' exposé, entitled 'Literature, Politics Mix Poorly at Yale'. The article was seminal in that it contained the germ of every stratagem that the *Lit*'s detractors would use against it for years to come. The only analogy that springs to mind is the part played in my grandfather's life, and for his generation, by the famous *Pravda* article which signalled, in February 1936, the ideological rift with the 'proletarian internationalism' that had reigned over cultural policy. Here 'the students of Yale' took on the role of 'the Russian people' as I opened the newspaper to read that

> the stupid and harmful babble to the effect that the Russian people, in the past, comprised a mass of lazy good-for-nothings, endless Oblomovs, Asiatic savages, and so on, has been repeatedly and decisively condemned by the Party.

It must be borne in mind that although my negotiations with the University administration had gone on unobserved by the Masonic eye of the academic community, by now the professors had had a whole year of meetings and lunches to ferret out the ugly truth. Not only was the *Lit* to continue publishing, but Yale was to have no say in whom it would publish. In the stormy atmosphere of the president's sermon on the enemy without and the enemy within, this disturbing intelligence, in bureaucratic terminology a 'leak', was promptly fed to friendly journalists on the culture beat. And here they were, those enemies, right in the president's back yard, poised to sever Yale from the rest of America, seize the Panama Canal and march through Mexico:

> To outsiders, it was known as *The Yale Literary Magazine*, the student-run, student-written review founded at Yale College in 1836. But to some of America's greatest writers, who began conceiving poetry and prose for its pages, it was the *Lit*, or more fondly 'The Old Lady in Brown,' one of the oldest and most hallowed literary magazines in the country.
>
> Today the *Lit* endures, but the non-student owners who bought the magazine when it was in financial trouble in 1978 have recently changed the Old Lady's face dramatically, leaving many former admirers and contributors outraged and raising embarrassing questions about one of Yale's most illustrious traditions.
>
> 'The Old Lady in Brown,' said a disgruntled Maynard Mack, former *Lit* writer and Yale English professor, 'now seems more like the Whore in Red.'

Funded by leading conservative foundations and businessmen and led by the son of a prominent Russian emigré, the *Lit*'s new management has since 1979 gradually converted the traditional booklet of student literature into an expensively produced, full-color magazine with a national circulation – a slick international review with a clear anti-Soviet, right-wing slant.

By this year, the contrast between the old and the new was striking. Where students like Sinclair Lewis once wrote poetry, professional writers now appear along with works appealing to what the magazine calls 'high cultural interests only' – little-known East European plays, British poetry and strident critiques of the *New York Times*, the *New York Review of Books*, and *Sophie's Choice*, a novel by William Styron, which the *Lit*'s reviewer called 'a hideous heap of platitudes.'

A few paragraphs later it emerged that the author of the article had been alerted by the 'disgruntled' English Department to the symbolic proviso in my deal with the university administration:

> The *Lit*'s transformation into a coffee-table item that is the toast of the New Right has caused growing anger and resentment among many Yale faculty members and *Lit* alumni, who contend that the new *Lit* is pretentious and filled with 'reactionary' politics. They also argue that a national magazine stocked with professionals and led by alumni, not students, should not bear the Yale name.
>
> 'The name of Yale has become an illegitimate banner to fly for a group of people and their ideologies,' said Peter Brooks, a professor of French and comparative literature who is among those pressing hard for the university administration to restore the *Lit* as a student review.
>
> American literary figures, like 1936 *Lit* editor Brendan Gill of the *New Yorker*, said they were 'absolutely stunned' and disappointed at the change in the magazine. Novelist John Hersey expressed 'a feeling of sadness about what has happened to the *Lit*'. And Styron, saying 'I can tell hollow rantings from serious critique,' called the *Lit*'s review of his book 'an extremely right-wing hatchet job.'
>
> But appeals for the *Lit* to go back to what it once was have had little effect so far on either Navrozov or university officials.

Quite apart from the hatchet job, Styron's motive for wishing that the magazine go back to what it once was did not surprise anyone who remembered that a decade earlier the author of *The Confessions of Nat Turner* had taken up an entire issue of the *Lit* with a polemic entitled 'William Styron Replies to His Black Critics'. If we had asked the author of *Sophie's Choice* for an update, perhaps under the title 'William Styron Salutes His Jewish Admirers', all would have been well. But as it was, the famous author could tell hollow rantings from serious critique, and so could his friends in the English Department. It was no more surprising that the University officials were standing their ground. After all, the 'new' *Lit* had now been functioning for over three years, during which it had moved from bankruptcy to insolvency on a grand scale. Our agreement had been signed and sealed for more than a year, during which the corporation had moved from insolvency to prosperity. To side with the openly political agitators of the English Department would be worse than legally impossible, it would be bureaucratically impolitic.

> Yale officials are privately dismayed by the magazine's national format and predominantly professional writers, but they say a check last year showed that students are involved enough in editing and making editorial judgments to justify the classification as a student organization.
>
> Navrozov and his non-profit American Literary Society have clear title to the magazine, have the right to publish freely and are not bound to publish student literature or even to remain a literary magazine if students decide otherwise, they said.

Good old diversity! The fact that half a dozen undergraduates worked on the magazine was turning out to be a blessing for the university administration, which now used them as a kind of *vox populi* to clear itself of the charge of complicity in a pact with the renegade branch of the Mellon family and other rednecks. But if the administration supposed that this would keep Mrs Epstein's avengers at bay, it underestimated the pain we had caused her:

> But Yale English professor John Hollander and other faculty members think Yale is being hoodwinked. 'When Yale investigated this, it showed less than the necessary attention,' he charged.

An historian of Yale traditions was trotted out to substantiate the charge, recalling the *Lit*'s good old days and its 'decline in the 1960s and 70s':

Some *Lit* traditions began to seem old-fashioned, like the stern, all-powerful *Lit* board that coldly rejected submissions and expected student writers to bow when they passed an editor in the street – attitudes that irked Sinclair Lewis in 1904. The *Lit*'s chairman, who once could expect an annual invitation from Skull and Bones, the most exclusive of Yale's secret societies, also lost some prestige.

This laid the historical foundation for the professor's main argument, namely, that the voice of our students was not as loud as the voice of their students and hence, if Yale really was as diverse and democratic as its president said, the voice of their students was the true *vox populi, vox Dei*, while the voice of our students was that of a cunning ventriloquist. Unbeknown to President Giamatti and his administration, the *Lit* was a Moral Majority front, a cuckoo hatching the redneck young of British poetry, little-known East European plays and strident critiques of the *New York Times* in the nest of Yale's silver-throated thrushes:

> Although students might not have been interested in the *Lit* then, they are now, Holiander maintains. Dozens of students are eager to work for and edit a student-oriented literary magazine, but starting a new magazine is too expensive and the *Lit*, because of its prestigious name, is the most realistic vehicle for Yale undergraduates, Hollander said.
>
> Others claim that the professors' arguments are merely sour grapes. 'In fairness to Navrozov, when he bought the magazine it had all but perished,' said Dorothee Metlitzki, the *Lit*'s former adviser. 'Why didn't the students do something about it then? Navrozov bought it, made something of it, and then of course, they all came and said "oh-oh" and made a noise.'

Professor Metlitzki was a medievalist. Now, and by her own admission for the first time in her life, she was in her colleagues' way. Shortly before, this quiet old woman with an international reputation for scholarship came to our office in tears, shaking like a leaf: 'They are ganging up on me in the Department. They know I've been talking to you.' It was a genre scene that could have been subtitled 'Moscow, 1936'. Equally ominous was the note on which the *Hartford Courant* concluded:

Hollander, Brooks and other *Lit* critics say they have not abandoned their efforts to 'recapture' the magazine for students, but they acknowledge that Navrozov appears to have a firm hold for now.

Good old diversity, I exulted, trying to imagine Mrs Epstein's fury. This is not Moscow, not yet.

31

Deceptively echoing my exultation, an editorial rebuttal of the *Courant* article appeared in *National Review*. In my own rebuttal, which had already been published in the *Courant*, I wrote that

one of the assortment of assailants your reporter has lined up implies that Sinclair Lewis, who contributed to the magazine in the good old days, 'wouldn't approve' today of a magazine so right-wing.

The trouble is that a certain American middle-class milieu has sequestered the right of considering itself the only true representative of the universal Left (synonymous with universal Truth, Good, and Beauty), all opponents being by definition 'anti-Soviet, right-wing.' Rather disappointingly for this milieu, Sinclair Lewis was in fact anti-Soviet when the New York intellectual community was almost solidly pro-Soviet. Another contributor to the magazine, unmentioned by the assailants, was Rudyard Kipling, who was neither pro-Soviet nor left-wing. Still another, John Dos Passos, was left-wing yet anti-Soviet.

By being so inquisitorial in their attempt to charge the magazine with a 'clear anti-Soviet, right-wing slant' the assailants evince their own total preoccupation with politics, which they brandish at the 160-year-old magazine for motives of their own. William Styron complains that our criticism of *Sophie's Choice* is 'extremely right-wing.' It is very convenient to write atrocious novels and imply that anyone who finds them atrocious is a right-winger, a reactionary, and possibly a fascist. It is this vicious circle of self-protection that has created the self-contained *New York Review of Books* culture we criticize.

By contrast, *National Review*, whose preoccupation with politics was as total as that of our assailants, was delighted that the debate had been polarized. It was us and them, was it not? Yale *v* Harvard? Cowboys an' Injuns?

> Deck the halls with commie corpses,
> Fa-la-la-la-la
> La-la-la-la!

As these 'conservatives', beleaguered and utterly impotent only a year before but now representing the universal Right synonymous with Truth, Good and Beauty, claimed that it was they who had put Reagan in the White House, so too they had every reason to take credit for the spread of their revolution to the intellectual sphere. No doubt my own considered decision, three years earlier, to buy the Brooklyn Bridge for a buck was just one of the many political manoeuvres they had been planning all along:

> The counter-revolution in the Ivy League continues, pitting liberal professors and administrators against conservative students.

'The *Lit*', boasted the *National Review* editorialists, has been 'transformed into a slick, full-colour quarterly with Rolls-Royce ads', which was only to be expected, of course, of any magazine that was virtuously 'conservative'. Oddly enough, *National Review* itself had difficulty selling advertising space to anyone more demanding than the Conservative Book Club, despite artless rumours that the editor now had a direct line to the White House. 'The table of contents began to include poems by people like Philip Larkin and Joseph Brodsky.' This too, apparently, was an unmistakable sign of 'conservative' virtue. Oddly enough, the only poet to grace the pages of *National Review* was a man by the name of von Dreele, who supplied politically relevant limericks inspired by the news of the week. 'Along the way,' the editorialists concluded their assignment of virtue by contiguity, the *Lit*

> ran pieces of a decidedly conservative cast: urging the West to summon its will, attacking the *New York Review of Books*, assaying the dogma of academic freedom. Now lo! the *Hartford Courant* has run a two-page blast ('Literature, Politics Mix Poorly at Yale'), the *Washington Post* has put reporters on the story, and New Haven echoes with the grinding of molars.

Where *did* that moralizing platitude come from, I wondered, that old chestnut about how the decadent West must be urged to summon its political will? Why, it sounded just like something our shrill summer neighbour would say. Then I realized that it came from one of the 'liberal professors' quoted in the *Courant*, to the effect that 'Navrozov wants his father to become a second or an even better Solzhenitsyn', except that here the polarities of good and evil were reversed. The platitude fitted the story seamlessly. It was us against them, conservatives against liberals, Western civilization against the barbarians of the East, angels against devils, and the only minor detail to be sorted out was the stubborn question of who was who to whom. Since Solzhenitsyn, to *National Review*'s editorialists, was on the side of the angels, they naturally thought they were doing me a good turn by standing the professor's analysis of my ambitions on its head. Henceforth, in 'conservative' circles, the *Lit* would enjoy a very special status. An ingrate might describe it as 'honorary Aryan', and I often recalled the phrase overheard by Dostoevsky in Paris: *Le Russe est sceptique et moqueur.*

32

But one scarcely finds words picturesque enough to describe the effect which the polarization of the controversy had on the *Lit*'s assailants. Where their own effort to polarize the issue along political lines broke on my insistence that they were narrow-minded timeservers calling themselves 'liberal', now their position was strengthened by their political opponents, narrow-minded timeservers who called themselves and my magazine 'conservative'. To be sure, *National Review*'s endorsement convinced many of our financial supporters that they had not backed a 'liberal' cause by mistake. Yet the representations which we, if not always our intermediaries, had made to them in the course of our fundraising had been deliberately subtle, while now the spectre of what Loeb, in his letter to the Maecenas from Palm Beach, called the 'meat axe approach' hung over the intellectual integrity of the whole enterprise. On campus there began a furore. In the autumn the *Yale Daily News* launched a front-page series of investigative reports on the magazine, in daily instalments of excruciating length, where cries of outrage from the English professors and their students were interspersed with cautious opprobrium from the University administration. The news, to me, was that the good Dean with whom I had negotiated the incorporation now told the student reporter that 'in addition to worrying about the legal situation, we have to weigh whether the advantages of getting the name back would be worth the awkward and embarrassing scandal in the press'. But as far as the rest of the 'Yale community' was concerned, the news *was* the *Yale Daily News*, which announced in a leader published at the conclusion of the series that 'undergraduates on the *Lit* act as fronts for its owner, Andrei Navrozov'. 'His backers are rich', this fearless indictment continued. 'They are conservative. They drive Rolls-Royces.' As a result,

> Yale officials seem reluctant to probe the *Lit*'s status. They are afraid of the messy and embarrassing legal fight which might develop in an attempt to get back the Yale name from the *Lit*. Such fears should not deter them, however. The *Lit* is not run by members of the Yale community; it therefore misrepresents the attitudes of Mr. Navrozov as those of at least a portion of that community. We think it's more embarrassing to have the name 'Yale' associated with the *Lit* than to have a legal fight with its editors.
>
> We hope the administration gives the *Lit*'s space to a deserving undergraduate publication. The University should be supporting undergraduate literary publications in every way possible, especially considering the enormous talent here at Yale and the dearth of funds and opportunity for publication or editing experience.
>
> Mr. Navrozov's father may get his works published in *Commentary* or even the *New Yorker*, but give the students back their *Lit*.

It was the dream of every campus Woodward and Bernstein to find a campus Watergate, and there it was. Yale was covering up for the Moral Majority! As found, of course, the story was less than perfect, but with patience, time and effort it would mature into the kind of explosive stuff the *New York Times* was always looking for. True, it was fraught with contradictions. Professor Joseph Hamburger, for instance, who had taken the place of Dorothee Metlitzki on the magazine's advisory board, was quoted by the student reporter as saying that he had advised Navrozov's gang on 'how to defend themselves against liberal and unjust attacks'. Now, in a letter to the Editor, the fink was changing his story:

The plain fact is that many of the critics demand a change of management and policy *and* complain that the *Lit* is anti-Soviet, ideological and reactionary, a combination that amounts to an illiberal call for censorship.

I am disappointed that the *Yale Daily News* fails to recognize this, for I thought all good journalists were quick to defend First Amendment values as a matter of principle and self-interest.

When I agreed to be a faculty adviser, the clamor against the *Lit* already was audible. As I explained to your reporter, this was why I regarded it as one of my functions to help defend the magazine against '*illiberal* and unjust attacks.'

I emphasized the word 'illiberal' and even spelled it to avoid misunderstanding. I certainly did *not* refer to '*liberal* and unjust attacks.' This was a gross and misleading misquotation. To attribute these words to me is to characterize me as one who thinks of opponents in terms of crude, politically partisan caricatures.

Partisan, shmartisan. But what about us students, whose magazine got stolen? Sure enough, there was a fink even among us students, in with another letter to the Editor:

As an undergraduate, I do not wish to be published in a magazine 'just for undergraduates' *just because* I am one. I do not think that this form of tokenism is intellectually satisfying. To the contrary, I find it conducive to egotistical delusions and unrealistic expectations.

Finally, I fail to understand your reporter's charge of partisanship. I do not work for the magazine because it is conservative, liberal, Catholic, Protestant, undergraduate or professional. I work for it because I like it.

Yes, these were setbacks. Perhaps the Moral Majority was not behind it after all. But nobody ever said that the life of an investigative journalist was all beer and skittles. Ah, here is a good idea. why not organize a student coalition to demand that we get our magazine back? Call it, let's see, 'Young Americans for Literary Excellence at Yale', YALE for short. No, too snazzy. How about 'Organization for an Undergraduate Literary Forum', or OULF?

The fledgling organization's statement of purpose declares: 'Our goal is simple, straightforward, and moderate. *The Yale Literary*

Magazine should be controlled by Yale students. We, as an under-graduate literary organization, can serve that role. We are ready, willing, and able to assist the University in any way possible.'

OULF will eventually ask for investigation of the *Lit*, according to OULF officer Seth Magalaner. 'We are trying to emphasize our role in regaining a Yale tradition. We're not rabble-rousers,' OULF officer Joe Andrew said.

While the *Lit* never had more than a dozen students on its staff, the *Yale Daily News* article promised that the 'undergraduate literary organization' would have a membership of 'at least 150 undergradu-ates by the end of the semester'. They had already stormed the Office of the Dean to submit their petition, which concluded:

> We are new students, with new enthusiasm for the oldest college literary magazine in America. We hope to cooperate with the administration in any way possible, for we are not fighting just for ourselves, but for Yale.

By the end of the semester, it seemed likely, the 'undergraduate literary organization' would storm our office as well, possibly bran-dishing hockey sticks and baseball bats in homage to the Yale sporting tradition. But just as suddenly as they began, the attacks stopped. The *Yale Daily News* fell silent. It was not until three years later that Brookhiser, covering the *Lit* affair for the *American Spectator*, explained why. Unlike Nixon, Yale's president had met with the Woodwards and Bernsteins to assure them that there had been no cover-up, and that they could count on him:

> Giamatti told the *News* the matter would be studied, and he told its editorial board to cool it. 'They were not doing themselves or anybody else any good by objecting to the content,' he remembers saying.
>
> Privately, Yale considered its options. In January 1982, Howard Lamar, Dean of Yale College, wrote to a disgruntled English professor that he and David Henson, Dean of Student Affairs, were 'trying to find ways to return control of the *Lit* to a proper Yale constituency.'

What bureaucrat does not know that silence, not argument, is the stuff of political solutions? Obediently, the professors piped down.

Obediently, their students cooled it. But then, suddenly interrupting the silence, came the voice of Yale's master and judge. A single glimpse of the headline above the news article told me that the campus fight was now irrelevant, and that in the history of my family Barbara Epstein had succeeded where Golda Meir had failed.

YALE LIT'S NEW TONE: TO SOME MELLIFLUOUS, TO OTHERS STRIDENT
Special to The New York Times.

It began by observing the stage conventions set down in the *Hartford Courant*. After a bow from the reporter, by now almost obligatory, in the direction of the Old Lady in Brown, Sinclair Lewis and the rest, the curtain went up on the familiar 'Gothic grey campus':

> The change began in 1978 when the financially troubled magazine was sold to Andrei Navrozov, a Yale alumnus who turned the modest undergraduate publication into a handsome journal with a national circulation. Now, Mr. Navrozov and his creation have become the center of a literary and political squall.
>
> To his admirers, Mr. Navrozov, 25 years old, is a man of exceptional vision publishing a magazine that not only strives for truth, but, as one eager supporter put it, 'contains truth itself.' To others, however, he is 'an intellectual thug' and right-wing iconoclast who has shattered a prized and venerable tradition.

At first I thought that my eyes were playing tricks on me. But through the cloak of theatrical objectivity, worn by every *New York Times* journalist from Walter Duranty to Harrison Salisbury, any urbane reader of the news article was sure to perceive a gentle slant. The *New York Times* was siding with the *Lit*!

> The *Lit* is published in an old gray stone building on a hill overlooking the campus. [Charming, simply charming!] On a cold day last week, a fire was going in the hearth. [Charming, and how very Yale!] Mr. Navrozov, a lithe man with a boyish face and a shock of wavy black hair, chain-smoked cigarettes and talked about his mission. [Charming, intense, and so terribly literary!] 'In this country, there is a cultural desert, and this desert has a political

coloring: it is left-wing,' he said. 'In this sense we are anti-left-wing. We are going to create an oasis.'

Even the quote was accurate. 'You see, President Giamatti,' I could now laugh as my father had laughed in Vnukovo, 'relationships with power are not always reciprocal. You may love the wield, but it does not return your affections. I hate the wield, but apparently it loves me in return.'

> His critics insist that the issue is simple. Should an 'outsider' – that is, someone who is not an undergraduate – own and run a publication that is recognized by the university as an undergraduate organization? Should he, they add, be allowed to use the Yale name and alumni lists to solicit funds when most of the material in the magazine comes from professionals off campus.
>
> That, at least, is the public cry. Privately, these same people talk about Mr. Navrozov's politics, his 'raucous, antiliberal, new cold war' politics.

Now it was the turn of the student Woodwards and Bernsteins to defend their professional reputation. Had they been telling the truth without fear or favour, in the aristocratic tradition which some day would be theirs to carry on amid the splendour of the kingdom so mouthwateringly described by Gay Talese, or were they plebeian rabble-rousers, insensible to First Amendment absolutes upon which the kingdom stood? It was a provocation worthy of the pseudotsargod. When Russian writers gathered in his presence to discuss 'socialist realism', they wanted to please him by talking Marx. 'Comrades,' he said, 'if you spend your time talking Marx, you will have none left for writing.' A mortified silence. Who would argue? Here, unbelievably, they began to argue. A letter to the Editor, signed by the little Liberal Levich and the little Conserva-tive Frum, 'respectively, an editor and a columnist for the *Yale Daily News*', appeared in the next day's edition:

> In 1978 *The Yale Literary Magazine* was misappropriated from its duly constituted board by legal chicanery. Your news article quite erroneously implies that this action has saved the magazine and that all criticism of the magazine in its new incarnation is politically motivated. This is untrue.

Oh, Levich! I thought. Oh, Frum! I pity you. How can you fling ugly words like 'erroneous' or 'untrue' in the face of your master and judge? In the face – and may I be forgiven my bluntness – of power? Was it an error in your youthful eyes to replace Ezhov with Beria at the head of the secret police? Was it untrue that Tukhachevsky was a Nazi spy? Did you doubt that enemy agents were everywhere, derailing trains and poisoning the water supply? Did you think, perhaps, that it was a tragic miscarriage of justice when Zinoviev and Kamenev were shot for the assassination of Kirov, or when his real assassins, Pyatakov and Radek, were shot afterwards? Did you weep for Bukharin as the hellish machine dragged him under? Were you surprised to hear that Shostakovich produced chaos instead of music? Or that the Poles at Katyn had been killed by Germans? Was it really just a fib that Jewish murderers in white coats had been plotting on behalf of imperialist aggression? Was it untrue? Then for Heaven's sake, why was it that when all these errors were later exposed by those who had committed them, you and your kind nodded dutifully over your favourite newspaper, murmuring that the truth is out at last? Oh, Levich! Oh, Frum! You are about to discover that life is not always a Yale game, with you on the *New York Times* team and your opponents where they belong, on the team of the *Lunatic Fringe Gazette*. You thought you were winning? *They can change the rules.* I pity you, really I do, I pity you at least as deeply as Orwell pitied the learned bore. There he was, remember, the archetypal, aboriginal learned bore. On the right team and everything. Humming a happy tune.

> When the sons of Hegel break through the line,
> Our team will never fail!
> Marx and Engels! Bow, wow, wow!

Dialectical materialism? Why, he knew it like the back of his hand. Literary criticism? Pasternak and Mandelstam had better be there, scribbling notes, when he lectured. Military theory? Sure. Take Warsaw, capture Berlin? No problem. But then the bore fell afoul of the pseudotsargod who, unbeknown to him, was everyone's master and judge upon this imperfectly dialectical earth. Made a little mistake, you might say. Strutted. Talked back. Everybody knows how it all ended. And here you are, two sycophants, polishing apples and whistling Yale, or Marx, or psychoanalysis, or Eldridge Cleaver, or whatever happens to be the banality of the moment, and then you make a little mistake. Why is it a mistake? Because the *conservative New*

York Times, your master and judge, wants President Giamatti to know that it is his master and judge too. Power, do you understand, power has spoken. Do not protest your innocence. And on your way out, please remember to hand over your Kremlin dining hall passes.

33

In January 1982, a new and fabulously wealthy private foundation with a policy arm called the Institute for Educational Affairs sponsored a conference on 'student publishing' whose proceedings became the subject of an article in *The Nation*. Although the Olin Foundation, directly as well as through the Institute, had made donations to the magazine, it was not among our best-loved sponsors, for the most part reclusive eccentrics in the wilds of the American West and South who sent us money out of the innate sense that somehow, somewhere out there, where people cared about such things, it would make the sort of trouble they liked to see, if only to be reminded, as they were likely to put it, that this is still a free country. 'I hate Yale, despise literature and never read magazines' was the characteristic response of one Yale alumnus rung up by *The Yale Literary Magazine*. He gave $10,000. That was precisely the kind of support we courted, because obviously it would never have occurred to a Texas oilman to protest that a poem by Michael Schmidt failed to express whatever political sentiments he had paid us good money to convey. By contrast, Olin's administrators had already begun encroaching on our editorial freedom, and every bit as brazenly, or so it seemed at the time, as Yale's. One afternoon I received a telephone call from Michael Joyce, the foundation's director, during which he let it be known in no uncertain terms that unless the *Lit* shared with him the names of its eccentric sponsors, further support for the magazine from his foundation, 'as well as from our whole conservative network', as he phrased it, would become problematic. I balked, out of nothing more than a sense of fair play. A lily-petal page cost us $1,000. I had not taken a penny in salary since the launch. The very important official with tens of millions of dollars at the end of a pen was trying to blackmail the editor of a shoestring literary magazine into surrendering its independence, what on earth for? 'What on earth for?' I asked him, dry-mouthed. 'What's the matter,' countered the official, audibly irritated, 'don't you want to help the cause?' 'What cause?' I hung on, naïvely. 'Well, the conservative cause!' came the inevitable reply, as it had come to my father from the lips of the New York judge. 'But the *New York Times* is now *conservative* too,' I mumbled, with Salisbury's book in mind. The important official rang off, leaving me mystified and more than a little uneasy. At about that time, as it happened, Mary was recruited to Olin as one of the foundation's programme officers, and immediately pumped for any information she had 'on how the *Lit* worked'. Apparently Joyce refused to believe that the reason our magazine 'worked' was that all the money we earned or raised went into producing it, rather than into the pockets of its directors. Acting as a kind of double agent, Mary went on to reveal that her employer had been hatching plans for a new literary magazine patterned on ours, 'with the difference', she added with her inimitably Teutonic sadness, 'that Joyce is going to run it himself'. Soon thereafter the *New Criterion*, financed by Olin, began publication. The veteran *New York Times* critic, Hilton Kramer, was appointed editor, presumably the better to teach Joyce and the rest of his emergent 'conservative network' how to reject a bottle of vintage wine at the Oak Room of the Plaza with the aristocratic insouciance to which they were beginning to get accustomed. The faint suspicion I had had all along, that should the 'conservatives' seize the collective eminences occupied by the 'liberals' nothing would change save the names of the occupants, was proving excessively optimistic, because now it appeared that even the names would stay the same. Salisbury's conversion was not an anecdotal fluke, a piece of political *trompe-l'œil* which only the *New York Times* could palm off on the faithful, but something in the nature of a vicious circle, a *perpetuum mobile* of self-stratification and self-adulation. I remembered what Rozanov wrote of the civil unrest with which this century began in Russia, and which the 'bolsheviks' would later claim was a 'dress rehearsal' for their 'revolution':

How do I regard my 'almost revolutionary' infatuation of 190 . . . no, from 1897 to 1906?

It was right.

The *repulsive* in man begins with self-contentment.

And then the self-contented were the officials.

After that the revolutionaries became self-contented. And I began to hate *them*.

But Joyce's attempt at blackmail in the name of the 'cause' in which he presumed I had enlisted was only the beginning. Olin was a 'neoconservative' presence, this new term intended to distinguish the *Commentary* strain of intellectual claimants to the spoils of Reagan's populist success from the older 'conservative' strain of *National Review*. From *The Nation*'s coverage of the Institute for Educational Affairs conference it emerged that during the past year both strains had turned their attention to 'student publishing', and that the *Lit*, like an exotic bird accustomed to sylvan solitude finding itself in a wire-mesh coop full of pigeons and ducks, was now part of a political trend:

> Conservative students have long been out of favor on campuses, and only the recent ascendancy of conservatives to national power has alleviated their ostracism. As a result, the conference took on the atmosphere of an exile's return. Participants talked far less about the nuts and bolts of putting out a newspaper than they did about plans for uprooting the liberal orthodoxy they see as still entrenched.

The Nation, which hovered at the other end of the political spectrum for generations and could not aspire to the ecumenical loftiness of the *New York Times*, spoke with unconcealed horror of 'some thirty conservative university-affiliated newspapers now being published'. The first, the *Dartmouth Review*, became 'the puckish mascot of the New Right' when, during a fast called by Oxfam, 'it picked up the tab for a champagne and lobster brunch to which the whole campus was invited'. *Counterpoint*, at the University of Chicago, 'was started by John Podhoretz, son of *Commentary* editor Norman Podhoretz'. There were also the *Harvard Salient*, the *Madison Report* at Princeton, and threats or promises of similar ventures throughout the Ivy League. Not only did the *Lit* scandal feature prominently among these, but the cartoon animating the article in the tradition of Kukryniksy drawings for *Pravda* showed a fat capitalist in a black shiny topper and striped trousers m-m-mes-m-m-merizing a copy of the *Lit* on thin and pitifully proletarian legs, Svengalian magnetism suggested by wavy lines streaming from the outstretched fingers of the Bourgeois Exploiter who is also, if *Pravda* circa 1937 or 1952 is more accurate than *Pravda* circa 1917 or 1942, the Jew Mason. So it was not unexpected when a Party of the Right friend of a friend of mine dropped by the *Lit* office with the idea of starting a paper at Yale along the lines of those sponsored by the Institute. Charlie's father was Robert Bork, widely touted as the next in line to become a Supreme Court Justice of the United States. The Party of the Right, which alone in the Ivy League had been cultivating the attitude of embattled ostentation since the 1960s, was the ideal launching pad for an enterprise like the *Dartmouth Review*. Charlie had already met with the Institute's trustees, and the first issue would come out in October. I was delighted. The *Yale Free Press*, as Charlie's paper was called, would give the *Yale Daily News* a run for the money. More important, its very existence would help to differentiate the *Lit* from the 'conservative network' in the ascendant, dispelling the impression that the *Lit* was an answer to the prayers of Podhoretz's 'neoconservatives', or a political manoeuvre devised by Buckley's 'conservatives' way back when I was almost stillborn among the lice.

34

While I was busy shadow-boxing with the people who everyone else seemed to think were my political allies, a left hook laid me out in all earnest. The blow came from where I might have expected it to come, what with the knowing looks on professorial faces in College Street, the deafening silence that followed the campaign against the magazine and the jesuitical public behaviour of the University administration. I suppose I had been relying on the *New York Times*, which seemed to have said the last word on the conflict between the mellifluous and the strident. The final quotation in the news article was from the University Secretary, who said: 'I've been around here for twenty-five years, and I remember when the *Yale Daily News* was a Maoist collective. This too shall pass.' The world-weary remark seemed to suggest that the administrators had put their trust in natural entropy, and that the University would leave us alone until we got tired, as young people do, of putting up barricades and printing subversive rubbish. If so, it was a deliberately wrong signal, because by the end of April a decision had at last been taken to suppress the magazine using quietly administrative rather than openly legal means. With cool detachment in place of visible glee, and without so much as a passing reference to the *Lit*, the *Yale Daily News* announced that a 'Manual for Registered Undergraduate Organizations' would be taking effect in the autumn. Everything fell into place. Did I not promise the good Dean that the *Lit* would abide by the innocently vague undergraduate regulations, for fear that my unscrupulous successors-in-interest might put a nude Miss Freshman on the cover in the photogenic company of the famous bulldog? So I did, and now, just like every other snivelling little Liber-al and pompous little Conserva-tive, I was about to discover that life was not always a Yale game. I thought they were losing? *They can change the rules.* Or at least they were about to try. Although the Secretary, the various Deans, the Office of the General Counsel and all the President's men had been working with the newly reinstituted Committee on Undergraduate Organizations since November to weave a net so fine that the renegade in their midst could not escape, initially they appeared to have overdone it, because even the housebroken student council objected that the 'new regulations' of the draft Manual were 'either too ambiguous or too extensive'. In fact, if enforced, the new rules would have precluded the *Yale Daily News* from advertising, the Yale Political Union from fundraising and WYBC Yale Radio from broadcasting. But the general thrust of the administrative initiative was clear. The new rules had been devised to prevent the *Lit* under my editorship from 'registering' as an 'undergraduate organization'. By the autumn the holes in the net would be enlarged, either formally, in the published final version of the Manual, or informally, by exempting all the other organizations which the Manual inadvertently affected. The helplessly thrashing phoenix would then be hauled in for processing into tinned dogfood. I'd been had. If I did not figure out how to get my firebird through the nylon meshing, come September I might as well not bother.

35

September came and I knew that my paranoid foreboding was right when the *Yale Daily News* announced that 'this year, for the first time, Associate Dean for Student Affairs David Henson will hold a meeting with leaders of Yale's many undergraduate organizations to explain the rules that govern their activities'. Lest a paranoid mind should read an unprecedented assault on diversity into the inexplicable fact that the explanation was being proffered 'for the first time' in the two hundred and eighty-first year of Yale's existence, the announcement went on, deadpan:

> This year many of the regulations appeared in writing for the first time, although Henson stressed that they had been in effect as unwritten laws for years.

A further piece of news, which would have been hilarious but for its lethal significance as far as the *Lit*'s future was concerned, was that Charlie's newspaper had been invited by the University Secretary, John Wilkinson, to 'register' with the Office of the Secretary:

> Because the newspaper is not staffed entirely by undergraduates, it had to register with Wilkinson's office rather than with Associate Dean for Student Affairs David Henson, who handles undergraduate organizations. The *Yale Free Press* managing board includes four undergraduates, one law student, one graduate student and one alumnus.

Obviously the *Lit* could not 'register' as anything other than an 'undergraduate' organization for the simple reason that I had promised, legally and in good faith, that it would do just that. One might think that a self-proclaimed right-wing scourge of commie pinko lefties everywhere like the *Yale Free Press* would have trouble getting accreditation from a university whose president had vowed that the redneck menace stops at the Porter Gate. Instead, such accreditation was thrust upon Charlie Bork by special invitation from the university, and this despite an angry *Yale Daily News* reminder that his father was the man of Watergate fame who

> worked for Nixon. Not only did Dad work for Nixon, Dad *fired* that impudent Archibald Cox when that wimp Elliot Richardson got cold feet. Your father is the ultimate Cox Sacker.

But the professors who wanted to suffocate the *Lit* did not mind if a paper at Yale threw a champagne and lobster brunch to disrupt an Oxfam fast. Barbara Epstein did not mind if a *Lunatic Fringe Gazette* was published with the word 'Yale' in its title. President Giamatti did not mind if the Party of the Right declared itself a Yale chapter of the

Moral Majority. It was the *Lit* they wanted to pacify, because the wars between little Conserva-tives and little Liber-als, like those between the *National Review* 'commies' and the *New York Times* 'fascists', were not wars but episodes in a struggle for power among corporate men, a soap opera of the intellect that could only incite the freethinker to Nietzschean denunciations of both its good and its evil, its heroes and its villains. The *Lit*, an upstart with a pedigree, was different. An outsider on the inside, it challenged the corporate model of The Game whose rules were laid down by the sponsors, insisting that outside the incestuous microcosm of civilization's culture, life isn't like that. It wanted war for war's sake, out of its editor's paranoid belief that truth, at any rate any terrestrial truth worth discovering, is born of the war of opinions, tastes or caprices, a war that is waged in earnest by whatever combatants it may please to enter the lists, with whatever weapons. And, not coincidentally, such war was precisely what the administrative measures of the new Manual were devised to prevent, by bundling up the dissenter into a straitjacket of corporate regulation introduced for the first time in the one hundred and sixty years of his magazine's and two hundred and eighty years of his university's existence. It was obvious, therefore, that the only hope of escape was to kick and scream bloody murder, as Mother had kicked and screamed in the middle of the Garden Ring when my birth was about to be similarly institutionalized. The difficulty was that by incorporating the magazine I had infected myself, as it were, with the institutional virus, and now that dormant contagion was upon me. Now I had no choice but to engage a lawyer, because as a director of a corporation I could not make use of Father's loophole to argue my case '*pro se*'. I hired the first ambulance-chaser who came along, asked him to prepare a court injunction to prevent the university from imposing its new rules on the magazine, and got ready to yell bloody murder in the form, favoured by dissidents since times immemorial, of an open letter to the authority most likely to claim that the canvas straitjacket in its hand is only a nurse's starched apron.

36

From the Office of the Dean I had already received a printed copy of the Manual, which was in the nature of a manifesto. Translated from its Dickensian bureaucratese and legalese, the message of the manifesto was Down with Rolls-Royce-driving Wall Street Magnates who Have Robbed the Students, the Only True Owner of *The Yale Literary Magazine*. Needless to say, the manifesto did not mention the magazine by name, because when John Doe must be hanged, the *ad hoc* law condemns *all* fair-haired men taller than 6'4" and residing in the shire where poor dumb John is the only fair-haired man that tall. 'If the full title of the organization includes the word "Yale" but does not identify it as an organization of students', ran the ominous wording of one of the manifesto's *ad hoc* laws, 'then the organization's publicity should state that fact.' The *Lit* did have the word 'Yale' in its *full* title. What a coincidence! *Ipso facto* it was henceforth to be known as 'an organization of students' rather than of those Wall Street magnates. But I was no longer a student when I bought the *Lit*, and could not now become a student retroactively any more than Kipling could. When the *Communist Manifesto* announced in 1848 that the Capitalists must be expropriated, a 'capitalist' knew that in the end he could at least go to work in a factory as an ordinary workman, and thus join the Proletarians. But for me to join the Students was impossible. Besides, even if I had re-enrolled as a freshman, just in time to hear President Giamatti's denunciation of the Moral Majority, in another few years I would have to re-enrol again, and all for the sake of belonging to the exalted revolutionary estate. Woe to those who are not the Students. Woe to the hundred-and-sixty-year-old magazine which must change its name to incorporate the sacred revolutionary word. The manifesto was stern as it gave examples of prescribed new names:

'The Weekly – A Publication of Yale College Students' or 'The Yale Backgammon Club – An Association of Yale College Students.' Permission to continue to use the Yale name is contingent upon maintaining the above and conforming to the regulations applicable to the organization.

All power to the Students, thundered the manifesto. 'Under the leadership of undergraduates', on the first page. 'Must be initiated and controlled by Yale College students' on the next page. 'In the hands of undergraduates' on the page after.

> Only registered students in good standing of Yale College can hold office or act on behalf of an organization in any official way.

On the last page:

> In keeping with the requirements that administrative, policy and managerial decisions are to be in the hands of undergraduates, decisions about the contents of each periodical, the editorial policy and the business policies and practices are to be made by Yale College students.

But why was All Power at *The Yale Literary Magazine*, founded sixty-six years before the very name 'Yale University' became official and forty years before the first Ph.D. degree in the United States was conferred, to pass to the Students and their professors all of a sudden? Was All Power at the Yale President's Office to pass to the Students as well? It did once, a decade earlier, when Giamatti's predecessor, President Kingman Brewster, faced in May 1970 what he later recalled as the 'invasion of New Haven by a horde of outside agitators bent upon burning Yale down'. What did *he* do then? Did *he* make a thunderous enemy-at-the-gates speech like Giamatti and write a set of new house rules aimed at excluding the interlopers? And was *I* an 'intellectual thug' as the *New York Times* put it, or a real criminal, threatening to soak the university in petrol and set it alight? No, President Brewster 'adopted a strategy of trust', as he declared in the University Annual Report for 1972. He refused to 'assume that all protesters were maliciously motivated'. Indeed, who is maliciously motivated in the twentieth century? Surely Pol Pot exterminated half of the population of Cambodia for his selfless love of the other half. The week before May Day, studies at Yale were suspended, so that the 'outside agitators' like Abbie Hoffman and Jerry Rubin could address the Students without the irritating interruption of university lectures. The university bureaucracy provided the 'outside agitators' with all the facilities and even funds they needed for their activities, because Yale now belonged to Abbie, Jerry and their comrades. Said the *de facto* President Hoffman, speaking at Ezra Stiles:

There's no such thing as a revolutionary culture without revolutionary politics. Work – W+O+R+K – is a dirty, four-letter word.
There ain't no work worth doin' out there in desolation row . . . We
gotta destroy the Protestant Ethic as well as capitalism, racism,
imperialism – that's gotta go too.

Speaking in Woolsey Hall, the *de facto* Secretary Rubin announced
that since all schools were concentration camps by another name,
Yale must be 'closed down for ever', a statement which the Moral
Majority might like to print verbatim if not for the fact that much of
it was unprintable. Later that week, in his sermon at Battell Chapel,
Chaplain William Sloane Coffin said that the surrender of Yale was 'a
Christian job'. 'We practised Christianity', Revd Coffin summed up.
The Master of one of the residential colleges, Master Trinkaus of
Branford, was even more positive:

Thanks largely to our effort, Yale is now in the vanguard of a great
movement in this country. This is one of the greatest events in this
college's history.

The vanguard of the great movement did not in the end burn down
Yale because the National Guard were not far away. There were only
what one might call revolutionary episodes. In Branford, the college
buttery was axed. Fires were started here and there, as in the Yale
Law Library, but all were put out by firemen after 'only books' had
burned. A bomb in Ingalls Rink went off, but did not kill anyone by
accident, and certainly no one would have been so churlish as to recall
serious injury or mutilation, considering the revolutionary greatness
of the moment. No, President Giamatti was much tougher than his
predecessor. I could see that he was going to brave my wrath as he
had braved the wrath of the Moral Majority, taking a stand where
many lesser men might have quaked in their booties. He was not
going to allow Yale to be intimidated and held to ransom by the
horde of outside agitators led by that thug Navrozov, no matter how
many Molotov cocktails they hurled at him. Still, I had no choice but
to try.

225

37

The aim of my open letter was threefold, I would almost say
dialectical. It was to introduce the protagonist. Then, rather than use
the standard polemical tactic and indict an antagonist, it was to
identify, and defend, the antagonist's victim. In so doing, it was to
present what to a stranger's glass eye might well look like a storm in
a teacup as a microcosm of the decline of civilization, which I saw
it to be as plainly as if Doré had lived long enough to illustrate
Spengler. Privately I abhorred and might wish to transcend, as the *Lit*
under my editorship transcended, any partisan labels attaching to the
good and the evil of the moment. Yet I knew that to all but a tiny
minority of my prospective readers, these labels represented realities
too habitual to be questioned. The letter was a cry of bloody murder,
and help would only come if I could convincingly relate the reader's
conventional conception of political reality to my own predicament,
political in only the broadest sense. 'Dear Dr Giamatti', ran the
preamble,

> Some sixty years ago in Russia, Evgeny Zamyatin – whose *We*
> anticipated George Orwell's *Nineteen Eighty-Four* by several decades
> – wrote an appeal which he entitled 'I Am Afraid'. If I were to give
> a title to this letter of mine, it would be the words of Zamyatin: 'I
> Am Afraid'.
>
> What was Zamyatin afraid of? He told my grandfather, then a
> young writer: 'Though I happen to be a Russian Marxist, I dread a
> society in which everyone must be a Russian Marxist.' Orwell could
> well have said: 'Though I happen to be an English Socialist, I dread
> a society in which everyone must be an English Socialist.'
>
> Paraphrasing, I could say today: 'Even if I were an American
> liberal Democrat, I would dread a society in which everyone must
> be an American liberal Democrat'.
>
> Indeed, even if I were an American liberal Democrat, I would be
> terrified by the fact that the largest periodical supporting the
> Republican Party in the United States is a weekly with a circulation
> of fifty thousand. If this is the scale of dissent in the press by one of
> the country's two major political parties, what hope is there for a
> lesser social group in this boundless sea of conformity?

Like any individual, I have my own political creed. Individuals with similar political creeds, such as immigrants from one country in another, have been known to form their own political parties and send their elected representatives to the legislature. In the United States this is impossible: we have a two-party system, the idea being that vigorous daily debate between the media of the two parties is so diversified that all political creeds can be heard.

But where is this vigorous daily debate in the media? Is it the 'debate' between the liberal Democrat giants, reaching all decision-makers through the quality press and the entire population through television, and several conservative Republican dwarfs?

My family left Russia in search of the freedom to dissent. Not in search of wealth: we belonged to the country's wealthiest. Not in search of physical freedom: we lived in splendid seclusion, and I never even attended school. It is the freedom of public dissent, called also the freedom of the press, that we sought.

But here we find many liberal Democrats who do not dread a society in which everyone must be a liberal Democrat. Quite the contrary. Even those among them who are exemplary conformists espousing a vast and practically unchallenged conformity in all spheres of national culture, from daily television news to academic scholarship, often behave as though they are heroic fighters for freedom of the press pitted against overwhelming odds. Thoroughly politicized, they pose as nonpartisan truth-seekers, always weighing everything and everyone on the scales of absolute impartiality. The weaker the dissent against them, the more jealously they want to destroy even its last vestiges.

After a recapitulation of what viewers of television drama know as the story so far, I turned to Giamatti's aptly named sermon on 'Liberal Education and the New Coercion'. For the first time in my life I was writing, as it were, in public. The pages of the *Lit* were just too expensive, as everyone who worked alongside me on the magazine agreed, for any of us to attempt anything of the kind.

The opening five paragraphs of your Address consist of the most general generalities to which practically every major institution of the twentieth century can subscribe, from the League of Nations to the National Socialist Workers' Party of Germany, the Communist

Party USA, the World Council of Churches, the Editorial Board of the *New York Times* and the Society for the Prevention of Cruelty to Animals.

You are for 'values that make us civilized'. For being 'responsive to the new'. For being 'tough-minded and open-hearted'. For the 'quest for truth'. For the 'whole person'. For 'reasoned judgement and humanity'.

You are 'for the freedom to assert the liberty of the mind to make itself new for the others it cherishes'. You are for law and order:

> The order necessary to keep that freedom from collapsing into merely competitive appetites or colliding gusts of anarchy is, first, in this country, a respect for law and the process of law. But it is also more than an order external; it is the internalized order that grows with self-government, self-civilizing. Order is the precondition of humane freedom, freedom the goal of responsible order.

The most general generality of these declarations stems from the fact that in the twentieth century all powerful institutions, no matter what they do or ever did, have been proclaiming liberation, freedom, genuine freedom, actual democracy, social democracy, humanism, peace, progress, altruism, justice, order, internalized order, and everything else their officials could find in dictionaries. Similarly, many such institutions have proclaimed the existence of the Enemy who stands for the antonyms of these words.

At the end of your preamble, we do discover the existence of such an Enemy:

> I have said what I believe because there are now in America powerful voices which attack and will continue to attack these very ideas I have raised.

But who in the twentieth century would attack these most general generalities of the twentieth century?

Yet there is such an Enemy, and the Enemy is apparently at the gates of Yale, since the rest of your Address is devoted to denouncing the Enemy and explaining how to overcome its power, cunning and cruelty.

My first guess as to who the Enemy was went to the following sentence from the University Annual Report for 1972 by your predecessor, Yale President Kingman Brewster:

> The critical test, of course, was the invasion of New Haven
> by a horde of outside agitators bent upon 'burning Yale
> down' in May of 1970.

Was a horde about to invade Yale again, with the intention of
burning it down?

My second guess was that you meant the totalitarian global war-
power which calls itself 'communism' and which is presently
advancing, with the inexorability of a chess game, on the Middle
East, Africa and Central America. But this was unfashionable, and I
am used to the fact that the political beliefs of many Americans
depend, like skirts or watches, on the fashion of the moment.

So my third guess was that the Enemy must be the Devil. A
university president's address devoted to the Devil's snares is also
old-fashioned, of course, yet who else could be threatening the
United States and Yale? But the Enemy proved to be the Moral
Majority:

> A self-proclaimed 'Moral Majority' and its satellite or client
> groups, cunning in the use of a native blend of old intimi-
> dation and new technology, threaten the values I have named.

Perhaps, Dr Giamatti, you did after all mean the Devil? Was not
the Moral Majority another name for the Devil you wanted to
exorcise from the souls of Yale men, for no other presence of the
Moral Majority was in evidence? Those hordes, to which President
Brewster referred, intended to burn down Yale. But the Devil's
hosts lay their siege ever so more subtly! Their intimidation is
invisible to the naked eye, nor is it detectable by any scientific
device. The Devil's hosts

> threaten through political pressure or public denunciation
> whoever dares to disagree with their authoritarian position.

Political pressure? How *do* they do it? By means of the *New York
Times* and the rest of the liberal Democrat media *you* can exercise
political pressure outside Yale. Through your subordinates you can
exercise even greater political pressure inside Yale, such as the
pressure you have brought upon the university to destroy *The Yale
Literary Magazine*.

But the only political pressure the Moral Majority can exercise is
to vote or not to vote for certain presidential and congressional
candidates. Do you consider this illegal or immoral? Are they

obliged to vote the way you do? Are you suggesting their disenfranchisement? Perhaps those 'hordes of outside agitators' who intended to burn down Yale should burn their houses if they dare to vote?

Public denunciation? But again, *you* have far more opportunities, in terms of mass communications, to denounce them than they to denounce you. You made your Address into a public denunciation of the Moral Majority, and off it went into the major, that is liberal Democrat, news media. How can *they* denounce you in reply, or at least defend themselves on an equal footing?

> Using television, direct mail and economic boycott, they would sweep before them anyone who holds a different opinion.

But liberal Democrats of the 'major' news media have thousands of hours of television prime time every year, reaching tens of millions of viewers daily, and not only do these thousands of hours not cost them a cent, they bring them hundreds of millions of dollars in profits. Now, the Moral Majority has to scrape and save to buy a paltry half-hour of television time, and you proclaim that they sweep before them anyone who holds a different opinion!

By the same token it can be proclaimed that Moscow dissidents, who manage to circulate several typewritten pages, sweep before them the readers of *Pravda* and *Izvestia*.

Similarly, direct mail is used by those who are denied access to large-circulation news periodicals reaching national decision makers. Again, direct mail is infinitely less effective than such periodicals, and costs millions of dollars instead of bringing in millions of dollars in profits.

It is curious that your Moral Majority opponents have only to replace several words in your denunciation, and the result will be their denunciation of you and the liberal Democrat establishment in general. Thus you denounce the Moral Majority:

> From the maw of this 'morality' rise the tax-exempt Savon-arolas who believe they, and they alone, possess the truth. There is no debate, no discussion, no dissent. They know. There is only one set of overarching political and spiritual and social beliefs; whatever view does not conform to these views is, by definition, relativistic, negative, secular, immoral, against the family, anti-free enterprise, Un-American. What nonsense. What dangerous, malicious nonsense.

Replace the word 'morality' above with the word 'culture', and so on as below, and you will have:

> From the maw of this 'culture' rise the Lenins of media and academy who believe they, and they alone, possess the truth. There is no debate, no discussion, no dissent. They know. There is only one set of overarching political and spiritual and social beliefs; whatever view does not conform to these views, is by definition absolutistic, chauvinistic, bigoted, ugly, against progress, anti-intellectual, fascist. What nonsense. What dangerous, malicious nonsense.

Or you proclaim, for example:

> If pluralism as a concept denies anything, it denies the hegemony of the homogenous, the rule by a single, over-mastering sensibility which would exclude all those who are different from the general benefits of citizenship.

This your opponents can copy without a single word changed with the obvious implication that it is the liberal Democrats who have established a hegemony of the homogenous in the news media, academic institutions and even government bureaucracies where they vastly predominate no matter who is president. Or, to take another example, you declare:

> The issue is that a reactionary mood, preying on the fears of those who feel dispossessed by change and bypassed by complexity, is growing and that there is a moral imperative, rooted in America's best traditions, to identify it and call for a cleansing of the air.

Only the word 'reactionary' would have to be changed for 'decadent' or 'nihilistic'. But the expression 'cleansing the air' rather belongs to the vocabulary of your opposition, except that the latter would wish to cleanse the air of child pornography, and you mean to cleanse the air of Puritanism.

38

Wenn ich 'Kultur' höre, said a denizen of militarization who at least knew that Browning is also the name of a poet, *entsichere ich meinen Browning*. The rage building up within me ever since my first brush with diversity in Professor Rockmore's class was now breaking all dams. I was feeling dizzy at the thought of those years of silently endured hypocrisy. To think that these people actually had the temerity to raise the spectre of pornography, *Hustler*, as they lured me into their authoritarian trap! My God, no wonder Kate could not believe it. Kate, the girl who had come to work on the magazine in her freshman year and was still here in the office now, two years later, the quiet, upright girl from Louisville, Kentucky, whose lucid letters managed to get a breathtakingly intelligent essay out of Annie Dillard for the current issue. Kate, who went last spring to hear a poetess promoted by Professor Hollander, a naughty poetess who was also, deliciously, 'a horse and dog trainer', with a veterinarian's vocabulary and range of interests, and fainted, yes, Kate fainted in the middle of the animal trainer's recital, passed out, came round, then burst into tears, because down there in Kentucky people do not use such words even with intent to shock, Latin words that belong in a veterinarian's office, not that they do not know how to swear in Kentucky, not that she was some hysterical Southern belle, not that attendance at the recital was mandatory, but anyway she fainted. Though why pick on Kentucky? I had just been to visit an acquaintance of Igor's who collected his paintings, a wealthy, hard-headed dowager, living in isolation on her farm in Pennsylvania among the Amish.

> Indeed, some liberal Democrats are determined to cleanse the air of Puritanism, but is not Puritanism an American tradition older than Yale? I have met Americans who consider it sinful to use electric lights, automobiles or telephones, not to mention abominations like movies or television, to drink tea or coffee, or to wear any but the plainest homemade clothes, preferably black and without such diabolical devices as zippers. During their worship the segregated women wear veils and no musical instruments of any kind are allowed.
>
> To them, and there are hundreds of thousands of them in

America, the Moral Majority is almost as permissive as you are. They fled to America centuries ago precisely because they had been tracked down and persecuted for their Puritanism. Evidently, some were as intolerant of those who did not want to drink tea or coffee as of those who wished to believe that the earth revolves. Today this desire to kill anyone who looks askance at, say, child pornography or incest or Updike's novels is still curbed legally in this country, but I sense its volcanic roar underneath your reiterative grandiloquence about 'human and intellectual diversity'.

A contributor of ours told me of a curious scene he recently witnessed at a New York beach. Right next to a fenced-off nudist zone, which was empty, he saw a hundred or so girls of grammar school age, splashing in the water, laughing, shouting. To his astonishment, as the girls emerged ashore exhausted from happiness, he saw that all of them bathed in full school uniforms down to white cotton stockings and shoes. This was a summer camp, and the management believed that bathing suits, even of the kind worn in the nineteen-twenties, are indecent.

Imagine the reaction of these girls, their teachers and parents, to that unspeakable pornography which Professor Hollander calls poetry – and you, liberal education? They are not against Professor Hollander's private life: they are against such professors', writers' and journalists' public imposition of their private mores through libraries or television under the label of culture, liberal education, or whatever you choose to call it.

In a stray issue of a Moral Majority publication I read the opinion of one of the contributors that after Bach mankind has not produced music equal to Bach's, after Raphael any painting equal to Raphael's, and after Tolstoy any literature equal to Tolstoy's. No one compels anyone to agree with this opinion. But is this opinion any more monstrous, pernicious or dangerous than the opinion propounded by the liberal Democrat media and academy that John Updike's amateur ill-mannered hackwork is literature, that the sound of billiard balls thrown by tenured professors into a piano rivals Beethoven's sonatas, or that a fellow who has painted a rather ordinary full-length portrait of Hitler deserves a government grant because the portrait is 'ironic'?

The most tragicomic stroke of your denunciation of the Moral Majority is your invocation of Cardinal Newman to define what a liberal education is:

It is an education pursued, as Cardinal Newman believed, in a spirit that studies a subject simply for and in itself, without concern for the practical consequences of such study. That would be the description of the proper attitude to bring to your studies.

Sir: John Henry Newman lived in a society in which ordinary lay people did not like to refer to the legs of chairs and tables for their undesirably vulgar associations. And in that society he was an ascetic, living in a quasi-monastery of his own and preaching the return to the 'ancient and undivided Christianity of the Fathers'.

What worried John, aged fifteen? Here is a translation from the Latin of his diary entry: 'In a few days I must go home. Then Satan will leap upon me with new though familiar enticements. Give me strength so that I may defeat the world, the flesh and the Devil.'

Liberal education? In a sermon of September 1831, Cardinal Newman says that it makes us 'trifling and unmanly', for an 'elegant and polite education', according to him, 'separates feeling and acting'. Even an art describing the glory and beauty of Christian life is 'a strain and waste of moral strength'. 'We should never allow ourselves to read fiction or poetry, or to interest ourselves in the fine arts for the mere sake of the things themselves'. Sciences? The Cardinal warned against the fashionable pursuits of 'chemistry, geology and the like', for rain, wind, rivers and the sun are 'the work of Angels'.

Yet you invoke Cardinal Newman to castigate the Moral Majority! Imagine Cardinal Newman attending a 'poetry reading' organized by Professor Hollander here at Yale. He would have thought he stumbled into a Neapolitan brothel, because even today there are robust college students who could not physically endure such an ordeal by pornography. Fortunately for the Cardinal, he would have fainted after a minute of such liberal education.

Your invocation of Cardinal Newman reminds me of my own liberal education at Yale. When I was asked to describe Hegel's view of freedom according to his *Phenomenology of Mind*, and I honestly wrote that Hegel upheld serfdom, with copious citation in support of my thesis, Professor Thomas Rockmore was so indignant that he refused to accept the essay as though the quotations from Hegel were so many ink blots. Professor Rockmore wanted to believe that Hegel was an American liberal Democrat.

Instead of citing some of the Moral Majority opinions before castigating them, your Address suddenly blazes forth with the evils of Nazism and the Ku Klux Klan:

> In December of 1980, the Anti-Defamation League of B'nai B'rith stated that reported anti-Semitic episodes, including vandalism, arson and cemetery desecrations, increased by 192 per cent in 1980, from 129 episodes in 1979 to 377 in 1980. The tip of the iceberg grew in a way that sickened all decent Americans. In the past few years, the Ku Klux Klan has increased its visibility again and claims to have founded or revived, in its name or in league with others, its paramilitary camps and training activities.

But what has all this to do with the Moral Majority? The Moral Majority, you say, has 'licensed a new meanness of spirit in our land'! Yet is this not a charge one can safely level at any dissenting source of spiritual influence one wants to suppress?

In 1919, the Yale-in-China Association's magazine launched the magazine's editor, Mao Tse-tung, on his political career. Up to the late 1970s, Mao was whitewashed or eulogized by the liberal Democrat media. After his Chinese successors exposed him, however, even the American media had to recognize that Mao's regime was more regimented than Stalin's or Hitler's. Let us conclude from this that Yale not only 'licensed a new meanness of spirit in the land', but also helped to rear the greatest mass murderer in history.

Do I rule out the origin and growth of powerful fascism in the United States? On the contrary, I believe that if the liberal Democrat monopoly on culture continues, the *real* growth of this *real* monster is inevitable. The more the liberal Democrat monopoly on culture smears as fascist or Nazi, the way you do, anyone who dissents or disagrees with their truth, the greater the likelihood that *real* fascists or Nazis will originate and grow in number and become powerful enough to smash – by *real* force, by *real* violence, by *real* coercion, by *real* intimidation – the liberal Democrat monopoly on culture.

The monopoly is not expressive of the views held by all Americans – or President Reagan would not have been elected. Yet the monopoly wants to speak for the American people, for all people on earth, for all mankind. It thus imposes its views on all American people regardless of their will. This is coercion, Sir, under the camouflage of the monopoly's endless grandiloquence about the freedom of the press and the quest for truth.

And coercion breeds coercion. Every day in the existence of the monopoly brings fascism or Nazism closer to your door. Neither your Address nor any other manifestations of liberal Democrat culture take notice of the *real* dangers to the United States, such as the latest measures of Soviet militarization. But these *real* dangers exist, they will *really* grow, they will produce *real* fear, and on this fear *real* fascists or Nazis will capitalize.

Your suggestion that your political opponents are by implication fascists or Nazis does not stave off *real* fascism or Nazism. On the contrary, this 'crying wolf' on the part of the liberal Democrat establishment for political purposes of its own merely brings *real* wolves a step nearer.

You create the impression that the Moral Majority *is* the National Socialist Party, and the National Socialist Party *is* at the gates of Yale, with only your heroic Address to keep them at bay:

> This is not a community that will tolerate the sexism, the racism, the anti-Semitism, the bigotry about ethnic groups, the hysterical rejection of others, the closing off and closing in, that is now in the air. The spirit that sends hate mail, paints swastikas on walls, burns crosses, bans books – vandalizes minds – has no place here.

The Enemy is at the gates! The Students of Yale must therefore

> have the courage to reject hysteria and coercion in all forms and have the courage to embrace the intellectual and human diversity of our community and our country.

The country has evidently forsaken the Students of Yale, fighting their titanic battle to the tunes of your lone bugle:

> What a shame such denials of our country's deepest traditions of freedom of thought, speech, creed and choice are not faced candidly in open debate by our political and religious leaders.

Apart from everything else, you have an interesting understanding of the word 'debate'. The Moral Majority has challenged you to a debate, and you have refused the challenge. A 'debate' is when you, or the *New York Times*, or *Time* magazine do all the talking, while those who dissent or disagree must be silent because they are reactionary or absolutistic or coercive, or simply unworthy of a debate with you.

Through rose-tinted glasses, your Address can be seen as an idyll. You shared with the freshmen your thoughts on liberal education. Struck by the newness, originality and wisdom of your thoughts, the major news media responded at once. Since Yale students and professors were also overwhelmed by these profound thoughts, their only reaction was a petition to support you.

With the rose-tinted glasses off, the matter looks quite different.

The Moral Majority is an important voting asset of conservative Republicans. You took advantage of these freshmen – after several banalities about freedom, education and Cardinal Newman – to make a zealously partisan political speech actually aimed against conservative Republicans, and the liberal Democrat media publicized it with no less zealous partisanship. Whether you did it because you want to use Yale as the springboard for a political career is irrelevant: your Address *is* a political speech hinged on your own ambition.

Now, sociologically, a university is a bureaucratic hierarchy where the students depend to some extent on their professors, and the professors, not to mention the other employees, on the apex of the hierarchy. By taking such a partisan stand intended to undermine conservative Republicans, you *coerce* the whole hierarchy into your political zealotry. The freshmen started a petition in support of their beloved President Giamatti? This is what many low-rung members of bureaucracies all over the world do, whether their boss has made a communist, an ecological or an anti-Semitic speech.

And if you think nothing of coercing Yale University into your political zealotry, small wonder that your subordinates have been coercing us in order to destroy our magazine as a source of cultural and political dissent. If, for the sake of ambition, you could take advantage of some freshmen to smite conservative Republicans, what chance does our magazine stand in your blatantly political game?

I conclude with a glimpse of the idyll you have painted:

> Yale is a diverse, open place, receptive to people from throughout our society, and it must and will remain so. It is a University community given to the competition of ideas

and of merit, devoted to excellence and dedicated to the belief that freedom of choice, speech, and creed is essential to the quest for truth that constitutes its mission. Those who wish such a place to teach only their version of the 'right' values and 'correct' views misunderstand completely the free market of ideas that is a great university; they misapprehend the intent to which the University serves the country best when it is a cauldron of competing ideas and not a neatly arranged platter of received opinions.

The experience of three generations of my family indicates that the more colorfully such idylls are painted, the bleaker the reality underneath, and the more dangerous the painter.

39

LIT SUES UNIVERSITY was the exclusive scoop for Charlie Bork's *Yale Free Press*, given advance notice of the court action on the condition that it publish the unabridged text of my open letter. The syndicated columnist James Kilpatrick, whose column was then carried by the *Washington Post*, was the first to pick up the story: BROUHAHA AT YALE. The 'conservative' columnist reiterated the word 'conservative' to describe the *Lit* and its embattled owners, despite the fact that throughout my open letter I had deployed the deliberately clumsy adjectives of political partisanship, 'liberal Democrat' and 'conservative Republican', to distance myself from the appositional neatness of Left and Right. But if the object of the exercise was to break the silence surrounding the impending arrest of the *Lit* at any price, obviously the letter had done the trick. 'It is not a pretty piece of business', wrote Kilpatrick,

Giamatti distinguished himself a year ago with a hysterical attack against the Moral Majority, whose followers 'threaten whoever dares to disagree with their authoritarian positions'. These right-wing reactionaries, said Yale's president, permit 'no debate, no discussion, no dissent'. And to demonstrate its fearless opposition to such conduct, Yale would now take a conservative magazine away from its conservative owners.

'The conflict', agreed William Murchison in the *Dallas Morning News*, 'is emblematic of what goes on – alas! – in late twentieth-century America':

> As I say: emblematic. I ask for a show of hands. How many believe that, if instead of a conservative aura the *Lit* gave off an effulgently liberal one, Yale would now be trying to wrest away control of it?

Time magazine was stung into giving national coverage to the story uncovered six months earlier by *The Nation*: CONSERVATIVE REBELS ON CAMPUS. As I had hoped, the launch of the *Yale Free Press* was forcing the media to acknowledge that the *Lit* was not a part of the 'conservative' initiative to infiltrate the academy:

> After prolonged internal debate, Yale ruled that to qualify to use the university's name, a publication must give undergraduates editorial control. Navrozov sued to forestall enforcement of the rule. Taking his side was another, even more conservative Yale journal, the *Free Press*.
>
> Whatever the merits of the *Lit*'s case, Navrozov is unusual among the new campus crusaders. Hardly any come from families of even modest literary celebrity or deep political involvements. (One notable exception: *Yale Free Press* publisher Charles Bork is the son of U.S. Appeals Court Judge Robert Bork, who, as President Nixon's acting Attorney General, fired Watergate Special Prosecutor Archibald Cox during the Saturday Night Massacre.) Most of the right-wing students are white, male, middle-class products of suburbia.

More 'conservative' commentators, emboldened by the snow-balling of the story which a mainstream magazine like *Time* had deemed important enough to cover, were leaping up in defence of the First Amendment. William Rusher, the publisher of *National Review*, wrote a column entitled 'A Yale Liberal Will Hear All Views – Conservative Views Excepted'. M. Stanton Evans, the head of the National Journalism Center in Washington, did likewise: 'The Limits of Yale's Commitment to Pluralism'. Within days, the grab-bag of nationally syndicated headlines grew to include 'Yale's Gag Rule', 'Totalitarianism at Yale, or How to Fight Dirty When you are Losing', 'Fighting the Good Fight ... At Yale'. In November, THE NEWS FROM NEW HAVEN: PLURALISM AT YALE made it into *Fortune*, the Time-Life stronghold of American Capital founded by Yale's own Henry Luce. Daniel Seligman described the *Lit* as 'an extraordinarily readable journal of ideas', suggesting that my struggle against 'the unprincipled middle-aged liberals who seem destined to always run things' had shown that I, an 'idealistic young conservative', was a worthy successor to Buckley:

> To be precise, it has been 31 years since your correspondent penned an editorial note in *Fortune* on the remarkable case of William F. Buckley Jr. We observed (in the issue of November 1951) that this highly principled young person had recently produced *God and Man at Yale*, a volume featuring extensive groaning about the anti-capitalist attitudes of the professoriate and the deadening conformity imposed by Old Eli's liberal establishment. Having attained condescension at an early age, we chuckled amusedly over this spectacle of youthful conservatism baiting its pinko elders.
>
> It seems to be time for an update. Yale's liberal establishment nowadays is headed by President A. Bartlett Giamatti, who has cagily positioned himself as a fearless foe of the Moral Majority, a supporter of free speech and cultural pluralism, and a passionate believer in a well-paid faculty – all things considered, a strong platform in New Haven academic circles. The only discernible fly in Giamatti's ointment is Andrei Navrozov (Yale, '78), an unabashable conservative who is the publisher of *The Yale Literary Magazine*.

The *Washington Post*, whose reporters had been hovering over the *Lit* scandal even before the *New York Times* condescended to it, now assigned its leading literary light, James Lardner, to the story, which took up the front page of the 'Style' section:

THE TUG OF WORDS OVER YALE'S 'LIT':

An Issue of Control:
Is it a Case of Conservatives vs. Liberals?

What magazine had published the work of John Dos Passos, Sinclair Lewis and Rudyard Kipling, currently lists Eugène Ionesco,

George Gilder and Irving Kristol on its advisory board, costs $8 an issue, pays up to $1,500 an article, and tells prospective contributors it is looking for translations, memoirs and 'no Barth, Doctorow, Styron, Kosinski, Talese, Roth, Capote, Updike, Mailer, Gardner, Oates – and certainly not those who sound like them'?

The answer to this riddle – and the improbable cause of a lively fracas pitting one of the nation's oldest universities against a young Russian emigré with backing from the New Right – is *The Yale Literary Magazine*, otherwise known as the *Lit*.

Reduced to its dramatic essence, the story has a familiar ring: an aristocratic Yankee father, a much-loved daughter, an unsuitable suitor, and a bitter battle. Yale, the paternal figure in the case, has been trying to effect a quick and quiet divorce between the 'Old Lady in Brown', as the *Lit* used to be called, and 26-year-old Andrei Navrozov, who has been running the magazine for four years and insists the relationship is for keeps.

Despite the inventive preamble, after the first three paragraphs Lardner's analysis settled down comfortably to the *New York Times* formula of benign 'objectivity' favourable to our case. A few weeks later, in the first days of January, a mortified *Yale Daily News* reported that

> Mike Wallace and the CBS *60 Minutes* camera crew descended on the Yale campus yesterday filming a story about the controversial *Yale Literary Magazine*, run by Andrei Navrozov.
>
> Wallace interviewed Associate Dean of Yale College Lloyd Suttle in the afternoon before retiring to the local Holiday Inn for the night. Wallace said he had already talked to Navrozov and conservative columnist George Will. The crew will meet with several students today. Wallace would say little about the content of the story, except that it would take 'the usual objective approach', and added that it will air in one to three months. He said that other media coverage of the *Lit* controversy had attracted *60 Minutes*' attention.
>
> Navrozov is suing the University, charging that recently written rules on undergraduate organizations, a category to which the *Lit* still officially belongs, were designed primarily to subvert the *Lit*'s operation. Wallace's reputation for fierce investigation has of course reached Yale, but University officials seemed to take the visit in stride. One commented to another in the halls of the Dean's Office afterward, 'There, that wasn't so bad, was it?'

A cockeyed optimist might have gloated, but I knew that none of this mattered. 'A sparrow that's been shot at', in the marvellously evocative words of the Russian proverb favoured by the criminal underworld, 'won't be fooled by chaff.' Neither the noise now being made in our behalf by 'conservative Republicans' like William Rusher or George Will, nor the benevolent attention of the rest of the 'liberal Democrat' media, including the *Washington Post* and CBS News, would make any difference. The only thing that mattered was what the liberservative Republicrat godfather of all the media would have to say, about the unexpected escalation in the war for Giamatti's turf in particular.

40

Of course the *New York Times* fooled me. The godfather's resourcefulness was quite beyond a poor sparrow's imagination. Besides, as an institution it could look back on a long history of conflicts, from World War II to the Vietnam War, which it had helped to foster with the attitude of Olympian objectivity, thereby increasing its prestige as a responsible, cool-headed and detached observer of world affairs. After a war had raged long enough in its view, the attitude of Olympian objectivity would help to foster peace, thereby again increasing its prestige as a responsible, cool-headed and detached observer of world affairs. It was with this attitude that the *New York Times* deliberately deleted Hitler's threats to exterminate the Jews of Europe from the published texts of his speeches, making a diabolical surprise out of a totalitarian dictator's openly stated intention. When the surprise came, years later, and the war was fought, years later, and Hitler was defeated, years later, it was with the same attitude that the *New York Times* began to make peace, concealing the fact that another totalitarian dictator was now poised to become the war's winner and beneficiary. It was with the same attitude that the *New York Times* egged on the government and the American public to defend democracy in Vietnam, neglecting to mention that what 'our boys' would have to stand up to was totalitarian militarization, and not just a bunch of slanties in straw hats. After the war had been splendidly lost, with much news coverage and even a Pulitzer for Harrison Salisbury, it was the same attitude again that enabled it to hail Henry Kissinger as both a peacemaker of evangelical stature and a negotiator of Machiavellian shrewdness, although America had already surrendered and he was only a fat guy in specs. So if all the Jews of Europe, not to mention the people of South Vietnam, could not shake the Olympian objectivity of America's newsmaker, what chance had I? In the middle of November I opened the *New York Times* to the front page of the 'Metropolitan Report' section to find a photograph of myself, laughing respectfully, with the Revd Jerry Falwell, laughing uproariously:

REV. FALWELL MEETS AN OUTSPOKEN ANTAGONIST, YALE'S GIAMATTI.

Special to the New York Times.

NEW HAVEN, Nov. 11 – The Rev. Jerry Falwell, the founder of Moral Majority, met here today with one of the organization's most outspoken critics, A. Bartlett Giamatti, president of Yale University, in a session arranged by Vice President Bush.

'Met'?! I knew nothing of that. I knew that the Yale Political Union had invited Giamatti to debate Falwell, but Giamatti had declined. I knew that the Union had finally mustered up the courage to invite Falwell to speak alone and that Falwell had accepted. I knew that he arrived in New Haven, dropped by our offices with a photographer to wish us good luck, and then made a surprisingly lukewarm Union speech in which he did not refer to Giamatti's attack at all. 'I went hoping for a rumble', a *Yale Free Press* staffer told me that night by way of summarizing what had transpired at the Union, 'but it was only the Jesus Christ stuff.' Only now I knew why.

Mr. Giamatti and the Yale administration did not publicly announce the meeting. Until 4 P.M., when Mr. Falwell mounted the marble stairs to Mr. Giamatti's high-ceilinged office, the official position was that Yale knew nothing of a meeting.

Mr. Giamatti did not come out of his office after the meeting to comment.

Mr. Falwell, however, said the men had discussed a variety of issues. He said they had agreed on most – 'some people might accuse Mr. Giamatti of being a conservative' – and disagreed on others, specifically prayer in public schools.

243

Boy, what a setup. Boy, did I walk right into it, with a *New York Times* photographer and everything. Laughing. So the only intellectual chasm between the grandiloquent bully and his redneck victim was, 'specifically', whether or not there should be prayer in schools. Mindful of the bucket of propagandist spittle running down that dumb red neck of his, unanswerable demagoguery that a hundred public-relations consultants would not have washed away in a hundred years, I had assumed that the chasm was as infinite as the insult. I had assumed that it was as deep as the old chasm between any mendacious power and any offended meekness. But in reality it was as imaginary as any old chasm between a 'liberal' and a 'conservative', and here they were, the two lovebirds I had brought together, like Rostand's Cyrano, by the beauty of my open letter, chirping beak to beak in 'Mr Giamatti's high-ceilinged office'.

> Charm, not conquest, characterized Mr. Falwell's day at Yale. He disarmed some with wit, found foes willing to hear him out and was welcomed as an ideological hero by the conservatives on this campus. The conservative owners of *The Yale Literary Magazine*, for instance, whisked Mr. Falwell to a reception moments after his plane set down at 3 P.M.

So it took the Jesus of Lynchburg, Virginia, less than an hour, not including the trip from the airport and the stroll from our office, to make peace with Pilate in his own mind before walking up those marble stairs. Both knew exactly what they wanted. PEACE, it oozed from every line of the news article I was reading. 'We can disagree and remain friends', and besides the erstwhile antagonists 'agreed on most'. They 'traded personally inscribed copies' of books, presumably to remind the public that the First Amendment was sacred. There was 'no war going on', it was a case of 'charm not conquest'. The suspicious were 'disarmed' with wit. Even the extremists 'hissed only a bit at the mention of Moral Majority', once evil incarnate but now 'a Christian fundamentalist political movement'. As for the Jesus of Lynchburg, he was presented to the college audience as 'a man recognized by *People* magazine as one of the twenty-five most intriguing people' in the United States, and went on to introduce himself as a 'badly misunderstood man'. Diversity at Yale, progress in America, peace on earth, they were all here in the pages of the *New York Times*, as the lion of cultural pluralism lay with the lamb of religious fundamentalism. And who took the credit? Why, Yale of course:

> The meeting with Mr. Giamatti – who addressed a reunion of the Class of 1943 at the same hour Mr. Falwell spoke – was proposed and arranged by Vice President Bush, a Yale alumnus and a friend of both men.

41

Fowler's *English Usage* had not reached the present generation of provincial American lawyers to which the *Lit*'s attorney belonged. When I saw the court papers he had filed in the magazine's name I felt physically ill, reviving only after it was confirmed that we were paying him a fraction of the hourly rate billed by Golda Meir's firm in her case against Father. In addition to the University's own legal powerhouse, its Office of the General Counsel, Yale had retained just such a firm. Wiggin & Dana's leading trial attorney looked, appropriately, like a bulldog, and never appeared in public attended by fewer than two of the firm's juniors, each of whom represented a different canine species. By contrast, our provincial resembled one of Zina's sixteen cats. His tiny firm could not cope with the impeccably typed documents, served on us by the trayful, any more than Kolya could pluck up the Ostankino television tower by its roots and throw it as far as the Black Sea. It is easy to say, in retrospect, that from the start it all came down to money. Admittedly, in the next two years we were to spend half a million dollars on our legal defence. Excluding the salaries of its house counsel, Yale would spend over $3 million, though it must be borne in mind that the University measured its financial prowess in the hundreds of millions. But my seminal error was one of naïvety. I sought to reassure myself by reflecting that, after all, law was law and not literature, that however humiliating it was to read through the illiterate pleadings filed in my name, bad English was probably good legalese. Beneath this gross error of naïvety lay an equally gross delusion of shrewdness. To hire a suave, clubbable, Yale College educated and Harvard Law School trained luminary with a nationally known firm at $300 an hour, I reasoned, was to court betrayal, as almost every famous law firm had proud links with Yale and open loyalty to its causes. Pressure could easily be brought to bear on the firm through known and established alumni channels to negotiate a surrender in the guise of a settlement. To be fair, if exaggerated, my fear was not wholly unfounded, as I discovered later when attempts to engage one of several major New York and Washington firms proved unsuccessful, with actual or apparent conflict of interest, or simply lack of interest, cited by way of explanation. To sue a great university like Yale or Harvard, and over a volatile issue which seemed to call into question its very greatness, was quite unlike suing any other large corporation, or for that matter the United States government. Moreover, as the unaccountable disappearance of Roy Cohn in Father's legal endgame had demonstrated, even in the absence of concrete evidence of any foul play the national reputation of a firm was in itself no guarantee that the lawyer would behave responsibly. All of which may explain why, when I finally dismissed the first provincial bumbler, I hired a second, equally cheap and just as illiterate. The farewell took place after the defendant's attorneys had filed a counterclaim to enjoin the plaintiff from using the name *The Yale Literary Magazine*, whereupon I was summoned to their offices to give a deposition in the case of Yale *v.* Yale, as it was now appearing on the court calendar. The deposition turned into a five-day, 9 A.M. to 6 P.M. interrogation, during the course of which I answered questions on subjects ranging from my private life to my view of modern prosody, all with hardly a single objection from my perfectly unclubbable counsel whom we were paying to raise them. Then came his turn to depose our adversaries, but instead of an interrogation, what I witnessed in every instance was more like a chat between girlfriends in an office cafeteria. With the wheels of justice already turning, their pinions already snagging the magazine and pulling all the living life out of me, I sacked him. The new bumbler at least resembled a dog. He was enormously fat, and every time he slapped his knee after making a joke, quite literally at my expense, I expected him to bark, which he did. This time I was determined not to repeat my first mistake. I telephoned everyone I knew to see if a high-flying professional would agree to team up with the local *Bleak House* bumbler, and not only explain to him at every stage how the case was to be litigated without charging us the $300 an hour we could not afford to pay, but also function as our trial attorney once the case got to court. Through Lee, my original partner in the *Lit* venture – who had finished law school at the University of Chicago and was now clerking for Judge Scalia, later a Supreme Court Justice – a suitable mastermind was found in the person of Robert D'Agostino. Young, nervous, literate, D'Agostino had recently quit his appointment as an assistant to the United States Attorney General and was sitting on his hands somewhere in Delaware. He agreed to lead the case *pro bono*, billing the *Lit* only for his time in court. The arrangement seemed to be working until one Monday in October 1983 when our two lawyers actually presented themselves before the face of justice, providentially impersonated by the Connecticut Superior Court judge called Zoarski. He ought to have been called Sodomski, I thought, grinding my teeth with impotent fury: 'And the sun was risen upon the earth when I entered Zoar'. In the sober words of the *New Haven Register* news report published the next day, 'Judge Zoarski's decision precluded a lawyer, Robert D'Agostino of Delaware, from entering the case'. In addition,

> Zoarski denied the magazine's request for a court order to gain access to all magazine-related legal files and documents received by the university's general counsel from 1978 to October of last year.

Whereupon Zoarski scheduled the trial to begin on Thursday. But the worst was still to come. In my files I still have a faded piece of paper headed WESTERN UNION: CONFIRMATION COPY OF THE FOLLOWING MESSAGE I sent to twenty journalists, newspapers and press agencies:

> 2036248400 MGM TDMT NEW HAVEN CT 126 10-18 04-14 EST LADIES AND GENTLEMEN OF THE PRESS: YALE UNIVERSITY VS THE YALE LITERARY MAGAZINE CASE IS SCHEDULED TO OPEN 10 AM THURSDAY OCTOBER 20 AT SUPERIOR COURT NEW HAVEN JUDGE ZOARSKI PRESIDING. MONDAY'S DECISIONS OF THE COURT DEPRIVE US OF A JURY, PREVENT OUR ACCESS TO DOCUMENTS VITAL TO OUR DEFENSE AND EXCLUDE OUR ATTORNEY FROM REPRESENTING US. EUGENE ROSTOW, OUR ADVISER AND FORMER DEAN OF YALE LAW SCHOOL, CALLS IT DENIAL OF DUE PROCESS. WITHOUT YOUR ATTENTION AND PUBLIC KNOWLEDGE AMERICA'S OLDEST MAGAZINE WILL BE SUPPRESSED AS A SOURCE OF INTELLECTUAL DISSENT. AND IF IT HAPPENS TO US TODAY IT MAY HAPPEN TO YOU TOMORROW.

The Dickensian Mr Vholes was not discouraged. He was deeply flattered. The judge had, in effect, ruled that he was not an unclubbable bumbler at all, but a worthy son of Connecticut, perfectly capable of taking on those legal eagles from Wiggin & Dana. The impression was strengthened when the legal eagles intimated that his talents were being wasted in the provinces. If he showed himself to be a responsible member of the legal community, by not pursuing, for instance, his client's insane ambition to have the case heard by a jury, many a major law firm would see these talents for what they were. D'Agostino left, disgusted. On Thursday morning, faced with the prospect of arguing a case which he had not prepared, my exquisitely unclubbable Mr Vholes, despite the judge's professed confidence in his abilities, locked himself in the lavatory and could not stop vomiting. What followed in the courtroom, in the sober words of another New Haven newspaper, the *Journal-Courier*, was mayhem:

> Immediately upon taking the stand, Navrozov told the judge, 'Your Honor, with all due respect, I will not testify in this trial.' Navrozov said he was being 'denied due process' through the court's refusal to admit Robert D'Agostino as a lawyer in the case. The judge told Navrozov there was no legal basis for his refusal and granted a recess.

The recess was called for the unclubbable bumbler to persuade me to change my mind and to enable the farce to proceed, a discussion that ended a few minutes later when Mr Vholes 'stormed from the court, gesticulating angrily' at his former employers.

> Navrozov took the stand a second time and again refused to testify, saying he had dismissed his attorney. 'I escaped from Russia to follow the dictates of my conscience,' Navrozov said, 'and my conscience tells me I have been denied my right.' The judge told Navrozov he was not interested and insisted that the trial would proceed with or without his testimony.

And so it did. The judge could have decided in Yale's favour right then and there, but this would have made the decision more vulnerable to a future appeal. To impress on him that my refusal to honour the legal farce with my participation was final, I resigned as director of the corporate entity publishing the magazine, American Literary Society, Inc. Zoarski could not compel me to testify because the last thing Yale wanted was for him to imprison me for contempt of court, something that I, needless to say, had hoped he was just glib enough to do. But he could and did compel the *Lit*'s bumbler to go through the motions as the attorney representing the corporate entity from which I had resigned, and during the next two weeks dozens of witnesses, from President Giamatti to the lowest Dean, were given ample opportunity to mend their tattered reputations as friends of free speech, diversity and American motherhood. Even without my participation, however, almost accidentally, some vital evidence came to light during the staging of the farce. Giamatti, according to the *New Haven Register*, offered testimony about that fateful train journey in February 1980:

> The university president said he had no objections to Navrozov's handling of the publication during his first years at the helm. In fact, Giamatti said he complimented Navrozov on the magazine when they first met on a train trip from New Haven to New York.
>
> At that time, Giamatti said, Navrozov introduced himself and they had an 'amiable' conversation. Navrozov appeared to be 'an affable young man', Giamatti said. Giamatti said he commented on the 'beautiful printing and layout of the magazine'.

A memo written by the good Dean of *Hustler* fame, now Associate Provost of Yale University, established how and when Giamatti was finally persuaded to move against the *Lit*:

> A university official testified he wrote a memo of January 28, 1982, that admits the magazine was sold to Navrozov by another organization, the *Yale Banner*. University Associate Provost Charles Long's memo to another Yale official said, 'In 1978, with the approval of the Secretary of the University and the General Counsel's Office, the *Yale Banner* did sell the copyright and assets to a group of students and alumni including Navrozov.'
>
> The memo, introduced as evidence, was written as a result of a complaint sent to the university by Archibald MacLeish, a recently deceased renowned author and alumnus of the university. After receiving MacLeish's complaint about the magazine in 1981, Long wrote a draft of a reply that mentions 'what appears to be the Navrozov group's legal right to the title' acquired in the 1978 purchase.

The draft letter was never sent.

A reply to MacLeish written by Yale President A. Bartlett Giamatti says at the beginning of its second paragraph that 'the Yale name was not sold to anyone in 1978.' The memo written by Long says of Giamatti's letter, 'It's OK as a response to Archie, but the first one-third of the second paragraph is incorrect in every respect.'

Thus I learnt that on the heels of our savaging of the *New York Review*, Archie MacLeish, the kingpin of the academic establishment and its poet laureate, had written to Yale's president, until recently but a lowly English professor, demanding to know how it was that the *Lit* had fallen into the hands of 'right-wing propagandists'. And that a fellow English professor, Ronald Paulson, wrote a week later:

> I will not regale you with stories of Andrei and his father – you must have heard them all before – but when everything I know about the pair is brought into conjunction with the proprietorship of the *Lit*, it spells out 'confidence game'. The Yale administration should feel very uneasy as long as one of its offices is filled by such a shady character as Andrei, and wonder exactly how it came about.

One Dean memoed in reply, even as the dastardly trap was being sprung: 'An off-the-record response to your letter about the *Lit*. I heartily agree with you.' Another Dean, Dean Henson of the Undergraduate Manual fame, perjured himself at the trial when he denied shouting to a student in his office that 'There will be no more *Yale Literary Magazines*!' The student testified under oath that the Dean was lying, and later wrote to him: 'Not only did you deny making the statement, but you claimed I had made it, and that you had "declined to agree."' The disobedient student went on:

> When I took the witness stand I swore an oath before God that I would tell the truth. I take such oaths very seriously. You have accused me of a crime in both the legal and the moral sense. I am innocent of this crime. It is you, not I, who have lied under oath.
>
> Therefore I must ask you to publicly retract your testimony and apologize to me. I came to Yale with little idea of what the University stood for. I was, however, sure of one thing: that it stood for the pursuit of truth. The lack of truthfulness you have shown in this matter can only reflect badly on the University.

The Dean resigned, and was promptly hustled out of the state. Still another Dean, according to the *Yale Daily News*, told the court that

> the right to free speech at Yale would not necessarily be guaranteed in the case of a 'very small group'. The Dean then explained: 'I'm thinking concretely of insanity in the Party of the Right',

prompting a student I had never met, one J. Kirby Simon '85, a member of the very class for whom Giamatti's attack on the Moral Majority had been composed, to write in a letter to the Editor:

> The notion that the freedom to express a given ideology should depend on the number of its adherents, directly repudiates the ideals of liberty and pluralism from which both our country and our university derive their strength. Particularly despicable is Dean Griffin's use of the term 'insanity' as a pretext for silencing those whom he dislikes.

Numb and immobilized, I watched the proceedings like a patient confined to the soft regime ward of a mental asylum, reading about the trial in the newspapers. In distant Virginia, the *Richmond Times-Dispatch* ran a leader entitled 'Yale's Falwells', concluding:

> Yale should worry less about having its name taken in vain by conservative iconoclasts than about its betrayal of true liberalism. The next time Mr. Giamatti feels moved to deplore intolerance, he need not look all the way to Lynchburg, Virginia.

The *Wall Street Journal* ran a leader on the case under the title 'The Illiberal Academy':

> Mr. Giamatti says he is a champion of free speech, open dissent and the like, and thus couldn't care less about the generally conservative leanings of the *Lit*, which tends to oppose the cultural hegemony enjoyed by such institutions as, well, Yale. It's a simple matter, Mr. Giamatti explains, of protecting the fabled 'Yale name'.
>
> Funny, though. We ran our thumb through the New Haven phone book and found references to the Yale Motor Inn, Yale Auto Parts and the Yale Comfort Shoe Center. None of these has been targeted.

'What is really afoot', the leader concluded, 'is an institution defending itself against unwanted "outsiders"'. On national television, when CBS *60 Minutes* finally aired, the columnist George Will agreed:

> It's not a minor flap about a minor journal. It's a semi-major-league flap about a major-league university, because what's at issue here really is not the fate of the *Lit*, which was anaemic a few years ago and might be anaemic again soon, but Yale as a powerful force. And there's a question here about the integrity of a major American university and its decision-making process.

The programme, featuring the great American media personality Mike Wallace, was entitled 'The One Dollar Misunderstanding'. It included footage of my father at his New York flat, smothered in papers, a perfectly photogenic Mad Russian Intellectual:

> MAD RUSSIAN INTELLECTUAL: What was insulting to the Yale bureaucracy was an assault on the cultural sacred cow, the *New York Times* as the greatest representative, or centre, or Mecca of culture —
> AMERICAN MEDIA PERSONALITY: Wait.
> RUSSIAN INTELLECTUAL: Yes?
> MEDIA PERSONALITY: What you did was to write an article which in effect said 'The emperor has no clothes'.
> RUSSIAN INTELLECTUAL: Right.
> MEDIA PERSONALITY: About the *New York Times*?
> RUSSIAN INTELLECTUAL: Right.
> MEDIA PERSONALITY: And you are telling us that this is the reason for the attack at Yale upon *The Yale Literary Magazine*?
> RUSSIAN INTELLECTUAL: Yes. Yes. Yes.
> MEDIA PERSONALITY: The polemics of the magazine are directed toward —
> SON OF MAD RUSSIAN INTELLECTUAL: Well, they're —
> MEDIA PERSONALITY: Advocating the conservative point of view?
> SON OF INTELLECTUAL: They're directed against the cultural desert made by people who call themselves and are called liberals, who have had the stewardship of culture for the past thirty years.

The new wave of publicity was not doing Yale any good. John Templeton, an alumnus whose Nassau-based international investment operations were legendary, informed the administration that in view of its position in the *Lit* affair he was withdrawing his gift of $3 million and directing it to Oxford, where a school of business administration would be established in his name. No longer steered by the University administration, unsettled by the hard line taken by the national media, worried that Yale's new gag rules might be used against it, even the *Yale Daily News* was now showing signs of fatigue, in headlines like 'Trial may Affect Other Organizations', 'Lit Battle may Last Several Years: University Expenditures Extremely High' and 'Trial Leaves Issues Unresolved: Administrators Divided on the Lit's Legitimacy'. Spiritual children of the *New York Times*, its brave editorialists were suddenly aware that it was more difficult than they knew to win the war they had helped to start. They were now suing for peace, peace at Yale, peace in American culture. But it was too late, if only because American culture had been at peace with itself for so long that I could not find a lawyer who would not lock himself in the lavatory at the mere thought of confronting this culture with its hypocrisy. Without such a lawyer, the battle for the *Lit* in the appeals court would be nothing more than another scene of the same emetic farce. Yes, it was too late. Confined to his bed at the soft-regime ward, the mad Russian intellectual's solebegotten son was blaming himself for having let his father down. He was twenty-seven. In the mirror he saw that the hair on his head was beginning to turn white. The *New York Times* quoted the lone inmate, whom it now openly called a 'conservative', on December 2, 1983:

> 'The history of *The Yale Literary Magazine*'s persecution by the Yale bureaucracy is the story of a political crime', he said. 'The trial began as a farce, and it is only reasonable that it should end as one'.

But is this not what all madmen say?

> Yale's general counsel, Lindsey Kiang, said yesterday that it was 'absurd' to characterize the dispute as a free-speech issue. 'We are not trying to silence him', he said. 'He can continue to publish whatever the heck he wants.'

There was an air of relief, however, about the *New York Times* headline:

LITERARY MAGAZINE IS BARRED
FROM USING 'YALE' IN NAME.

PART THREE

THE GINGERBREAD RACE

1

An ancient Russian epic describes the poet's thought as following the outline of a tree. A similar tree is found in Anglo-Saxon epos, where 'gleo-beam' or 'gamen-wudu' are used as synonyms for the singer's harp, cut from the tree of human imagination. But another culture is on the move, leaving its imprint on the asphalt, and our eyes may follow that outline instead. Police indicators have blocked off the area. On the pavement is a silhouette of the victim, executed simply and without the artistic nuance becoming a figure of sacrifice, in chalk or white tape. There lies a gingerbread man, a modern, progressive man, a man of the West.

> And then you scream. I'm no fool! Oppressors!
> I lived as you live . . . Only who's to know?
> For history is not what made the dresses,
> But what was driven naked through the snow.

There goes Pasternak's thought, following the Byzantine contour of a prostrate silhouette. It is a figure bounded on all sides by calm preconceptions, comprising what is called received wisdom. If I push back these boundaries, challenging the preconceptions to expand the figure of thought indefinitely, there will be no recognizable 'figure' left on the asphalt. Then, to put it bluntly, no one will know what the hell I am talking about. So I say a name like 'Kipling', or a word like 'husband'. A newspaper hack says 'Kipling', or 'husband'. The mother of a friend says 'Kipling', or 'husband'. Then we, all of us, leave it at that, because the name, or the word, is a recognized concept, a piece of official police tape, and although we could pursue the matter indefinitely through biographies, dictionaries and primary sources, our effort must be commensurate with the thought to which the name, or the word, relates and always be in proportion to its importance. This is a definition of philistinism, and the reason why the Western man is so startled when he is executed in the middle of

Dallas, gunned down like a dumb animal. 'There', he thinks, 'I am not going to listen to this. Why Dallas, for Heaven's sake?' But even as the wind bloweth where it listeth, answers the freethinker, so knowledge of man spreads capriciously, its branches intertwining overhead, and the trunk alone is only good for a gallows. A doctor, another Western man, might say: Paranoia. He is right in the sense that this or any other mental disorder displaces philistinism, which prides itself on seeing all things in proportion to their obvious importance. Unfortunately, neither Kipling's obsession with Kim, nor a wife's obsession with the man who is her husband, nor Einstein's obsession with time, nor any obsession in history to bear the fruit of knowledge which philistinism, always with Olympian equanimity, now claims for its own in perfect harmony with nature, was ever in proportion to the subject's obvious importance. Who cares who Kim is? So your wife loves you, and I think that's just great. Everyone knows how to tell time. All of which is unfortunate for the philistine, because when his world ends and he is gunned down in the middle of a city street, when the city itself is sacked and his daughters are raped, when his civilization disappears under the desert sand, his most visible emotion is surprise. As that other obsessive paranoiac, Nietzsche, would say, he blinks. But all of this is unfortunate for the freethinker as well, because in the civilization which he inhabits there is hardly ever room for his obsession, only the occasional eminence, enclave, crevice or gutter. There he makes a garden of knowledge, with a tree of thought all his own, whose outline he can follow with his mind's eye from dawn to dusk, when it is time to go to bed and nurture his obsession with slow, dark sleep, thick as mead. When the surrounding civilization begins to totter, it is his garden that is the first to be destroyed and uprooted. His eternal consolation is that he is never surprised. He has had this mental disorder since childhood, these visions of the future arising from an obsession with knowledge, and despite the doctors, the lawyers and the accountants, he has spent a lifetime secretly pushing back the limits of his fellow men's preconceptions. Unlike theirs, his garden is not of this world. His body has never strayed beyond the gate. He has never believed in progress, and consequently his silhouette will never be found taped to the asphalt. But what if the civilization he inhabits has been designed from scratch, from top to bottom, from sea to shining sea, on the philistine assumption that any eminence, enclave, crevice or gutter would spoil its beautiful evenness? Then he must roll like the rest. Die like the rest. At times even think like the rest. And when a man's silhouette is cordoned off by police in a busy street, it is wrong to point at the pitiful cross of its arms and legs as if to say: 'There lies a gingerbread man.' Our civilization being what it is, we could be mistaken.

2

1984 was my twelfth year in America. It found me in a straitjacket, pinned down by corporate bureaucracy, tormented by lawyers, sedated by the press. A legal case in New Haven which had recently stolen the local headlines was a perfect projection of my mood. The class-action suit had been brought on behalf of victims of illegal wiretapping conducted by the FBI in combination with the city authorities between the late 1950s and the early 1970s. The Southern New England Telephone company immediately settled out of court for a prudent $150,000. The city held out until the attorney prosecuting the case bought newspaper space to publish the full text of the action, naming some 3,000 citizens targeted by the operation of whom 1,285 were his clients, whereupon it finally capitulated, paying $1.75 million. The wiretap victims included lawyers, poultry farmers and a rabbi. Three thousand dangerous subversives under surveillance in a city with a population of 137,000, and still that horde of outside agitators intent on burning Yale down had invaded, no doubt with help from the inside. Perhaps the FBI had been secretly filming New York's cockroach population as well, I reflected, monitoring their telephone conversations, perlustrating their private correspondence. Be that as it may, John Williams was the man who exposed this Kafkaesque conspiracy to forestall a conspiracy. I found out that as an undergraduate Williams was at Harvard, where during the 'radical sixties' he sat on the executive committee of the Young Republicans. After graduating from law school at Georgetown, he took a job in the legal department of an insurance firm, which involved a certain amount of work *pro bono*. 'In the course of handling misdemeanours for indigent clients', according to an article in the *American Lawyer*, 'he decided to devote himself to righting the injustices he was seeing clearly for the first time.' And here he was in the 'conservative eighties', a bearded, bespectacled leftie on the legal-aid trail of police misconduct, accepting a retainer of $10,000 from the ultimate victim, an immigrant who had bought the Brooklyn Bridge which was now being taken away from him to shrieks of laughter in the audience. The magazine was allowed to publish pending an appeal, and I knew that it was on the success of the appeal, rather than on any of our editorial successes, that its fate depended. Third time lucky, I retained Williams to handle the appeal, as well as a parallel First Amendment case he was planning to file in Federal court. When I saw some of the preliminary appellate motions submitted by the bearded, bespectacled leftie in the *Lit*'s name, it seemed to me that I understood for the first time the phrase 'Jeffersonian prose'. I did not remember admiring anything this much since I read Schirmer's poems, watched Leonard adjust the presses, or heard Mrs Jones hypnotized by the Southwestern dulcimer. It may sound implausibly corny, but that wad of legal papers made the immigrant proud to be an American.

3

Into my life and the *Lit*'s offices, which shortly before I published the open letter to Giamatti had moved off campus to a five-storey townhouse of our own at the intersection of Crown and High Streets, walked a strange young man. He had on a torn tweed overcoat, its lining hanging out like horsehair from an old armchair, and because he held his head sideways, as though to look in as many directions at the same time as possible, which predictably he did by means of abrupt, jerky turns, he resembled a sparrow. On closer inspection, he looked as I imagined Orwell must have looked to his calmer contemporaries. His Christian name was Steve, and of course I had known him by sight because not to notice someone who looked so different in a place where, as John Laing said, everyone was so bloody calm, was impossible. But now he had sought us out. My associates and I gathered round to hear what he had to say. Steve's surname was tinged with Colonial antiquity, and vast tracts of Connecticut, including some of the land upon which Yale stood, had once belonged to the family, which had since all but died out. He had an obsession with American intellectual history, which he treated as his own with a lucid straightforwardness that was wholly autobiographical, speaking of Yale and Harvard as though they were a tea caddy and a canteen of Georgian silver that he remembered his great-uncle auctioning off to pay a few bills. I mention the two American universities, rather than any of the Founding Fathers, any historic dispute or polemic such as the Civil War or the Federalist Papers, any key document of nationhood like the Constitution, and for that matter any specific writer or thinker, because for Steve the historical juxtaposition of Harvard and Yale was the basis of all intellectual and hence political life of the United States, while everything subsequent to the eighteenth-century schism was only a makeshift superstructure. Where Harvard took the open road, Steve explained, preparing men for public service as schoolboys are prepared for university, Yale took the shortcut. Since the early 1800s, which, independently of Steve, I had identified as the generation of Fenimore Cooper, the object of the Yale game was to internalize experience, fashioning the four undergraduate years into so lifelike a microcosm of the future that nothing about that future, when it came, could mortify, excite or seduce. This insight would have struck anyone with first-hand knowledge of the great English public school debate, and especially those who, like Orwell, had observed themselves eating 'everlasting strawberry ices on green lawns to the tune of the "Eton Boating Song",' as nauseatingly familiar. The political implications, drawn by those who believe that even if the Battle of Waterloo *was* won on the playing-fields of Eton, 'the opening battles of all subsequent wars have been lost there', would if anything be more familiar still. But as Mandelstam said,

> With the Imperial world I had but a child's connection,
> Oysters I feared, upon guardsmen I gazed with suspicion . . .

Dear God, I recall what I thought to myself as I took in word after word of Steve's disquisition, how well this would have suited young Orwell. And later in the poem, where Mandelstam wonders why the sudden passing of that world is even subjectively a tragedy, one again sees the cocky author of 'Such, Such Were the Joys':

> Ponderous, in a mitre of beaver, with furrowed brow,
> I did not linger beneath a great bank's Egyptian portico,
> And o'er the lemon Neva, to the rustling of a crisp note,
> No gypsy ever strutted her stuff for me.

But the sudden passing of that world was what it was none the less, and why this is so a poet could explain better than the freest of freethinkers:

> Was it not because I had seen in a storybook picture
> Lady Godiva unfurling her long auburn mane . . .

I am not suggesting that Steve's autobiographical insights were as beautiful as Mandelstam's or as profound as Orwell's, but something about them, some storybook image of a moment or an attitude that had set history awry, struck me as genuinely original. I listened. In halting half-sentences, Steve explained that he had made up his mind to come and introduce himself after reading newspaper reports of my refusal to testify at the *Lit* trial, concluding from my obvious wish to be imprisoned by Judge Zoarski that I was 'serious about winning this fight', as he put it. I confirmed that this was indeed the case, and told him that Williams was already writing the appeal in Jeffersonian prose. I also mentioned the Federal case. The grounds for this were yet to be established, I confessed, because it seemed doubtful that the mere fact that Yale was receiving Federal educational subsidies was enough of a legal toehold to launch such an action. There were other specialized legal questions, most of them apparently unanswerable because so much of the inner workings of the university was routinely hidden from view. Besides, as Steve already knew, once the *Lit* case came to court the university's Sterling Library closed its archival section to visitors without special passes. It was then, in reply to my confession of weakness, that I saw a maniacal grin stretching the visitor's face from ear to ear and heard his offer to read to me a series of informal lectures on the institution that shaped America. I accepted. The next few months were a period of intensive reading and study. Not since delving into the Gnostic mysteries had I had such a keen sense that the sole difference between a cult and a culture is power. At last I stood before the idol of the establishment that had the wherewithal to make all the rules. I had entered the inner sanctum of American culture. Like Mandelstam's poem, it boasted an Egyptian portico for the initiated to linger beneath, whether fumbling with their keys or pausing to light a cracking good cigar. As for the dancing gypsies, apparently on this important point historians differed.

4

High Street intersects with Crown, Chapel and Elm as it runs in the direction of the university burial ground. It is the main thoroughfare traversing the campus, with the quad of the Old Campus, comprising all the freshman dormitories, to one side and a row of three residential colleges, out of a total of twelve where upperclassmen reside, on the other. Some fifty yards from the corner of Crown Street, where the *Lit* kept house and Steve was hired as my Virgil, a bridge-like extension spans the width of the street, connecting the old and the new Art Gallery buildings. The architectural confusion punctuated by the Street Hall bridge, as it is known, arose from a quirk in the will of the painter John Trumbull, who had left his collection to Yale on the condition that his body would not be parted from it even in death. Few recall the charming subterfuge, with the likes of which the history of every institution of some considerable antiquity is no doubt replete, as they pass under the bridge, sauntering past the Old Campus on their right. What emerges on the visitor's left, however, framed by the light sandstone of Jonathan Edwards College, is a structure in the Egyptian style. The colour of congealed blood, it has stood here since 1856 and has not changed since 1871, when the following objective description of it was published: 'It is a grim-looking, windowless, tomb-like structure, of brown sandstone, rectangular in shape, showing a front of about 35 and a length of 44 feet, and is at a guess 35 feet in height. The entrance in front is guarded by a pair of massive iron doors, a dozen feet high, finished off in panels, and of a dark green color.' The roof is nearly flat, according to the observer, 'and is covered with half-inch plates of iron'. There is also in the roof 'a skylight, similarly protected'. In the back of the structure 'are a pair of small windows barred with iron, and close to the ground there are two or three scuttle holes, communicating with the cellar'. The total value of the premises, estimated in 1871, was 'upwards of $30,000', easily borne by the owners who incorporated themselves at the May 1856 session of the Connecticut legislature as the Russell Trust Association. Apart from William H. Russell, an 1833 graduate who had founded the association while still at Yale, the youngest of the six named incorporators were Henry D. White and Daniel C. Gilman. All were Yale alumni and none, at the time of incorporation, was an undergraduate. 'The society', notes the observer, Lyman Bagg, whose book was published anonymously by Henry Holt and Company under the title *Four Years at Yale, by A Graduate*, 'was originated in 1832 by fifteen members of the class which graduated the following year. General Russell, the valedictorian of that class, is its reputed founder, and the best known of his associates is Judge Alphonso Taft of Cincinnati'. The society arose, in a Yale of 'pathfinders' and in a nation with an increasingly imaginary 'frontier' for them to roam, from the General's idea that there existed a system to enable the fittest to survive, and that this system could naturally take root at Yale under the name of 'the society system'. Take root it did, and the social history of the university in the nineteenth and early twentieth centuries is an excruciatingly complex outgrowth of the General's seemingly rational idea, with dozens of sophomore, junior and senior societies struggling to remain on the scene dominated from the start by his creation. 'Whatever be the facts as to its origin,' comments Bagg, 'the mystery now attending its existence is genuine, and forms the one great enigma which college gossip never tires of discussing.' The General imported his enthusiasm for the system from Germany, where he had spent time in his youth, and Bagg notes that the fact that the society's founders are listed in its catalogues 'as belonging to the "third decade of the second period"' supports the theory that Russell's creation had been conceived as a chapter of a German society. The Germany Russell had visited was not only the Germany of Hegel, with its systemic view of the universe, but also the university Germany of revolutionary oaths, conspiratorial dreams, and secret passwords which the Russian exile Herzen mocked in *My Past and Thoughts*. Russell realized that by transplanting the masonic mumbo-jumbo of the Illuminati to politically tranquil and law-abiding Connecticut, he could instill great zeal in the hearts of young men without exposing them to the physical danger which, as the events of 1848 would show, was but one unpleasant consequence of revolutionary activity. Daniel Coit Gilman, later the first president of both Johns Hopkins and the University of California, as well as the first president of the Carnegie Institution, Andrew Dickson White, later the first president of Cornell as well as the first president of the American Historical Association, and Timothy Dwight, later the twelfth president of Yale, were all among the post-1848 initiates into the Russell cult who travelled to study at the University of Berlin under prominent 'Young Hegelians' like Karl von Ritter. But it was the social aspects of revolutionary activism, adapted for use in a country without, as yet, an established ruling élite, that made Russell's plan to form the nucleus of that élite so everlasting a success. In the first place there was the name.

5

'The senior societies', wrote Bagg some forty years after the Russell experiment commenced, 'are such peculiarly Yale institutions that it will be difficult for an outsider fully to appreciate their significance. Nothing like them exists in other colleges, and Harvard is the only college where, under similar conditions, they possibly could exist.' During the nineteenth century the 'society system' spread to every educational institution in the United States, to the accompaniment of ritual incantations improvised by Greek-letter fraternities, as even the grubbiest colleges began to imitate the Yale model often with little or no knowledge of the original. The Russell original, however, did not take its name 'from the initials of a Greek motto, but from the peculiar emblem adopted as a badge', and Yale College proved the only suitable breeding ground for its perpetuation. By the middle of our own egalitarian century, only the Porcellian at Harvard and the famous dining clubs of Princeton remained as scars left by the society fever, yet these were merely gentlemen's clubs for the sons of gentlemen. At Yale, by contrast, Russell's original took hold and soon produced a replica of itself, then another, then a third, and these clones have flourished to this day without, however, ever challenging the original's pre-eminence. When Bagg published his book, only the original and the earliest replica were deemed worthy of serious consideration. This too is true to this day. 'In the first place', explained Bagg, the two societies are unique in that their 'transactions are really secret. Their members never even mention their names, nor refer to them in any way, in the presence of anyone not of their own number.' Hence the term 'secret society', which by the time I came to Yale had supplanted the older designation, 'senior'. 'There are two of these societies,' Bagg explained,

> but as one takes its tone from the other it may be well to treat first of the oldest and most famous member of the modern system. Its

name is 'Skull and Bones' – formerly printed 'Scull and Bone' – and its badge, of solid gold, consists of the face of a skull, supported by the crossed thigh bones, with a band, bearing the number '322' in place of the lower jaw.

There is neither the electioneering associated at many American colleges with 'pledging' for the society of one's choice, nor any of the paraphernalia of democracy generally associated with university life. Fifteen juniors are chosen, or 'tapped', on a Thursday in mid-May by the fifteen seniors comprising the society's undergraduate member- ship. The society has three whole years to study the faces and the dispositions of twenty or thirty suitable candidates in a class pool which today consists of approximately a thousand men, while the older members are always on hand to supply whatever information about the candidates and their families that the seniors need to make the correct decision. In practice, little of that information is required, as most of the future initiates are known to the society since prep school days, or rather since their grandfathers' and great-grandfathers' prep school days. When Bagg published his book, thirty-nine initia- tions into the society had taken place and the total membership stood, logically enough, at 585. During the next century it increased only as the life expectancy increased, so that today in the world there are no more than eight hundred living graduates of Yale, out of a total of one hundred thousand, likely to 'leave the room', as the old custom demands, at the mention of their society's name. Naïve as this may sound to anyone who has heard the breathless phrase used many times before in praise of clubs, restaurants and airport lounges, the list of the living members 'reads like a *Who's Who*' of American politics, business and finance, yet it is only when that list is read as a fragment of the society's history since 1832, with the names of the deceased echoing the names of the living, that the reader begins to form some notion of the American aristocracy. And that, not to put too fine a point on it, was precisely the homunculus General Russell sought to incubate, except that because American society as a whole was as hostile to the notion of hereditary aristocracy as its European counter- part was to the notion of bloody revolution, the homunculus was to be kept under wraps. The mumbo-jumbo of secret handshakes that concealed the 'Young Hegelian' doings on the Continent from French gendarmes or Prussian spies would serve to keep the nascent aristocracy from the prying eyes of democracy in America. But the most curious feature of this aristocracy, which made it so unlike the nobility of Europe whose influence it wished to emulate and even more unlike the beleaguered revolutionary movements whose methods it adopted, was that it was born of peace.

6

Initially the invasion of the university by some of the old graduates intent on lording it over some of the undergraduates gave the administration pause. 'It is said,', Bagg reports, 'that the faculty once broke in on one of its meetings, and from what they saw determined upon its abolishment, but by the intercessions and explanations of its founder, then serving as tutor among them, were finally induced to spare it.' By the time the Tomb was built, the society had produced three hundred and sixty initiates, many of whom joined the faculty to give it a voice in the administration of the University. Every department from Chemistry to Law found new blood in young professors like Chester Lyman, Cyrus Northrop, Lewis Packard, Benjamin Silliman and Thomas Thacher, dynamic young men from good families with a vision of a new Yale. When, thirty years later, Timothy Dwight succeeded Noah Porter as President of Yale, the society had the University in the palm of its hand. Porter was the last of the uninterrupted succession of clerical presidents to rule the University since its origins in a theological schism with Harvard, and all that remains of his memory today is a pointedly invisible Porter Gate of wrought iron lace opposite the Old Campus. In 1899, Dwight was succeeded by Arthur Twining Hadley, an economist whose sole public claim to distinction was a volume on railroad transport but who had been initiated in 1876. Hadley would preside over Yale until 1921, producing further volumes that probably startled his natural audience of meatpackers and longshoremen, including one entitled *The Conflict between Liberty and Equality*. By then 'Yale University', incorporated by Dwight and superimposed upon the modest 'Yale College' of his predecessors, had become accustomed to its main role as the society's public persona, not to mention its recruiting ground. Hadley, Dwight,

Silliman, Farnam, Woolsey, Wright, Chittenden, Phelps, Davenport, Taft and Whitney are but a few of the 'society names' familiar to every freshman today because they are borne by university buildings, though hardly anyone realizes that the very architecture of their environment, the Gothic nightmare designed in the 1930s by James Gamble Rogers for President Charles Seymour, initiated in 1908 and later Professor of History at Yale, is a grandiose apotheosis of its private mythology. I certainly never realized this, even after ten years in New Haven, until my Virgil produced detailed drawings and close-up photographs of some of these landmarks, where sculptural reliefs of Lenin, God and the Devil attitudinized as gargoyles in poses that would have made Diego Rivera blush. So prominent is Yale in all its aspects in the collective mind of New York publishing that during one of our field trips, to inspect buildings no more than a hundred yards away from the *Lit*'s office, I asked Steve why he had not written a biography of James Gamble Rogers. He answered that it was far more important to write a biography of Averell Harriman, and that the secret history of Yale since the Great War, of which I was yet to have a glimpse in his course of lectures, would be the foundation for such a work. Whereupon he produced from his coat pocket a contract with Harper & Row to deliver a life of Harriman by the end of 1985. As for the architecture, here with an eloquent wave of his hand Steve circumscribed the Sterling Memorial Library, almost completely shrouded in scaffolding. He explained that Yale had got wind of his research and was determined to alter or remove some of the potentially embarrassing reliefs under the guise of renovating the Rogers buildings. The *Lit*'s lawsuit, he said with a frightened rather than a triumphant look, was not the only reason that Sterling had closed off the university archives. None of the concerns and interests attendant on Steve's obsession, it must be noted, were echoed by the student population when I was at Yale in even the smallest degree, including clever boys who could name the capital of Cambodia and find Guam on the map. But even those who had been hearing since childhood about Goethe and the Freemasons, Mozart and the Illuminati, Pushkin and the Decembrists, John Wilkes and the Hell-Fire Club, Boss Tweed and Tammany Hall, Bakunin and the Anarchists, Hitler and the Brownshirts, proved utterly indifferent to the possibility that, whether good or bad, talented or giftless, writers or terrorists, free men sometimes form clandestine combinations whose activities have an effect on the lives of their fellows and on the course of history.

Whereas, in militarization, such combinations are invariably the result of a provocation by the rulers or a pretext for one, in civilization their effect may be lasting and profound. Yet my classmates' eyes were fixed upon the government, its agencies and the concomitant struggle of the two political parties as the sole mutable star in an unchanging world, where the Vietnam War was wicked, the *Lit* was a stapled freebie and the Tomb at the corner of High and Chapel was there because it had been there always. My own ignorance during those years is only partly excused by the avalanche of new impressions and facts which I had to evade on arrival at Yale, and quite possibly I was the only son of my Alma Mater to depart unburdened by the knowledge of what 'love-all' means or how the game of baseball is played. But at least I knew who lived in the Tomb, while Gene Meyer, a junior in Jonathan Edwards, a frequent Political Union debater, a sometime chairman of the Party of the Right and the son of a writer who had been Bill Buckley's intellectual mentor, once asked me, a freshman, what that godawful thing next to his college was. The one distinguishable focus of campus opposition, or for that matter aware-ness, of the Tomb's inhabitants were the University's feminist organ-izations, who objected to the society on the grounds that since Yale is a 'co-educational' institution, every 'club' on its premises must admit women as 'members'. To make the point, every year or so paint was thrown at the Tomb in an attempt to deface its façade. What the protesters did not know, and I would never have learnt had I not met my Virgil, was that much of their University occupies premises owned by the Russell Trust Association, not the other way round, and that as a landowner in New England the society, whose corporate name was a mystery to them, rivals Trinity College in the England of their ancestors. Doubtless they would have been as surprised to see the land records as I was when Steve showed them to me, but not nearly as surprised, I wager, as I had been to learn that Bill Buckley entered the Tomb as an initiate in 1950. To hear that George Bush, the incumbent Vice–President of the United States, is also a member was, at the time, something of an anti-climax.

7

Conformity was, however, a characteristic only gradually acquired. In those distant days, long before Walter Camp arrived on the scene to make the newly incorporated University worthy of the name by expressing President Dwight's vision of the future in pigskin and astroturf, Yale College had been populated by students as restless and as inquisitive as any that Russell and his young friends might encounter on the Continent. It is very hard indeed to imagine a sceptic of the stature of Mark Twain catching on with a reading public whose tastes had been shaped by an educational system hostile to the free exchange of ideas. Where the professoriate, with families, salaries and careers to consider, had assented, accepting the conqueror within as a fact of life, the students, with hardly anything to consider but the occasional bottle of booze, rebelled. The society's practice, by then firmly established, of 'tapping' every chairman of the *Yale Daily News* and of the *Lit*, and later the chairman of the *Banner* yearbook and of the frivolous *Record*, had effectively shut down discussion of the 'society system' in the college media, but individual undergraduates continued to fight by whatever means they could against its increasing dominance over every sphere of student life. A kind of *Bildungsroman* by Owen Johnson, whose title, *Stover at Yale*, is still widely remembered although no one I knew as an undergraduate had ever read it, was published in 1911 and became a best-seller on the strength of its author's dramatization of the football hero's struggle against, and final capitulation before, the power of the 'society system'. Yet Dink Stover already belonged to the rococo age of the struggle. Its golden baroque, in a Yale where non-competitive chapel rather than pseudo-competitive sport was socially compulsory, transports the historian to the last decade before Dwight tightened the society's grip, the Porter decade of the 1870s.

> We represent no clique or clan, but honest men and true,
> Who never will submit to that which *fifteen* men may do,
> Who feel the shameful yoke that long has on the college lain,
> And who propose to do their best to break that yoke in twain,

began the October 13, 1873 issue of *The Iconoclast*, its first and last, put out by the avowed 'Neutrals' who declared in their preface that 'Skull and Bones, directly and indirectly, is the bane of Yale College'.

If they have grounds on which they base their claim as just and true,
We challenge them to set them forth exposed to public view,
That all may know the reasons why this oligarchy proud
Elect themselves as lord supreme o'er us, the 'vulgar crowd'!
We offer no objections to their existing clan, –
No one disputes with them this right, we question but the plan
On which they act, – *That only he who wears upon his breast*
Their emblem, he for every post shall be considered best.
We wish this understood by all. Let none who read this say
That we are moved by petty wrongs or private spite obey;
It is for principles of right that we with them contend,
For principles which they've ignored, but which we here defend.

From the conclusion of the anonymous versifier's polemic, among other documents of the Porter decade, it is clear that if the debate on the 'society system' was to advance beyond *The Iconoclast*'s position of 1873, it would do so by marshalling new facts, because the intensity of feeling was already so great that nothing short of armed rebellion could have increased it.

Shall none assert the right to act as to each seemeth best,
But cringe and fawn to him who wears a *death's head* on his breast?
Nay, let us all rise and break the spell whose sickly glamour falls
About all that originates within these brown stone walls.
And if they will not hear our claims, or grant the justice due,
But still persist in tarnishing the glory of the blue,
Ruling this little college world with proud, imperious tones,
Be then the watchword of our ranks – DOWN, DOWN WITH SKULL
  AND BONES!

A pamphlet swept the campus in 1881, prefaced on the title page as follows:

Let it be stated in advance that this pamphlet is published solely with a view to clear away the 'poppycock' which surrounds the greatest society in college. It has no malicious intent. The sole design of the publishers and those who made the investigations, is to cause this Society to stand before the college world, free from the profound mystery in which it has hitherto been enshrouded and to lessen, at least in some degree, the arrogant pretensions of superiority.

271

What followed was an updated version of an earlier pamphlet, which had proven equally incendiary when first circulated in 1877. The irreverent investigators, who had taken 'great risks to disclose the inner parts of our Yalensian Juggernaut', described how they broke into the Tomb that autumn by cutting through the cellar window bars, a feat replicated in the spring by another team using 'a small crow bar, a hatchet, cold chisel and jimmy' to pry open the skylight.

> As long as Bones shall exist, the night of September 29th will be to its members the anniversary of the occasion when their temple was invaded by Neutrals, their rarest memorabilia confiscated and their most sacred secrets unveiled to the eyes of the uninitiated.

The investigators, who called themselves and published under the name 'The Order of the File and Claw', reported their findings and even inserted a detailed plan of the Tomb into the text of the exposé:

> Room B, called 322, is the 'sanctum sanctorum' of the temple. Its distinguishing feature is a fac-simile of the Bones pin, handsomely inlaid in the black marble hearth, just below the mantel, and also inlaid in marble is the motto: 'Rari Quippe Boni,' in old English text. This room is furnished in red velvet.

Marked 'H' on the plan was 'an old plain lock safe' in 'Room B', wherein 'nothing save a knife covered with blood stains' was found. Other rooms were discovered to contain, in addition to such evidence of the members' literary and sporting interests as 'a complete set of the *Lit*' and a display case 'containing a large number of gilded base-balls', a collection of objects that once belonged to the society's detractors, including 'a well-thumbed textbook' inscribed with the name of a student who had been 'Bones' irrepressible annoyer' as well as society badges of ephemeral adversaries like 'Bull and Stones' or 'Spade and Grave'. These they confiscated, along with 'a few pieces of memorabil', noting that 'the second thief is the best owner'. Finally, after exhaustive scrutiny of a proudly displayed German engraving of an open burial vault bearing the device '*Ob Arm, Ob Reich, im Tode Gleich*' ('Poor or Rich, Equal in Death'), inscribed 'From the German Chapter, Presented by Patriarch D. C. Gilman of D. 50', the intruders departed. Their considered conclusion went as follows:

Bones is a chapter of a corps in a German University. It should properly be called, not Skull and Bones Society, but Skull and Bones Chapter. General R—, its founder, was in Germany before Senior Year and formed a warm friendship with a leading member of a German society. He brought back with him to College authority to found a chapter here. Thus was Bones founded. The 322 on the pin has been commonly supposed to mean, founded in '32 and 2nd chapter. But the Bonesman has a pleasing fiction that his fraternity is the descendant of an old Greek patriotic society, dating back to Demosthenes, 322 BC.

I took the battered copy of an old *Oxford Dictionary of Quotations* we had in the office and looked up 'Demosthenes' to see if some platitudes of the Russell generation would throw light on the schoolboy mystery. There was only one quotation, from 1837, at any rate not too anachronistic. It was from Macaulay: 'With the dead there is no rivalry. In the dead there is no change. Plato is never sullen. Cervantes is never petulant. Demosthenes never comes unseasonably.'

8

Unlike its famous counterpart in the slightly older Cambridge Apostles, with which the secret order at Yale has sometimes been compared, Russell's *'conversazione'* was onanistic rather than homoerotic. The initiation ceremony undergone by each of the chosen fifteen, who had to give a full account of his intimate experiences before 'dying' to be reborn as a 'Knight' of the order, centred on masturbation in the sacred coffin. While no alcohol was ever allowed on the premises, a ban extended in later times to drugs, I did meet several Yale co-eds who were known on campus as 'Bones whores'. To recount one's experiences one needs to have had them, and it is likely that rumours spread by the girls in recent years were responsible for at least some of the indignation with which the feminist sorority regarded their weird brethren. In practical terms, one formidable advantage of the initiation ceremony was that not one of the 2,280 members initiated in the society's history had ever broken the code of silence and published a memoir. Beginning with William Dougal Christie's personal account in *Macmillan's Magazine* in 1864, by contrast, scores of books and articles on the Apostles have been published, and the most recent and widely known study, Richard Deacon's *The Cambridge Apostles: A History of Cambridge University's Elite Intellectual Secret Society*, includes a sizeable bibliography. Apart from instilling mortal fear of embarrassment in the event of disclosure, which, in a tolerant community or at least a self-consciously philosophical one like the Cambridge of Coleridge and Tennyson, would not have attended homosexual intercourse in either a literary or a legal sense, in the residually Puritan social context of New England the unusual rite served another purpose. The young knights of the order had been chosen for their ambition as well as their fidelity, and to affirm that they had, to use a uniquely Yale term with origins in President Hadley's railroad era, the 'grit' to get ahead in the new life into which they were born, they had to sacrifice such trappings of the old life as honour or dignity. It was the reluctance to do so, on the part of a number of many otherwise suitable candidates in the first decade of the society's existence, that led to the founding of its earliest replica and only formidable rival. The motto of Scroll and Key, established in 1841 and incorporated in 1860 as the Kingsley Trust Association, was 'To Not Compromise Dignity', the scroll in question being described in a pamphlet of 1845 as a 'Declaration of Independence from the Scull and Bone'. It was the founding of Keys, the upstart's motto unsportingly parodied by Bonesmen at the time as 'To Give Community and Sweetness to the Eating of Sour Grapes', that in part precipitated and in part helped to dissipate the baroque age of student rebellion against Bones, giving the term 'Neutral' its dignified meaning of opponent of the 'society system' generally and not merely of the one society that counted. On the crest of this opposition rose the 'Diggers' of Spade and Grave, mentioned as long vanquished by the intruders of 1877, under circumstances that had direct relevance to the legal predicament in which I found myself a century later. Bagg described these as follows:

> The immediate cause which banded them together in the scheme was a quarrel in the class of 1864. Of the five *Lit* editors in that class, three had been chosen to Bones and two were Neutrals. One of these two published, as a leading article in the magazine for February of that year, a piece called 'Collegial Ingenuity,' reflecting on the mode

by which men may worm their way into Bones, and, it was claimed, making personal insinuations against a particular member of that society; and on this latter ground the Bones editors, who formed a majority of the five, voted to suppress the article, and requested its writer to produce another to take the place of it, – themselves meanwhile seizing upon all printed copies. The Neutral editor refused to obey, and called a class meeting which voted to sustain him, and commanded the Bones editors to surrender the magazines within a certain time, or be expelled from office. As they paid no attention to the order, the class elected three Neutrals in their places, and these, with the two original Neutral editors, duly brought out a new edition of the February number, 'Collegial Ingenuity' and all, and edited the two following numbers, – with the latter of which their term in office expired. The Bones editors meanwhile issued the February number, with an explanation of their action printed in place of the obnoxious 'leader' but otherwise unchanged, – and duly published the two remaining numbers of their term, still keeping the five original names at the head of the title-page, as if nothing had happened.

The five rebel Neutrals and ten of their classmates, Bagg went on, 'have the credit of founding Diggers'. I rushed to the shelves which held the complete set of the *Lit* we had exhumed from the attic of Woolsey Hall, dusted and lovingly restored since our move to the new offices. Sure enough, no trace of the obnoxious leader could be found. In a legal sense, the *Lit* I had bought was a Bones bastard.

9

Neither Bagg's book nor any other outsider's account of Yale life to contain more than a passing mention of the society, or for that matter any of its past rivals, could be found in the public libraries of America. I once asked a writer staying in Washington to look up Johnson's innocuous *Stover at Yale* in the Library of Congress. He wrote to me as follows: 'Here is what happened. On March 26 I arrived at the Main Reading Room as the Library opened, at 8:30 A.M. I was given a computer slip with an edition of the book, which I then ordered. An hour later the lady librarian came over to say that someone must be reading the book, as it is not on the shelves. I expressed surprise. It's only nine-thirty in the morning and somebody's already at it, reading *Stover at Yale*! The reading room was nearly empty. I went back to make another computer search, and came up with three more copies. I ordered them. The librarian returned in an hour, announcing that the books are not on the shelves. I expressed even greater surprise. The reading room is still nearly empty, yet I am asked to believe that four people are busy reading *Stover at Yale* at eleven in the morning! At 11:45 I queried Special Research, in one of the radial anterooms of the Main Reading Room. The librarian returned after ten minutes, and said there were not four, but five copies of the book: "All five have been stolen." He explained at great length how he knew that they had been "stolen" rather than "misplaced", as well as why the theft had not been discovered until the afternoon of March 26, although because I am not an employee of the Library of Congress I confess that to my lay ears the explanation sounded obscure. He spoke of some "markers" and, holding up these invisible symbols, kept exclaiming: "They were removed, you see? Removed!" If he had been a Brooklyn cop he would have spoken of "perpetrators" in the same convoluted way.' The anecdote may help to explain why Steve's lectures, and the collection of rare pamphlets and documents in his possession, came as such a revelation. The only public scandal in which the Bones name had recently figured was the publication in the September 1977 number of the magazine *Esquire*, on the centenary anniversary of the Diggers' intrusion, of an article immodestly entitled 'The Last Secrets of Skull & Bones'. The obnoxious number was torn from the bound volumes of *Esquire* in most public libraries soon thereafter, despite the fact that the malevolent outsider's darkest hint was that during the initiation ceremony 'one can hear strange cries and moans coming from the bowels of the tomb'. Still, to an innocent like myself, it would have come as a surprise that such prominent Americans as Supreme Court Justice Potter Stewart and President of the Ford Foundation McGeorge Bundy began their adult lives naked in a coffin, 'chanted over and reborn into society'. I am sure that if it had not been so half-hearted, my attempt at the time to get hold of a copy of the *Esquire* article in New Haven would have been as anecdotal as my correspondent's experience at the Library of Congress. What I learnt from Steve's lectures, however, was that these efforts to conceal were noteworthy not only for the tenacity with which the society kept its secrets, but rather for the significance of the felonious acts themselves. The custom of committing such acts originated in the youthful zeal of the Knights – as the initiates are called during the senior year at Yale before they graduate and become Patriarchs – but after many success-ful escapades became an accepted norm of conduct, as the Knights rifled through the university and later the adult universe beyond as if these were mere drawers of a grandmother's bureau, stealing what totems they could usefully add to the Tomb's collections. By the time Steve walked into the *Lit*'s office, the society had come to possess a set of Hitler's personal silver, rumours of which had reached a number of Keys men. These rumours had come on the heels of a theft which they found especially provocative. Shortly after Giamatti, a member of Keys, had been inaugurated as the nineteenth President of Yale, a ceremonial item of jewellery known as the President's Collar was stolen. Though some months later the necklace reappeared far more mysteriously than it had vanished, with most newspapers following the *New York Times* lead and reporting the theft as if it involved da Vinci's *Gioconda*, the message had hit home. Like his predecessor Kingman Brewster, who had had the audacity to turn down a tap from Bones and remained a Neutral, Giamatti, a Keys man, was an illegitimate president. To teach the Keys upstart a lesson, his dignity was publicly compromised. Tantalized by the rumours and intent on vengeance, a group of Keys members, led by a student whom I had known since freshman year, replicated the Diggers' feat and broke into the Tomb through the skylight. They found the silver, and much more besides.

10

It was on the basis of the Keys report of their findings that Steve had taken what he believed to be the most dangerous step of his life. He had written to Dr Ned Anderson, Tribal Chairman of the San Carlos Apache Tribe in Arizona, to inform him that the skull of the Indian chief Geronimo had been stolen in a Bones raid led by Prescott Sheldon Bush, the vice-president's father, and had been in the society's possession since 1917. Apart from eyewitness accounts, Steve supplied Dr Anderson with copies of secret Bones documents purloined by Keys, including one of the society's anniversary histories, and these he now passed on to me for safekeeping, along with the tribal leader's reply:

THE SAN CARLOS APACHE TRIBE

San Carlos, Arizona 85550

October 15, 1984

Dear Mr —

I've never written a more important letter than this. I suppose it's because it's very difficult to convey on paper the magnitude of sincerity with which I am writing. Suffice it to say that everything in this letter is from the bottom of my heart.

I've thought about your request to postpone our planned action. I've also discussed it with Tribal Attorney Joe Sparks. While I appreciate the risks that are inherent in our planned action – to you and to us – I believe the timing is right for action on our part. I tend to think that we've waited too long already. I'm afraid that if we wait further the task is going to become all the more difficult, if not altogether impossible. You yourself have stated in the past, for example, that the building holding the remains has been fortified several times since last year. (This was indeed evident when our tribal attorney and I made an on-site inspection.)

You mentioned that you have a New York publisher interested in your material. It appears to me that you would be in a position to strike a better deal if you helped us carry out the task – directly, that is – as opposed to your not assisting at all. This is because by then you would be talking about a real situation as opposed to what may seem like a hypothetical one. I say this because the piece that was written by Ron Rosenbaum for *Esquire* came across just like that. Is it any wonder, therefore, that that article did not attract much attention? At any rate, I sincerely believe that by helping us you would be helping yourself.

You indicated that you were afraid of retribution on the part of the wrongdoers in our case. You know, I think the wrongs committed by the guilty ones will be considered so atrocious that society will completely ostracize them once their deeds have been exposed. It is my opinion that virtually the same thing that happened to Nixon and his men will happen to them.

278

The letter continued for another two paragraphs, in which the tribal leader again mentioned his plans for criminal as well as civil action against the thieves, and expressed the Indians' hope that Steve would testify as a witness. Despite Dr Anderson's prediction of the thieves' fate, Steve was not convinced. Watergate, in his private history of America, was just another Bones prank, somewhat less audacious than the theft of Giamatti's necklace, and in the end no Bonesman cared 'what happened to Nixon and his men'. Why, Nixon was a nobody, Whittier College and Duke University Law School, more of a nobody than Giamatti, a savage who at least made it into Keys. As for the President's men, those barbarians never even went to Yale, and so could not possibly know how funny it was when he insisted that he was not a crook. Ha-ha-ha! I now remember that Steve's laughter, on the rare occasions I heard it, sent even more chills up my spine than his historiography.

11

'Crooking' acquired its secret meaning in 1883, when George Crook, promoted to general ten years earlier for his raids against the Paiute Indians of Idaho and the Apache of Arizona and having further distinguished himself in the 'Sioux War' of 1876, led his mountain expedition against the Chiricahua Apache in Arizona and captured their chief Geronimo, though Geronimo later escaped. In the larger, national perspective, the object of General Crook's grand theft was land. But in the intellectual universe of the Tomb, revealed in the manuscript of Timothy Dwight's fiftieth anniversary history of the society, of a copy of which I am at present the sole uninitiated possessor, Crook was the greatest American hero of his time while the practice of 'crooking' was the civilized answer to the Indian practice of scalping the vanquished. Recalling in 1883 the 'humiliating' moment to which Bagg alludes in his book, when, during the administration of President Day, 'a portion of the Faculty appeared at the door of the old Temple' and 'demanded entrance', subsequently commanding the society's 'adjournment', Professor Dwight, who would become President of Yale in 1886, poked gentle fun at the naïvety of his sometime predecessor who assumed that the resolution would stick:

> The same generous desire to save the head of the College from any undue or dangerous excitement was manifested many years later during the administration of President Woolsey, in the delicate manner in which his room in North College was relieved of the presence of the Punch Bowl. The good President told his son-in-law, our fellow-patriarch Hermance, of the club of 1858, some three or four years ago, that he was quite confident that I knew where the precious relic was. But I never gave him any ground for such confidence.

A few pages earlier, a rather more sombre acquisition is celebrated, as follows:

> I may state at this point – somewhat aside from the straightforward progress of my discourse – that a new and interesting relic has just now unexpectedly come into the possession of the club; – namely, the Presidential robe which President Woolsey wore on Commencement days during his administration, and which President Porter has used since his administration began. The College having arrived at such dignity and such a condition of wealth,

he continues sardonically, that 'Dr Noah Porter can be arrayed with new insignia of royalty, while our presiding officer is for the future in possession of the old and better ones'. 'Happy life, that of a pirate,' he exclaims in connection with yet another triumph, 'if only one sails on the right seas with the Bones flag! The victims and the victor rejoice together, and nobody tells even his nearest neighbour what he has suffered.' One of *The Iconoclast*'s poets saw it in a similar, though less kind light:

> The sign they bear, in former days,
> The pirates of the seas,
> The foes of God and scourge of man,
> Unfolded to the breeze . . .
>
> Are these the pirates of our day?
> Have they with petty crime
> Together joined in evil league
> In this, our later time?

Whate'er they be, and whence they come,
Where'er they seek to go,
Their badge defies an honest world
And brands it as their foe.

Invoking the society's 'Demosthenic' goddess, Eulogia, to whom the Temple is dedicated, Dwight describes how their revenge on the outsiders grew in sophistication:

With the wisdom which the Goddess gives to us more liberally as the years go on, we have provided a better arrangement for the era of President Porter. We have secured his right-hand agent, Professor Dexter, and his left-hand agent, Mr. Hotchkiss, in our membership and in our interest. The result is that when a good thing is to be obtained for the Club, the President makes no opposition. And thus we discover that the tombstone of Governor Yale himself has recently appeared here, and, in immediate connection with it, a new representation of Demosthenes. The old fashioned system of 'crooking' which was sometimes carried beyond bounds and was offensive to the consciences of some – my own among them – is, by this means, done away.

By coincidence, actually, the Hotchkiss School was established shortly thereafter to serve, along with Groton, Andover, Exeter, St Paul's and Taft, as the initial link in the chain of recruitment for the society, although today hardly any of the students boarding there realize why the fact that the school's main building is a Y-shaped structure pointing in the direction of the Governor's tombstone is more than a tribute to Hotchkiss's original name, 'Yale Preparatory School'. Today's young Hotchkiss preps are equally surprised to discover that the school anthem, 'Fair Hotchkiss', bellowed to what they assume is the tune of 'Bright College Years', is in reality 'Die Wacht am Rhein' so beloved of the Hitlerjugend. But even in 1883 there was ample opportunity for gloating:

But the days of conflict with the Faculty came to their end long since. They terminated, not in the mortifying way in which the early meeting already referred to closed – by motion of the Faculty – but by the judicious action of the far-seeing. As the Club found itself in 1833 in danger from a threatening rival society and accomplished its freedom from the evil by swallowing its rival – that is, absorbing all its members into itself, so it proceeded in this case. Or to limit ourselves to a comparison with the meeting of which we have spoken, the Club turned the tables on the Faculty and, adopting their own course, presented itself at the doors of that venerable body, demanding admission. The demand was soon answered and the door opened. The founder of the Club himself became a Tutor in 1835, and in 1843 a permanent hold upon the body was gained through the entrance of the Elder Professor Thacher upon his professorship.

President Day and his associates, when they had accomplished their temporary purpose, retired from the field and left the Club to itself. Not so, the sons of Eulogia. They pursued the policy – noble and wise when the cause is good and the end, as well as the means, is best – of getting all that they could and keeping all that they got. Gradually, the Faculties of Arts and Science and Theology and Medicine and Law were all inroaded, and even the Corporation began to transform itself into a chapter of our Order. The Club did not follow President Day's rule and retire from active life at nine o'clock in the evening. He taught the club a valuable lesson, but its members practised it to a later hour and with more permanent success. President Day made the great mistake of going to bed too early in the evening and getting up too early in the morning. He was, because of this mistake, asleep while the club was awake; – and the Faculty was transformed and glorified.

At the time he was composing this 'Historical Address', Timothy Dwight, it must be borne in mind, was not a frolicking youth, nor was he living in a barbarous era. He had been born in 1828, the same year as Tolstoy, whom he would outlive. He was the grandson of Timothy Dwight the Elder, the prominent eighteenth-century clergyman, preacher and leader of the 'Connecticut Wits', who himself served as President of Yale College from 1795 to his death in 1817. The elder Dwight, in his turn, was the grandson of Jonathan Edwards, the great American theologian and metaphysician who graduated from Yale at the tender age of seventeen, two years after the college had been founded in the schism with Harvard, and went on to become not only the architect of the 'Great Awakening' of New England but also, in the last year of his life, the President of the College of New Jersey, now Princeton. Considering the focus of Steve's obsession with the period, and his determination to write, some day, a historical novel entitled *The Devil and Jonathan Edwards*, it always amused me that my Virgil walked about with a copy of Edwards's writings edited by a man called Faust. But the relevant point here is that the younger Dwight had come from a long tradition of elder statesmen, and had himself reached the ripe age of fifty-five, when he rose to deliver his address to his fellow Patriarchs. I have said that the homunculus of American aristocracy conceived by General Russell, who was, alas, a general in name only, was born of peace. It is not surprising, therefore, that something that was, by its very conception, so infinitely infantile, should have found foes where an outsider might find only playmates, and should have seen in Crook, whom the uninitiated might see as a bully, a national hero. Richard Deacon, who sees the Cambridge Apostles very differently from the way Steve saw the Yale Patriarchs, as a curious phase in the intellectual development of Britain rather than as the central pivot of American history, writes in his study:

> Gradually the Society developed its own coded jargon and indulged in a love of what they call 'coded language', something which non-Apostles could not share. There was an element of the schoolboy about all this and letters of the period reveal how extremely immature the early Apostles were.

In keeping with this, according to Deacon, 'anything to do with the Society and its members and environment was arrogantly described as "Reality"'. In stark contrast to this immaterial yearning for the paradoxical, appropriately found in the children of an existing, ancient, real aristocracy and those raised in its chivalric spirit, for Dwight the outside world was literally divided between the Barbarians and the Savages. The latter term originally designated members of other Yale societies and the former, the Neutrals, though in current use the latter extends to all those who have attended Yale and the former to all those who have not.

> The time of warfare for the Club, however, did not end with the discomfiture or surrender – or rather the absorption – of the Faculty. The student world took up the conflict in the vain thought that they could rush in where the angels had not succeeded in forcing an entrance.

283

The Patriarch goes on to tell the story, apparently unknown to Bagg, whose book he frequently mentions in his address as 'the well-known volume entitled *Four Years at Yale*', of a 'Savage' intruder who 'penetrated into many of our secret places' in the Tomb, having availed himself, 'by a theft, of the keys'. It is to that incident, of course, that the latter part of the rival society's name refers, the intruder having availed himself of the keys, as every Keys man knows, in a card game. A second story, unrecorded even by the Digger pamphleteers of the Porter decade, tells of the first-ever invasion by the Neutrals:

> In the same year, 1865, the Barbarians, inspired by the example of those insane men or impelled by a blind fury, made a similar assault on the Temple . . . But their names became known, and they were visited, to their great astonishment, by Professor Thomas Thacher in the name of Demosthenes. What he said to them has never been fully revealed, but I surmise that he intimated to them that there was a representative of Eulogia in the Medical Faculty, and that there were ways known by which obnoxious persons could be placed in charge of that faculty. At all events, the treasures, with the exception of a silver ink stand, were at once restored.
>
> These young men – I remember hearing at the time – proposed to the Professor to return the valuable property on condition that, when they should reach the Senior year, they should be elected into Bones. Strange as it may seem, however, they never reached the Senior year. I suppose this may have been due to the fact that the Faculty and the sons of Eulogia had, long since, begun to see eye to eye. One of these misguided young men threatened some years later, it is said, – when he had fled to the other side of the continent, – to publish what he knew, and, like all his blackmailing tribe, at the same time offered to suppress the publication for a sum of money. But Eulogia looked at Demosthenes and Demosthenes at Eulogia. Nothing was said on either side; only a pleasant smile illumined the face of each. No money was paid, and no publication appeared. The elder Professor Thacher has rendered many valuable services to Yale College, but never, perhaps, a greater one than when he recovered for our Goddess, on this occasion, the possession of the symbols and records of the life which she had given her worshippers.

Many Keys men, who are the only ones at Yale to have a fortified temple of their own where secret records may be kept at least as safely as in the Tomb, believe that the fate of the unfortunate Barbarian intruder who fled to California is explained by the knife found by the Diggers in the safe designated 'H' on their plan of 'Room B'. After this, their first political assassination, the bond tying the Russell aristocracy together was no longer a bond of make-believe blood. But it will be understood that at the time I was far more interested in preserving my own journalistic venture than the memory of America's first, and perhaps last, real investigative journalist. And so, with trepidation, I thumbed on and on through the manuscript until at last I found, among all 'the other conflicts with the barbarian world', Dwight's own account of the incident:

> The Editorial Board of *The Yale Literary Magazine* in that year – instead of being composed, as it should have been, of five members of the Bones – had in it only three sons of Eulogia, who were associated with two barbarians.

The facts enumerated by Dwight were in agreement with Bagg's published version. Several handwritten pages later, 'Spade and Grave', the rebel society founded by the *Lit* dissidents, makes an entrance:

> The name proved most appropriate, for it soon dug its own grave with its own spade, and no one remained who was so base as to do it honor. No society arising in opposition to our Club, up to the present date, has ever lived for a long season, except that of the Savages; and that lives because there must be, or may well be, some place for the meeting of those who would be worshippers of Eulogia, if they were fitted to be so, but who cannot, by reason of their lack of fitness, become such worshippers.

One way of dealing with dissidence in the outside world, goes Dwight's history lesson, is by ignoring it. So it was with each of the rebel student groups: 'Because it was ignored, it died.' In the university faculty, by contrast, the leader of the rabble rebellion against the society élite, Dwight reveals, was Law Professor William R. Townsend, a Bonesman. This 'brilliant manoeuvre' was a classic provocation.

> 'Our Club,' said he, 'had all the Townsends.' It impressed me thus deeply because I knew that one of these Townsends was the Bones

Devil, the author of all mischief. I suppose he stirred the wrath of
the barbarian multitude for his own amusement, knowing that no
real harm could befall the Club.

Provocation, as anyone who has read Dostoevsky's *The Possessed*
knows, is the Devil's business. To nurture an opposition, to foment
dissent, to spearhead a social movement, to speak of an uprising, to
run guns, to manipulate political assassinations, to land troops on
foreign soil – and then, with a beatific smile, to abandon the credulous
victims of the provocation to their fate – is to carry out what might be
called the Bay of Gadarene Pigs manoeuvre. For much of the twentieth
century the Bones Devil was Averell Harriman, but here again it was
with even greater disbelief that I learnt that while the Bones Devil is
intent on grave mischief outside the Tomb, another title obliges the
bearer to make *frivolous* mischief. It is that of the Jester, and since his
initiation the Bones Jester has been Bill Buckley, sometime chairman
of the *Yale Daily News*, author of *God and Man at Yale* and pied piper of
American 'conservatism'. By light-hearted though long-established
tradition the Jester is allowed to sit while even the Patriarchs in the
Tomb are standing, while in compensation his bottom may be
smacked, at any time, by any member so inclined, a tradition which,
as far as I have observed, has shaped the special relationship between
the White House and *National Review*'s offices on East 35th Street in
New York. But, as I said before, even in 1883 there was ample
occasion for gloating:

> I find, by a summary made about two years since, that there were, at
> that time, on our list 295 lawyers; 103 merchants and bankers; 38
> physicians; 108 ministers of the Gospel, of the Congregational,
> Episcopal, Presbyterian, and other denominations; 40 farmers; 25
> editors; 88 teachers, including six College presidents and forty-two
> professors – twenty of these being in our own College; and twelve
> officers in the civil service of the country, one of whom was recently
> Secretary of State of the United States and another is Chief Justice
> of the United States Supreme Court.

The Chief Justice was Morrison Waite, whose interpretation of the
post-Civil War constitutional Amendments was a benchmark of
judicial orthodoxy for nearly a century. Among the merchants, Dwight
might have added, were two men whose achievements would help his

hero, General Crook, finally to prevail in his courageous war against the red menace, Wesson's revolver and Hotchkiss's machine-gun. The aristocracy born of peace was finally acquiring playthings of real consequence for its future Yale game, one that would take its Patriarchs through two World Wars and many others besides. Meanwhile, their secret had to be vigilantly guarded, and Dwight closed his jubilee address with the fear that an outsider's glimpse of the initiation rite, in particular, would end the society's progress toward dominance over the Barbarian world. And fear this well he might. Among the Patriarchs gathered in the Tomb for the jubilee was a young prosecutor for Hamilton County, an initiate of 1877 and the son of Judge Alphonso Taft of Cincinnati whose early ministrations had helped to nurse Russell's homunculus to adulthood. In 1909, coincidentally the year Geronimo died, William Howard Taft was inaugurated as President of the United States. It is highly doubtful that the American electorate, then as now, would have taken any but the harshest and most cynical view of the opening pages of Dwight's address in which the initiation ceremony is tenderly described:

> But the initiation itself is not changed. The same gelatinous mass is made of the barbarian stranger in every case, by the same process and by the same solemn rites. The new candidate is recreated; ceases to be a Him; finds a new spirit within him, which casts out the old; knows more of Demosthenes in a few moments than his teachers had ever taught him, and, as he gains for himself the accurate meaning and pronunciation of the word, 'Toby-fkliwizi-firo-catlicko-carricks-carnicksi-carnickso-macpherson-o-phane', begins to understand and to speak the sacred language. And so we all become some of the Skull and Cross Bones, to whom all others are but contemptible foemen.

I hope that I have read the scratchings of the Patriarch's quill correctly, because it would be embarrassing to hear feminists, who can always be relied upon to yell at presidents, whether of Yale or of the United States, yelling at President Bush what amounts to incomprehensible gibberish. The difficulties of the 'sacred language' worried Dwight himself, as he jestingly proposed that even a Patriarch of the 'early, uncertain, mythical, heroic time' of old might balk at the newfangled ritual questions, who are the Gorillas; and is there a process of evolution by which a Gorilla can become a Him, and a Him can, grammatically or otherwise, be changed into a He, and a He into a Knight; – and is this the way in which a gelatinous mass is developed by slow degrees into Demosthenes, and Demosthenes sublimates into the divinity of speech, and dies in and into 322 and into utter abnegation and annihilation of himself? What questions these, for the uncultured mind!

I am certain, however, that the average American, to say nothing of the average intellectual thug like myself, would sooner plunge a tomahawk into Dwight's benighted skull than acquire the culture of the mind which President Taft, twenty-six years later, would bring to the White House and, twelve years after, to the Supreme Court. In a unique episode of American history which scholars other than Steve have oftentimes pondered, in 1921 the former President of the United States became Chief Justice. Yet, as Steve reasoned, it was essential for Taft to seize that eminence. In 1921 a University of Chicago psychology professor, James Rowland Angell, a graduate of the University of Michigan with a postgraduate degree from Harvard, replaced Patriarch Arthur Hadley as President of Yale. A firm hand on the tablets of the law was needed to keep the Barbarians from getting restless. In 1936, Patriarch Charles Seymour took over the Yale presidency and again all was well in the Tomb. It was time to build the Sterling Library.

12

Confusion in the mind of a newcomer to Steve's intellectual laboratory, with its sudden telescoping of 'social' norms and its mad oscillation between 'presidents', is perfectly natural. Every student of American history soon discovers that such confusion is inherent to the very object of his study, and ceases to be amazed by such insights as this one, from Hadley's biographer: 'Theodore Roosevelt would term Arthur Hadley his fellow anarchist and say that if their true views were known, they would be so misunderstood that they would both lose their jobs as President of the United States and President of Yale.'

What ought to astound the student of history, of course, is not that a prominent American was an anarchist, but how artlessly the two offices are confounded in one sentence. Thus such confusion grows by what it feeds on, and the more the newcomer to American history comes to know of America, of its toxins and of its tonics, the more compromised he is by the knowledge already gained. As an initiate into a fully developed religious culture, or one of its mysteries, may find, his ability to take an independent view diminishes as his understanding of the mystery increases, so that in the end a student of the Renaissance, even if he is a Buddhist, cannot look at a lily without a 'Christian' thought in his head any more than a Yale graduate like myself can look at a newspaper picture of George Bush without seeing a skull. But unlike Apostolic Christianity, to say nothing of its origin in an act of self-sacrifice, the cult I am describing here was conceived as a schoolboy game. As it developed into a national culture, its ideal of sacrifice evoked a tribal world, one in which it is invariably *we* who crucify *others*:

> As flies to wanton boys, are we to the gods;
> They kill us for their sport.

Between the pagan cult and the pagan culture, however, lay a whole century of nods and winks, pranks and escapades, stolen jam tarts and pulled pigtails, lapel stickpins and messages in invisible ink, white lies and occasional canings, dime novelettes and forbidden adventures. Generation after generation of upper-middle-class Americans not only absorbed these tales of derring-do and Derrida at Yale, but learnt to identify them with 'culture', 'education' and 'influence'. The closer they got to the secret of success, the less immune they became to the appeal of its cruel infantility. The more they thought of themselves as belonging to the club, the more its spirit possessed them. The confusion increased. The victims and the victor rejoiced together, as the Patriarch had prophesied they would, and nobody told even his own kin of the subjugation he had suffered. Although the Yale Law School, for instance, is almost as far removed from the magic crucible of national political power as the Open University is from Whitehall, as witness such ineffectual alumni as Gerald Ford, Gary Hart and Pat Robertson, it is a mark of the same confusion that Wesley Sturges, its sometime Dean, used to tell his students that if money was what they were after they ought to be at Harvard, while 'the function of the Yale Law School is to train presidents of the United States'. The same confusion led an anonymous wit of the 1940s to decipher the acronym of the OSS, the CIA's wartime predecessor, as 'Oh, So Social', while the fact that no fewer than forty-two members of a single social class, forty-two graduates of the Yale class of 1943, got jobs with the agency is typical of the historical riddles which scholars have since come to meet with a blank stare. It is remarkable that my classmates, who thought of themselves as insiders and supported the insider team in party politics as they supported it at the Yale Bowl during the football season, were oblivious of the truth that its victories had been scored on the field of bureaucratic rather than electoral approval. Apart from a number of Patriarchs who, alongside other Old Blues, have always been prominent in Congress and in the Senate, only Taft and Bush made it to Washington as presidents, but even they got there on the backs of their populist predecessors, Roosevelt and Reagan, naïve enough to allow themselves to be used yet not so naïve as not to regret it later. It is hardly surprising, therefore, that the student of his own confusion would start by looking for the best example of an insular bureaucracy beloved of those who seek political power unburdened by public accountability, and find it in the CIA. To an outsider like my father, since its inception the agency has epitomized civilization's suicidal inability to comprehend the predator of militarization. For an insider like Steve, the self-destructive ignorance of this bureaucracy had a predominantly self-serving side. Yet both men were self-confessed obsessive freethinkers, beyond the pale of institutional respectability. Its salaried inhabitants, by contrast, lived off the object of their study – known since 1943 as 'The Campus' – and their vested interest in increasing rather than diminishing the public confusion of which I speak naturally extended to their own minds. One of these inhabitants, said at the time 'to have an eye on Steve' and appropriately named Winks, was Master of one of the residential colleges and Townsend Professor of History at Yale. Two years after the events I describe, Robin Winks published an academic volume entitled *Cloak and Gown: Scholars in America's Secret War*. Since neither Steve's biography of Harriman nor anything else he was planning to write on the subject was ever to appear, and since campus rumour served me well in the past, I assume that the scholarly tome was undertaken with a view to absorbing some of my Virgil's more heterodox representations into the orthodoxy of corporate romanticism. If so, Professor Winks has failed, because the very facts which his work of temperate sycophancy was intended to absorb not only justify the charge of self-serving but provide startling evidence of self-destructiveness. Like the maxims of America's robber barons, 'The business of America is business' or 'What's good for General Motors is good for the country', its animating sentiment is directly descended from the intellectual worldview of Louis XVI.

13

My interest in Professor Winks is psychological, of the kind I myself have always generously attributed to historians who spend their lives seeking to document Hitler's personal responsibility for the annihilation of European Jewry, although any denizen of totalitarian militarization could point in the direction of their own academic bureaucracy and remind them that any pyramid of power is made up of subordinates who guess their superior's innermost wishes. I am not in the least bit interested in the workings of the American government or any of its agencies, including the CIA, and even the shared life of the academy and the media concerns me only in so far as it has affected mine. My obsession is with the pitiful anthropomorphism of modern civilization, and hence with the collective brain that is the source of both its ultimate vulnerability and its occasional beauty. Professor Winks's brain, like Mr Rose's *Britannica*, fascinates me as a specimen of the greater whole, and I never tire of asking myself why this internationally known scholar did no more than 'have an eye on' the only person who might have enlightened him, never bothering to challenge Steve or confront him in debate. How could this university elder, immersed in a book on the CIA unrivalled for its scholarly footnotes and arcane sources, have failed to acknowledge that the subject of his brainstorm, no less than the university paying him to have one, was but a convenient lodge of an order of naughty schoolboys with headquarters less than a hundred yards from his study? My command of Winks's spy language is no better than average, but commonplace truths may on occasion speak for themselves. As every educated American knows, American intelligence began with the martyr of the American Revolution, Nathan Hale, who 'went to Yale'. Thus Mr Rose, ever proud to flaunt his family links with the culture Dr Steiner spent a lifetime re-defining, named the block of flats where my father lived 'Nathan Hale Gardens':

Nathan Hale
Went to Yale.

Similarly, every American who happens to have an interest in World War II knows that modern American intelligence began with William 'Wild Bill' Donovan, a graduate of Columbia, and his Yale friends. Yet only a Yale insider can feel, as Winks does, a delicious *frisson* at the discovery that e. e. cummings had written of Donovan: 'And how do you like your blue-eyed boy, Mister Death?' The truth was that America's secret aristocracy finally had an all-seeing eye, and Winks is only too proud to say what even a poet could not guess, that its colour was actually Old Blue. It hardly troubles the urbane academic and former diplomat that the hasty conversion of the Office of the Coordinator of Information, itself hastily established two years after the war for Europe began, into the Office of Strategic Services took place in the summer of 1942 at the Sterling Library at Yale, where many of the leading lights of the new profession, intelligence, hatched an embryonic Research and Analysis section. Why should this trouble the Townsend Professor of History at Yale? *He* was not killed fighting that war, as my grandfather was. *He* was not denied access to the library archives, as I was. 'Seldom', coos the distinguished historian, 'has a project so clearly been part of an old boy network.' Indeed, apart from Yale's own Donald Downes to whose antics Winks devotes a whole chapter, central to the OSS 'Library Project' were the son of the Wall Street tycoon Walter Pforzheimer, a Yale graduate of 1935 whose family would later endow the opulent gymnasium at Horace Mann; a Yale graduate of 1932 who was a professor of History at the university; and a Yale graduate of 1923, a professor of English, Joseph Toy Curtiss. Whether or not the appetite for the infantile came to the latter with his middle name, from the same genetic source as it came to Winks, is not as significant as the historian's insistence that 'at Yale no one else, including the president, Charles Seymour, was informed of the goings-on at the university library.' Was President Giamatti *informed* that the *Lit* was a menace? Was Chancellor Hitler *informed* that the Jews had conspired to bring about Germany's downfall? No, of course not, and even as his onanist brethren lined up in Washington, '*Ob Arm, Ob Reich, im Tode Gleich*', to take charge of their blue-eyed boy, Seymour remained in the dark. Yet the same historian says proudly of the university librarian, who was so 'well connected' that he 'addressed cabinet officers, senators and presidents by their first names' and swapped Nathan Hale stories with OSS comrades: 'With his law degree from Harvard, Knollenberg was a sojourner at Yale but an accepted one'. The same historian goes on to describe Curtiss's first meeting with Downes, arranged, though disappointingly not by means of a note written in sow's milk at midnight, by yet another Yale professor called Notestein, who was in turn, as 'an OSS man who knew him well observed, "a natural conspirator"'. First the conspirator 'slipped into Curtiss's suite' in Jonathan Edwards College. Then he 'closed the windows, checked on the doors so that the undergraduates who lived above and below Curtiss would hear nothing'.

> Notestein told Curtiss to go to the Yale Club, opposite Grand Central Station in New York City, to its cavernous second-floor lounge; he was to wear a blue suit and a purple tie – not a combination Curtiss cared for – and look for a man who would be seated in a corner near the portrait of President William Howard Taft; the man would light a cigarette and immediately put it out. Notestein then left for the golf course, where he spent many of his afternoons.

I remember my own feeling of pride, and another of those rare twitches of patriotism, when I learnt that the PanAm skyscraper towering over Grand Central was commissioned by the airline's founder, a Yale man who had not done well in the social game, with express instructions to the architect to make the building tall enough for him to spit on the roof of the Yale Club. Others, like Pforzheimer's father, whose Wall Street firm became the future CIA's first money laundry, welcomed the slightest chance to get in with the right crowd. But for a social man like Curtiss, nothing but a good, old-fashioned initiation would do. He was met in Baltimore 'by a man wearing a red carnation' and taken to 'a large verandahed house' an hour west of the city for his 'training'. Here new recruits 'crawled through a cellar with .45s in their hands, to have a figure dressed as Hitler leap out upon them'. If this was not exciting enough,

> They were sent to Baltimore (or, in some instances, Philadelphia, Pittsburgh, or Richmond), where many ships crowded the harbors

> and trains sat on the lines and much military and government work was being done, and with forged papers were told to obtain a job in the defense industry and return, within three days, with 'a secret'.

Momentarily enthralled, Winks feels obliged to re-establish scholarly detachment:

> Curtiss, to whom most of this little game was not applied, thought much of the activity smacked of the Boy Scouts, but since the training he did have had been fun, he emerged happy enough.

As every educated denizen of militarization knows, in the 1940s the intelligence facilities at the disposal of totalitarianism were as limitless as any facilities it required for global expansion. Despite this, as every denizen of militarization with an interest in World War II knows, intelligence penetration of one totalitarian regime by another proved impossible. In the West, by contrast, where a former spy may lie or boast as much as he likes and the plausible is what works on the cinema screen, Donovan's men had put away their telltale red carnations to don the costumes of extras in *Sullivan's Travels* and infiltrated the ports and railway stations of Russia and Germany as easily as they had swarmed Baltimore or, in some instances, Philadelphia, Pittsburgh and even Richmond. For Curtiss it was Sweden or Turkey, although 'he spoke neither Swedish nor Turkish', but since 'he had travelled fairly widely in Turkey, especially in 1937 when he had visited Asia Minor, Greece, Cyprus, and Portugal', Turkey it was. Others, with parents rich enough to have taken them to see the Pyramids or the Taj Mahal, presumably found themselves in Egypt or India, 'gathering information' as American tourists have been gathering it since Mark Twain's *Innocents Abroad*. Yet what, one may well wonder, was the ultimate destiny of that information? Here I leave Curtiss and move to another junior member of the OSS fraternity to whom Winks devotes a chapter in his book, William Langer. While being a Harvard man Langer was an outsider rather than a 'barbarian stranger', the fraternity accepted him as it accepted the librarian Knollenberg, as a sojourner. The holder of the Coolidge chair in diplomatic history had made his career by travelling to Mexico to meet his archetype, the learned bore of my earlier narrative, and to persuade him to give some of his private papers to Harvard. Obviously anyone able to convince a learned bore, forgotten by the world and waiting for death, to allow his view of history to be enshrined in the annals of a world-famous university was cut out for intelligence work, and Langer duly became the man responsible for 'methodology' at Research and Analysis, 'a liaison to the world of scholarship'. In this role new triumphs awaited him, such as 'the case of Super-Secret Document No. 33876' furnished by another OSS fraternity, Secret Intelligence,

> in which Robert Lee Wolff of R&A's Balkan section was asked to come to Langer's office to examine a six-page SI document on an eyes only basis. The document was said to give the German order of battle in Russia and to have been received from 'Fighting French sources'. Thirty seconds of inspection revealed the document to consist exclusively of verbatim excerpts from official Soviet communiqués published months before in the *New York Times*.

The Yale boys in SI might have put one over on Langer, but what they did not reckon on was that the Yale boys in R&A read the *New York Times* the same as they did! One eyewitness of these escapades had come from Dartmouth and must have felt excluded, because a peevish Winks writes that

> from his memoirs one could conclude that the professors were petty in the extreme, fighting with him for bigger and better desks, jealous of those who had window views, even demanding that they, like their military counterparts, should have official cars while overseas. Vanity ruled, Alcorn concluded, though he exempted Langer from this charge.

Even the Dartmouth innocent was not so clueless, in other words, as to criticise his superior. Equally, when Secretary of State Cordell Hull, later the winner of a Nobel Peace Prize, asked Langer to produce 'a dispassionate analysis' of America's policy toward Vichy France, the policy analysis was produced without fear or favour, regardless of any party, sect or interest involved. Unfortunately Langer made the mistake of publishing it in book form in 1947, whereupon *Our Vichy Gamble*

> created a storm of protest from those who had been anti-Vichy, and Langer was accused of a whitewash.

At the time, apparently, America still had a press capable of protest. But when libel actions ensued from Frenchmen mentioned in Langer's dispassionate analysis,

> Langer turned to Allen Dulles and Henry Hyde, old friends from the OSS, for help on the French flank, and after agreeing to make minor changes in future editions, and the forthcoming French edition, Langer was relieved to see the libel actions withdrawn.

Petty or not, one mind stood out among the academic intellects gathered by Langer, unsurpassed for its analytical prowess on the one hand and its perfect impartiality on the other, and that mind belonged to Langer's brother. Writes Winks:

> In his presidential address to the American Historical Association, 'The Next Assignment', Langer took up the cause for the role of psychology in history and, by implication, in intelligence. In part this may have arisen from the work his brother, Walter C. Langer, had done for the OSS, for – with unnamed collaborators and researchers – Walter prepared a secret report on 'the mind of Adolf Hitler'.

Unfortunately in 1968 the report was declassified and published in the 1970s as *The Mind of Adolf Hitler*, whereupon my father included a generous mention of the book in his essay on mediocrity and the West published in our launch issue. Father's attention was drawn to the book because reviewers, from the *New York Times* to *Newsweek*, found this masterpiece of predictive analysis 'amazing', 'fascinating', 'gripping', 'absorbing', 'far-reaching' and 'significant':

> Racing against time – for as Dr Langer notes, the course of World War II and subsequent foreign policy might have been different had the report come later – the research team finally discovered in 1943 the clue to Hitler, the German people, and the history of Germany. By combing through all the available hearsay, the team established that Hitler suffered from an unbearable sense of guilt, shame, revulsion, and that his life was one long attempt to conceal and suppress them.
>
> How did the American experts learn about this heinous secret

across the ocean? In a pile of amassed hearsay they discovered that young girls, movie actresses, were said to come 'alone to the Chancellery late at night and departed in the early hours of the morning'. That was it. What do a man and a girl do at night? *Alone?* The question is superfluous, according to Dr Langer. She urinates on him. What else? With what many of his colleagues in New York would no doubt call amazing perspicacity, Dr Langer notes that a girl would be 'alone with Hitler behind closed doors so that not even his immediate staff knew what transpired between them'. If the girl had not urinated on Hitler, he would have thrown the doors open, so that his immediate staff could see what was transpiring between them. But he had the doors closed. What for, except the concealment of his heinous secret?

Besides, Hitler did not drink beer, according to Dr Langer. Actually, Hitler did drink beer, favouring the Holzkirchen Brewery, but since all of Dr Langer's statements can be replaced by the opposite statements, it can be assumed that Hitler did *not* drink beer. Now, beer is 'almost synonymous' with urine, and by forgoing beer, Hitler suppressed his disastrous passion for being urinated upon by movie actresses.

The rest easily falls into place. Urine is filth, dirt, according to Dr Langer, apart from being a symbol of beer. At one time, Hitler 'not only looked like a lower-class Jew but was as dirty as the dirtiest'. He loved dirt, filth, for it reminded him of urine. But he had to suppress his heinous love. So, 'as the perversion developed and became more disgusting to Hitler's ego, its demands were disowned and projected upon the Jews'. But what about the Gentiles?

The answer, which might have been vital for German Gentiles like Hindenburg, von Papen or Roehm, was less important for Langer's audience. The collegiate world of rival fraternities – with its kegs of beer, its marching songs, its urine and vomit in dormitory entries, its secret vices, its alienation from women, its regimentation, its professorial all-seeing eyes – was projected with the help of Freudian gossip on to the totalitarian universe, and it hardly bothered Langer's audience, Gentile or Jewish, that the fate of Europe in some measure depended on his infantile fantasy. Quite apart from his unsuccessful attempt to create a militarization to rival the already existing one, when he died Hitler was responsible for the death of at least twelve million civilians. But none of that was as important to the collegiate mind as his 'secret', which had to be 'crooked' by *our* fraternity before his fraternity could 'dig' into *our* secret:

> Father, Mother and Me,
> Sister and Auntie say
> All the people like us are We,
> And everyone else is They.

Well, what of them? The pretty Eva Braun became Hitler's mistress when he was only an unsuccessful politician, twenty-three years her senior. '*Mein liebes Tschapperl*, my lovey-dovey, please don't worry about me,' Hitler wrote to her after the attempt on his life in 1944. '*Geliebte*, beloved,' she answered, 'you know, and I told you many times, that I won't live without you. From the moment I saw you, my pledge has been to follow you wherever you go, even unto death.' Such pledges are common enough in the collegiate world in peacetime, but one may doubt that the pledges exchanged by Dr Langer's superiors in the Tomb some hundred yards from Professor Winks's study would hold up in wartime, as Eva Braun's did in another tomb. Nor are relationships between men any more suspect in militarization. Goebbels, who had been private secretary to one of Hitler's rivals, heard the future dictator speak in 1925 and remarked on his 'blue eyes'. First to speak was Goebbels himself, a product of *eight* European universities at which he had studied and taken degrees, not some cockamamie Columbia, like Donovan. Then spoke Hitler, a former corporal with only a school education, an autodidact. Goebbels wrote in his diary: 'Then he spoke. How small I feel!' And the doctor of philosophy, like the young woman, remained faithful to the pledge unto death. I am not an admirer of Hitler. Yet it is clear to me that the peacetime pyramid of power of which Professor Winks is a specimen was far more collectivist, inhuman and hypocritical even in wartime than anything totalitarianism had seen.

14

Langer, Curtiss and the rest of the professors, SI and R&A, Donovan himself and the OSS as a whole, all these were, in the words of the Russian proverb, only the flowers. The berries were yet to come, though by the time I got to them the former Director of Central Intelligence was well on his way to becoming the President of the United States. The trail began with Steve's documents, of course, and in particular a degree thesis written by one of Winks's research students. While the author made no reference whatever to Yale and its mysteries, his thesis explored a single episode in history: an American businessman's trip to Russia in 1925 to negotiate concessions to mine manganese deposits at Chiaturi, in the recently conquered Georgia. In fact, that was already the businessman's third entry into a market under his country's embargo since 1917. In 1921 and 1922 the Barnsdall Corporation obtained concessions to drill for oil, and in September 1922 *Pravda* ran an article on Barnsdall which concluded that 'American capital is going to support us'. Barnsdall was owned by Patriarch Averell Harriman, in partnership with another Patriarch, Frederick Winthrop Allen, and the Guaranty Trust Company of New York represented by Eugene Stetson, whose son, Eugene W. Stetson Jr., would be initiated in 1934. The chairman of both Barnsdall and Georgian Manganese was Matthew Brush, a Dickensian nobody who began his life in remote Stillwater, Minnesota, and later became a clerk for a Chicago firm owned by Patriarch Franklin MacVeagh, Secretary of the United States Treasury during the presidency of Patriarch Taft. It must be borne in mind that at the beginning of the century Russia had been producing half of the world's crude oil and more than half of the world's manganese. Steel was foremost in the mind of every aspiring dictator of the day, especially one who had chosen the word as his lifelong sobriquet, while oil was necessary to power the armour made of that steel. By 1925, when the city of Tsaritsyn was renamed Stalingrad, the pseudotsargod had his eye on Averell Harriman. But what the pseudotsargod giveth, he taketh away, and before long, though not before Harriman and his partners had had the opportunity to invest millions of dollars in industrial development of the Caucasus, the concessions were 'nationalized'. In return, 'government bonds' to the value of the expropriated investment were offered and gratefully accepted. Harriman was grateful because at the time he began gambling with his father's fortune he was still in his twenties, and it was vital for him to make believe that he too was a tycoon. His old man was a legend when he died in 1909, the aboriginal American robber baron who had hijacked Union Pacific Railroad, among many other piratical expeditions, before going into partnership with J. P. Morgan. In 1904 Edward Harriman gained notoriety in the Northern Securities fraud, when, in the words of the Interstate Commerce Commission investigating it, 'it was admitted by Mr Harriman that there was about $60 million of stock and liabilities issued, against which no property had been acquired and this is undoubtedly an accurate estimate'. Despite the efforts of Papa Harriman's personal biographer to whitewash him, the transparent truth is that the robber baron kept himself out of prison by responding to Theodore Roosevelt's call for political contributions with a donation of $250,000 to the Republican National Committee. Despite the gift, two years later President Roosevelt described the party's greatest benefactor in a letter as a man of 'deep seated corruption', an 'undesirable citizen' and 'an enemy of the Republic'. In short, it is easy to understand that the next generation of Harrimans, Patriarchs Roland and Averell, was determined to fill the old man's shoes without, however, repeating his mistakes, those elementary, uncouth mistakes in which most rags-to-riches stories abound. At Yale the boys got lucky, because what they found there was a humming power machine which not only put a man in the White House when Averell was only an impressionable freshman, but more important, was uniquely suited to project its grey eminence into the bureaucracy of democracy. A US Department of State exchange in January 1925 shows how much better adept in bureaucratic machination than his father the young pirate was. When Assistant Secretary of State Wilbur Carr was alerted to Harriman's expedition to Moscow, an expert from the Division of Eastern European Affairs called upon to clear up the mystery replied:

Dear Mr Carr:
    With respect to the attached letter from Mr Miller, Liaison Officer with the Department of Commerce, there are certain and very definite reasons why I consider it very unwise for the Department to initiate any investigation with respect to the reported manganese concession.

The young pirate did not need to drop $250,000 into the coffers of the grand old party of business. Why, he was even a registered Democrat. Education, culture, prestige would be *his* spokesmen, not vulgar lucre. A few years after graduation from Yale, Harriman hired the sympathetic biographer mentioned above to whitewash the life of his father, published, in two volumes, by Houghton Mifflin in 1922. The author's name was George Kennan, and this first in a series of Harriman retainers became the architect of the Truman policy of 'containment', a policy he later repudiated just as easily as he had put it forward in the first place. But now came the Russian fiasco, which Harriman recalled in an October 1967 issue of *Look* magazine as follows:

> In the early twenties my firm participated in credits to finance trade with Russia. We found as others did that the new government was most meticulous in meeting its financial commitments.

In the same article, entitled 'From Stalin to Kosygin: The Myths and the Realities', Harriman analysed, as the CIA had been analysing since 1945 and would continue to analyse until 1985, that

> On the Russian side, one of the most troublesome myths is that America is run by a 'ruling circle', made up of Wall Streeters and industrialists who have an interest in continuing the cold war and the arms race to prop up the 'capitalist' economy. Anybody who knows American politics knows what nonsense this is.

Nonsense or not, Harriman's 'Russian experience' of the 1920s served the ruling circle well when the war began. In 1941 Harriman went to Britain as head of Lend-Lease, because now that the pseudotsargod was openly on the side of peace and democracy he could be openly supplied with strategic commodities. From London he went to Moscow as US Ambassador, and after Yalta, where by all accounts a jolly time was had by all, to London he returned as US Ambassador. In 1946 he was appointed US Secretary of Commerce, and after that year his life was a never-ending stream of government appointments and agency posts. Even President Kennedy, who trusted the Harrimans as much as any president since Theodore Roosevelt, was compelled to appoint him 'Ambassador At Large', though what some whispered was exile ended with Kennedy's assassination and the ensuing farce of the Warren Commission, whereupon Harriman was himself again. In 1968 he was at the Paris Peace Talks, to make sure his newest retainer, Henry Kissinger, would not inadvertently offend the North Vietnamese. The retainers, it may be noted, came and went, but the 'ruling circle', whose existence has always been a popular Marxian fantasy of course, remained. The Harriman family bank, known since 1930 as Brown Brothers Harriman and looked after by such coryphaei of American finance as Patriarchs Roland Harriman, Prescott Bush, Knight Woolley, Robert Lovett, Eugene W. Stetson Jr. and, lest I forget the Uriah Heep of the tale, Matthew Brush, grew and prospered. The other family bank, J. P. Morgan's old Guaranty Trust of New York, known since 1954 as Morgan Guaranty, grew and prospered too, looked after as it was by such equally capable Patriarchs as Harold Stanley, Averell Harriman, Knight Woolley, Harry P. Whitney, Percy Rockefeller, George Chittenden, Henry P. Davison Jr. and Daniel P. Davison. The two companies, through a myriad interlocking directorships, and with few scandals of the kind that operators of an earlier generation like Harriman, Morgan or Mellon could scarcely avert in their era of trust-busting paranoia, reached into every financial honey-pot. With American business and finance increasingly dependent on government regulation, and with the government increasingly dependent on the resources of business and finance, there was no foreign policy initiative which the incestuous offspring of a dozen families, bonded together by the mumbo-jumbo of the Tomb, could not launch or scuttle. It was the high point of The Game. The cowboys wanted to shoot some Injun, the Indians wanted to shoot back, but it was the city slickers who financed the gun manufacturers and sold the guns to both sides that made the profits and, more important, the rules of the game. So long as the city – civilization – was at peace, a bottle of claret gently breathing an arm's length from a darn good cigar, who cared if the barbarians raged? Who cared if Geronimo killed some rednecks before he went down, for go down he would no matter how many rifles they had sold him. Angola was a Cuban military base? South Africa did not want to become one? Who cared what these black-arsed Africans wanted, so long as Cuba protected our refineries in Angola and our banks did business in South Africa. North Korea invaded 'our ally' South Korea? North Vietnam invaded 'our ally' South Vietnam? True, some American savages might be drafted if the farce got out of hand, some barbarians also, even a Patriarch or two. But the important thing was that the adversary's military power had come

from Chiaturi manganese and Azneft oil, Guaranty Trust's Ruskom-
bank and J. Walter Christie's tank designs, Roosevelt's lend-lease and
Truman's United Nations. It had come from the 'Eastern' Europe of
Yalta and the 'Red' China of Henry Stimson. Germany invaded
Russia? Its military power had come from Thyssen Steel, happily
financed by the Union Banking Corporation in New York, whose
eight directors in 1932 included Roland Harriman, Knight Woolley,
Ellery Sedgewick-James and Prescott Bush, four Patriarchs of the club
of 1917, and two Nazi financiers, H. J. Kouwenhoven and Johann
Groninger. Ah, happy was the life of a pirate with a secret cove an
ocean away! Taft, Wadsworth, Gilman, Stimson, Perkins, Whitney,
Phelps, Bundy, Lord, Harriman, Rockefeller, Davison, these were no
longer mere family names in the Social Register, they belonged to the
'ruling circle' of whose existence the totalitarian oligarchs were only
too well aware. Moscow propaganda? It was when the circle began to
rule in all earnest, in that auspicious year immortalized by Orwell, that
the propaganda in Moscow stopped. Sixty years earlier, when the Bone
Devil was in their trap, both sides agreed a make-believe scenario and
arranged a make-believe reprieve. Now it was time to do the same for
the whole 'ruling circle', and for the blind civilization it ruled.

15

Pirate tales was what these were, to be sure, gruesome tales that
reached me in badly photocopied fragments of US government
archives, shreds of newspaper cuttings, carbons of interoffice memo-
randa. Yet they corresponded with what I already knew of civilization's macrocosm, and of the microcosm I had stumbled into with my
Lit. One question, beginning with 'Who knew?', tormented me then,
although later I realized that the question was as ambiguous and
unanswerable as that other classic question, beginning with 'Who
believed?' Who believed, in 1917, that totalitarian militarization was
the best hope of all progressive mankind? Who knew, in 1937, that
every tenth man, woman and child could not have been an enemy
agent? Everybody except paranoiac grumblers 'believed', and nobody,
including the suspected enemy agents, 'knew'. Once a culture is at
peace, whether civilized or militarized, it hardly matters what people

believe or know. It hardly matters if Mr Rose, a private citizen in a democracy, knew of the Tomb, and if he believed that it was best for Yale and for the country. It hardly matters whether he ever asked Dr Steiner, another private citizen, to consider the subject in his lifelong re-definition of culture. It hardly matters what the privately owned *New York Times* believed or knew, because none of them, Mr Rose, Dr Steiner or the *New York Times*, would have risked their lives, careers or prestige to confront a cultural reality that existed side by side with the cockroaches rather than in the cultural imagination of their milieu – a milieu which 'believed' in the existence of a 'Red Menace' in the 1920s but not in the 1930s, and 'knew' that the enemy in the 1950s, but not in the 1960s, was 'Communism'. Of course Dr Giamatti, Scroll and Key's house historian, knew everything there was to know about Skull and Bones, but it was the denunciation of Moral Majority rednecks that he believed would advance his career. Of course Herr Hitler believed that Jews were a bad lot, but it was the promised expropriation of their property and influence that he knew would help him to win power. Of course the Revd Falwell knew that he had been used for political gain, but he believed that by making peace he would make gains of his own. The final result was that here as elsewhere only fools or madmen stood up in defence of their beliefs and knowledge, and here as elsewhere they were so marginalized by the culture of the 'ruling circle' that they might as well have been dining in Vnukovo. It was as if a generation subsisted on television dramas featuring actors who could not act. Boys and girls enacted what they absorbed in real life, synchronizing their sentiments like watches. This generation, in turn, produced television stars who were even more homogeneous, to act out the dramas absorbed by the next generation. Boys and girls finally came to believe that what they absorbed and enacted was real life, and by now there was nobody left who knew any better or believed any different:

> We are merely the stars' tennis-balls, struck and bandied
> Which way please them,

as Webster has it in *The Duchess of Malfi*. Who could blame these boys and girls for doing whatever else their homogenous culture commanded or condoned, whether it was marching in support of South Korea or North Vietnam, joining the Peace Corps or the Hitlerjugend, saying 'This must be a very expensive car, sir' or 'Hey, man, that's some set of wheels you got there'? Who the hell knew?! With this ambiguous and unanswerable question, which at the time I supposed to be vital and real, I approached the life of James Jesus Angleton, not a private citizen but the chief of counterintelligence to whose rise and fall in the CIA Winks devotes the longest chapter of his sycophantic epic. If the revelations, first publicized in 1979, that members of the Cambridge Apostles, notably Burgess and Blunt, had been spies, exposed the insularity of an élite which forgot that insularity was not what had made it an élite, it was clear that Angleton was the star in a drama of far greater proportions, if only because insularity was every Bonesman's middle name. Not surprisingly Steve believed that Angleton, with whom he conducted a lively if somewhat incomprehensible correspondence of handwritten nods and winks, 'knew everything', which of course, having turned down the tap from Bones in 1940, he did. Angleton was conceived, and supplied with the exotic middle name, when his father, accompanying General Pershing on a punitive expedition against Pancho Villa in 1917, captured the affections of a seventeen-year-old Mexican girl. Later the Angletons moved to Italy, where the paterfamilias represented an American corporation, and at sixteen Angleton was sent to an English public school, Malvern College. At Yale he founded a literary magazine, *Furioso*, which, Winks reverently comments nearly fifty years after the fact, 'was clearly intended for an audience outside the University, and despite its origins, was not a "campus publication"', attracting contributions from William Carlos Williams, Wallace Stevens, e. e. cummings, Ezra Pound and William Empson, among others. They were the famous men of their day, of course, but there was another important difference in the University's reaction to Angleton's venture: President Seymour approved of it, as did another Patriarch, Archibald MacLeish, who supplied the introductory benediction for the first number in 1939. But then Angleton became an editor of the *Lit*, and a funny thing happened:

> The *Lit* tried to shock the university with a mild attack on the senior
> societies, but this created hardly a ripple, and Angleton concentrated
> on trying to get more original poetry onto the pages of the journal,
> helping to attract unpublished work from MacLeish, who had once
> been an editor of the *Lit* himself.

In short, he chickened out. Similarly, while in 1939, titillated by what he perceived as intellectual dissent, he persuaded Pound to give a reading at Yale, and another at Harvard where, according to Winks, 'Pound spread his anti-Semitism on thickly', come 1943,

> when the Department of Justice was gathering a dossier on Pound, Angleton provided information on the poet's fondness for Mussolini and Fascism.

Nor were Angleton's 'best friends on the literary side', like the young English professor Andrews Wanning whose undergraduate contributions to the *Lit* I looked up, the best critics to question what Winks calls 'his sincerity and conviction, the complete loyalty he gave to his literary heroes, and his determination to change a Yale establishment' to which they happily belonged, one in which Wanning shared a set of rooms in college with Charles Seymour Jr., the President's son. Thus by the time he left Yale in 1941, Angleton had acquired the intellectual characteristics of a sheep in wolf's clothing, a provocateur posing as a dissident, a *Kulturhändler* masquerading as an innovator, a sycophant telling the truth without fear or favour, a thinker savage enough to dig for the answers but tame enough not to find them, a Neutral sufficiently ambitious to accept the facts of social life yet reluctant to compromise his dignity. Soon after graduating, this promising recruit

> was put through the OSS Schools and Training course pursuing the usual fun and games routine, including infiltrating the office of the chairman of Western Electric, and was assigned to the Italian desk in Washington.

After this he was posted to London to work for X–2, or counterintelligence, under the Yale English professor Norman Pearson who headed the Ryder Street branch. Here he pondered what Winks calls the 'methodology' of counterintelligence, the aim of which is 'to live in a real world while thrusting the enemy into an unreal one':

> Such a world view contained many dangers. This year's friend might be next year's enemy, so that one limited even a friend's view of the real world to the short range. The enemy might be induced to act on false information and yet act in a way inimical to one's own interests, or reach a right conclusion from the wrong information. One would need always to be testing one's own colleagues, for one of them

might be an unwitting dupe of an enemy deception and thus misevaluate information.

Here Winks, like Mark Twain's Sid Sawyer, again feels the need to put some distance between himself and his subject, fearful that democracy's Aunt Polly may misunderstand his breathless summary of Tom's exploits:

> One might, indeed, become confused oneself. Further, there were ethical questions, profound ones in a democracy in which deception was considered wrong. And that which might be accepted as necessary in wartime would not be accepted in time of peace. But then, in a time of undeclared war, but war nonetheless, a cold war, a war of subversion, a war against terrorists, what standards were to prevail?

Apart from giving free rein to those who had formulated Angleton's methodology back in 1832, the system had another advantage. One could be a bumbler, a fantasist, a dilettante or a fool with total equanimity:

> While others – William Hood, Gerstle Mack, John Marquand, Jr. ('a bit weedy, but nice'), and Kim Philby ('reliable and charming') – seemed to have fun, Angleton's pleasure took other forms. When free he would visit with T. S. Eliot.

So poetic, incidentally, is the whole business of spending taxpayers' money that Winks is compelled to introduce one of Pearson's departmental colleagues, none other than Professor John Hollander, who 'published a remarkable book-length poem, *Reflections on Espionage*', the first, avers Winks, 'to reveal the work of the Twenty, or XX, or Double-Cross Committee (from which X–2 may have derived its title)'. Having fun, after all, is a social norm. When a Harriman retainer, Robert McNamara, taught business at Harvard while Angleton was learning his craft in London, nobody could say that what one taught or the other learnt was nonsense. By contrast, when McNamara went to preside over the Ford Motor Company and masterminded the Edsel fiasco, the fact that the new motor car did not sell was a hard fact, a cold reality which directly affected the shareholders. Not surprisingly, McNamara resigned to become Secretary of Defence. There he could safely bumble, fantasize and fool away American taxpayers' money and their children's lives while prosecuting the war in Vietnam, a war he did not know how to fight, or win, any more than he knew how to build, or sell, a motor car. Seeing that the war was about to be lost, he went on to become President of the World Bank where, once again, there were no criteria for success except having fun and doing right by those who mattered. Angleton's methodology, whether or not he 'knew' it or 'believed' it was best for America, merely brought these intangible criteria to the world of intelligence, where 'one might, indeed, become confused oneself' about who the enemy was, but where there was no confusion whatever as to the identity of one's bureaucratic superiors. After the war the OSS became the CIA,

> with the same close-knit atmosphere that Angleton had liked in X–2 and at Yale – three communities in which people had a strong awareness of their responsibilities to each other and a certain 'we–they' view of the world.

Unable to catch even a glimpse of totalitarian militarization, incapable of infiltrating so much as a Moscow caretaker's boiler room, the giant CIA bureaucracy would spin its wheels for half a century, occasionally treating the taxpayers to a fable, a prophesy or a piece of analysis like *The Mind of Adolf Hitler*. None of its chiefs understood the totalitarian creation, with its charades of 'communism' and 'socialism', any more than the learned bore understood the pseudotsargod, if only because the bore was a dilettantish mediocrity like Angleton and the ruler a formal creator like Eliot. 'I am on to you', Angleton once frightened Philby over lunch, according to Winks, 'until Philby learned that this was Angleton's idea of a good joke', while on another occasion, 'when Philby had remarked that England needed a good dose of socialism', Angleton promptly informed Allen Dulles 'of his suspicion that Philby was well to the left'. Philby had been oversubtle, as he had been in Britain with MI6 and MI5. In September 1949, 'confirmation that the Soviet Union had the atomic bomb', with a bang sufficiently unsubtle for the Yale boys to acknowledge as a reality, 'led to a distinct change in CIA estimates'. Equally unsubtle was the outcome of a series of juvenile pranks intended to 'destabilize' Albania and overseen by Philby – who had finally caught on – for which 'pixies', as the Yale boys called their Albanian *émigré* recruits, had been 'trained', presumably by making them crawl through a cellar firing at cardboard cutouts of Enver Hoxha. Still more anecdotal was the episode of Khrushchev's allegedly 'secret' policy speech of 1956, which had been disseminated to tens of millions of Russians and the text of which the CIA finally 'obtained' two months later, on April Fool's Day. Allen Dulles passed the text on to the *New York Times*, in whose pages the February speech became the scoop of the decade when finally published in June. Some, according to Winks, said the text came 'directly from Palmiro Togliatti', others 'through Israeli intelligence', while Harrison Salisbury reported in the *New York Times* that it 'was obtained from a member of the Polish Communist Party'. Nobody knew just how those Yale boys managed to pull off such a coup, for 'there are certain matters', said their chief, no doubt with a significant wink, 'that you take to the tomb'. In October, when I was born, the Budapest provocation engineered by Ambassador Andropov began and ended bloodlessly, with the deaths of only 1,945 Hungarians, and the Yale boys were only too happy to take the credit: 'The CIA', writes Winks, 'actively encouraged the rebels'. So left out of the triumph was a University of Virginia graduate, Frank Wisner, head of the National Security Council's Office of Policy Coordination within the CIA, that he 'had a nervous breakdown' and 'committed suicide soon after retiring from the agency'. An alternative so Shakespearean was not available, alas, to the two or three Russians lured by their consciences into spying for the heirs of Nathan Hale, and until the 1970s military intelligence officers in Moscow would be entertained by the footage of one of the victims incinerated alive in an open coffin. Amid such indubitable triumphs, meanwhile, Angleton's ultimate superiors were wined and dined at the Kremlin, conducting a foreign policy that was based on the wishful presumption that their blue blood, their money and their country would be as indispensable to totalitarianism in the twenty-first century as it had been in the twentieth. Angleton was ambitious enough to accept the facts of life, but sooner or later the increasingly transparent futility of the whole exercise had to compromise his dignity. There had to have come a time when he realized that he was not in control of his own actions, clandestine or otherwise, for although in retrospect it may seem that there were no actions to control – so delinquent, amateur and haphazard was the whole CIA operation – there had to have come a time when these struck even him as ominously Kafkaesque. He was a patsy, more highly placed than Lee Harvey Oswald or the exiles of the Bay of Gadarene Pigs, but a patsy none the less, and, like Kafka's hero, he began to look for the answer among his ultimate superiors. Like the 'mild attack on senior societies' of his youth, the Great Mole Hunt 'hardly made a ripple' among them because *all* of them, collectively, had created the social system based on exploiting the weakest, deceiving the weak, courting the strong and surrendering to the strongest. Some said that Angleton had become insane, which seems implausible, because even the judicious supposition that the brain of the assassinated President of the United States had ended up in a glass jar on the library shelf of a clubhouse in a small university town was not bizarre enough to have driven a Yale man insane. The cult had become the culture, and this was but one of its shrunken heads.

16

Steve never got round to telling me who wrote the centenary anniversary history of the society, which told of the 'mad expedition' undertaken by Vice-President Bush's father as a young Knight to rob Geronimo's grave at Fort Sill, Oklahoma, made for the Indian chief by the US Army which had trailed him, unbelievably, into the twentieth century. The skull brought back to New Haven in 1917 by the future Senator Prescott Bush was 'fairly clean, having only some flesh inside and a little hair'. The world, at least as civilization had understood the term for a millennium, was collapsing into the crucible out of which totalitarian militarization would spring in the autumn of 1917, but the great white hope was on a summer holiday. At last, after 'an axe prised open the front door' of the tomb, 'Bush entered and started to dig'. The red enemy, conveniently a dead Indian, was finally vanquished. If only life could always be so simple! To procure the skull of the Mexican revolutionary Pancho Villa, which even General Pershing and the elder Angleton had failed to obtain, one Knight paid $25,000 to 'an adventurer' who promised to bring it to him, but according to Steve neither the trophy nor the adventurer ever materialized. Still, $25,000 seems not too heavy a penalty for an attempted prank of this kind, considering that nowadays every Knight receives from the society's trust managed by Brown Brothers Harriman the gift, understood to be entirely symbolic, of fifteen thousand dollars to defray some of his summer's unanticipated expenses. Then it's off to Deer Island, on the St Lawrence River, a present to the society from Patriarch George Douglas Miller, an enchanting place and one of the few 'if any', in the words of its present keeper, 'where the B-n-s life thrives in such luxuriance outside the thick and tomblike walls in New Haven'. Refreshed by convivial discourse with the most senior Patriarchs, having listened to their lurid tales of daring and intrigue, a young Bonesman is ready to enter the world. All this sounded splendid to me, and I would have liked to hear more, but soon thereafter Steve vanished. In his book Winks coyly describes as 'moderately ridiculous' the types of communications that were 'standard at my first encounter with many professional intelligence officers', boasting that 'one person would call me only from telephone booths and would take my calls only at other booths'. I now found myself on the receiving end of such communications from Steve, who explained that his rooms had been burgled and many documents went missing. He was on the run, staying in fleabag hotels all over the Eastern seaboard where on occasion I would send him money. There was nothing even moderately ridiculous in his predicament. I had been brought up in a culture where just about anyone who could read and write was at one time or another followed, watched, photographed or tapped, to say nothing of the consequences, and friends of our shrill summer neighbour in Vnukovo, infrequent guests though they were, tired us with their own true stories beyond endurance. Even in Rome, after we had received a call from Igor Galanin, still in Moscow, the telephone rang again and the entire tape of the conversation was played back from the first hello to the last goodbye. But now the dark underside of civilization was uncovered for me, as the dark underside of militarization had been uncovered for many by our shrill summer neighbour, and it hardly surprised me when, months later, I learnt that the person responsible had been committed to a mental institution. Why not, I thought. Another Vnukovo story. And what could I do to save my Virgil, if I couldn't even save myself? If I had not been an autodidact from Mayakovsky Street, alienated since birth from the culture beyond the fence painted forest green, I would have thought I was mad too. 'Spooked', as Steve used to say. But of course he had to be put away. The cult he had uncovered, while de facto the culture of educated Americans for generations, was not ready to become a culture de jure, and even its secret hold on such bureaucracies of power as the Supreme Court, the State Department or the Central Intelligence Agency would not have prevented its aristocracy from being swept away in a wave of plebeian fury at such revelations. The Revd Falwell might be happy to strike a deal with the aristocracy's chamberlain, President Reagan might be manipulated into one and the *New York Times* might take the long view of the matter, but tens of millions of uneducated rednecks, the aristocracy's cannon fodder, would not be co-opted so easily. With so much less to lose, if they could not void all the deals of previous generations by the ballot box, they would smash these deals by force, along with their makers and the ballot box itself, under the command of a military leader whom they would welcome as an *open* dictator. For such is the inevitable outcome in any civilization which suppresses the natural struggle among men, and the enmity that openly raises some above others as noblemen, in favour of a secret hostility and a secret aristocracy. The nobility that created Europe cannot be claimed to have been superior to those it trampled in the process, as one minute of conversation with a Russian Grand Duke who is an investment advisor in Paramus, New Jersey, will convince anyone who does not share this republican view. But it was open, with open rules of accession and open principles of succession, open standards of conduct and open criteria for admission, open luxury, open history, open literature. This openness, in turn, was transmitted to and ultimately reflected in the life of the public at large, through the conduit of guilds, associations, commerce, politics, fashion, middle-class aesthetics and civil-service ethics. Yet even in that old world conformity continued to rule, making a mockery, on more than one historical occasion, of the diversity written into the social constitution from the outset by the enmity that abides among free people. Here, by contrast, the entire edifice of democracy was gradually converted into the masonic pyramid represented on the dollar bill, and none but the all-seeing eye at the top was to know any of the rules of success save the rule of money. In peacetime that was enough for many, perhaps for most, certainly so long as America remained the imperial, enchanted island that Britain had been. But how would the secret aristocracy fare once the spell was broken, after the island had been surrounded by totalitarian militarization, with a versatile, competitive, dynamic culture of its own and an aristocracy that, within the context of that alien culture, was a meritocracy? Britain's open aristocracy, exhausted by the old world's first, and probably last and only, totalitarian war, openly withdrew, openly retaining for itself what little there remained of its former empire. By contrast, America's secret aristocracy would arrange a secret surrender, hoping in all its pacific innocence to save itself from eternal oblivion. The surrender would later be publicly unveiled as the New World Order, and although with its advent the United States was certain to lose an empire, the 'ruling circle' believed that it would find a role. Their hopes and beliefs were not entirely fantastic, of course, or altogether without historical precedent. Geronimo, for example, had enjoyed the privilege of marching in Theodore Roosevelt's inaugural procession.

17

Thus I was not in the least surprised to read in the newspapers that militarization's new rulers had launched a policy of 'openness', familiar to me since my university days as 'diversity', nor to learn somewhat later that Averell Harriman was the first American to be received in Moscow by the architect of the policy since the death of his bushy-eyebrowed predecessor. It was already clear to me and to my father that militarization had come to control Lasker's 'thirty-two squares of the board', for which in the opinion of the autodidact chess master there is no substitute. America, in particular, was now in the same strategic position as Russia had been from the moment of Einstein's departure from Germany. But we also knew that Einstein's emigration was a fluke or a miracle, and that civilization was viable because it was life, itself a fluke or a miracle. Harriman's meeting with Andropov, and the subsequent 'restructuring' of totalitarian militarization for the needs of the twenty-first century, was not, however, the miracle we yearned to see. Such a 'restructuring' was inevitable, because territorial wars, border fortifications, spiked helmets, fluttering flags and marching soldiers, obsolete for a century, could not possibly figure in the microelectronic future of global totalitarianism. By the 1980s these martial antiques were being preserved as symbolic anachronisms, whose inadequacy would be deliberately paraded in Afghanistan before they would be consigned, along with 'communism' and other ideological artifacts of a bygone age, to the kind of purge even Russia had not seen since the 1930s.

313

Yet even to me, informed as I was by the culture of Yale and of the *New York Times*, they still seemed alarmingly real, and their retirement only a hopeful prospect. Still, I was looking upon the triumphant perambulations of Western statesmen with the eye of Tiresias, blinded by Hera for his insolent prurience, with the documents inherited from Steve for company. It was 1985, and I did not know where to turn. Reagan's original redneck *apparat* had long been replaced by the Vice-President's retainers, for whom the *New York Times* showed far more tolerance. I was meeting with some of the stragglers, such as the stalwart Edwin Meese, in the hope that they might persuade Giamatti to call off the lawyers. The undergraduate view of the *Lit* battle had been shifting. A year before, in April 1984, a student who was now the editor of the *Yale Daily News*, Crocker Coulson, published an article entitled 'Hiding Behind the Rhetoric' which described Giamatti's ongoing effort to suppress the magazine as 'a nasty little political turf battle' and moved to this ominous conclusion:

> Yale's administration must ease up on the stranglehold which it exercises upon information, and open up the decision making process. President Giamatti should redirect his efforts towards solving Yale's problems rather than merely concealing them.

The *New York Times*, omnipresent as ever, ran its version of Coulson's conciliatory admonition in February 1985, even mentioning that the magazine 'savaged' what my father saw as the 'ignorance, mediocrity, inaccuracy, hypocrisy and sad cultural omnipotence of the *New York Review of Books* and the *New York Times*'. When I met the star reporter, Colin Campbell, I had the feeling that he had come to the *Lit* office with the article already written in his pocket. The article, entitled 'A Magazine That Was Sold By Yale Fights to Keep Name', ended as follows:

> The other day, in the magazine's small but comfortable offices on Crown Street, Mr Navrozov said he was really more interested in culture, in quality, than in politics per se.
> 'We didn't want to take on leftists,' he said with the barest hint of his native Russia in his accent. 'We wanted to take on provincials.'
> The magazine has also been shifting, he said, toward a less explicitly political identity, and he has the feeling that the magazine's opponents 'no longer burn with the same intensity'.

Of the nine university officials and two professors who had testified against the *Lit* in the trial, only Professor Hollander survived unscathed. The other professor left for Johns Hopkins. The good Dean of *Hustler* fame was demoted, another Dean resigned, a third returned to teaching, a fourth died. The General Counsel's contract was not renewed, and his assistant did not replace him. This left the President and two of his executive appointees, and the news was out that Giamatti would retire in June 1986. With the apparent change of climate at the University, the *Lit* was now widely viewed as an institution that had won its right to eccentricity. After some manoeuvring by Henry Finder, an undergraduate Secretary of the Elizabethan Club whose brother had recently refused a tap from Bones, and sympathetic members like Anthony Appiah, I was elected to the club, a stronghold of the English Department. Such consolations of notoriety did little, however, to relieve my growing anxiety and hopelessness. John Williams was leaving no stone unturned in the appellate court, but the Federal complaint, into which Steve's secret lore was to be incorporated, was delayed. The illegal takeover of the *Lit* a hundred years ago by a society incorporated and governed by graduates – an organization whose secret links with the University were to be scrutinized in the complaint – would be the bombshell of the Federal action, but its preparation would take enormous research and effort. If, in the mean time, I could get Giamatti to let the *Lit* alone, using the change in the under-graduate mood to justify a change in university policy, the Keys man would be trading another's secret for my editorial freedom without compromising his dignity, which struck me as a reasonable bargain. It was then, in April 1985, that I found an unexpected letter in my morning post. It was neatly typed on thick paper and signed with a blue biro:

THE VICE-PRESIDENT

Washington

April 22, 1985

Dear Friends:

Thanks so much for sending me the latest issue, which I will read with pride. I appreciate your thoughtfulness. With best wishes,

Sincerely,

George Bush

315

I did not have to interrogate my colleagues. Nobody on the magazine would have been crazy enough to send anything to anyone mentioned by name in the forthcoming Federal action without clearing it with Williams beforehand. 'Friends' indeed! The Vice-President of the United States wanted to negotiate a settlement. My reply was in Steve's best tradition of society doublespeak:

THE YALE LITERARY MAGAZINE

Box 243-A Yale Station
New Haven, Connecticut 06520

April 29, 1985

Dear Mr Vice-President:

Thank you for your letter of April 22nd. The last few years have been difficult for all of us here at the *Lit*, and it is from letters of support like your own that we have learned to draw strength. We are very grateful to you for the acknowledgement.

While I hope that you have followed to some extent the controversy surrounding the *Lit* under our management, I wish, in particular, to bring to your attention the latest account to appear in the *New York Times*.

We are pleased to see the *Times* take a conciliatory attitude to the entire matter, and can only pray that this can in some way be transmitted to the Yale administration. Now that President Giamatti has announced his plans to leave the University, an opportunity to settle the dispute he initiated may present itself in the nearest future.

I sincerely hope it does, before it is too late. We are tired of fighting for our independence, tired of spending hard-earned publication dollars on a lawsuit into which we were inadvertently forced. We are a part of Yale spiritually, as we have been since 1821 and as we wish to remain for all time. But we are not prepared to submit our editorial traditions to the soulless bureaucratic control of a politicized administration.

We trust, Mr Vice-President, that from distant Washington you may cast a concerned glance in the direction of our office at High Street, and perhaps find a moment to suggest to us some suitable remedy. We are open to suggestions from anyone in the Yale community; but your suggestion, I know, will have about it the full authority of the law.

316

'Law' meant political power, of course, 'suitable remedy' meant an alternative to the Federal action, 'at High Street' meant the corner of Crown but close enough to worry, 'trust' and 'distant Washington' meant good will, 'soulless' meant that I was an unpredictable Russian, '1821' meant older than 1832, 'tired' meant that I was not a fanatic, 'too late' meant once the Federal complaint is filed, and so on. Despite my overwhelming gloom I could not stop laughing as I wrote the letter, reminded of an English fairy tale I once read in childhood. An eccentric lord of the manor insists that his servant must use special euphemisms like 'white swans' or 'red cockerel' when referring to mundane realities like bedclothes or the kitchen fire. The servant runs to tell his master that there has been an accident, but by the time he finishes, the manor house has already burnt down. I wrote the letter only partly believing that I had not somehow imagined the whole thing, but sure enough:

GEORGE BUSH

(self-typed)

May 15, 1985

Dear Mr Navrozov:

Thanks for your good letter.

I regret that I have not followed the controversy and thus am not able to comment on the matters that you so thoughtfully called to my attention.

I wish I were in a position to be helpful, but, unfortunately, I am not.

Sincerely,
George Bush

I knew that it was mid-May, that Tap Day was upon us, that in a few days Bush would be in New Haven for the reunion of the Patriarchs, that the Tomb was more than ever on his mind. But I would not have been able to believe my eyes if like Argus I had a thousand of them. 'Self-typed', he had typed at the top. Even a White House secretary who came across the letter accidentally would have thought it mighty strange that the date had been left blank and then filled in using a second typewriter: month, *space for date*, comma, *space for year*. If he had left only the date blank, I might not have understood the message, assuming that he simply did not know when the letter would be sent and decided to fill in the date later. But surely he knew that the letter would go out sometime that month, since 'May' was typed using the first typewriter, and that the year would still be 1985. The message was: '15'. I was being shown up. My letter to Bush, which I wrote thinking that it was in the best tradition of social doublespeak, was in fact ridiculously heavy-handed, an uncultured, savage *faux-pas*. I was being taught a lesson in patriarchal subtlety: '15', nothing more. I had to show that I was able to learn:

June 28, 1985

Dear Mr Vice-President:

Thank you for your letter of May 15th. I have thought about it a great deal.

I am enclosing for your perusal a copy of a collection of news articles dealing with the controversy surrounding the magazine.

It would be presumptuous of me to hope that you would have the time to review this issue in detail, and yet I know of many unlikely things by which literary ventures have been delivered throughout history. May I, then, continue to believe in your interest in this matter?

With all good wishes.

Nothing but an acknowledgement of the message, in other words, and a reference to the Bones takeover of the *Lit*. The reply, on a stiff correspondence card adorned, as were the two earlier communications, with the White House escutcheon of the American Eagle, showed that the deal was on:

July 16, 1985

Dear Mr Navrozov:

I just got back from Europe to find your packet and letter of June 28.

I will try and review it in the not too distant future.

Sincerely,
George Bush

I asked Williams to cut the complaint down to the bone, so to speak, limiting his use of Steve's material to what was legally indispensable. Then I began phoning around to people we knew at the White House,

318

to see if the Vice President's office was about to intercede with Giamatti. Word came back through Ed Meese that this was the case. I waited until Christmas.

18

'Dear Little Lady in Brown', wrote a Patriarch of the club of 1887 in an anniversary number of the *Lit* in 1936, 'Now as I sit in my library in Woodley and let my fancy run back over the half century which has intervened',

> in the depths of my heart I still feel the pang of that winter day when you rejected my suit. Life hardly seemed worth living without you. Older voices of friendship urged that a bachelor future might still hold a modicum of charm, – some possibility of useful endeavor. While my mind accepted their cold reasoning, my heart yearned for my first love.

That a grown man, with whiskers if you please, should be so tortured by an experience of rejection he suffered fifty years ago in being passed over for the editorship of what was, after all, only a literary magazine, a trifle which his own society cronies had already crooked, lock, stock and barrel, some twenty years earlier, may serve as the historical *mise-en-scène* to the pose of sporting nonchalance I assumed in the bizarre correspondence with the future President of the United States. Steve was mad? *I* was mad? *They* were barking mad, all of them. The poetic author of that heart-rending memoir of the *Lit* was Patriarch Henry Stimson, launched in his political career by Patriarch Elihu Root, McKinley's Secretary of War, Theodore Roosevelt's Secretary of War, Wilson's special ambassador to Russia and the first honorary chairman of the Council on Foreign Relations, later chaired by Patriarch Winston Lord. Barking mad! Between 1911 and 1946 Root's protégé held cabinet-level posts in the administration of every American president except Harding: Taft, Wilson, Coolidge, Hoover, Roosevelt and Truman. His Washington home, Woodley, purchased in the 1920s for $800,000, served as the summer White House to the last four. A historian of the period has written of Stimson:

> The guiding maxim of his life was that 'the only way you can make a man trustworthy is to trust him'. It was a lesson, he often said, that he learned as a member of Skull and Bones.

It was Patriarch Stimson who advised Truman to drop atom bombs on Japan in August 1945. And it was the same man who, a month later, in the words of the same historian, wrote, signed and submitted to the same president 'the first formal proposal for a Soviet–American atomic arms control "covenant"', although it might have been obvious even to an idiot child that no such 'covenant' was necessary to control the only atomic arms in existence, American atomic arms.

> When the President called on him that afternoon, Stimson spoke eloquently and off the cuff. The only way to avoid a devastating arms race, he argued, was a direct offer to the Soviets to share control of the atomic bomb. The Russians had 'traditionally been our friends', he said, harking back to the Civil War and the sale of Alaska. There was no 'secret' at stake, for the scientific principles were common knowledge. And once again he imparted his gentleman's faith that trust was the way to beget trust.

Barking mad, all of them. Averell Harriman was at the Kremlin on August 9, the day the bomb was dropped on Nagasaki, to discuss 'Japanese-occupied Manchuria':

> Stalin also had another subject on his mind, but he was careful not to appear overly concerned about it. 'He showed great interest in the atomic bomb', Harriman reported, 'and said that it could mean the end of war and aggression but that the secret would have to be well kept'.

Kept by whom? The big men on campus, of course. From whom? The savages. As for obnoxious diggers like myself, they were, as I was about to discover, not worthy of the trust extended to gentlemen:

320

THE VICE-PRESIDENT

Washington

January 8, 1986

Dear Mr Navrozov:

I appreciated your post Christmas letter (December 27, 1985), but I simply am not in a position to intervene with Yale regarding the *Lit*.

I am all for reconciliation of disputes, reconciliation that leaves all parties happy, but I can't – in this case – be the intermediary. Good luck,

Most sincerely,
George Bush

I had written to Bush because during the Christmas recess US Army trucks had been seen parked along High Street. Soon thereafter we lost in the appeals court and I left New Haven. The last issue of *The Yale Literary Magazine* closed with an essay by Lewis Lapham, 'The Wealth of a Nation', later expanded into his book *Money and Class in America*. Lapham's father was in Bones. With all the passion of an illegitimate child of society Lapham understood the cruel dialectic of patriarchy, and I recall the last paragraph of his essay because in a sense it was my own farewell to Patriarch Bush:

Remarking on the effects of life in the sanctuaries of wealth, Charles Francis Adams in his autobiography observed in 1908 that after forty years in the railroad business, amassing a considerable fortune in company with E. H. Harriman and J. P. Morgan, he wished he had gone elsewhere. The subsidiary power of money becomes clear in the perspective of time. Who can remember last year's tycoon? Who can name the ten most important citizens of St Joseph, Missouri, in 1845? The American press delights in crowding its pages with the names and faces of new fortunes; journalists drape their adjectives on the shoulders of the walking dead. Whenever I read the rosters of the glorious heroes I think of the patrons disguised as angels and shepherds who stand around in the foreground of Renaissance religious paintings. They have paid for the space, and they expect to be introduced to the best people in Heaven. With an anxiety born of the fear of oblivion they peer at the Madonna with expressions much like that of Henry Kissinger staring into a television camera.

Perhaps I *am* beginning to lose my mind, I thought anew as I dialled to book one-way tickets to Heathrow for myself and my future wife, reading too much into those bizarre people and their cryptic trivia. Then again, I am but mad north-north-west. When the wind is southerly, I know a hawk from a handsaw. It was they who came after me, not vice versa, just as it was Bush who wrote to me, not I to him. Those people were certainly ruthless, I had to give them that, and thorough, very thorough. But then again, they were simply mad, barking mad. Like Steve, like Geronimo, I had been swallowed up by them on the sly. Yet I pitied them. For what is the good of strength tested only on weakness? Of bureaucratic cunning in the face of eternal oblivion? Of philistine madness in the steel grip of totalitarian reason? They, *they* were the gingerbread men, and the fox was waiting for them here on earth as God used to wait up for naughty children in heaven before putting out His light.

19

I often imagined the scene. It is winter. Park Avenue is quiet, except for a liveried doorman, here and there, exchanging chuckles with a departing Carmen, Macy's carrier bag in her dusting hand, or solemn, manly words with a waiting limousine driver. In the library of Mr Rose's duplex, or is it a triplex, Dr Steiner, the eminent cultural critic, and his host, the American billionaire, are lingering over brandy. 'George,' says Mr Rose, 'George, I want to tell you something, in confidence for the time being. I have this feeling of unease, depression almost, and I think there is a story in it somewhere, not in a journalistic sense, of course, but in the cosmic sense which you, of all people, should be able to grasp. As you know, although I am a Yale man, I am not a writer or a thinker, and so all I can do is share my anxiety, and you do with it what you will. I am also, like you, a Jew, and I am as conscious of this in my business career as you, my coreligionist, are conscious of it in your writing. I am grateful to this country for the opportunities my family has had, but we both know, you and I, that the world has seen many places where similar opportunities existed, only to disappear as suddenly as they appeared. Opportunities, after all, are merely latitudes, not freedoms. I do not wish to be remembered by future generations of my family as an opportunist, but rather as someone who, in a small way perhaps, did something to preserve their freedoms, and so I have decided to make this confession. George, America is run by a bunch of crooks, by a bunch of—' He trails off, looking for a word to suit his darkest conviction and bravest sentiment. Dr Steiner's cigar ash drops on the Aubusson rug. 'Dan?' Neither seeing nor hearing his interlocutor, the host paces the floor of the room. 'Of wankers, as you say in England, and I mean this quite literally. Just as when I use the word bunch, I mean no more than twenty or thirty white Anglo-Saxon males, and you know something? I don't care if I sound like a lesbian feminist.' He looks up to see if his guest is laughing, then again stares at the floor. The guest, unable to decide whether to look intrigued or amused, downs the remains of brandy in his balloon. 'I can tell you exactly who they are,' Mr Rose resumes, 'and although I haven't the foggiest idea of what they are up to, I know as well as I know you're sitting here that whatever it is, it's not good for America. If somebody overheard me right now, he'd probably say, Why should this rich Jew decide what's good for America? George, let me tell you what I know, and you can answer for me.' The clock ticks away, more brandy is poured, the eminent cultural critic shifts in his seat as he listens, fascinated, to his informant. Other civilizations are rushing past, parading their secret weaknesses before his Socratic mind's eye. Other excited, incoherent men try to expose, to prepare, to warn, facts and figures tumbling from sweat-stained tunic bosoms, from inside broken boots, from the folds of torn chitons. He recalls that title of Browning's, 'How it Strikes a Contemporary'. How odd, he thinks, for no reason at all that he can discern, Browning, there is a revolver by that name. He is the pre-eminent cultural critic of his day. He writes for the *New Yorker*, and anywhere else he may wish to publish. Serious newspapers from Los Angeles to Bombay wait on his every word. The *Times Literary Supplement* said of one of his books that 'no more comprehensive survey exists of the problems that press on civilization's mental life in the second half of this century'. C. P. Snow in the *Telegraph* said of another that his was 'the kind of criticism which others could not easily emulate'. Philip Toynbee in the *Observer* said of a third that 'knowledge is marshalled here with the skill and authority of a great general'. Well, those books were only a beginning, a limbering up, a trial of the pen. He, Dr Steiner, knows that they added nothing to man's understanding of civilization, and the reason for this, to develop young Toynbee's simile further, is that they contained no hard intelligence, no maps of troop movements, no names of enemy towns, no reports of conspiracies in the making, no strategic insights or tactical solutions. Because to stay news, an utterance must begin as news, as letters bearing some intelligence of great import to the lives of their recipients, not as speculative observations on the back of a postcard from Rome or Moscow, such as one educated man may send to another, containing a tourist itinerary of world culture that can be looked up in any encyclopedia, even that new *Britannica* over there on the corner shelf. Whether it brings news of language or of behaviour, every art is a study of conflict among gods and men, because thought itself is disobedience to matter, insubordination to power, a slap in the face of what is. And now his time has come. He, Dr Steiner, has finally heard the kind of news that bridges the gap between Xenophon and the Sunday tabloids, the kind of news that, once made literature by an eyewitness and published by history, fills future textbooks with end-of-chapter exercises. 'I did this in order that the enemy might not hear.' He, Dr Steiner, will show them all that he is not an encyclopedia salesman mistaken for the inspector general, Dr Arnold, but a Tolstoy, a Dickens, a Grossman. 'All right, Dan,' he says slowly, 'you leave this with me.' Beyond the vast expanse of window glass, snow is beginning to fall on Park Avenue. Dr Steiner is in a spacious guest room, writing down impressions of the confidential interview with his host, the first of many native informants to follow. From the horse's mouth, so to speak. 'I did this in order that the enemy might not hear.' Optative active, he dimly remembers. Translate. Use the aorist.

20

Alas, no such conversation can be inferred to have taken place, nor is there in Dr Steiner's work a reference to the cockroaches. The lushness with which I imagined the scene was a natural issue of its improbability. As Pasternak said of Balzac,

> He dreams of freedom like a lackey,
> As grey accountants dream of pensions.

I spent the months before my scheduled departure testing the improbability experimentally. The first victim I attempted to lure into the labyrinth of that imaginary dialogue was Colin Campbell, the star reporter of the *New York Times* who had written the last of its articles on the *Lit* controversy. I asked him to lunch at the Yale Club, hoping that its Dover sole and my intimacy with the waiters would check his creeping conviction that, whatever the substance of the controversy he had been covering, I was a 'conspiracy nut', a 'singlespacer', or at the very least a 'paranoid Russian'. He might well have thought all those things anyway, of course, but what startled me was that while paying close attention to every detail of the evidence, he seemed to know its general outline as well as I did. The *New York Times* was sitting on the story, I concluded, in order to use the scandalous material for the protection of its own interests, much as I had attempted to use it to protect the *Lit* from Yale. Its owners knew perfectly well that theirs was the only media organization in a position to blackmail the Washington establishment and, if necessary, to bring down a president. The *Washington Post* had been tied to the 'ruling circle' for decades, by the Harriman investment in *Newsweek* in particular, and the fact that it brought down Nixon did not mean that it could take on the big boys. *Time*, Luce's magazine, was a Yale creature through and through, and when, later in 1986, two of its editors, historians Walter Isaacson and Evan Thomas, published a history of the Washington establishment entitled *The Wise Men: Six Friends and the World They Made*, I was not surprised to find the following blurb on its dust jacket:

> '*The Wise Men* is a fascinating portrait of the friendship of six extraordinary men who, in shaping the modern world, saved the possibilities of freedom. This is an insightful and compelling account of the dedication of these "wise men" to the service of our country on behalf of principles beyond partisanship.' Dr Henry Kissinger.

In fairness it must be noted that the Isaacson and Thomas volume was something of a watershed, in that it was the first book by historians no less conservative than Professor Winks, and with an equally respectable publisher, to refer to Skull and Bones by name with the regularity of the old Yale bell. The *New York Times*, meanwhile, maintained its commitment to obliqueness. It behaved like a politician who, having ferreted out the secret that the married opponent's secretary is his mistress, makes a meaningful pause during a televised debate between the words 'Take my opponent's secretary' and 'Under his tax proposals she would have to pay more'. Inept as its owners ever were at understanding the global concept of nuclear blackmail, now that they had in their possession a neutron bomb of their own, they were demonstrating its political applications with a chess player's subtlety. In February 1986 the *New York Times* magazine came out with a cover story by Campbell, 'The Tyranny of the Yale Critics', which ridiculed the academic establishment the *New York Times* had been fostering for a generation. Into this unexpected and unprecedented act of cannibalism any Old Blue with a mind for inference could read the threat that, should the main exposé ever need to materialize, it would blow Yale and all its secrets to kingdom come. That spring in New York, in that atmosphere of highbrow suspense, I made a second attempt to tell the whole story. This time the victim was a transatlantic journalist, British by birth and American by adoption. I had met John O'Sullivan on a number of occasions in Washington, where he had edited a 'conservative' magazine called *Policy Review*. Most recently he had been my fellow speaker at a Washington conference, organized by 'neoconservatives' to combat what they regarded as the bane of American media, namely, the assertion of a 'moral equivalence' between totalitarianisms and democracies. I had accepted the invitation in order to plug the *Lit*. 'I will admit', I said in my speech,

> that under certain extreme conditions, the 'absolute zero' of freedom, such as existed in China in the 20th century AD, under Mao, or in the 3rd century BC, under a man named Ch'in, the forbidden walls separating the official culture from the subterranean are blasted away, and all independent intellectual activity ends. But in what can be described as merely a *harsh* political climate – Schubert's Vienna, as Sir Ernst Gombrich reminded us in a recent issue of *The Yale Literary Magazine*, was also Metternich's Austria – culture has been known to blossom like Connecticut laurel after a summer rain.

The organizers of the conference, I explained, were the product not of Schubert's Vienna but of the *New York Times'* New York. It was their culture, with its parochially Manichaean, crudely politicized discourse, that lacked the subtlety with which the question of 'moral equivalence' could be addressed without equating Afghanistan with Vietnam. Needless to say, the speech did not go over very well, and the only 'conservative' or 'neoconservative' in the audience to take it in stride was John O'Sullivan, which I, already contemplating an escape to England, took as a providential sign. Now I was lunching with him at the South Street Seaport in nether Manhattan and, sure enough, he was listening to me as I imagined Dr Steiner might listen to Mr Rose. After all, Buckley's 'conservatives' and even, though to a lesser extent, Podhoretz's 'neoconservatives' had been brought up on stories of cultural intrigue and political conspiracy, 'gossip' that never made it into the *New York Times* any more than Kremlin 'gossip' ever made it into *Pravda*. Besides, as I was lucky enough to see for myself later, even the serious press was immeasurably less monolithic in Britain, where, in addition to this oasis of competitive journalism, a vast, uncontrollable subcontinent of daily and Sunday tabloids, completely unknown and without an equivalent in America, routinely slung mud at the great and the good. O'Sullivan had never heard of Skull and Bones before, yet he was a product of Fleet Street, that fabulous milieu at whose existence I could then only guess, and it seemed that the scandalous titbits he was eagerly swallowing over lunch were no more controversial than the prawns on my plate. Until I mentioned Buckley. Here the urbane, witty Englishman choked and looked at me, glassy-eyed. The noise of the restaurant, sudden like a special effect in a horror movie, became deafening. The Americanized ghost of Fleet Street looked with suspicion at the Deep Throat before him, and saw trouble. The ghost of Vnukovo returned the look, and saw a gelatinous mass of conformity across the table. Buckley had body-snatched him, thought one. He is one of those conspiracy nuts Buckley warned me about, thought the other.

21

Still later, when I was already in England and Buckley appointed John O'Sullivan the editor of *National Review*, I realized just how importunate the attempt to lure this veteran of Fleet Street into my labyrinth had been. The uninitiated, clueless, loyal Brookhiser had been groomed by Buckley since Yale to take over upon his mentor's retirement, faithfully pushing the 'conservative' editorial line in the correct direction. One of my erstwhile friend's articles, which struck me as particularly brazen, appeared in the magazine on November 7, 1988, a day before Bush was elected president. It was cheerily entitled 'The Establishment Man', and its message was that 'George Bush has a rare opportunity to institute a new establishment, uniting conservatives and pragmatists'. The trouble with the old establishment, apparently, was that it was too heterogeneous, too diverse, too open, and what it now needed was a bit of bow-wow unity. Even at its most slavishly Salisburian, the *New York Times* showed more fear, more favour. And yet, when Buckley retired, it was not Brookhiser but O'Sullivan who replaced him at the helm. Buckley's sights had been set on Britain, and quite shrewdly too, because the spectre of an uncontrollable press, the very spectre that so belatedly beckoned me, must have been haunting him in his nightmares. Despite Yale's fawning anglophilia, despite the traditional Bonesman sojourn at Oxbridge and Rhodes scholarships by the gross, despite Harriman's marriage of symbols at age seventy-nine to Pamela Churchill, not one member of the 'ruling circle' understood England any more than they understood Turkey or India, to say nothing of the culture of militarization. Their insularity, which had some of the properties of a convex wall-mirror, so surreal that no genuine outsider could ever find himself intruding upon its innermost recesses, had been obliquely portrayed in the many novels of Louis Auchincloss and, more recently and spectacularly, in Tom Wolfe's odyssey of Sherman McCoy's Yale chin, published when I happened to be reviewing books for *The Times*. When I sent Wolfe, with whom I had corresponded throughout the *Lit* affair, a cutting of my review of the novel, he wrote to say that 'not only the author of *The Bonfire of the Vanities* but also everyone he talked to' could hardly believe that 'complex points' of the novel's argument, such as the social role of the *newspaper*, could be 'illuminated' in a *newspaper*. Wolfe is not alone in his incredulity. Hardly an American now living remembers what newspapers are, just as hardly anyone in Britain ever bothers to imagine what life would be like without them. Buckley must have reckoned that by drawing in a Fleet Street insider, American 'conservatives' would be better equipped to put out whatever stories happened to catch fire across the ocean. Equally important, such insiders were valuable as a collective conduit by which

American 'conservative' policies and practices could permeate the Conservative Party, just as some of the men and ideas of Margaret Thatcher's campaign had been borrowed by the Republicans in 1980. The cross-pollination, American 'conservatives' reasoned, would help to Americanize the academic establishment in Britain and give them still more leverage in the British press. My final attempt to interest an outsider, the editor of a London paper, in visiting my labyrinth showed that Buckley's hopes were not as wildly misplaced as I had at first supposed. I do not name this Old Etonian, who is no longer with the paper, because he was one of the most astute, open-minded and kind editors I knew. Some weeks before the popularity contest between Bush and a barbarian with the Greek name Dukakis on Tuesday, November 8, 1988, I submitted an article entitled 'Why I am Not Voting', raising an issue that even a foreign audience would agree was elementary:

> Bush's membership in Skull and Bones has hardly been mentioned during the campaign. It is astonishing that this chapter of his biography has totally escaped public scrutiny, especially considering the American media's interest in the candidates' private lives. But with this as with ostensibly more important issues, such as defence or intelligence, the media in America focus on the predictable. Just as the CIA is often criticized for its excesses and never for its inadequacies, so revelations about a politician's life are equally ritualized: 'marital infidelity', 'use of controlled substances', 'history of mental illness'. Certainly a *respectable* newspaper like the *New York Times* would never drop its mask of omniscient objectivity and chase after a spurious story such as this one.

One week before the election the article was accepted and set up in type. Too late for the story to hit home, I thought, but it was a start. On Monday, November 7, I received a telephone call from the editor who asked me whether it was true that William F. Buckley Jr. belonged to the 'club' I described in the article. I confirmed this, whereupon the editor got round to the point of his call, which was to tell me that the article could not run. The next day I received a cutting of the following article from a friend in New York:

YALE SOCIETY RESISTS PEEKS INTO ITS CRYPT

Special to The New York Times.

NEW HAVEN – In a sylvan pocket tucked off High Street, masked by blank slits in an ancient stone building called the Tomb, barred from the world by a padlocked iron door, Skull and Bones keeps its secrets closely. But it casts a shadow across the country.

The article, given the front page of the 'Metropolitan' section on Friday, November 4, had been timed to preclude any further investigation of the story – in the editors' possession at least since my lunch with Campbell two years earlier – while the election was still news. What could a television news crew, for instance, have done over the weekend, apart from filming the outside of a building that had stood there since 1856? The *New York Times* had decided to flex its muscle, but not so much as to cause damage to the Bush campaign.

> If Bonesmen say anything at all, they portray their association as a venerable fraternity whose rituals instill honorable and selfless values in youthful initiates and forge intimate bonds of friendship that last a lifetime. But their cloak of secrecy suggests something considerably more cabalistic.

What that 'something' was the American voter would not be told, although the reporter did mention, thirteen equivocating paragraphs later, that the youthful initiates

> recount their sexual histories while lying naked in a coffin. Within the Tomb are the purloined skulls of Pancho Villa and Geronimo, the latter obtained by a raiding party that included the Vice-President's father, Prescott S. Bush.
>
> Not a word of this may be true. But efforts to get the truth are met either by silence (Jonathan Bush, the Vice-President's brother and a member of the 1953 delegation, declined to answer questions on the subject) or by carefully crafted misinformation.

The article ended with a membership list, carefully crafted to titillate the voters without in any way suggesting that their democratic ballot

330

would disturb the peace of history about as much as a candy wrapper thrown into the Potomac:

> Prominent alumni from these years include William F. Buckley, Jr., editor of the *National Review*; Senator John H. Chafee, Republican of Rhode Island; R. Inslee Clark, president of the Horace Mann School; the Rev. William Sloane Coffin, Jr., president of SANE/Freeze; Daniel P. Davison, chief executive officer and chairman of the U.S. Trust Company, and his brother, Endicott P. Davison, partner in Winthrop, Stimson, Putnam & Roberts.
>
> There are William H. Donaldson and Dan W. Lufkin, founders of Donaldson, Lufkin & Jenrette; William H. Draper 3rd, administrator of the United Nations Development Program; Evan G. Galbraith, former Ambassador to France, now managing director of Morgan Stanley, and Judge John M. Steadman, of the Court of Appeals in the District of Columbia.
>
> It is tempting – perhaps too tempting – to see Bones at every turn.
>
> The 1955 group includes Ray C. Walker, the Vice-President's cousin; Robert H. Gow, who was president of the Zapata Corporation, the oil company founded by the Vice-President, and Richard C. Steadman (Judge Steadman's brother), who was an associate partner of G. H. Walker & Co., the investment banking house founded by George Herbert Walker, the Vice-President's grandfather.
>
> Is this Bones at work? Yes and no. Mr Gow's friendship with Mr. Walker went back to boyhood days at Groton. And Mr. Steadman had befriended Mr. Walker when they were freshmen, several years before they were tapped.
>
> 'Don't place too much of a web where there is no web,' Mr. Steadman cautioned. As if to emphasize his point, he added, 'I'm for Dukakis.'

No better gloss to the issue I raised in the spiked article was needed, but it was now too late to address elementary issues. The Game was played. Yale won. And if it had lost, well, what difference would that have made? So long as you are the one making the rules, it really does not matter whether you win or lose. 'It's the taking part', as they say at Eton.

22

Haunted wherever I went by memories of the quivering mass of conformity across the table, I had ever greater reason to reflect on the subject of sanity, which so captivated Michel Foucault and, fifty years earlier, a great-uncle of mine, a psychologist who studied at the Sorbonne and published a journal called *Madness and Genius*. A normal denizen of a Western democracy does not look at the page, much less feel his heart contracting in a spasm, when an immigration officer stamps his passport with some meaningless figures. My heart did, when I saw '322' stamped in my passport at the O'Hare Airport in Chicago. A normal literary journalist, sent a book to review, does not pay attention to pagination. Can I lie and say that I did not notice that the chapter on Angleton in Professor Winks's scholarly monograph begins on page 322? A normal reader of the *Sunday Times* would have read its interview with the newly appointed US Ambassador to the Court of St James's, 'a key negotiator for a reunited Germany', with only a slight interest in the fact that he is '6ft, elegant, a Yale man'. I could hardly keep still when I read the interviewer's account of Ambassador Seitz's appointment:

> Bush's offer took Seitz by surprise as he was dining out in Brussels after a day of Nato meetings. Called to the phone by the barman, he feared he was about to be sent on another trip, and his first thought was damn, he'd have to find some place to get his laundry done. But it was James Baker, the secretary of state, to say the president would be calling in five minutes to offer him the Court of St James's. Later Seitz made a diary note of what was said – first spelling out to Baker the correct dialling code for Brussels.

A normal person would not say to himself: 'Wait a minute. Why should the first thought of a man described here as "a symbolic Grip-Fix on the Anglo-American entente" rush to his dirty laundry? This is like something out of *Macbeth*, or from the Apocalypse: "Happy are those who wash their robes"! Besides, Baker had just phoned him in Brussels. Why should he spell out the code unless it has some hidden significance, as codes do? What *is* the Brussels code, anyway? I bet it's 322. Ah yes, so it is.' For what is the standard by which a normal denizen of a democracy measures his sanity? Why, his culture of course, and for generations his culture has been teaching him that the Townsend Professor of Entrails Divination and Numerology at Yale is among its high priests, while a taxicab driver who makes a note of the licence plate of a chauffeured limousine involved in a hit-and-run is only its voiceless worshipper. That a highbrow cultural critic, who quotes Nietzsche and angers no one by what he writes, is closer to its Olympian ideal than a two-bit reporter on a mass-market tabloid who wants to make a name for himself by disturbing the peace of its hypocrisy. That a 'conspiracy nut', beyond the pale of its notional properties and proprieties because his Letters to the Editor are typed single-space, is best ignored. That the culture itself is a Janus, whose public face represents enlightenment, progress and diversity, while its secret face, revealed only to those it has educated, promises power, comfortable insularity and a bit of crumpet on the side. And yet, I reasoned, even measured by this double standard, I was no more insane than Averell Harriman:

> Harriman regularly went back to the tomb on High Street, once even lamenting that his duties as chief negotiator at the Paris Peace Talks on the Vietnam War prevented him from attending a reunion. So complete was his trust in Bones's code of secrecy that in conversations at annual dinners he spoke openly about national security affairs. He refused, however, to tell his family anything about Bones. Soon after she became Harriman's third wife in 1971, Pamela Churchill Harriman received an odd letter addressing her by a name spelled in hieroglyphics. 'Oh, that's Bones,' Harriman said. 'I must tell you about that sometime. Uh, I mean I can't tell you about that.' When Harriman carried secret dispatches between London and Moscow during World War II, he chose as the combination on his diplomatic case the numerals 322.

Why should I lie then, and conceal the horror I felt upon reading in *The Times* of the sudden death in Oxford of a former President of Yale and the then Master of University College, Kingman Brewster, on Tuesday, November 8, 1988? Should I lie, and conceal the disbelief I felt a year later, reading in the *New York Times* of the sudden death, 'after apparently suffering a heart attack at his summer home', of a former President of Yale and the then Commissioner of the National Baseball League, A. Bartlett Giamatti, aged fifty-one? They too were gingerbread men, these savages among barbarians, hoping to flee yet haunted by knowledge, running for their lives yet unable to call for help. In the peace of their culture they tried to think for themselves, and thought only of their own salvation. They balked at compromising dignity, yet they were much too civilized to slap reality in the face, to disturb the peace, to yell bloody murder, to read a single-spaced letter. They opened their mouths, but nothing except progressive platitudes came out. They tried to yell, but all they could manage was the occasional highbrow wink. By the time they decided that the game of peace had gone far enough, they had already lost it, and when they realized that the beast was sly, they were already in the sly beast's belly. Let us see if my Greek is up to the revelation of the beast, which 'forces everyone, great or small, rich or poor, freeman or slave, to engrave on the right hand or on the forehead the mark, so that nobody can do business except if he wears the name of the beast or its number'. Here, adds John, who did not want to be called insane any more than I do, is where *he sophia estin*, where wisdom comes in: 'Let the guy with a brain figure out what that number is.'

23

And so it is with the shrinking macrocosm of civilization, unlike the microcosm only in that it is circumscribed by the front page, rather than by page B1 of the 'Metropolitan Report' section, of the *New York Times*. In one as in the other, the Leibniz curve of progress, the Hegelian dialectic of development and the Darwinian theory of evolution are all mutely contradicted by the modern science of mass destruction, with its power to intimidate, and by the modern technology of mass control, with its power to marginalize. Yet this science and this technology now exist, independently of civilization, elsewhere on earth, and the reality of mass destruction and mass control is a global reality, one that has made the very etymology of 'civilization' an object of nostalgia, a storybook picture of Lady Godiva, an antique bauble Winston finds in Orwell's old curiosity shop. Show me a civilian of the twentieth century, and I will show you a deaf-mute philistine who deserves to warm the Arctic permafrost with his mortal remains. This science and this technology are more than two yards of the rope which, as one of the founders of militarization promised, civilization would sell him the better to hang itself with, as it soon did. They are also the hooks which allow the big fish, swallowing the small fish the fisherman uses as bait, to celebrate victory even as they feel the water rush by at unfamiliar speed. No doubt what they experience at that moment, glutted with oxygen, is the feeling of euphoria, a concept which also exists in law to characterize the state of mind of the party induced into a contract under duress. On the face of it, the bucolic scene is an episode in the life of the food chain which only an eighteenth-century sentimentalist would find objectionable. In reality, it represents the deception of the fisherman and the self-deception of his bait, made universal for all of humanity in the twentieth century by the ineluctable convergence of 'East' and 'West'. The power to intimidate and marginalize, once it has levelled civilization's historic eminences of freethinking individualism like so much asphalt, has been used by the self-deceived aristocracy of American democracy to produce a global myth of civilization's invulnerability. The architects of the Maginot Line had only their individual folly to underwrite such a myth. The architects of the future world order were moved by their misconceived self-interest, the cultural duress which compels the big fish, even if it is the biggest in the sea, to take the bait and prompts the corner grocer, even if he is the most honest in town, to sell out to the supermarket chain before retiring to Coral Gables, Florida. What have they done, these wise men, with their corporations and institutions, their universities and newspapers. What have they done, these gingerbread men, rolling into the totalitarian abyss from which mankind will never emerge. What have they done!

> Sun! Do you hear? – Fill your purses.
> Pine, are we dreaming? – Must endure.
> O life, our name is – dispersal,
> Unknown by sense and to your cure.
>
> O Duncan of grey guesses! – Fate.
> O hosts of legions in his omens!
> O God, my Lord, what hast thou made
> On our sale to the commons!

So it was in the microcosm of Pasternak's life. So it is with the macrocosm of civilization. How can it be otherwise? The East, the

East! Life comes from the East, where the sun rises, where, from the dust and clay of fallen civilizations, the gingerbread man, whom the Russians called Kolobok, was made.

24

The fairy tale is unambiguous. He was made from the leftovers. He possessed the zest of life, yeast, gist, barm, from the Greek *zestos*, fervent, like the Germanic Dionysus, Kvasir, from whose froth the ancient Slavs made their beer, called *kvas*. He was barmy, and where an ordinary sort of bun would have stayed put in the frying pan, he ran away from his makers. Out of the frying pan, out of paradise. On and on ran the gingerbread man Kolobok, the currant-eyed refugee with a soft spot for what he called individualism, and by and by his was the race. The race built cathedrals, mastered navigation and engineering, found the cure for scurvy, designed the steam locomotive and the machine-gun, survived a world war. The animals in its path were fierce but slow, and although they had muscle and brawn where he had only his exuberant individualism, he outwitted them. He was very proud of his record, which he believed was the history of his race rather than a biography of its outcasts and martyrs. Alas! This was a philistine delusion, and although it could not be logically reconciled with the true story of his origin, he decided that from that moment onward all would be for the best in this best of all possible worlds. 'No one can catch me,' was how he actually put it. Just then he met the beast of prey named Chronos, identified in the fairy tale as a sly fox. The fox was the youngest of his brood, already famous for having lured to their doom all the nightingales in the forest. 'Stop,' said the fox, 'I want to talk to you. Let us reduce the tension I feel between us. Let us strive for peace.' The gingerbread man referred to the beast's sly suggestion by a variety of names, none of which belittled either the strength of the predator or the intelligence of the prey. Sometimes he called it diplomacy, sometimes international dialogue, sometimes currant-eyed pragmatism. Meanwhile he kept running, because everything in what he believed was the history of his race told him that if he should ever stop, the fox would eat him. 'You can't catch me, because I'm the gingerbread man and I never stop,' whispered his vestigial instinct of self-preservation. 'Stop,' said the fox, 'actually I'm running after a fighting cock, a childhood enemy of mine called Fritz, well, not an enemy actually, we used to be friends — ' Here the fox paused to catch his breath. 'But now Fritz and I are enemies, and I'm only pretending that I'm after you, sweet Kolobok!' Kolobok believed the cock-and-bull story, but the vestigial instinct of self-preservation told him to keep running. Then the fox tried a different tack. 'I'm only running because you are. I don't want to catch you, I just want to talk to you.' Because after about fifty years of running the fox knew that if the gingerbread man kept running, as he had since the beginning of time, no one would ever catch him. Just then they came to a wide river, called Europa. 'Wait,' said the fox, appealing to Kolobok's self-interest, 'let us make a deal. Jump on my tail, and I will carry you across the chasm. But you must tell your inborn nobility to keep quiet, because the rationale of our bargain is something which irresponsible, volatile, hysterical spirits can easily misapprehend.' The gingerbread man knew that if one of those freethinking aristocrats of the spirit, perennial outcasts and martyrs of his race, set his mind to it, not only could the river be crossed, but Chronos would be rendered hydrophobic, as if by magic, and left behind for ever. But he chose Chronos's way, which the fox said was the way of peace, because that way he, a civilian doughboy, could actually use the dangerous predator for his own benefit, and without sharing any of the credit with his race! So he jumped on the fox's tail and the fox began the descent, down the river bank and into the water. Again, many words were used to describe this process, scholarly terms like bilateral disarmament, détente, or necessary coexistence, and many explanations of its utility were put forward. Sometimes the gingerbread man spoke of new markets, justifying his course of action on economic grounds. Or he would simply say that the world was a small place and everybody must work together. At times he even spoke of an impending ecological catastrophe, deliberately irritating himself with apocalyptic memories of the frying pan where his race began. Again, this was illogical, because if one is a civilian doughboy, death by fire may well be less ignoble than death by water. But since the freethinkers of the race had been silenced and only institutional toadies remained, no one dared to say that it was philistine hubris and blind ambition which made him decide to embark on the suicidal voyage. And then the sly fox pretended, as only sly foxes can, that it was unwell. They were now wading in shallow water, and Kolobok could

337

still leap back ashore. 'I'm positively collapsing,' said the fox. 'You are too heavy for my tail! As you probably know, the state of my economy, I mean my health, is so much sly propaganda. Jump up on my back.' The toadies, who always agreed with everything, agreed that the fox had always been one for sly propaganda, failing to note that this too was sly propaganda. So the gingerbread man jumped up on the fox's back. Oh, he was more proud than ever of his noble race. He felt euphoric. He *had* to feel euphoric, because by now there was no turning back. Ornate covenants were signed, orchestras played patriotic tunes, fireworks lit up the sky, and the reunification, as it was called, of the predator and the prey was celebrated all over the world. To the spectators they seemed inseparable, a kind of mythical centaur progressing through the stream of existence, Europa, a realization of some ancient dream of the lion and the lamb, until suddenly the fox said, sharply: 'It's no use. You are too heavy for my back. If you don't jump on my nose I will drown, and you will drown with me.' Suddenly frightened, the gingerbread man did as the fox said. 'It's a funny old world,' Kolobok whispered to himself, momentarily chastened. Time itself seemed to stop, and though he was no thinker, it now occurred to him, apropos of nothing as it were, that sufficient fear can relativize history as surely as sufficient speed relativizes time. 'Well, that wasn't so bad, was it?' said the fox to reassure him, and added, to distract him from that sinking feeling of powerlessness which he had never before experienced: 'Not many of your race have ridden on a fox's nose!' This kept him from fidgeting. As they reached the other side, the gingerbread man felt himself tossed into the air. For a moment he thought it was an accident, worried only that his dignity had been compromised, although the famous Archaic smile did not leave his raisin lips even then. But the fox's teeth snapped. 'Oh dear,' said the gingerbread man, 'my toadies are gone!', because, oddly enough, the toadies are always the first to go in such situations. Then he cried: 'My freethinkers are gone!', because in such situations the freethinkers are not far behind the toadies. And after that, the gingerbread man said nothing more, because he was inside the fox and the fox was the world. Then time finally stopped, because the inanimate does not need to keep time while it is being digested.

25

Oxford was where Kingman Brewster came, to die as it later turned out, a few months after the contents of the Tomb were moved out of New Haven. I too came to England. Brewster was never to hear, in the deceptive safety of his sun-drenched and rose-scented exile, of the restructuring of the society that killed him, an evolutionary leap that would replicate the changes in the totalitarian macrocosm. By the time Brewster became the President of Yale, Bones no longer needed Yale: it *was* Yale. Now, whoever became the next President of the United States, Bones would not need America: it *was* America. The Tomb, General Russell's peacetime incubator of secret aristocracy for the only global military power in civilization, had done its job, and could finally be dismantled. The 'ruling circle' no longer needed Yale to blue its blood, because the generations now living would be the ones to preside over the symthanatosis, the reciprocal totalitarianization once known as a diplomatic dialogue, an academic disputation, an abstract *conversazione*, but now finally ushered in as the New World Order. What would that new order be like? Like America on the day after tomorrow, initially. But potentially and, worse yet, inevitably and to the end of time, like Russia on the day before yesterday. Worse yet because as the English poet prophesied, not for the electronically-tagged powerless of this impending apocalypse are the old-fashioned consolations of madness and eternal sleep:

> And worse I may be yet. The worst is not
> So long as we can say 'This is the worst.'

The new compromise would be equally global, centring on national sovereignty rather than individual dignity. The restructuring militarization would initially mimic the mass culture of demilitarized civilization – with its ballot booths and its symbols of diversity, its social hypocrisies and political deceptions – as competently as it once simulated the aristocratic culture of old Russia. Then it would foment a Thirty Years War of a thousand local Vietnams, a pseudoreligious, pseudoracial, pseudopolitical fragmentation to which a centralized power able to bring about global peace would be the progressive answer. Equally progressive would be its use, limited at that juncture by nothing whatever, of the entire modern scientific and technological apparatus to reduce the individual to the status of an electronically tagged sheep in a tribal flock, which it would shepherd with Mosaic zeal all the way back to Creation, whereupon the Indo-European *vartanna* of time would end. Could I help it that I came to England when the chariot wheel was in its last revolution? Oxford was something I had to see with my own dying eyes, as a leukaemia patient, obsessed with blood, might decide to visit an abattoir just to watch it flow. And here it was at last, nature's bounty, *fecunditas augustae*, red-green fruit of Indo-European myth, piled sky-high under the roof of the Oxford market. I walked up to the man with the tomatoes. I had eaten these red-green fruit – which we call *pomi d'oro* in Russian, 'golden apples' of the Romance languages brought from America to Europe by the conquistadors – many times since the day Mother offered me the sacrifice in the hospital ward, thinking as ever of the late Tsevyanov my saviour. But the ones I had eaten, from New Jersey, from Long Island, from as far away as Louisiana, always the first of the season, had been more luxuriant, somehow less real. Oh, they had been real enough I suppose, ripe and home-grown, not like the tennis balls at the local supermarket, pink and resilient. But these, these were somehow meaner, poorer, more honest if you like, modest in size, with wilted green stars on top, and the grocer's name was Smith, as in *The Wealth of Nations*. Out of intellectual habit, unconsciously subjecting him to cultural duress, I appealed to his self-interest. Could I buy a whole crate of his English tomatoes, I asked, the first of the season. Smith looked at me sadly, as one looks upon the feeble of spirit, as Dostoevsky describes hardened criminals eyeing him in prison. Overcoming his pity, he finally said: 'If I sell you all my tomatoes, I won't have any left for my other customers.' Babylon, Babylon has fallen, he might have said instead, and I would not have been more amazed. I recalled Herzen's first impression of the England of John Stuart Mill, the only nation in Europe, wrote this itinerant freethinker, 'where the iron in the blood has not been displaced by gold'. I walked through Oxford on that day in summer, and my amazement grew. I remembered the title of a book I had seen in a catalogue in New Haven, though I never ordered the book or found the author's name again and it was quite possible that I simply imagined the title, *The War on Light: The Destruction of the Image of God in Man Through Art*. That was what James Gamble Rogers had done. He had vanquished sunlight, which flowed and throbbed on the sandstone of these buildings named after Christian saints, buildings that were actually sun traps, forcing frames, tomato greenhouses. At the centre of each was an expanse of succulent grass, where one could just as easily imagine vegetable beds, or grazing cows. The society that laid their foundations recognized nature and, like nature, kept its secrets openly. That sunlight makes the grass grow was a mystery held up to public inspection here, even as the membership list of a private club may be made known to the public without destroying the club's social purpose. Nature kept its secrets without making secrecy into a cult, and here civilization followed suit by exposing its culture to sunlight. I never went back to America. I realized that I did not come here, like Kingman Brewster, to escape persecution, as Elder William Brewster had done when he sailed from Southampton on the *Mayflower*, but because it was time for me, another hereditary dissident, to share civilization's fate. It was time for the freethinker to stop running. The civilization now before me was as vulnerable and mortal as the one I had left behind at Kennedy Airport, perhaps more so, yet its culture was open, based on open conflict. Here money and education had not conspired to hide the natural enmity among men, the enmity whose obverse was freedom, and Smith would not have parted with his tomatoes if I had been the prime minister. Call me a dreamer but I saw what I saw, and here for the first time in my life I saw a press that was diverse, competitive, bloodthirsty. Here editors did not sit on stories, because here proprietors had to shift papers to stay afloat, and when I first came to see a man about work at *The Times* he did not ask me whether I had been to university, or who my roommates were, or what I thought of the Tory Party, but threw a book at me, still in the publisher's jiffy bag, and barked that I had three days to review it or never to bother him again. Here, in this pre-revolutionary enclave and non-progressive backwater, part Mark Twain's Connecticut and part King Arthur's court, part Dostoevsky's Paris and part Rastignac's illusions, I found books that still expressed the fallible opinions of their authors, books published not because they enhanced the prestige of infallible editors who commissioned them or appealed to infallible reviewers who praised them, but simply because, like Smith, their publishers had been in the business since anybody could remember and, like nature, never thought of retiring to Coral Gables, Florida. Here the men and women reared on the aristocratic culture of natural conflict were not so surprised to see politicians who spoke their mind that they rushed to vote for them, yet still some persisted in speaking their mind, and whatever it was that Norman Tebbit or Tony Benn was saying at any given moment, even a child could tell that it would not advance the man's political career to say any of it. Here one major political party might be run by the trades unions and the other by big business, but no one, however honest, would insist that both were run by the same people. Here the academy influenced the media and the media influenced politics, but only a superficial observer would conclude that the influence was superficial and that in reality somebody else was pulling the strings of partisan interest. Here membership in a gentleman's club might be prized, but only a sourpuss would argue that it was more unattainable than a peerage, and besides, neither distinction was a secret any more than a writer's fame or a businessman's wealth. Here games were played, and the back pages of newspapers did cover sports, yet at every level of society I met people who had served in the army, which meant that when all was said and done this civilization did not leave its games to gladiators. Instead of the Camp dialectic of Harvard crimson and Yale blue, at Royal Ascot it was the colours of Arab sheiks and Liverpool jockeys that mattered in the social game which even the Queen's own horse rarely won. Here I listened to the fusillade of champagne corks popping away at the last picnics of Ladies' Day. Here I watched the last rays of sunlight fall sideways on history's last manifest empire. Here were the men in their blacks and charcoal greys, and the women in their improbable hats. Unlike the denim of the student or the broadcloth of the corporate class, the wearing of these uniforms within this enclave had been openly commanded by Her Majesty's Representative, and those who obeyed the command had no secret illusions that their individual acts of conformity were in reality acts of fearless individualism. Here they were, the Englishmen with their quinine and the Englishwomen with their red-maned disdain, drinking champagne beside the Rolls-Royce in the meadow. Bearing roses? Call me a dreamer, but I dreamt they were drinking champagne because they knew that the millennial picnic of life, called civilization, was over, and that in the new, fierce and timeless existence to come there would be neither champagne nor Rolls-Royces bearing roses to destinations unknown. Call me a madman, but I imagined that when their race ended, and their civilization finally followed mine into the gaping maw of totalitarian darkness, its culture would not crumble like the gingerbread man, but die as the Russian poet died, with his eyes open. Call me an optimist, but here at last I thought I was among the undeceived.

26

Bloody-minded, they called themselves. I realize that the Oxford market grocer with his tomatoes and the Royal Ascot racers in their peculiar garb are haphazard examples. But are they any less convincing, as specimens, than Mr Rose's *Britannica* and New York's cockroaches, any less instructive than John's Southwestern experience and the destiny of the *Lit?* The plain fact is that the England I found was more different from the America I left behind than the militarization where I spent my childhood was different from the civilization where I spent my youth. I think this would be the case for every freethinker who envies, or emulates, the artist's interest in the still-life. Here the older generations had been through a world war, and although a conventional experience of this kind is no panacea for the social ills of naïvety and hypocrisy, in the bloody-mindedness they had been cultivating since the Blitz I found temporary relief. Temporary, because as I look back on the broad native lands I have left behind, one of sly, inexorable pacification and the other of conceited, bumbling appeasement, it is clear that all my escapes have been an illusion. The twain have met. The nightmare of world peace on totalitarian terms is almost manifest, and what remains of English bloody-mindedness may keep it from reaching Greenwich, where time begins, but not for long:

> The dark eleventh hour
> Draws on and sees us sold,

as Kipling has it. In one way or another, first by hook and later by crook, the destiny of the American press may be shared by the press here, and by the rest of the institutions and eminences which have been fostering the antagonism of debate – the soul of a national culture worthy of survival – since Mill's day. Exactly how this, or any other aspect of Europe's totalitarian future which I envision, will come about is a subject for another writer, or another book, which, if I am right, may never see the light of day. 'Every time I try to tell you how, you ask me what, and every time I try to tell you what, you ask me how', as Orwell shouted at H. G. Wells in August 1941. I have tried to concentrate on the individual 'what' of civilization and militarization, letting history deal with the collective 'how' of progress and peace, still dimly aflicker on the wall of Plato's famous cave. As I look, for what must be the last time, to that theatre of shadows called democracy in America, I recall a forgotten, though once fashionable and widely read, history of the earth's antediluvian past by Dmitry Merezhkovsky, *The Atlantis of Europe*. The original philistines of the Old Testament, Merezhkovsky believed, were the Cretans, last survivors of civilization's archetypal deluge which has haunted the West ever since. Their hubris inspired the prophet Amos to write that the sinners of his own people, deserving of death, are those who would say 'This evil shall not overtake us.' Jeremiah, too, hoped that 'the Lord will spoil the Philistines, the remnant of the land of Caphtor'. Crete, the Caphtor of the Bible and Virgil's *cunabula gentis nostræ*, the cradle of our race, was the birthplace of Europa, mother of Minos, from whom the Minoan civilization took its name. And what a civilization it was, the happy Philistia of Icarus! How passionately devoted to art and science! How deeply dedicated to commerce and trade! How resolutely opposed to argument and war! When I visited the islands of Greece and saw with my own eyes the portrait statuary of that civilization, I finally understood the meaning of the ubiquitous enigmatic smile for which its artists are famous. The term 'cretin', used by the Greeks to describe the philistines of the Biblical Caphtor, is still as widely used as their word 'barbarian'. Unbeknown to Virgil, the ancients must have coined the term to describe the peaceful and placid demeanour of Philistia's perpetually smiling inhabitants. Like modern gingerbread men, they smiled at everything because nothing could possibly threaten them, and wished everyone in the world to have a nice day because they could hardly imagine that their own days were numbered. No wonder the Southwestern salesman wept when he saw how calm America's future leaders were in their Yale *cunabula*. Any cynic would, but only the freethinker is free to think them cretins.